OFFSHORE PETROLEUM POLITICS

OFFSHORE PETROLEUM POLITICS
Regulation and Risk in the Scotian Basin

Peter Clancy

UBCPress · Vancouver · Toronto

21 20 19 18 17 16 15 14 13 12 11   5 4 3 2 1

Printed in Canada on FSC-certified ancient-forest-free paper (100% post-consumer recycled) that is processed chlorine- and acid-free.

Library and Archives Canada Cataloguing in Publication

Clancy, Peter, 1949-
Offshore petroleum politics: regulation and risk in the Scotian Basin / Peter Clancy.

Includes bibliographical references and index.
Also issued in electronic format.
ISBN 978-0-7748-2054-7

1. Offshore oil industry – Nova Scotia. 2. Offshore gas industry – Nova Scotia. 3. Petroleum industry and trade – Political aspects – Nova Scotia. 4. Offshore oil industry – Government policy – Nova Scotia. 5. Offshore oil industry – Government policy – Canada. 6. Offshore gas industry – Government policy – Nova Scotia. 7. Offshore gas industry – Government policy – Canada. I. Title.

HD9574.C33N8 2011   338.2'728209716   C2011-903540-5

Canada

UBC Press gratefully acknowledges the financial support for our publishing program of the Government of Canada (through the Canada Book Fund), the Canada Council for the Arts, and the British Columbia Arts Council.

This book has been published with the help of a grant from the Canadian Federation for the Humanities and Social Sciences, through the Aid to Scholarly Publications Program, using funds provided by the Social Sciences and Humanities Research Council of Canada.

UBC Press
The University of British Columbia
2029 West Mall
Vancouver, BC V6T 1Z2
www.ubcpress.ca

Contents

Part 3: Case Studies in the Offshore Petroleum Chain

Maps, Figures, and Tables

Maps

Figures

Tables

Abbreviations

BOE	barrels of oil equivalent
CAPP	Canadian Association of Petroleum Producers
CEAA	Canadian Environmental Assessment Agency
COGLA	Canada Oil and Gas Lands Administration
COPAN	Cohasset-Panuke
CNOPB	Canada–Newfoundland Offshore Petroleum Board
CNSOPB	Canada–Nova Scotia Offshore Petroleum Board
CPA	Canadian Petroleum Association
LNG	Liquified Natural Gas
MNP	Maritimes & Northeast Pipeline
NEP	National Energy Program
NSRL	Nova Scotia Resources Limited
OSEA	Offshore Strategic Energy Agreement (Nova Scotia)
PIP	Petroleum Incentive Program
SOEI	Sable Offshore Energy Inc.
SOEP	Sable Offshore Energy Project
UARB	Utilities and Review Board

Conversion Table

Volume:

cubic feet gas	× 0.028	=	cubic metres gas
cubic metres gas	× 35.3	=	cubic feet gas
million tones LNG	× 48.7	=	billion cubic feet gas

Energy:

cubic feet gas	× 1,025	=	British thermal units
British thermal units	× 1,055	=	joules
gigajoules	× 0.95	=	thousand cubic feet gas

Acknowledgments

Sometimes it is difficult to pinpoint the moment that a research interest begins. I suspect that the politics of petroleum exploration in the Scotian Basin first came to my attention during work on a different frontier. Northern Canada experienced its own oil and gas boom in the 1970s and 1980s, when offshore exploration touched a number of basins and the Beaufort Sea received special attention. At that time, land claim negotiations were under way between the Inuit and the Government of Canada, and the Canada–Nova Scotia joint management arrangement of 1982 attracted considerable attention as a possible model for Inuit-Crown resource governance. After moving to Nova Scotia in 1986, my interest was reinforced by an article in the excellent but, sadly, now-discontinued *New Maritimes* magazine. The title – "Oil and Gas, She's Fadin' Fast" – was an apt comment on the day but, fortunately for this project, premature.

Perhaps because of its ongoing cyclicality, the Scotian Basin has not attracted the scholarly attention it so richly deserves. In Newfoundland, Doug House produced a pivotal study of that province's petroleum industry to 1985, but no companion piece emerged in Nova Scotia. Eventually my curiosity got the better of me, and the present effort is the result.

Along the way, I have had assistance and support from many quarters, and it is a pleasure to acknowledge them, beginning with the Social Science and Humanities Research Council of Canada (SSHRC), which supported the project under Research Grant No. 410-2002-1798. I also thank the University Council for Research at St. Francis Xavier University, which awarded seed funding in the period before my SSHRC application. The Aid to Scholarly Publications Program of the Social Science Federation of Canada approved a grant in support of publication, for which I am most grateful.

Over the years of working on this project, I have been fortunate to have had the help of some very talented student research assistants. They include Emily Burke, Jeff Burns, Brian Francis, Alison Maunder, Leah Podetz, Courtney Strutt, and Ian Yap. Their contributions were considerable, and I hope they will recognize their efforts in the final product.

At St. Francis Xavier University, I wish to thank Dr. Mary McGillivray, academic vice-president, Dr. John Sears, retired professor of business administration, and Marcy Baker, secretary of the Department of Political Science. I am grateful also to my colleagues Dr. Xu Yi-Chong, who shares an interest in global petroleum politics, and Dr. Brendan Murphy, who has generously helped me to understand some rudiments of petroleum geology. Several of the chapters that appear in this book began as conference presentations, particularly at the annual meetings of the Atlantic Provinces Political Science Association, and I am grateful to my discussants for their comments. The manuscript benefitted substantially from the careful attentions of two anonymous academic reviewers. Their pointed and constructive appraisals are much appreciated.

The staff at UBC Press has been supportive and encouraging throughout the publication process and I wish to thank Randy Schmidt and Holly Keller in particular.

As always, my partner, Mary Ellen, has had an immense influence on the course of this work, and she has lived its progress through the years. I know that she shares my excitement that it is now, finally, complete.

Permission Note

I am grateful to the following individuals and organizations for permission to use certain materials in this book:

Paul Illsley for the photograph that appears on the front cover of the book.

Canada–Nova Scotia Offshore Petroleum Board, Halifax, Nova Scotia, for images from *Joint Public Review Panel Report: Sable Gas Projects*, 1997; and *Decision Report on the Application to Amend the Cohasset Development Plan*, 2004.

Emond Montgomery Publications Ltd. for sections from "Offshore Petroleum Politics: A Changing Frontier in a Global System," in *Canada's Resource Economy in Transition: The Past, Present and Future of Canadian Staple Industries,* edited by Michael Howlett and Keith Brownsey (Emond Montgomery, 2008).

Institute for Research on Public Policy (www.irpp.org), Montreal, for an image from Thomas J. Courchene, "Confiscatory Equalization: The Intriguing Case of Saskatchewan's Vanishing Energy Reserves," in *IRPP Choices* 10, 2 (2004): 1-44.

Nimbus Publishing for an image from Atlantic Geoscience Society, *The Last Billion Years: A Geological History of the Maritime Provinces of Canada* (Nimbus Publishing, 2001).

Scotia Capital for an image from the *Scotiabank Commodity Price Index*, 2010.

OFFSHORE PETROLEUM POLITICS

1 Introduction

Half a century after the Canadian petroleum industry first turned its attention to the Atlantic offshore region, the Scotian Basin remains a promise unfulfilled. This is not for lack of effort by either industry or government. Significant investments, in both business finance and public policy, have been committed to the search for hydrocarbons on the continental shelf. Tens of thousands of kilometres of seismic lines have been shot, and more than two hundred wells have been sunk in Nova Scotia waters. Two fields have reached the production phase – the Cohasset-Panuke oil project (1992) and the Sable offshore energy project (1999). A third, Deep Panuke gas field, is under development and is scheduled to flow in 2011.

In a comparative context, however, these results are disappointing. In the North Sea, where exploration also began in the mid-1960s, a series of world-class discoveries were confirmed within a decade, and an elaborate ocean infrastructure soon linked dozens of fields in both the British and Norwegian sectors. North Sea production peaked in the 1980s, and by the turn of the millennium the basin was considered a mature petroleum play. Nonetheless, the region, which has hundreds of producing fields and a northerly advancing exploration frontier, remains important in a global context. In Western Australia, the offshore sector also kicked off during the late 1960s. Here, too, a rapid series of discoveries led to a dramatic run-up in production. By the close of the century, the petroleum industry encircled the Australian continent, and the "elephant" gas finds in the North West supported a world-class business in liquefied natural gas. Finally, and most dramatically, the US sector of the Gulf of Mexico emerged from promising beginnings in shallow water to cover the outer continental shelf. The first twenty-year boom came to an abrupt end in the late 1980s. Renewed deep-formation drilling, however, together with expanded operations on the deepwater continental slope after 1995, opened an entirely new horizon.

This book delineates the economic fortunes of the Scotian Basin, from the earliest airborne magnetometer surveys of the 1960s to deepwater exploration efforts of the early 2000s. It is a political and economic history of an offshore petroleum formation in contemporary times. It explores why things happened the way they did. What underlying forces drove the industry through its various phases? How did wider currents in this highly globalized business affect events in the Scotian Basin? Equally significant, what part did state authorities play in shaping these outcomes? How have the political complications of federalism, Crown title, and administrative intervention shaped the offshore oil and gas industry? To answer these questions, it is necessary to explore the complex interplay of regulation and risk.

If the commercial results of Scotian Basin exploration have been modest, it has not been for lack of political effort. In Canada, the state sector was certainly aware of the potential of discovering offshore hydrocarbons. Aided by the terms of the 1958 Geneva Convention on the Continental Shelf, Ottawa fashioned a licensing and rights-holding regime for so-called Canada lands. East Coast resources also assumed a strategic dimension under the 1960 National Oil Policy. By its terms, the Ottawa River divided the country into a western sector supplied by Alberta and an eastern sector supplied from abroad, principally Venezuela. The Organization of Petroleum Exporting Countries (OPEC) price spike of 1973 illustrated the exposed character of the eastern market and underlined the economic significance of an Atlantic offshore production base. At the same time, the federal government was obliged to take a national view of new petroleum sources; in the process, the Scotian Shelf and Newfoundland's Grand Banks emerged as two potential basins. Ottawa's National Energy Program (NEP), unveiled in 1980, again redefined the relationship. Along with the territorial north and offshore British Columbia, the Atlantic petroleum shelves were treated as frontier lands. In other words, the federal government sought to use its Crown jurisdiction to shift exploration and production beyond the western sedimentary basin. This policy resulted in a rapid if brief explosion of industry activity that laid the groundwork for East Coast production in the 1990s.

Then the federal Conservative government rapidly undid the central terms of the NEP after 1984. With a broad marketizing sweep, oil prices were released from controls, pipeline regulation was liberalized, and rich fiscal incentives for frontier exploration were eliminated. In short, Ottawa was a major player in the story of offshore petroleum exploration. In the chapters below, the effects of this prominence can be seen.

The East Coast provinces were also keenly aware of the value of an offshore industry. In a petroleum-consuming region, provincial leaders could perhaps be forgiven for grandiose visions of energy self-sufficiency, not to mention a new industrial sector on the crest of a burgeoning world hydrocarbon trade. In Nova Scotia, the Liberal government of Gerald Regan cast envious glances westward, where Peter Lougheed in Alberta was fashioning a long-term growth strategy based on "seeding the oil."[1] The Calgary oil patch not only dominated the western sedimentary basin, it also fed an emerging petrochemical sector, underwrote the province's Heritage Savings Trust Fund, and generated powerful export earnings. In 1971, images of a beaming Regan, holding a small vial of dark Sable Island liquid and exclaiming "It's Oil!" appeared in newspapers throughout Nova Scotia.[2] Six years later, the premier joined his Maritime counterparts in signing an intergovernmental agreement with Ottawa that covered petroleum revenue sharing and established a single administrative and regulatory regime for exploration and production. Although that particular deal was never fulfilled, it inaugurated a period of federal-provincial collaboration on joint offshore petroleum authorities that continues today. The agreement generated some innovative institutions that lowered the political risk quotient for capital while entrenching some resilient rules of offshore governance.

In subsequent decades, the province's leaders carved out different priorities in the offshore sector. For Conservative premier John Buchanan (1978-90), the focus was exploration benefits, including equity participation (through the state corporation known as Nova Scotia Resources Limited) and onshore commercial linkages in supply, employment, and manufacturing. For Liberal premier John Savage (1993-97), the focus shifted to securing offshore production, particularly pushing the Sable subbasin to the next phase of development. To this end, new royalty and tax regimes, along with streamlined regulatory protocols, were instituted to support the Sable offshore energy project. Under Russell MacLellan's Liberal government (1997-99), policy shifted to transporting and marketing Sable gas. MacLellan left his signature on two important fields. The first was the licence for the Maritimes & Northeast Pipeline, built to carry offshore gas across the

Maritimes and for export to New England. The second was the launch of a new natural gas distribution system to make the product available within Nova Scotia. When the Conservatives returned to power under Premier John Hamm (1999-2006), the prospect of offshore exploration could not have looked better. A new exploration boom was under way, commercial gas was flowing, and Hamm's attention turned to securing maximum provincial revenue benefits for a generation. His "campaign for fairness" marked a return to a traditional provincial concern – seeking to win complete Crown revenues without prejudice to the province's equalization entitlement. Hamm's successor, Rodney MacDonald (2006-9), inherited the fiscal fight with Ottawa, which ultimately contributed to the defeat of his government. The election of Nova Scotia's first New Democratic government in June 2009 opened yet another chapter whose shape is not yet clear. Nova Scotia's strategic outlook on its petroleum resource is, therefore, far from static. As with Ottawa, a kaleidoscope of shifting forces has driven the province's approach to offshore politics.

Parenthetically, it should be mentioned that across the Cabot Strait in Newfoundland, Conservative premier Brian Peckford charted a different course in the 1980s. His inspiration came from the North Sea, where Norway was fashioning a development strategy with more statist overtones. Its National Petroleum Directorate exercised unified regulatory control over all phases of offshore licensing. In addition, the state oil company, Statoil, was designated a compulsory partner in all development projects. Finally, the Norwegians took a firm regulatory position on industrial supply and service linkages to the onshore economy. Not surprisingly, as exploration results turned favourable in the Jeanne d'Arc Basin, Peckford established his own petroleum directorate and the Newfoundland and Labrador Petroleum Corporation. Unlike the unitary Kingdom of Norway, however, the province found itself locked in a jurisdictional tangle with Ottawa. Subsequent premiers have followed Peckford's lead and championed offshore jurisdiction as a non-negotiable provincial birthright. Indeed Danny Williams, the provincial premier from 2003-10, revived Peckford's style as a "fighting Newfoundlander" to devastating electoral success.[3]

Over the past generation, then, Canada's two Atlantic offshore petroleum-producing provinces have been linked with the national government in a complicated political dialectic, and private petroleum capital has usually provided a third animating force. The geopolitics of federalism has meant that Nova Scotia and Newfoundland can be allies or rivals. They share a provincial interest in maximizing political leverage with Ottawa and the petroleum industry. However, since they claim authority over separate tracts of the continental shelf, and thereby separate offshore petroleum basins, they are sensitive to matters that could give them a political or business advantage in the promotion and management of their resources. Halifax and St. John's have each harboured ambitions to become the Houston (or Aberdeen) of the Atlantic offshore play.

Clearly, the political economy of the Scotian Basin is complicated, and the complications begin with the physical setting. Offshore petroleum deposits are found principally under the earth's continental shelves, the geological formations that are submerged today in relatively shallow water. Although depths vary considerably, the shelf surrounding Nova Scotia is about 90 metres deep on average. On the Atlantic coast, the depth can reach up to 100 metres in the initial 25 kilometres offshore. Beyond this, the water depth increases only gradually over the next 175 kilometres to 150 metres. The Scotian Shelf seabed is not uniform, however. It is punctuated by multiple basins and banks. One of the best known of these banks surrounds Sable Island. At the outer edge of the shelf, the continental slope marks a sharper decline toward deepwater. The depth drops by several hundred metres in a surface distance of 5 to 10 kilometres. Beyond that, the seabed plunges thousands of metres to the abyssal ocean floor.

Not all parts of continental shelves are petroleum prone. However, in places where organic materials were deposited in volume over the past four hundred million years, often by the work of massive prehistoric rivers flowing off of the continents, the materials could be trapped in sedimentary layers and compressed and heated. The root meaning of *petroleum* is "rock oil," and the challenge of oil and gas exploration is to locate sedimentary formations in which significant volumes of rock oil is trapped. Although the resource was first discovered and exploited on land at a time before petroleum geology emerged as scientific discipline, the modern industry could not have materialized without this knowledge domain. It is at the exploratory phase of the petroleum cycle that geological science plays a determining role. In addition, the move from terrestrial to offshore petroleum activity has required a series of engineering and technological adaptations to make exploration and production feasible.

The story continues with the entry of corporate and industrial agents that locate commercial reserves and develop petroleum extractive systems. This is an extremely complex field of business interests – sometimes particular and sometimes shared – that have coalesced and dissolved with the passage of time or with the shift from issue to issue. In Houston or Calgary, the oil patch is justifiably regarded as a bastion of competitive individualism. Firms may engage in a series of distinct activities in exploration, production, servicing, transport, refining, and retailing. The players range along a continuum from super-majors (such as ExxonMobil, Shell, and Chevron) to majors (Petro-Canada and Imperial Oil), independents (Kerr-McGee and EnCana), and juniors (Canadian Superior and Corridor Resources). Douglas House captures the industry's spirit of risk and rivalry in the phrase "the last of the free enterprisers."[4] However, he also stresses the partnerships and allied ventures that are integral to this sector. It is precisely the scale of risk that has made the joint venture and the farm-in such crucial relationships in the oil patch as a whole.

It would be wrong to focus on petroleum capital alone. A number of well-established industries responded to the newly emerging energy segment by defending economic and political interests of their own. The Atlantic fishery recognized the dangers of petroleum exploration and development: threats to freedom of movement, damage to gear, ecological degradation from spills, blowouts and routine discharges, and lost catch. On the other hand, a series of land-based manufacturing and supply-and-service businesses – ranging from shipyards and design-engineering services to well, scientific, pipeline, diving, air transport, and marine supply services – stood to gain significantly from the presence of offshore exploration and production. By 1980, the Offshore Technology Association of Nova Scotia had been formed as a trade voice for these interests.

A third pillar of power is the federal and provincial states. From the point of view of politics, it is the combined properties of petroleum extraction and sea-based operations that make the offshore sector distinctive. But they also render the offshore domain considerably more involved than its terrestrial counterpart. As the two jurisdictions have asserted their rival claims to sub-sea resource ownership and to broader offshore jurisdiction, the industry has faced a dilemma. Political uncertainty constitutes a significant dimension of business risk. The prospect of intergovernmental warfare, divergent legislation, multiple regulatory regimes, and cumulative royalty and tax burdens is a nightmare. Tactically, petroleum operators had two choices: to withhold activity until the jurisdictional smoke cleared or to ally with one or the other of the sovereign authorities. In many respects, it was a classic case of market interests being "caught in the vise of federalism."[5] When the underlying co-ordinates of Canadian energy policy eroded several times during this period, relationships within and between states were complicated further.

The history of Scotian Basin petroleum comprises a series of political challenges, accommodations, and settlements. Among them are the negotiation of serial intergovernmental agreements and accords, the passage of detailed pieces of legislation in both Ottawa and Halifax, and the delegation of a multitude of legal and regulatory mandates to diverse administrative boards and agencies. The joint management agency known as the Canada–Nova Scotia Offshore Petroleum Board (CNSOPB) has played a central role in the disposition of the Crown resource during the exploratory and development phases. Authorized in 1986 and operational three years later, it continues to be integral to offshore governance. However, it does not exhaust the range of government authorities. The comprehensive delineation and assessment of the offshore petroleum state is a central concern of this book.

Themes and Variations in the Literature on Offshore Exploration

Offshore petroleum is best understood as a staple resource domain poised between local, national, and international forces.[6] Local conditions are a significant variable for an industry that operates in many basins and under many state authorities. At the same time, local interests have often struggled to have a voice in offshore policy regimes controlled by higher powers. For their part, sovereign states have guarded their jurisdictional claims to continental shelf formations while adapting terrestrial petroleum policies to subsea regions. This policy, in turn, has engendered tensions between central and regional authorities on questions ranging from rights allocation to environmental protection to industrial and employment linkages with onshore economies. The policy also helps account for incipient "national traditions" in offshore practice. Finally, over the past half century, offshore petroleum has evolved rapidly into a global domain. Although its commercial roots are on the US Gulf Coast, where Texas independents underwrote early exploration in the 1940s, international oil giants and their subsidiaries soon rose to prominence. By the time new offshore basins were attracting attention in Europe, Latin America, West Africa, and the Asia-Pacific, a fully rounded multinational complex (including not only operators but also supply and service sectors) had assumed a predominant competitive position. The development of second- and third-generation prospects therefore led to sharp tensions between host states and overseas capital, particularly over the respective terms of domestic and foreign participation. All the while, offshore areas have come to constitute a global frontier in a physical sense as advances in technology, finance, equipment, and expertise have pushed operational prospects into ever-deeper waters and more severe climate zones. This trend is likewise transforming the calculus of commercial viability and posing formidable new challenges to state authorities.

A Distinctive Political Economy

Offshore petroleum can be treated, commercially and politically, as an industry *sui generis*. From the 1950s, US oil interests have pressed both Congress and the administration with arguments that offshore operations are by nature qualitatively different from those on land.[7] Government has been urged to legislate, tax, and regulate accordingly. Geography was not the only consideration, however: the offshore industry could not be fully severed from the national energy and hydrocarbon policies of sovereign states.[8] Indeed, early legal and policy templates were forged in terrestrial contexts.

Over time, however, the differences between offshore and land-based operations have become as pronounced as the similarities, in both corporate and state circles. Offshore petroleum exists by virtue of complex engineering and technology systems that are among the most dynamic on the globe.[9] Moreover, the transfer of these technologies from one hydrocarbon basin to another may be affected by interfirm or intrafirm transactions. At the same time, developments in the law of the sea have extended and deepened jurisdictional claims by national and regional authorities, enabling states to regulate commercial activities through novel and experimental development strategies.[10] Finally, the offshore sector has had to reckon, in political terms, with complications not encountered onshore. Overlaps and intersections with other ocean businesses – marine transport, communications, fishing, and so on – have complicated the management of hydrocarbon resources. Most recently, a new challenge has emerged in the form of ocean policy and governance, a framework predicated on the integrated resource management of extensive marine spaces, usually for ecosystem health. To date, this approach has no counterpart in terrestrial oil and gas administration, where a pillared regime separates petroleum from the administration of adjacent resources such as agriculture or forests.[11] Offshore, however, the growing presence of policy metaframeworks threatens to complicate, if not entirely overturn, normal sectoral practice.[12]

Spatial and Temporal Dimensions

Policy diffusion can be explored in at least two dimensions: the spatial and the temporal. The spatial is evident on any global petroleum map that highlights the interplay of offshore basins and geopolitical authorities. Each emerging basin in the expansion of the offshore frontier has drawn lessons from its predecessors, from the Gulf of Mexico in the 1950s to the North Sea in the 1960s to Australia, Brazil, and West Africa in the 1970s. As this set of offshore frontiers has expanded, it has become a political and a geological reference group. For example, when operations were pioneered in the Gulf of Mexico after 1945, coastal states vied with Washington for legal jurisdiction. The judicial settlement confined Louisiana, Texas, California, and other states to a coastal strip of three nautical miles, while the balance of the offshore continental shelf fell to the Department of Interior and its Minerals Management Service.[13]

By the time offshore plays were contemplated in the North Sea, the coastal nations had a different preoccupation. Negotiating boundary limits, they carved the ocean into a series of national sectors. Beginning in southern waters adjacent to the Netherlands, Denmark, and the United Kingdom, the exploration frontier pushed out across the North Sea.[14] In subsequent decades, most of the world-class fields were found in mid-basin, where the major state beneficiaries proved to be the United Kingdom and Norway, unitary states in which the central government enjoys exhaustive jurisdiction.[15] In the 1990s, the frontier moved again, this time into the far northern reaches.

Perhaps Australia comes closest, in political-economic terms, to matching the key institutional and structural characteristics of Canada. It is a British dominion with Westminster-style parliamentary arrangements and a federal state based on former colonies in the Empire.[16] At the same time, Australia is a settler society with an Aboriginal minority, and it is endowed with extensive physical resources to fuel a primary industrial base.[17] Not surprisingly, a considerable amount of learning took place in the formative decade of 1965-75. Since then, however, Australia's offshore petroleum sector has far outpaced that of Canada; now entering its fifth decade, it has upstream activities on multiple coasts and operations in all phases of the product cycle.[18] In key respects, Australia suggests what the future might hold for Canada, if and when the Scotian Basin advances toward maturity.

Three other offshore regions have become significant since 1990. The first is in Brazil, where continental shelf petroleum has grown explosively through discoveries of several vast basins off the Atlantic coast. These discoveries have enabled the Brazilian state oil company, Petrobras, to follow the Norwegian path and emerge as a sophisticated global leader in offshore development. The second region is the West African coast from the Gulf of Guinea south to Angola, where a series of states – including Nigeria,

Ghana, Equatorial Guinea, Gabon, Cameroon, Congo-Brazzaville, Angola, and Sao Tome and Principe – have joined the offshore club. Geological prospectivity is high, and international oil capital has negotiated extremely favourable terms with the largely autocratic ruling state elites.[19] The third region is in the Russian Pacific around Sakhalin Island, where one of the world's largest liquefied natural gas production systems has recently come on stream.

The temporal dimension is equally significant to offshore development and is evident in all longitudinal analyses of offshore fields or basins. This dimension highlights the life-cycle stages of an offshore play and its tightly woven policy correlates. Four stages are generally posited. The first covers the exploration stage, beginning with legal permits that require a stipulated work program over a designated period of five to ten years. Prospective explorers are invited to nominate blocks of seabed space that they judge promising or the selection is determined by state authorities. Bids are then invited, and awards are made based on the highest level of work commitments pledged. When the results are sufficiently suggestive to warrant further investigation, permittees move to exploration drilling, by which holes are sunk at designated locations to test for hydrocarbon reservoirs. Significant finds are generally followed up by delineation drilling to establish field boundaries and volumes.

The second development stage begins when a commercial discovery is declared. Exploration permit holders have the opportunity to convert their rights into longer-term development leases tapered to the expected life of the field. At this point, plans are designed for petroleum production systems, including subsea wells, seabed control facilities and gathering lines, production platforms, and pipeline or ship-based transport and storage facilities. It is at this phase that major capital commitments are required. The rights holders often turn to global engineering and construction contractors to deliver complex facilities. As well, state authorities exercise regulatory approval over development activities as they unfold.

The production phase begins when oil, natural gas, or other petroleum liquids begin to flow. Rates of flow will vary over the life of a reservoir, and extraction practices can affect both the volume and duration of production. Reservoir management, then, is a central challenge if maximum returns are to be realized. Although the production phase is more modest in its capital and labour commitments, supply and service is a continuing function over the life of a project. As fields mature, it is also common for the initial investors to sell their holdings and with new ownership can come new business strategy. The public policy challenges of managing field or basin transitions from emergent to expansive to mature conditions are complex and have not always been sufficiently acknowledged. For example, the state has an interest in maximizing and extending hydrocarbon extraction, even as the rate of flow declines. The state's interest can be at odds with the operator's desire to terminate a project as soon as marginal returns on the field fall below those of bellwether corporate holdings. State authorities once took a rather passive stance in the face of such corporate decisions. In recent times, however, state interests have been projected more actively to put the right field in the right hands.

The hydrocarbon yield eventually diminishes to the point where closure takes place. This final phase entails the permanent seal off of seabed well facilities and the decommissioning of offshore installations. Developers first dealt with this challenge in the Gulf of Mexico. Since then, hundreds of offshore platforms have been abandoned, and thousands will face this prospect in future years. Seal offs began in the North Sea in the 1990s, and the famous *Brent Spar* dispute was its signature controversy.[20] A variety of industry protocols and state regulations have emerged in response. Options range from the complete removal of facilities above the sea floor to partial dismantling below navigable depths to virtual abandonment in situ. The US Rigs-to-Reef program promotes the potential for abandoned jacket structures to sustain pelagic and benthic ecosystems that originated during the production years.[21] On the Scotian Shelf, the only offshore system to reach this stage is the Cohasset-Panuke project, which quit flowing in 1999.

As with any cycle framework, there is no strict linearity. Stages can be arrested, reversed, or reset. For example, the Gulf of Mexico was widely regarded as a spent basin (the so-called dead sea) by the early 1990s, when exploration stalled and production volumes plummeted. Yet a new boom began in 1995 sparked by the advent of deepwater drilling (in subsurface depths exceeding 305 metres) and deep structure drilling (more than 4,500 metres below the seabed). These new technologies gave dramatic life to what had been regarded as a mature and declining sector.[22]

In sum, the prospects for offshore comparative analysis, on both the spatial and the temporal dimensions, are both rich and promising.

Offshore Petro-Capital as a Political Factor

The offshore petroleum industry is sufficiently unique in its upstream operations to be considered a distinct subindustry within the hydrocarbon sector. Yet a plethora of intriguing questions remain. How does the offshore segment express its shared interests on political and policy questions? Is the field or basin a relevant political denominator? The role of farm-ins and joint ventures has long been evident as a source of industry solidarity.[23] What are the prospects for coalition building along the offshore value chain? Alternatively, how does offshore petroleum relate to other ocean industries in terms of alliances or rivalries? Do associational structures give voice to offshore interests?

These are complicated questions. Few if any firms restrict their operations to offshore settings alone; rather, they assemble portfolios of property interests of varying degrees of risk in a comprehensive effort to acquire proven and commercially exploitable reserves. They are likely to combine fields and basins in many locations. An intricate process, internal to the firm, dictates where exploration and development funds are spent in a given year, and regional and project managers bring rosters of projects to the corporate table, where they compete for support. Relative attractiveness can change quickly over time, according to exploration results, market conditions, and political contexts.

So long as the zone of operations is confined to a single state's jurisdiction (as, for example, in Alberta during the period from 1918 to 1958), the lines of political mobilization and response may be relatively concurrent. The upstream industry depended upon provincial tenure and licensing policy, and the Alberta Petroleum Association (renamed the Canadian Petroleum Association in 1952) functioned as the collective voice of the major companies when dealing with the government in Edmonton. As activities proliferate into multiple state jurisdictions, however, the challenge of aggregating and articulating the political interests of shifting corporate subsets grows. The Canadian Petroleum Association, like other trade associations that service increasingly diversified memberships, opted for specialized internal sections or divisions where relevant business constituencies could coalesce for shared concerns while remaining part of the umbrella association. The Saskatchewan and British Columbia divisions emerged in this way.

A separate vehicle, the Independent Petroleum Association of Canada, represented companies whose activities were concentrated in the upstream exploration and production stages. This organization sprang in part from postwar tensions between independents and the integrated "majors" over the shape of the Canadian oil market. Wishing to supply the largest possible domestic market (at a time when oil exports were tightly controlled), the Prairie independents pushed for a coast-to-coast pipeline network. The foreign-owned majors, who already supplied Quebec and Maritime markets from non-Canadian sources, pushed for a west-east divide, which was ultimately put in place.[24] Although the Canadian Petroleum Association and the Independent Petroleum Association of Canada had memberships of similar size by the 1970s, the companies securing acreage off the East Coast were largely, though not exclusively, foreign-owned majors.

In the United States, a specialized offshore association emerged shortly after the war. The Offshore Operators Committee was created to speak for the offshore upstream segment of US petroleum operators and to aggregate the concerns of firms active in the Gulf of Mexico. Still active, the committee focuses on regulatory rule-making processes in federal government agencies. By 2002, the group included seventy operating firms and twenty-five service companies.

In Canada, an analogue to the Offshore Operators Committee appeared in two frontier regional associations following the start of offshore drilling. The Arctic Petroleum Operators Association represented the federal northlands. On the Atlantic continental shelf, the parallel body was the East Coast Petroleum Operators Association. According to the newsletter *Offshore News,* each numbered about a dozen firms, and the costs of collective action were met by an assessment on acreage-holding member companies. A decade later, in 1983, the eastern association was absorbed into the Canadian Petroleum Association as its Offshore Operators Division. Three years later, the Arctic section followed suit. (This consolidation coincided with a mid-decade market slump and massive industry retrenchment.) The arrangement continues today in the Atlantic section of the renamed Canadian Association of Petroleum Producers.

Even within the Canadian Association of Petroleum Producers, it would be wrong to assume a uniformity of corporate purpose on offshore matters, for structural tensions permeate the membership. For example, corporate mega-mergers at the turn of the twenty-first century created a new tier of internationalized interests that have dwarfed all other oil producers. The appearance of supermajors such as ExxonMobil, Chevron Texaco, Total, and ConocoPhillips has altered the offshore business in a number of ways. First, it has halved the number of giant players in the international corporate game, significantly curbing rivalry in the exploration field. In addition, the rationalization of budgets, staff, rights holdings, and planned projects has significantly cut the amount of exploration capital being directed at high-risk basins. This, in turn, has had a knock-on effect in the offshore services and supply sector, which has been squeezed by the same developments. Furthermore, consolidation reinforces the tendency of megafirms to limit their interest to truly giant finds, passing over promising prospects whose profit potential fails to match their newfound scale. Of course, there are many firms of lesser scale that can exploit this situation. Instead of targeting global elephant fields, they seek more modest portfolios, concentrating either on the prospects that the supermajors decline or abandon or on secondary or tertiary extraction from maturing fields that have been cast off by their initial developers.[25]

The Technological Imperative

One of the strongest sources of business and political solidarity for offshore petroleum has been its reliance on advanced technology. Indeed, technological breakthroughs were instrumental in creating the offshore sector.[26] It is worth noting the primitivity of early offshore exploration in the Gulf of Mexico region and the dramatic innovations that have followed. In the 1940s, drill barges were simply dragged into shallow swamp-water positions and submerged. As ambitions turned toward open water, military surplus landing ships were refitted with derricks and drill support systems.[27] The first true standing rig, the Kerr-McGee 16, was placed some eighteen kilometres offshore in 1947 to drill in 5.5 metres of water. In the half century since, however, the Gulf's geological province (along with its industrial and political regime) has been transformed repeatedly.

Successive waves of innovation have been dramatic, as evidenced each year at the Offshore Technology Conference in Houston.[28] The results have improved the prospect of locating petroleum deposits; opened access to ever more remote sites; altered the techniques of hydrocarbon collection, processing, storage, and transport; and (through resurvey and rediscovery processes) turned apparently mature or exhausted sites and basins into new, high-growth prospects.[29] In exploration, three- and four-dimensional seismic image measurement has dramatically refined the accuracy of pre-drill intelligence. (This innovation has had major implications for offshore regions that have been inactive in recent decades, either because of formal moratorium policies or lapses in interest. The reopening of such areas allows for qualitative reappraisals through new seismic campaigns.) Directional drilling has likewise become far more sophisticated, allowing for both angled and horizontal access to reservoirs and the subsurface linkage of small, complex deposits. In offshore environments, this innovation allows companies to drill multiple wells from a single platform site or in dispersed configurations and to utilize seabed lines to gather the product together. Finally, techniques of measurement while drilling allow ongoing well data to be compiled as drilling proceeds. In high-cost settings, where single wells run from $50 million to 75 million in shallow water and twice that amount at greater depths on the continental slope, all of these innovations represent dramatic economies.

In production, the most visible symbols of technology are new above-water structures, including a variety of production platforms, from jacket and compliant towers and semi-submersibles to floating production, storage, and offloading (FPSO) vessels that offer an alternative to pipeline transport. Until recently, the latter option was restricted to oilfield development. In the past few years, however, it has been extended to gas fields, where ship-based plants liquefy and store natural gas before offloading it to liquefied natural gas (LNG) tankers, the so-called floating liquid natural gas (FLNG) system.

Although the technical and engineering dimensions of offshore operations have been widely celebrated, the societal implications of offshore operations have been neglected. Yet one promising analytic school – the technology assessment system school – seeks to assess the societal dimension. In the mid-1970s, an Office of Technology Assessment was established in the US Congress, and the Science Council of Canada took up the theme in Ottawa. Technology assessment was advanced "as a policy tool for alerting public and private policy-makers to the likely consequences of making a decision either to deploy a particular technology or to choose from among competing technologies."[30] A celebrated first-generation technology assessment project, based at the University of Oklahoma, tackled US outer continental shelf oil and gas operations. In Canada, the Science Council mounted a similar program that shed considerable light on the emerging offshore petroleum frontier.[31]

For its part, the offshore industry expressed frustration that step changes in technology were not adequately acknowledged or appreciated by either the policy establishment or the interested public. This perceived neglect was a cause of ongoing frustration because, it was argued, many of these advances altered, sometimes decisively, the risk equations that apply to offshore activities. Technological advances were especially pertinent to a sector whose periodic political crisis moments – the Santa Barbara oil blowout of 1968, the Mexican Ixtoc 1 blowout of 1979, the Ocean Ranger rig loss of 1982, and the Piper Alpha platform fire of 1988 – seemed increasingly distant from contemporary practice. Of course, the situation changed on 20 April 2010, when a blowout destroyed the Deepwater Horizon rig at BP's Macondo well and released five million barrels of crude oil into the Gulf.[32]

Sharp questions once again attend the design, installation, and operation of complex systems, particularly in deepwater basins. The report of the presidential commission on the Macondo blowout highlights these questions, along with the urgent need for regulatory renewal.[33]

Even without the Macondo catastrophe, the relentless drive to develop new technologies raises questions about reliability, transferability, and risk of unintended consequences. In Western states, the organized public will continue to pose such questions as long as offshore operations are under way.[34] Indeed, as offshore operators seek and obtain permission to drill in water depths exceeding 1,000 metres and to subfloor depths of 10,000 metres, it could hardly be otherwise.[35] As a result, project assessment, both environmental and socio-economic, is a central and politically charged terrain. It demands continued monitoring by regulatory authorities as it triggers policy debates on optimal regulatory instruments and policy mixes, particularly the role of prescriptive and performance-based regulations, different kinds of industry self-regulation and third-party certification, and the dangers of regulatory capture.[36]

Federalism and the Offshore Domain

The history of commercial petroleum in federal systems is in large part a history of intergovernmental conflict.[37] Petroleum has pitted national governments against provinces and provinces against one another in struggles over jurisdiction, resource ownership, fiscal policy, environmental security, and industrial linkages, to name only the most prominent issues. What began on land has carried over to the water. Washington faces coastal states from Louisiana to Maine to Alaska. Ottawa deals with provinces and territories on all three coasts. Australia has a similar dynamic. In all these cases, there has been a proclivity for constitutional litigation, in which rival governments advance sovereign claims that are determined by judicial review, and central authorities have emerged legally dominant. Supreme Courts generally found the national governments' case for sovereign power over continental shelf resources to be superior to provincial and state arguments. This is far from the end of the story, however, for provincial and state authorities have spent the past half century seeking alternative paths to control over the resource.

In the first generation of offshore petroleum exploration and development (1950-75), central jurisdictions appeared to be self-contained and exhaustive. That is, all political questions pertaining to title and management fell to central state institutions. Indeed, if continental shelves were significant only for their petroleum reserves, this arrangement might have lasted longer. Federal authorities would administer leases, collect royalties, and regulate projects in much the same way that Texas and Alberta did on land. However, the very fact of ocean jurisdiction introduced complicating factors. One was the presence of parallel and potentially rival industries – such as fishing, marine transport, and coastal tourism – that had prior claims to ocean use.[38] Their effective political mobilization not only challenged offshore resource administrators to expand their policy repertoires but also provided provincial and state authorities with avenues to reassert an offshore presence.

Another key force, which began in the 1970s, was growing awareness of ocean ecology. This awareness owed much to damaging environmental episodes such as the blowouts, along with tanker spills, marine animal welfare campaigns, and a growing appreciation of the scale of shore-based pollution. The ocean commons were revealed to be profoundly complex and fragile systems in desperate need of integrated governance.[39] Where the ocean is concerned, policy issues are linked, overlaps abound, and intergovernmental and interagency conflicts are latent in almost all commercial and regulatory questions. Recognition of this reality has hastened the breakdown of traditional sectoral approaches to continental shelf resources. Previously separate domains – oil, fish, transport, communications, parks, and protection – are now increasingly connected, pointing toward a new era of ocean governance. A new repertoire of policy instruments and planning tools is emerging, one that includes cross-jurisdictional coastal and open-ocean initiatives.[40]

Although the institutions of ocean governance are still rudimentary, they point to a new political space that is being actively contested by an expanding range of interests. The risks of this situation have not been lost on the offshore petroleum bloc, which recognizes that holistic ocean policies have the potential to erode or even supplant sectoral resource regimes. Much will depend on how existing regulatory arrangements are reconciled with new initiatives and on where the seats of ministerial and bureaucratic authority are lodged. As a result, the interface between management regimes will be politically contested in the foreseeable future.

State Strength and Capacity

Much of the struggle of offshore politics ultimately comes down to the coastal states' capacity to manage hydrocarbon resources. An understanding of capacity can draw on some classic analytic debates about strong and weak states, policy coherence and fragmentation, and institutional autonomy and permeability.[41] The need to unpack these complex problems became clear as offshore studies progressed. It seems that part of the answer lies in the properties of state management institutions.[42] Another part lies in the properties of the policy subsectors being assessed.[43] In addition, a panoply of policy instruments figures in any offshore management effort. Policy borrowing, learning, and diffusion is common among offshore agencies.[44] Linda Weiss offers a helpful insight with her observation that "states are not uniformly capable across all policy areas."[45] Just as a state's capacity may vary among broad policy areas such as fiscal management, industrial adjustment, and social redistribution, so too can it vary among the several subsectors of offshore oil and gas policy.

Offshore petroleum exploration and development on the East Coast is a curious institutional hybrid that has emerged over the past twenty-five years. Its roots lay in a succession of federal-provincial disputes over offshore resource ownership that were exacerbated by the twin energy (OPEC) price spikes of the 1970s. When exploration began to yield significant discoveries (particularly the Venture gas and Hibernia oil strikes) in the late 1970s, the need to resolve uncertainties over state jurisdiction became more urgent. Industry hesitated to move forward so long as the status of tenures remained cloudy. It was at this point that the rival ownership dispute was transformed into a joint management regime by means of a series of negotiated intergovernmental accords.

The concept of a joint federal-provincial management board has a mixed provenance that originated in the 1970s. Parallel negotiations over power sharing arose in northern Aboriginal land claims talks and in renewable resource co-management.[46] In petroleum, however, the prototype was the tri-province Maritime Offshore Mineral Resources Agreement of 1977. It was succeeded by the Canada–Nova Scotia Agreement on Offshore Oil and Gas Resource Management and Revenue Sharing of 1982, which was modified in turn by the Canada-Newfoundland Atlantic Accord and the Canada–Nova Scotia revised deal one year later.[47] Talks on a parallel Pacific accord between Ottawa and British Columbia were under way after 1987 but came to a halt when it was decided that the West Coast's long-standing moratorium on drilling would stay in place. Interbasin comparisons can, however, still be made.[48]

A new template for offshore management was established by the East Coast accords: jointly appointed petroleum boards, supported by professional staff, exercise delegated regulatory powers under federal and provincial statutes and with a mandate to coordinate the essential administrative functions of exploration and production. Although the boards enjoy substantial autonomy as Crown agents, they are responsible to designated federal and provincial ministers, who also have the power to review, confirm, and override selected types of decisions through "an elaborate series of trumping arrangements" vis-à-vis the boards.[49] At each level of government, a range of bureaus and agencies are bound into the board structure by formal memoranda of agreement, while industry and public interests enjoy access through a shifting network of advisory committees.

The joint-board design raises a number of questions. How open is it to organized lobbying? Within its broad jurisdictional template, what are the formative or valence issue areas? How meaningful are the options for ministerial appeal? The literature on capital-state bargaining certainly has a role to play here, particularly given that petroleum basins have to date been developed largely on a project basis, by which each sponsoring consortium advances an omnibus plan to be adjudicated by public authorities.

Also relevant here is the question of issue boundaries and characteristics. In policy terms, how can the offshore development field most usefully be delineated? In response to this question, Derek Fee advances the concept of the petroleum exploitation strategy, which consists of "those instruments, both legal and fiscal, that define the relationship between the state and the oil companies involved in the petroleum exploitation process."[50] For Fee, this concept highlights a range of critical elements of which three – the exploration agreement, licensing policy, and taxation – form the core. It is worth noting that this framework was developed in reference to leading oil supply states during the years of OPEC hegemony. A more nuanced version can be established in reference to offshore petroleum regimes.

This Book

When this study was conceived shortly after the turn of the millennium, I expected the Canada–Nova Scotia Offshore Petroleum Board to be the centrepiece of the analysis. This assumption derived in part from the board's distinctive institutional traits and its role in resolving the jurisdictional uncertainties of earlier decades. A uniquely Canadian response to a problem faced by many federal states exploiting offshore resources, the board has not yet attracted the attention it deserves. As the investigation proceeded, however, it became evident that the board, although a central protagonist in Scotian Basin politics, accounted for only a part of the story. The reasons for its prominence were in part circumstantial. The first generation of offshore activity was confined overwhelmingly to exploratory efforts. As the Crown administrator of petroleum rights, the board stood squarely in the centre. Even then, however, there was evidence of a broader state presence and a more complex state structure overseeing the offshore industry. A more sweeping inquiry was needed to fully reveal the actors, settings, and issues affecting petroleum exploration and development in the Scotian Basin. The existence and importance of this wider structure has become increasingly evident in the past ten years as exploitation has followed exploration and as a variety of downstream businesses have entered the fray, along with terrestrial public interests.

Although the life and times of the CNSOPB loom large in this analysis, this book also offers a comprehensive picture of state involvement on the continental shelf. It captures the key role of federal agencies such as Environment Canada, Fisheries and Oceans, the National Energy Board, and Natural Resources Canada, to name only the lead players. On the Nova Scotia side, the Departments of Energy, Economic and Rural Development, and Environment and Labour enjoy a similar status, as does the Utilities Review Board. The local state is also added to the mix in recognition of the stakes of coastal counties, municipalities, and the communities they represent and to highlight the complications associated with this relatively disaggregated and weak state structure.

To illustrate the existence of multiple political contexts and potentially distinct governing structures, the offshore basin is placed in a regional geographic context. Map 1.1 offers one perspective, identifying a series of settings in which critical issues can arise.

The offshore Crown arena is the field in which Crown title is administered and corporate exploration and production activities are regulated. It is the domain of the CNSOPB, the agency that manages Crown title to seabed petroleum. In this sense, the board is the offshore equivalent to provincial departments that oversee the Crown's interest in terrestrial oil and gas. Simply put, the board is the licensor of exploration rights and production leases that play a critical role in shaping the pace and direction of initial field development. The board concentrates on the classic upstream activities that extend to the point of extracting petroleum from the ground. As will be discussed, the board links back to its parent authorities in a number of ways that allow policy direction from senior political levels. It also connects horizontally to other departments and agencies.

A spatially adjacent setting connects commercially viable oil or natural gas fields with points of onward sale. This involves field or project corridors

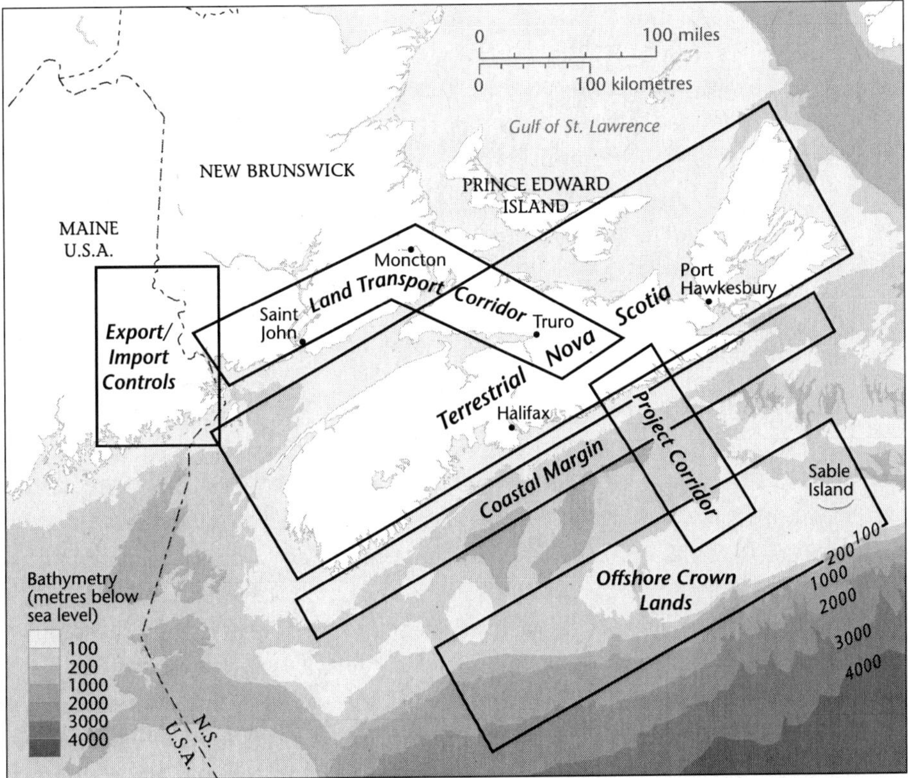

Map 1.1 Political contexts for offshore petroleum

that connect offshore wellheads with processing facilities. There are several possible configurations, including a FPSO (to tanker) facility for crude oil and a pipeline-to-shore based processing-plant system for natural gas. A key point is that new commercial interests, investments, and works emerge within the gathering-processing-storage infrastructure. The regulatory jurisdiction over these activities also tends to fall under separate authorities. For a FPSO system, the federal Ministry of Transport looms large; for offshore gas pipelines, the National Energy Board holds the lead.

A third setting is the territorial coastal margin, where shore-based authorities begin to play a role, particularly at the provincial and local levels. Any facility that is sited at tidewater, or otherwise directly connected to offshore industry, is affected in this domain. For example, natural gas processing plants, natural gas liquids separation facilities, and liquefied gas-receiving terminals exert a significant footprint on the coastal margin. Senior jurisdictions hold environmental impact review powers for such installations, while local authorities exercise crucial zoning and taxation powers. Another aspect of coastal margin politics involves industrial linkages between offshore operators and onshore contractors.

A fourth arena with distinct political concerns is the province as a whole, which can be described as mainland Nova Scotia. It plays a role in so far as interests and issues arising from the terrestrial community are directed at offshore activities. Since there is little to no political community resident within the offshore belt, it is not surprising that certain interests may be asserted on the basis of adjacency. Nova Scotia citizens have raised pointed questions about the range and distribution of benefits from offshore petroleum. How do citizens benefit from provincial Crown title to the resource, by way of royalties, taxes, and other fiscal transfers? What benefit are petroleum supply, security, and use to citizens? Some have argued that provincial consumers should be given full and even preferred purchase rights to the landed resource. If accepted, this has implications for market-building policies targeting local gas distribution and petrochemical manufacturing facilities. Another possibility is the assertion of a new category of interests in offshore petroleum, over and above the general provincial community. It has been suggested, for example, that Aboriginal peoples in Nova Scotia possess an interest by virtue of their constitutional rights.

The fifth and final policy setting is the onward transmission and sale of hydrocarbon products to final consumers, which normally entails long-distance transit by pipeline or other means. This phase can also involve the shipping of products abroad. In a sense, this step completes the industry chain for offshore petroleum products by realizing a commercial return. Notably, the transit and export steps are each subject to regulatory regimes that constitute discrete political fields of action. When shipment has an interprovincial or international component, the federal National Energy Board plays a central role. As a result, a wide range of interests tend to coalesce at this point: commodity owners, rival shipping interests, rival buyers, host provinces, and civil society groups. In Map 1.1, these stages are represented by the "land corridor" and "export controls" designations.

Taken together, the policy domains that have grown up around these spatially defined functional steps capture the full complexity of offshore politics on the Scotian Shelf. In principle, the domains can apply to any offshore petroleum basin. Examining the basin at the level of institutions, interests, and decision processes allows for the identification of the distinguishing features of basin politics. Yet several points should be clarified. First, the sequential logic of commercial production, as specified above, is seldom replicated literally in business and political practice. Put another way, there is no reason to expect that each stage stands alone and apart from the others. Indeed, the history of modern commerce suggests that corporate interests will adapt organizationally to prospective market uncertainties (as represented by external chain steps, for example) with strategic behaviour – equity partnerships, mergers and takeovers, or other business alliances. As a consequence, it is not surprising to find overlaps between these power arenas. In fact, the defining patterns of connection can offer crucial insights into prevailing power relations.

Second, the temporal logic of the industry chain seldom unfolds as a series of discrete steps. In other words, although commercial scale hydrocarbon discovery may be necessary to trigger other arenas, corporate planning and political reaction may proceed virtually simultaneously at multiple points along the chain. Infrastructure consortia may be formed and commence preliminary planning even before viable reserves have been confirmed. Similarly, long-term downstream delivery contracts are normally formalized between suppliers and buyers before oil or gas owners make regulatory applications for processing or transit.

Third, there is no reason to expect political processes to mirror, in structure, the industry chain. Indeed, discrepancies between the organization of the two, with all that this implies for interest holding and strategy, can account for much of the animating tension between market and state. Public authorities bent on petroleum exploitation have all discovered, sooner or later, that the political management of these endowments involves far more, in modern times, than getting the product to the surface and then stepping aside. Consequently, one of the most important questions for any authority is how the grid of sovereign institutions intersects with the chain of industry functions. This issue is one of the seldom-noted features of offshore petroleum management, and it is central to understanding the process. The configuration of agencies and authorities is commonly as diffuse as the business chain that it faces. Specialization is deeply embedded. Offices administering offshore Crown title, regulating indigenous business supply and labour use, enforcing environmental standards, licensing marine infrastructure, licensing terrestrial infrastructure, and conferring rights of export are scattered throughout multiple jurisdictions. It is important to consider that state authorities can achieve adaptive strategies different in form but parallel in function to those of business.

Offshore Politics and State Policy

The signature feature of offshore petroleum politics is that its sectoral unity breaks down under close analysis. Consequently, it cannot be captured on a single plane of analysis but only through a series of distinct, though still connected, policy domains. In effect, offshore petroleum politics consists of multiple arenas in which power – understood as the mobilization, clash, and resolution of organized interests – is exercised and affirmed. Each of these fields of power involves a potentially distinct and shifting configuration of interests, and the hierarchies of influence may vary from one field to the next. Insight into the cumulative patterns, or the ultimate distillation of offshore petroleum power, can only be drawn after a detailed study of the key constituent parts or policy subsectors, followed by their re-aggregation into a political-economic whole. It bears repeating that not all subsectors will be coordinate and equal in importance. To capture this reality, Rayner and colleagues advance the useful concept of the critical subsector, which plays an anchor role "capable of blocking or enabling overall levels or directions of sectoral policy change."[51]

Power can be a difficult and elusive concept. It may be manifest in a visible contest between organized interests that advance distinct agendas fulfilled only at the expense of rivals. This is the realm of organizational and group politics, where firms, industry advocates, and popular groups express concerns and pursue the desired outcomes. This visible plane represents only a part of the political domain, however, if we consider what it leaves out. On the one hand, it neglects political stakeholders who have not achieved the effective threshold of formal organization because of disproportionate skews in the possession of material or symbolic resources or biases in participative procedure or decision-making rules. In either case, potential interest holders can be discouraged or outright excluded. At the least, such constraints mean that the associational universe is an incomplete reflection of political interests. On the other hand, the visible plane can also overlook the significance of institutional interests within the very state structures called upon to adjudicate conflicts. The premise that governmental channels offer neutral conduits to balance interests has long since been abandoned. More accurately, state interests need to be seen as integral to political decisions and manifest in concepts such as bureaucratic politics and clientelism, among others. All of these considerations underline the need to explore the biases of institutions.

Part 1 of this book explores the physical as well as the political-economic terrain of the Scotian Basin. It locates offshore petroleum in geological terms and highlights the problem of oil and gas exploration. This is only a start, however, since commercial and political imperatives are also considered. Chapter 2 offers an alternative interpretation of offshore corporate politics based on the notion of basin development, a generic process that unfolds as a series of steps or stages. Analogous to the literature on product cycles in business and policy cycles in state decision making, I argue that the prime orientations and interests advanced by firms and governments evolve as a basin develops. Put simply, the priorities of firms at the early exploratory phases differ qualitatively from those of commercial exploitation. As a basin matures, new sets of issues arise; as it declines, the agenda shifts again.

Part 2 explores the processes of state building associated with Nova Scotia's offshore petroleum resource, beginning with the formative decades of the 1970s and 1980s and continuing to the present. Chapter 3 details the joint (federal-provincial) offshore Crown rights management regime, which emerged from a series of intergovernmental accords that were struck to clarify the rules and procedures for resource rights access. Although the accords dealt with more than management structures alone, the centrepiece was the Canada–Nova Scotia Offshore Petroleum Board. A product of institutional experimentation in the 1980s, the board has been a central force in Scotian Shelf development. Its origins reveal much about the state's expectations, and the board's mandate reveals its reach. The chapter offers an institutional analysis of the board's structure and identifies the logic and values embedded in its architecture.

Chapter 4 extends the investigation to the board's operational procedures, centring attention on the responsibilities the board has assumed and its means of translating mandate into action. The chapter reveals that the board exercises delegated powers in a number of policy fields. Questions of personnel, licensing processes, and reporting relationships loom large. The range of regulatory powers is impressively diverse and is illustrated by a case study of the first project to extract petroleum from the Scotian Basin, the Cohasset-Panuke oilfield. Ultimately, the chapter paints a picture of an offshore board practising regulatory politics in multiple dimensions.

The Crown rights regime does not exhaust the range of state policy options offshore, and the board was not its sole instrument. Not surprisingly, in light of the wider petroleum politics of the 1980s, the question of rent collection loomed large. Governments at all levels sought to supplement resource royalty and tax receipts with earnings from state corporations. Federal and provincial authorities both took this route. Petro-Canada was established explicitly as Ottawa's instrument for catalyzing new oil and gas development, particularly in frontier areas. The Crown corporation played a significant role in the Atlantic offshore booms of the 1980s, and its story is relatively well known. Far less prominent but no less revealing is the history of the provincial rent collection vehicle known as Nova Scotia Resources Limited. Its story is the subject of Chapter 5.

Part 3 offers a series of case studies on decision making and power relations in the offshore petroleum commercial chain. The pace of commercial production is a critical indicator of basin development. In this respect, the Scotian Shelf remains at an embryonic stage. Chapter 6 presents a detailed analysis of the only major natural gas production system to date, the Sable offshore energy project. For the Scotian Basin to achieve commercial takeoff, this system will have to be replicated many times over. For the moment, however, the Sable project offers significant insights into the complicated politics of linking fields to markets.

Chapter 7 explores the policy sector known as industrial benefits. Around the world, host states understandably want to maximize the domestic economic enterprise and employment advantages from offshore development. States also recognize that all phases of the offshore industry – from seismic work and rig construction to exploratory drilling, field development, and supply and service – has long been dominated by global firms. Left on their own, these firms, which are based in Houston, Singapore, Holland, or South Korea, will draw on prior networks of contractors to meet their needs, regardless of geographic location. As a result, host states have for decades stipulated domestic participation as a requirement for gaining and holding licences. The design and application of an industrial benefits regime to the Scotian Shelf is the subject of Chapter 7.

In a federal state such as Canada, the federal-provincial encounter over offshore jurisdiction is more than a matter of who has regulatory primacy. The fiscal dimension is also important, and Chapter 8 examines intergovernmental struggles over royalties, taxes, and equalization transfers. This matter was sufficiently fundamental to be written into the 1982 and 1986 accords. To a large extent, the subject remained dormant until commercial exploitation began. Beginning in 1999, however, the fiscal issue moved to centre stage. A satisfactory resolution to the question for Nova Scotia lay at the centre of Premier John Hamm's "campaign for fairness" over the course of his tenure. The offshore revenue question haunted Prime Minister Paul Martin in his early years in office. In 2007, the issue reignited, in spectacular fashion, when the Stephen Harper Conservatives again proposed modifications for the treatment of offshore revenues for purposes of equalization finance. That the fiscal issue, above all others, has dominated the partisan and electoral dimensions of offshore development is highly revealing.

Chapter 9 explores the interests of land-based consumers of shelf petroleum. One of the advantages held out for Nova Scotian society as a whole has been secure and affordable local access to oil and gas. By 1997, provincial authorities, who had the prospect of landing Sable gas by the millennium, were planning to make good on this legacy. In this field the Government of Nova Scotia has taken a lead role and the outcomes offer a test case of the province's capacity to deliver results. The process of forging an entirely new industry structure and then licensing local gas-delivery franchises proved to be far from straightforward, illustrating not only the limits of provincial industrial planning but also the dangers of political overreach in pursuit of legitimacy.

The coastal margin represents a boundary between the offshore and onshore worlds. It is a complex social space that may be thought of as a frontier of colliding political interests that links shore-dwelling residents, harbour communities, municipal authorities, and a variety of occupational interests. The prevalence of political cross-pressures is a signifying feature of the coastal margin. Chapter 10 considers the rise of a new potential industry that is pre-eminently coastal, that of liquefied natural gas import and processing. This sector arrived in Nova Scotia in the early 2000s, when several consortia announced plans to build shipping, storage, and regasification facilities on the Atlantic shore. For several years, liquefied natural gas import and processing was the most dynamic segment of the hydrocarbon industry and promised to both extend and upgrade the economy of the Scotian Shelf. Although the initial promise was not fulfilled in the expected fashion, the industry's early years offer important insights into power relations offshore.

Political margins can, of course, be measured socially as well as geographically. Chapter 11 explores a relatively recent and potentially profound challenge from the margin. Evidence is mounting that Aboriginal peoples in Nova Scotia may hold a position, in relation to resource title and use, that is coordinate with the federal and provincial authorities. Since the 1970s, Status and Non-Status Indian groups have asserted claims to lands and resources. Their claims are based on both the Mi'kmaq treaties of Peace and Friendship and the legal doctrines of Aboriginal rights and title recognized through litigation. Although a series of judicial rulings has confirmed a set of rights connected to hunting, fishing, and logging, the possible inclusion of offshore resources, petroleum in particular, is a relatively recent turn. Although these matters are far from resolved, it may be that a third constitutional interest will be acknowledged within the domain of offshore governance.

The concluding chapter synthesizes analytic themes and explores their interconnections, allowing for a second look at questions of power and conflict, disaggregated state structure, and diffuse governance. The discussion underscores how an extended case study of the Scotian Basin speaks to a variety of concerns: the place of hydrocarbons in the regional energy mix, the challenges of locating and extracting petroleum, and the complications of regulating a strategic industry in a dynamic offshore polity. The offshore state in the Scotian Basin is revealed as a complex structure. Despite the innovative impulse of the joint management mandate, federal and provincial structures are far from fully coordinated. A variety of policy instruments have been deployed by federal, provincial, and joint agencies in attempts to shape the pace of oil and gas development. Integral to this is political pressure from petroleum capital that has fluctuated along with the identifiable cycles in upstream industry development. The struggle between governments and civil interests to secure "prime beneficiary" status is inherent in offshore management and is ongoing. In the future, lessons from the Nova Scotia experience may inform political practice on other coasts and in other basins.

PART 1

The Political Economy of Offshore Petroleum

2 The Politics of Offshore Basin Development

This chapter introduces the notion of hydrocarbon development as a discrete sequence or cycle of events. The cycle figures as a significant conceptual device for upstream petroleum politics, and it can be usefully applied to both offshore fields and basins. A field is a reservoir or series of rock reservoirs that contain threshold quantities of crude oil or natural gas or both. A basin is a broader geological entity with sedimentary rock formations that may generate hydrocarbons. A basin normally contains multiple fields of varying sizes and physical and commercial attributes. By providing a dynamic portrait of upstream events, the cycle model characterizes fields and basins as developmental processes and identifies and compares them in terms of stage of advancement. Although it begins with a geological focus on discovering oil and gas "in place," the model also conceptualizes the field or basin as a system of resource exploitation with important business and political dimensions.

Geologists explore cycles of sediment deposition and petroleum formation as basins are filled over millions of years. Engineers and economists approach field exploitation on the basis of differential levels of reserve recovery or reservoir depletion. Companies plan and assess their offshore investments according to each project's life-cycle costs, from initial reconnaissance to final asset disposal. State regulators require proponents to file and gain approval for detailed project descriptions that cover activities from cradle to grave. Many public policy measures figure as "pacing tools" to shape the tempo and direction of these projects across the developmental cycle.

Field exploitation unfolds over time. It begins when an area within a basin is subject to petroleum analysis, an ongoing process that generates data about potential and proven reserves and their locations. Most areas are abandoned, and the dollars invested are lost. For the more promising areas, attention focuses on field development for purposes of production. Exploration is likely to continue, and positive results stimulate further investment in the design of production facilities. This stage marks a qualitative break, for commerciality gives rise to investment in the infrastructure required for production, but it also has the potential to lower the costs of extraction and transportation in the future. During this phase, the engineering challenge is to maximize field output. Eventually, there comes a point when output levels off and begins to decline. These signs of field maturity signal to operating companies that a new stage is imminent. Attention shifts from managing extraction to managing closure, which involves capping wells, removing machinery, and disposing of some assets while preserving and relocating others. Industry insiders call this decommissioning, and it marks the termination of field activity.

How does the notion of the cycle fit within the higher plane of basin development? Basins are described as immature when levels of exploratory drilling and hydrocarbon extraction are preliminary; as transitional when the pace, scope, or intensity of activity seems to shift; and as mature when growth calms to a steady state or perceptible decline. Shifts between phases can be sudden. A promising discovery can quickly move a basin from immature to transitional and unleash a flood of exploration licensing and drilling. Shell's 1969 gas strike at its Onondaga well near Sable Island led to further exploration, as did Mobil's gas find at nearby Venture a decade later. A prolonged period of dry-hole exploration can likewise downgrade a basin to inactivity, as was the case on the Scotian Shelf after 2005. Within a basin, attention can also shift in response to new geological thinking. A variety of conceptual plays have been drill tested over more than four decades in the Sable Basin.

Another tendency is to compare offshore basins in macro-terms. Such comparison is based on the assumption that past experiences provide benchmarks for future expectations. As the first and most extensively exploited offshore region, the shelf of the Gulf of Mexico is frequently put forward as a standard for assessing the success of exploration, technological innovation, onshore industry linkages, or return on capital. Indeed, one graphic illustration prepared by Nova Scotia authorities superimposed a map of Atlantic licensed areas on a map of the US Gulf region to establish a context for work in the province.[1] However, with dozens of offshore basins now in some state of play around the world, the grounds for comparison are far more extensive. For example, if five hundred exploratory wells were sunk before the first major discoveries were made in the central North Sea, should industry be discouraged after drilling a mere two hundred holes on the Scotian Shelf? If deepwater drilling in West Africa has a success rate three times that of northwest Europe, will companies accept smaller ratios for discovery elsewhere? If Norway can successfully build a national production and supply industry through the terms of offshore licensing, can Newfoundland do likewise? These are not unreasonable comparisons to make, either by companies allocating exploration budgets or by state authorities framing regulatory policies in the nation's or their provinces' interests. In recent years, the Nova Scotia offshore area has been analyzed as a conjugate margin whose geological evolution implies that the closest analogues are the Moroccan and Mauritanian shelves in Africa.

This is not to say that the linear sequence is cast in stone. Early promise may be consolidated or cancelled out. Discoveries that point to oil can turn out to hold natural gas. Basins that seemed endlessly prospective can lose that reputation after a string of dry holes. Despite pioneering the offshore industry after the Second World War, the Gulf of Mexico had become the "Dead Sea" by the 1980s because of the prolonged absence of new investment. Yet, as seen earlier, the advent of new technologies, together with significant public policy incentives from the US Minerals Management Service, returned the region to global leadership by the mid-1990s.[2] By 2000, more US oil was flowing from the deepwater zone than from the shallow water gulf.

In sum, hydrocarbon resources are found in reservoirs confined by traps. Companies search for fields that consist of multiple oil- and gas-bearing sands and sufficient reserves to permit commercial exploitation. States, for their part, claim ownership and assert jurisdiction over continental shelves and subsurface basins. The complex dialectic among these physical, commercial, and political dimensions drives the political economy of petroleum. The focus shifts constantly from the microsetting of the reservoir to the mesosetting of the field and the macrosetting of the basin. To oversimplify a complex situation, it can be said that the petroleum geologist focuses on the first setting, the business economist on the second, and the public policy maker on the third. All three draw upon a version of the cycle model in their work.

Finding Oil and Gas: Geological Basins and Geological Plays

Offshore petroleum activities are typically based on the world's continental shelves, where the deposition of layers of sediment over basement rocks extends offshore until the layers taper in thickness as the seabed extends into progressively deeper waters. Compared to the 4.5 billion year history of the earth, the crust that underlies modern oceans is relatively young, less than 200 million years old. Accordingly, most offshore exploration occurs in sedimentary strata laid down over the past 200 million years, a period of geological time when the continents separated, the oceans formed, and ice ages alternated with tropical climates. A geological basin is a section of the earth's crust that was pulled or forced apart, creating a low point in which sediments accumulated.[3] Rather than picturing a uniform saucer-style depression, one should imagine a basin as an irregular assemblage of high (ridge and mountain) and low (rift and valley) formations. Among the sedimentary layers are sands and muds that were transported from adjacent continents by the work of ancestral rivers and seas. The sands and muds include organic material from plants or animals that are crucial to the formation of hydrocarbon deposits. In addition, there are chemical or biochemical deposits that are not formed by transport but by the ocean itself. They include salt deposits left by the evaporation of seawater and limestone and chalk deposits that result in carbonate banks. The time frame is so long and the forces are so relentless that sedimentary rocks can be up to 20 kilometres thick in continental shelf areas. And there are dynamic forces that transform the rocks long after they have been laid down. The earth's crust has been stretched and fractured. In places where plate boundaries are active, forces of compression (pushing together) or tension (pulling apart) can generate movement along fault lines. Complex structures are the result.[4]

During the late Triassic and early Jurassic periods (248 to 200 million BP) the Fundy and Scotian basins began to form, and sediments from the erosion of the Appalachian Mountains were deposited. As the Atlantic Ocean opened to the south, the edges of the continents were stretched, and the basins expanded and joined into one large Scotian Basin that had progressively deeper sediments. During one of the hottest periods on record, shallow seas intermittently flooded the continent and then evaporated, leaving salt deposits. During sea-level declines in the early to mid-Jurassic

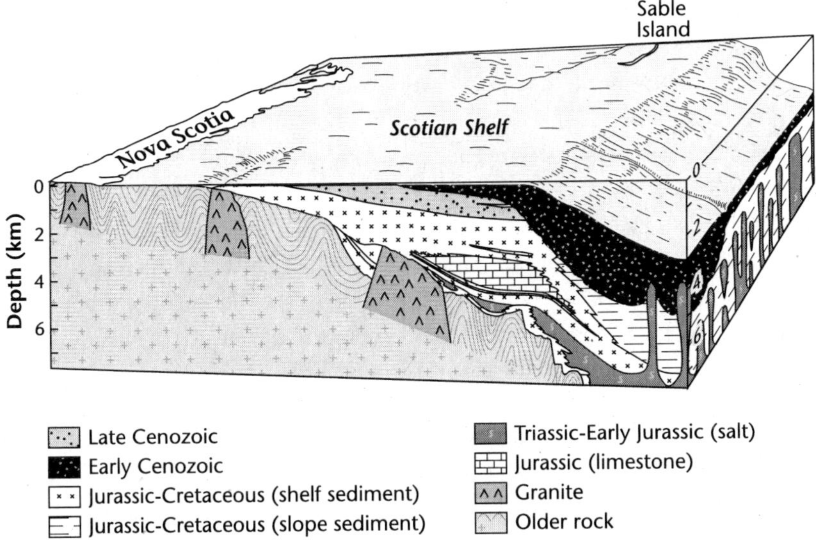

Figure 2.1 General geology of the Scotian Basin
Source: Atlantic Geoscience Society, *The Last Billion Years: A Geological History of the Maritime Provinces of Canada* (Halifax: Nimbus Publishing, 2001).

period (200 to 160 million BP), parts of the basin became vegetated lowlands, and sedimentary deposits concentrated at the mouths of the Laurentian and Sable rivers, fanning out into deeper waters. In the Cretaceous period that followed (140 to 65 million BP), the northern part of the Atlantic Ocean began to form, and marine sediments spread across the shelf as sea levels rose around the globe. The Sable Delta was fed by the dominant river. Extensive limestone deposits were part of the late Cretaceous period, which ended with a major extinction event. During the Tertiary period (65 to 2 million BP), the Atlantic took on a more modern shape. With much of the coastal lands above sea level, erosion made a powerful impact, and basin sediments shifted from mud to sand. In sum, the petroleum deposits of the Atlantic offshore area are a product of the past 200 million years, when the continents separated and sediments accumulated in the resulting basins. Complex and uneven patterns of sedimentation characterize the shelf area, and modern petroleum geology is practised by reading and interpreting the potential of rock formations to contain oil and gas. Not surprisingly, explorationists have been drawn to strata ranging from the Jurassic to the Cretaceous and Tertiary periods. Figure 2.1 is a simplified geology of the Scotian Basin.

Although Figure 2.1 offers a useful summary profile of some seven to ten vertical kilometres of sedimentary geology, it fails to capture the complexity of the offshore region. The Nova Scotia sector covers a spatial (surface) area of about 200,000 square kilometres, from the Yarmouth Arch in the west (today's Canada–United States border) to the Avalon Uplift off the coast of Newfoundland in the east. Along the way, from west to east, there are a half-dozen subbasins: Georges Bank, Shelburne, LeHave, Sable, Abenaki, and Banquereau. The Laurentian Subbasin at the eastern edge has recently passed by legal ruling to the jurisdiction of Newfoundland.[5] Subbasins differ according to time of subsidence and corresponding variations in sedimentary fill; in other words, the general profile varies substantially across all three dimensions.[6]

From a topographical and geological point of view, the Scotian Basin is made up of two components: the shelf and the slope. Accounting for three-fifths of the basin area, the shelf is the submarine terrace that extends seaward from the coast in water up to about 200 metres. Its breadth (shore to slope) ranges from 125 to 240 kilometres, and its length is approximately 850 kilometres. The shelf's broad expanse is characterized by shallow banks, seabed basins, and channels running between them. Although there were times in prehistory when much of the terrace was above water, only Sable Island remains today as a reminder.

The continental slope extends from the shelf's edge to the deep ocean abyssal plain, a decline of thousands of metres. The Scotian Slope has an average width of about 100 kilometres, as measured from the 200-metre to 4,000-metre depth mark. It represents an area of some 80,000 square kilometres or two-fifths of the total basin area.[7] The deepwater slope is far from uniform. From a depth of 200 metres to 2,000 metres, the average gradient is approximately 1:17, but below that point the gradient decreases to a 1:35 slope.[8] A number of transverse canyons cut the eastern Scotian Slope, the largest of which is known as the Sable Gully, a biologically diverse environment on the same vertical scale as the Grand Canyon that was designated a federal marine protected area in 2002.

The state of offshore exploration (especially drilling) technologies shapes the timing and selection of test sites. Historically, offshore exploration began on coastal shelves in extremely shallow waters. The first offshore well in Atlantic Canada was drilled as a wartime project in 1943. An artificial island constructed in shallow waters off Prince Edward Island, the well proved to be an expensive dry hole. In the intervening decades, the US Gulf was the crucible for industry innovations such as the shallow water barge, the jack-up rig that rested on the ocean floor, the semi-submersible (floating) rig, and the drill ship equipped with a mid-ship derrick. When drilling began in the Scotian Basin in 1967, the first derrick was erected on Sable Island. However, the second well was drilled from the *Sedneth I,* a Dutch-chartered floating rig that worked in 58 metres of water. In successive waves over the next half century, new technologies allowed global drilling and production to take place at ever-greater depths: 170 metres by 1970, 700 metres by 1980, and 1,300 metres by 1990. After several decades drilling in the Sable Subbasin, the exploration and production industry shifted its attention to the deep-water slope. Beginning in 1997 and accelerating through 2004, an exploration-licence boom took place in deepwater blocks.

Although general geological sequences are a necessary part of sedimentary appraisal, petroleum exploration requires a more exacting understanding of resource formation and trapping. The goal is to identify geological plays – formations or trends that have consistent rock or reservoir characteristics conducive to hydrocarbon prospects. Three ingredients are needed: a source rock that contains abundant organic matters (up to 5 percent), a reservoir rock that stores the hydrocarbons, and a trap to block upward-migrating hydrocarbons from reaching the surface. Hydrocarbons are formed in source rocks from decomposing organic matter (supplied by terrestrial or marine animals or plants) and a combination of pressure, time, and heat.[9] The process occurs in an environment that is essentially starved of oxygen. Oil and gas are lodged in tiny spaces or pores in sandstone, limestone, and other grainy formations. In places where the rocks are permeable (i.e., places where the pores are interconnected), the rock is known as reservoir rock, and oil and gas can migrate over time. The migration may be driven by buoyancy, since petroleum is lighter than the formation water that often accompanies it. Upward migration may also be facilitated by the exploitation of weaknesses, such as faults or fractures that allow oil or gas to travel long after the source rocks are fixed. Petroleum may find its way to the surface in seeps, but its vertical movement more commonly stops underground, when it is trapped by impermeable overlying rock structures.[10] Such traps are the targets of petroleum explorationists; without them, most of the oil and gas formed would have migrated to the surface and been dispersed.

Because deposits are buried and drilling is expensive, a variety of indirect methods have been developed to image potential deposits. Tools such as magnetometers and gravity instruments and methods such as seismic wave imaging highlight prospective areas of interest. Adopted during the 1930s, the magnetometer measures variance in subsurface magnetic strength and direction (most oil-bearing rock is non-magnetic). Airborne test results were among the first reconnaissance done in the Atlantic offshore region after 1959. The gravity meter, which measures variations in gravitational force exerted by rocks of different densities, also emerged around the same time. Salt domes in particular register anomalously low gravity and provide important clues to possible reservoir location. The final and most important method is seismic surveying. Although more expensive than the other methods, it provides more accurate images of potential reservoirs. Shock waves are set off on predetermined paths, and an array of sensors measure dense data streams as the sound is refracted back to the surface. The result generates partial pictures of rock structures, including prospective traps. When it was first used in the 1930s, seismic imaging captured two dimensions, effectively rendering a slice of a profile that could be broadened by successive sweeps. Postwar advances in electronic data processing dramatically enhanced the power of seismic surveys, and in the 1980s three-dimensional imaging became possible, vastly enriching the ability to map petroleum features.

Although these remote methods marked essential advances in the exploration process, they did not substitute for more direct methods. To confirm a promising play, exploratory drilling was still required. A drill stem can confirm oil- or gas-bearing strata by making a strike and allowing for the measurement of flow and structure. Even in the event of a dry hole, valuable evidence is acquired in the form of drill log data and core samples that can be analyzed post facto to help delineate the geological evolution of the basin.[11]

Over several decades, geologists have identified a variety of play types in the Scotian Basin, and they have been conceptualized and refined with the passage of time.[12] Some play types involve traps created by the upward penetration of salt structures and the seal formed by impermeable layers of shale. In each case, oil or gas is trapped in the anticlines (the upward folds created in sandstone strata above or beside the salt), and their migration is blocked by impermeable shale. In other types, traps are created as a result of faults that generate anticlines and channels for petroleum migration. These anticlines and channels tend to occur along the margins of subbasins and may involve vertically stacked reservoirs. Two other types are the classic rollover anticline, which formed in the Jurassic-Cretaceous period, and rollovers that occur at greater depth and tend to feature high pressures in the formations. A fifth type of structural trap is formed from the drape of sediments over a basement layer, as is found in the high basement levels of the LeHave and Canso ridges. Other types include stratigraphic traps, which are created by juxtaposition of permeable and impermeable sedimentary layers. They may be associated with dense river or delta depositions, or they may be of the carbonate bank variety, in which the impermeable shale layers trap the oil and gas within the limestone strata. The latter trap is common in areas such as the Abenaki Subbasin.

Once a reservoir is located, a key concern is the size of the trap. Explorationists usually consider three factors: the geologic period in which the sediments were deposited, the depth at which the sediments reside, and the average thickness of the pay zone. The notion of a petroleum field is somewhat imprecise. Although a single large pool may constitute a field, it is also common for multiple pools to overlie one another. In such cases, a production well may draw on a number of pools. In the case of the Cohasset-Panuke (COPAN) light oil project, for example, the larger Cohasset field consisted of ten sands in the Lower Logan Canyon and Mississauga formations, at depths from 1,700 to 2,300 metres. Panuke included two Mississauga sands between 2,300 and 2,400 metres.[13] In the production phase, these fields were drawn together to two surface platforms for processing and storage.

Nova Scotia's offshore region is vast, and geological knowledge about various parts of the basin varies. Some subbasins remain terra incognita. On the western and eastern edges, the obstacles to exploration have been more political than geological or economic. For example, the Georges Bank Subbasin straddles the Canada-United States ocean border, which was before the international court until the 1980s. An exploration moratorium was declared in 1989 on the initiative of the Nova Scotia government, which was seeking to protect the fishery. The moratorium remains in place today. As a result, there is virtually no drilling data for the region. At the opposite end of the shelf, the Laurentian Subbasin also remains unexplored. Much of the subbasin was put under moratorium in 1967 as Canada and France sought to resolve an offshore territorial dispute over the seabed attached to St. Pierre and Miquelon. The dispute was settled in 1992, when France acquired a 40-kilometre zone around the islands and a 17-kilometre corridor extending 330 kilometres toward the shelf edge.[14] A secondary dispute between Nova Scotia and Newfoundland over the boundary between their respective offshore administrations was settled in 2003 (largely in favour of Newfoundland). The Canada-Newfoundland Offshore Petroleum Board has since issued exploration licences, but only one well had been drilled by 2010.

Other subbasins have attracted substantial geophysical investigation but have not been drilled extensively in the four decades since exploration began. They include the Shelburne Subbasin (two wells), the Sydney Subbasin (two wells), and the Orpheus Graben Subbasin (seven wells). The lion's share of drilling has concentrated in the Sable Subbasin, where two-thirds of all exploratory wells have been located since 1967, generating the most detailed geological knowledge and several dozen significant discoveries. Seventeen wells have been drilled in the Abenaki Subbasin, located to the northeast of the Sable Subbasin (see Map. 2.1).

The Scotian Slope has a different configuration guided by different conceptual plays. The area gained attention in the 1990s following developments in other deepwater margins, including the Gulf of Mexico, Brazil, and south west Africa. The advent of three-dimensional seismic techniques revealed distinctive slope structures around salt domes and at deeper levels. These continental slopes were especially attractive because of the larger size of prospective reservoirs and the high production potential of deep formations. This speculation was rapidly proven out by major finds in all three analogous regions. Driven also by the modest (and to the industry, disappointing) results of exploration on the Nova Scotia Shelf, attention turned to the deepwater slope. In 1997, the third major wave of offshore licensing began. Within five years, fifty-seven exploration blocks had been taken up, more than half of them in contiguous positions along the full front of the deepwater slope from the Georges Bank moratorium area to the Newfoundland boundary. Wildcatting was not new to the slope. The first hole had been drilled in the 1970s, and four more followed in the 1980s, but all proved to be dry. The second deepwater wave saw six additional wells drilled between 2001 and 2005 and one discovery. This led the CNSOPB to assess the slope's potential for gas from 15 to 41 trillion cubic feet (420 billion to 1.1 trillion cubic metres), according to differential levels of risk.[15]

From Exploration to Production: Field and Reservoir Development

Business economics offers a different perspective on basin development. Petroleum exploration and production firms exist to discover and develop commercially profitable fields of oil and gas. Although this process depends heavily on the applied geological disciplines, the range of operative

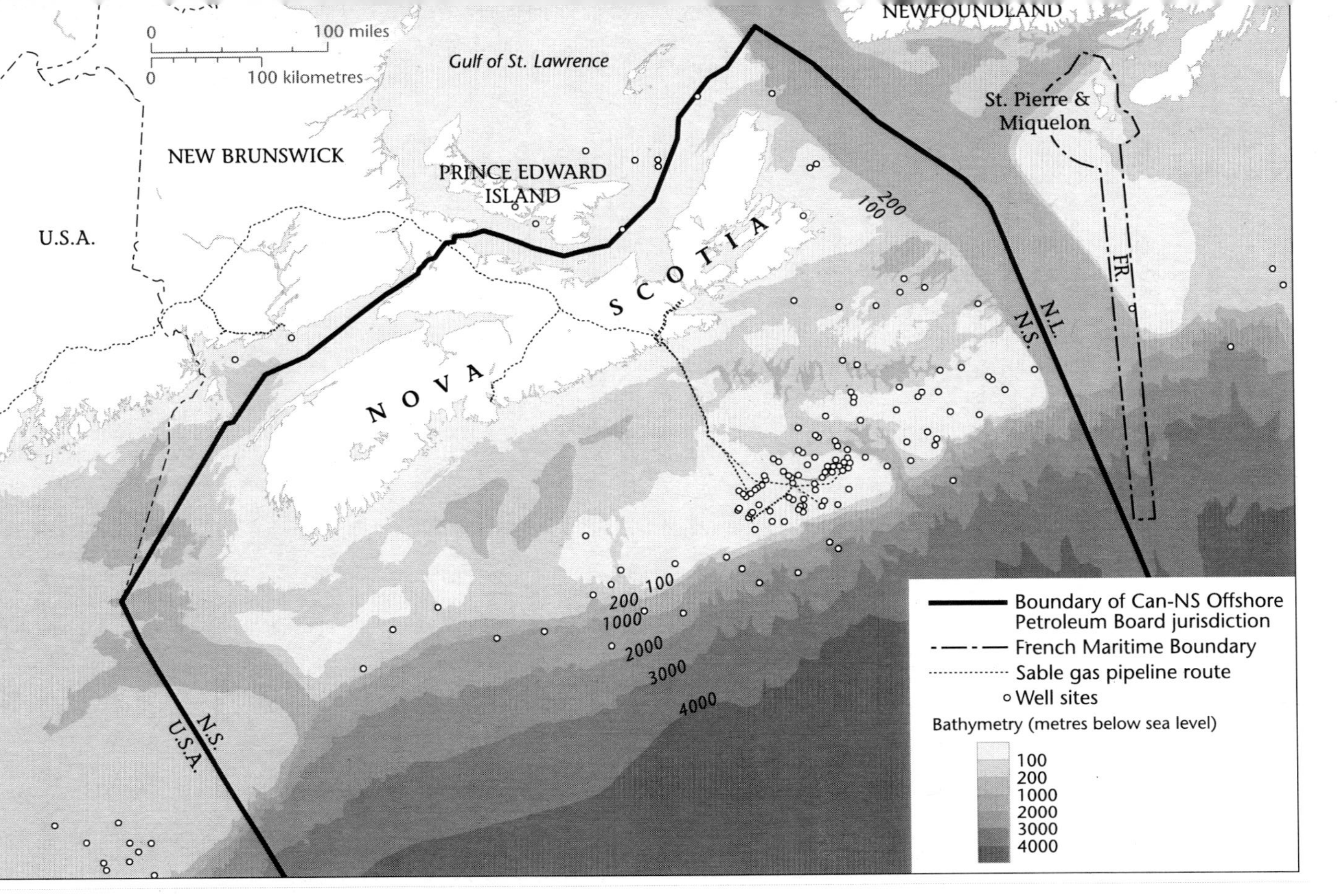

Map 2.1 Scotian Basin boundaries and wells
Source: CNSOPB Maps.

determinants is much wider. *Upstream*, the premier publication for the global industry, describes this world in detail each week. The newspaper provides an ongoing account of exploration block leasing, field discovery, exploratory drilling, project design, and production performance. As far as field development is concerned, the firm's analytic framework (or epistemic outlook) stretches from geology to engineering and economics. Organizationally, the corporation or operating syndicate is the central decision-making agent. This fact is aptly captured by a comment by an unnamed oilman who "would never hire an exploration geologist who is not an optimist or a petroleum engineer who is not a pessimist."[16] Every play carries the prospect of future discoveries. However, not all prospects are confirmed, and not all discoveries can be translated into commercial results.

When an offshore basin is first opened for exploration it is, in the terms of petroleum geology, largely unknown. The first reconnaissance tends to apply geophysical techniques to highlight features worthy of further investigation and set the stage for wildcat drilling to test attractive prospects. Major fields tend to be discovered in the early phase of basin exploration since large reservoirs are most likely to be highlighted at the seismic stage. However, each prospect has its own potential history that is contingent on an exploration path. Upstream firms make key decisions about the allocation of exploration budgets that typically involve a comparative assessment of available prospects and their prioritization in annual increments. There is, in effect, a political process by which field teams put forward the cases for their prospects, and senior officials hammer out a program. Once activated, however, these deliberative choices are tested in the unpredictable context of field exploration. Subsequent results, whether positive or negative, feed back into new decision chains. At the micro level of specific land parcels, this decision process can be mapped out in a series of steps.[17] The process begins with the decision to acquire exploration rights and continues with the decision to drill on that acreage, either before or after seismic work is done. A dry hole forces a choice between dropping the project or drilling further with a second wildcat well. Within a firm, an initial dry hole may be discounted and a follow-up well drilled, but a second dry hole will increase the probability of killing the project. Conversely, a large find virtually guarantees further exploration, while a marginal find carries positive but inconclusive probabilities.

Despite the high levels of risk associated with the exploration phase, upstream firms ultimately focus on results. A hydrocarbon find is commercially appraised in both qualitative and quantitative terms. Is the find crude oil, natural gas, or both? light or heavy crude? sweet or sour (sulphurous) gas? under high or low pressure? These factors affect marketability. On the quantitative side, how large is the petroleum-bearing rock body? Following a discovery, its size can be delineated by drilling step-out wells and by flow testing wells to establish natural rates of flow. Further geological analysis is done on the basis of drill data such as core samples and well logs. Ultimately, a prime point of determination is the estimated petroleum volume. The oil or gas "in place" in the ground – that is, the total volume trapped within reservoir rock – falls under the category of differential measurement criteria. It is never possible to extract 100 percent of this amount. In fact, given the attributes of the host rock, the limits of well positioning, and the changes to field pressure over time, extraction rates of 50 percent can be considered promising. The term *recoverable reserves* is used to indicate the volume of the total resource that can be extracted by reliance on the best available techniques. For example, the Venture gas field in the Sable Subbasin was discovered in 1979 by the pivotal Venture D-23 well. After delineation, the recoverable gas reserves at Venture were set at 2.5 trillion cubic feet (70 billion cubic metres).[18]

Discoveries are then placed on a scale for further investment. A significant discovery is a reservoir or field of sufficient quality to merit ongoing interest, in contrast to a small show of oil or gas beneath realistic thresholds. Such a find may not, on its own, justify exploitation. Further along the continuum, a commercial discovery merits exploitation on a stand-alone basis under prevailing market conditions. This designation is determined by an assessment of production costs and prospective revenues, which are often measured in terms of barrels of crude or cubic metres (or feet) of natural gas. Since costs tend to be markedly lower on land operations, the profitability threshold will be lower than on offshore operations. A similar relationship is evident when conventional oil and gas exploration is contrasted with synthetic (oil sands or shale) sources. It is possible to model the comparative break-even points for petroleum products, and Figure 2.2 offers an estimate for 2008.[19]

These designations are obviously dynamic categories subject to reappraisal over time. For example, during the peak market of 1980 and the slump that followed, there was some doubt about whether the Venture field reserves were sufficient to support a stand-alone project. The recoverable reserve estimate was scaled back, and because the price slide was sufficiently unfavourable, the Venture project was abandoned in 1986. On the other hand, it is possible to combine significant associated discoveries to create a

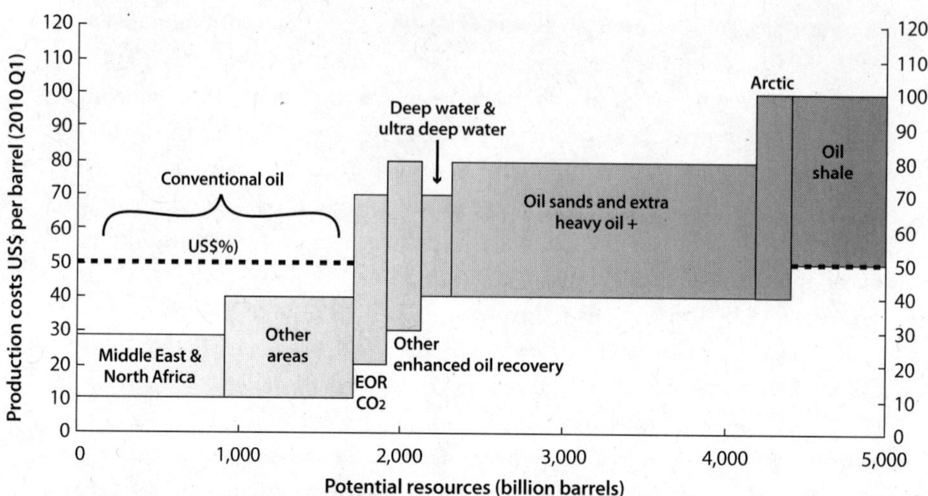

Figure 2.2 Global oil supply cost curve, 2008
Source: Scotiabank Commodity Price Index and International Energy Agency estimates, 2010.

commercial asset. In the 1990s, for example, six contiguous Sable fields with estimated reserves of 3 trillion cubic feet (84 billion cubic metres) of recoverable gas were pooled. Alternatively, an isolated significant discovery may be deemed commercial if access to existing infrastructure can be secured. The Deep Panuke gas field was initially estimated to hold 935 billion cubic feet (26 billion cubic metres) of recoverable gas, a volume sufficient to support a stand-alone pipeline.[20] However, the project was reconfigured after a corporate "time out," and for a time the newly consolidated firm EnCana judged the project to be viable only if it could tie into the existing Sable pipeline (the stand-alone option was later reinstated). In the future, a similar logic may also make possible the exploitation of significant Sable discoveries such as Arcadia, Chebucto, Citnalta, and Onondaga.

For many reasons, levels of confidence during reservoir assessment tend to become stronger as exploration proceeds. However, there is often an inclination or need to assess petroleum volumes in a broader geological context – for instance, a play type, a subbasin, or even a whole basin. In this regard, the move from field to basin raises a new set of complications, particularly the challenge of extrapolating estimates for largely unexplored areas from limited data. This greater band of uncertainty is reflected in the distinction between proven, probable, and possible reserves. In effect, these three declining levels of confidence indicate potential and help guide investment decisions about the ongoing process of field or basin development.

The techniques are often described as resource assessment techniques. The most publicly available formulations have been generated by state agencies such as the Geological Survey of Canada, the Canada–Nova Scotia Offshore Petroleum Board, the National Energy Board, and the volunteer Canada Gas Potential Committee.

During the 1970s, the favoured method of assessment was to calculate volumes by comparing geological features in the target area to other basins with known volumes. In later decades, the statistical distribution of proven pools within a play was calculated and extrapolated throughout the play. For example, in 1983 the Geological Survey of Canada produced a widely quoted estimate for the entire Scotian Shelf of 18 trillion cubic feet (504 billion cubic metres) of gas and 454 million barrels of oil.[21] A variation of this approach was also applied to plays with no proven results. The CNSOPB conducted just such a conceptual assessment for the deepwater slope region in 2002, when it drew on seismic results to identify twelve types of play and forecast 15 to 41 trillion cubic feet (420 billion to 1.15 trillion cubic metres) of deepwater gas and 2 to 5 billion barrels of oil.[22] These ranges highlight another necessary technique for assessing unproven formations, that of risk. Such forecasts are calculated as a series of probability distributions and presented on a scale ranging from minimum risk volumes (90 percent probability of occurrence) to mean risk volumes (50 percent probability) to maximum risk volumes (10 percent probability).

To fully capture the interplay between basin, field, and market, the firm must also be considered. A variety of enterprise types are active at the upstream level, ranging from super- and multinational majors to national independents and regional junior firms. Historically, all have been significant hunters and discoverers of petroleum. Although firms of each type may operate autonomously – handling seismic work, rights acquisition, exploratory drilling, and production – they may also be connected at any step in the chain. Seismic results can be shared in an effort to assemble a joint venture among firms. Rights holders can negotiate farm-ins by which the financial costs and prospective returns are syndicated among clusters of firms. Assets can also be bought and sold in the market, allowing firms with significant discovery properties to cash out their values before development. This culture also enables large firms to consolidate and balance their petroleum reserve assets outside of their own exploration programs. Finally, expansionary companies may adopt corporate takeover (merger and acquisition) strategies to extend their reach and restructure their operations. With every downturn in the petroleum equity market, firms whose asset values exceed their capitalization are vulnerable to outside takeover. The early 1980s brought an unprecedented level of corporate instability related to what Yergin terms "the shootout at value gap."[23] Throughout the decade there were extraordinary struggles at all market levels, such as Pennzoil and Texaco battling over Getty Oil or Mesa Petroleum and Chevron attacking Gulf Oil. These struggles ushered in a dramatic and permanent shift in oil business strategies, for firms entered the 1990s believing that share value management was equal to or even more important than cash flow or profit. Similarly, with every upturn in petroleum markets, senior firms swallowed up prosperous junior firms as a quick way to kick-start new exploration and production campaigns. These takeovers also opened the door for a new generation of junior firms to expand into niches vacated in the market. All of these tendencies were and are significant in shaping the level of interest, effort, and success attendant in a petroleum basin.[24]

In offshore operations, extra layers of expense arise at all levels. Although these additional costs are not necessarily prohibitive, they certainly present challenges to independents and junior firms. In addition, the opportunity structure in the offshore business is extremely time sensitive. For example, when the Gulf of Mexico first drew attention after 1947, access was unusually open to new entrants. Independent oilmen had ready access to bank loan capital, which could be secured by proven assets in the ground. Ready capital enabled a host of terrestrial exploration and production firms to embark, on their own and in concert, into the shallow waters of the Gulf with the relatively simple technologies of the day. Yet, by the time the North Sea opened up in the 1960s, in far harsher physical conditions, the price of corporate entry had jumped an order of magnitude. Only the international majors, the largest independents, and the newly created state oil companies had the capacity to lead this new play. Although oil and gas were found almost immediately, it took six to seven years before the first major fields were discovered in the UK sector (in the Forties and Brent fields) and a decade before petroleum flowed. Indeed, having the financial staying power to underwrite hundreds of preliminary wells is a critical aspect of basin development. A similar pattern applied to the Scotian Shelf after 1967. In Nova Scotia, Mobil Canada and Shell Canada were the pioneer explorationists, and Texaco, Chevron, and Petro-Canada soon joined in. However, the threshold of early exploration has not yet been fully achieved – 204 wells have been drilled in total as of 2010.

The life-cycle model is frequently used to explain the exploration and production business. The model highlights a series of discrete stages, each of which involves distinct business, operational, and management challenges. As mentioned earlier, the model has been applied to several distinct levels of activity, including the analysis of projects, fields or reservoirs, and basins. In the commercial development of a producing field, the project cycle is normally delineated in four steps: discovery, development, production, and decommissioning. However, this framework conceals a plethora of discrete operational challenges that must be addressed within each stage. Matthew Simmons aptly captures the processes that are embedded in each stage as an inwardly evolving spiral of field development.[25]

The exploration stage is a gate-keeping phase in which seismic testing and exploratory drilling result in discoveries whose size and significance are delineated by further well drilling. Before the 1980s, these so-called drilling programs often entailed drilling clusters of holes offshore for many years. A wildcat well success rate (in finding oil or gas) of one in ten was widely accepted as a measure of risk. However, recent advances in seismic data gathering and basin modelling have led to higher expectations of early success, particularly in the hunt for large fields. Today, the standard of success is closer to one in three. Moreover, the costs of offshore exploration are several orders of magnitude larger than terrestrial plays: continental shelf wells cost $30 to $60 million per unit and slope wells, $80 to $100 million or more. The time duration can be similarly scaled: land wells take one to three weeks to reach target depths, while continental shelf wells require up to three to four months and deepwater slope wells as much as six to eight.

Considerable analytical work is required between discovery and project start-up, including determining the oil in place and recoverable reserves, figures that in turn feed into the commercial analysis of project economics and ultimate return. A strategy for depleting the field is embedded in the analysis, and the process also includes preliminary design work for the offshore extractive system, including seabed facilities, undersea lines, and surface platforms. The design work involves choosing production systems for gathering, processing, and transport. Field planning evolves into field installation when the corporate sponsors give final approval or sanction. Drilling production wells follows field installation, and manufacturing and service specialists who serve a worldwide market complete the staged installation of equipment.

The next phase begins when the oil or gas starts to flow. With reserves projected to flow at predetermined rates over a stipulated duration, a project will pay out the sunk capital costs and generate profits thereafter. It should be noted that these calculations are far from self-evident. Agreeing on a production regime involves strategic decisions among both the project partners and state regulatory authorities, including estimates of ultimate recoverable reserves, depletion strategies for the fields, the financial structure of the development consortium, and royalty and tax scenarios. Modern resource management is geared to adaptive learning – the adjustment of strategy on the basis of feedback on prior interventions. The petroleum field is a case in point, and models are continually adjusted as reserves are drawn down. In the latter stages, secondary or tertiary recovery techniques can be applied to enhance flows, through gas or water injection or compression facilities beyond the wellhead.

When the commercial life of a field approaches its end, firms focus on closure, removal, or decommissioning. Decommissioning takes on special significance offshore because pipelines, platforms, storage vessels, and associated infrastructure cannot easily be abandoned. Post-production disposal plans form part of a development proposal from the outset, and decommissioning costs are factored into project economics. Given the magnitude of these obligations, the opportunity to extend a facility's life through tie-ins to new fields and related projects is extremely attractive. Thus there is a strategic component to decommissioning obligations that is recognized by both industry and government authorities. New discoveries can renew the life of both the project and the common infrastructure and can provide the stimulus to create joint ventures and partnerships among firms.

A different type of cycle model can be applied to the management of a reservoir or field after a discovery is deemed commercial in scale and planning gets under way for development. Obviously, the engineering goal is the maximum recovery of the asset. This cycle, which comprises the property's production life, begins with a ramping-up phase, when output is steadily increasing. In time, the daily rate stabilizes at a plateau, and steady output follows. Eventually, the reservoir can no longer sustain this level of flow, and decline sets in. Ultimately, the field enters a tail-end phase that includes closure and abandonment. The art of reservoir management depends on increasing and extending recovery levels. Firms can repressure a field by injecting gas or water, or they can fracture tight rock formations (those with low permeability for petroleum movement) by forcing new channels of flow. Other techniques include drilling new wells, using mechanical lifting machinery, or balancing flows from multiple sources to prolong extraction.

The various cycle models are most effective in understanding discrete reservoirs and projects. At a higher level of aggregation, however, when a field or basin is involved, the basic linear model is of questionable value.

First, a field or basin is likely to host activities and projects at several phases of progression. Hence, its status on the development continuum is ambiguous and contingent upon the analytic question of greatest urgency. Is a field in its growth phase only so long as new exploration activity remains high, thereby signifying expanding operator interest and commitment? Or is exploration a distracting preliminary to the reality that growth begins when oil or gas begins to flow? The pattern of subbasins also figures strongly, for they may be in different phases of readiness. The logic of the geological play suggests that absolute produced volume output is less important than the outcome per unit effort. The latter may be gauged by the volume of barrels of oil equivalent added for each fifty or one hundred wildcat wells. On the other side, when should a basin be considered mature? when total production trends downward, as occurred in the UK North Sea sector in the 1980s? Or perhaps maturity is marked by a decline in the level of newly discovered reserves or in the average new field size per year? Such considerations underscore the limited value of the simple linear model for explaining complex activities.

Governing Petroleum Basins

There is another way that shelves and basins do not necessarily correspond. State authorities assert sovereignty in large part on a territorial basis. Thus national and provincial boundaries, rather than physical or geological features, define the scope of both terrestrial and marine jurisdictions. In the case of continental shelves and oceans, international law has been incremental and cautious in affirming sovereign space. The long-standing convention of a three-mile coastal jurisdiction continued to the middle of the twentieth century, leaving the balance of the ocean as unregulated high seas. During the 1950s, states began to make claims to broader offshore economic rights of exploitation. The United Nations Convention on the Continental Shelf was signed in 1958 and ratified in 1964. State parties to the convention acquired sovereign rights to explore and extract resources to a depth of 200 metres or to whatever further depth exploitation was feasible.[26]

Canada did not ratify the convention until 1970. However, the federal Public Land Grants Act and Territorial Land Grants Act asserted statutory authority over the subsea Scotian Shelf and similar areas for the Government of Canada. The Canada Oil and Gas Land Regulations were issued under this authority. Several provinces chose to differ, claiming pre-Confederation rights to offshore areas and asserting regulatory powers of their own. Although the Supreme Court of Canada ruled in favour of the Dominion in

Reference re *Offshore Mineral Rights of British Columbia* (1967), the offshore legal jurisdiction remained more nuanced and found its way onto the federal-provincial constitutional agenda after 1965. As well, ongoing political uncertainties constituted a significant risk factor for firms contemplating offshore investment. The Government of Canada eventually proposed to set aside the title question in favour of joint resource management. In 1982, a unified Canada–Nova Scotia authority was established to manage petroleum rights in a defined Nova Scotia Offshore Area. The area's territorial jurisdiction included parts of the Fundy Basin, the Magdalen Basin, the Sydney Basin, and the greater part of the Scotian Basin. The boundary arbitration between Nova Scotia and neighbouring Newfoundland in 2002 had the effect of enlarging the latter's share of the Laurentian Subbasin. Evidently, the contours of state sovereignty follow a different logic than those of both shelf and basin.

Nonetheless, any sovereign state with continental shelf jurisdiction holds potential levers to regulate offshore petroleum activities. This power springs from the bundle of legal rights that states claim over subsurface resources, and it is from this foundation that management regimes are typically fashioned.[27] The potential range of statutory authority is extensive and includes powers of state title or ownership; rights powers to apportion commercial access and its terms; powers to declare the terms of extraction, including fiscal matters of royalties and taxes; powers to regulate impacts that are external to the flow of oil or gas but integral to the extractive endeavour (work safety, environmental integrity); and powers to close and dispose of post-production assets.

In fashioning and maintaining such a legal and administrative regime, a state not only draws from a broad inventory of policy tools but also invests them with substance. These decisions tend to reflect an understanding and an expectation of how petroleum resources should be explored and developed and for what purposes. They also constitute a potential set of control points for shaping basin development. Put another way, key policies can serve as pacing measures that, when exercised by state authorities, shape industry progression at the project, field, or basin level. This strategic dimension of management powers was recognized explicitly in the text of the 1986 Canada–Nova Scotia Offshore Petroleum Accord. The first objective is "to achieve the early development of Petroleum Resources in the Offshore Area for the benefit of Canada as a whole and Nova Scotia in particular."[28]

In petroleum management, legal and administrative rules are often geared to a particular stage of exploration and production activity. For example, the initial phase in scoping potential hydrocarbon deposits requires access for remote exploratory sensing through geophysical or seismic testing. This phase is generally regulated through some form of operator licence whose modest cost is tantamount to open access. However, activity rights can be enclosed or restricted at subsequent stages by means of exclusive exploration permits or licences. Should this lead to a hydrocarbon discovery, the proponent may convert the claim into a stronger form of exclusive property right by obtaining a certificate of significant discovery or commercial discovery carrying a longer term. Later still, the proponent may seek an approval for installing a commercial project that will extract oil or gas over the commercial life of a field.

Once production begins, the operator is subject to ongoing review of reservoir extraction practices, on engineering and conservation grounds. At the same time, the state, as resource owner, collects rental or royalty payments and, as fiscal sovereign, collects business taxes (which in the petroleum field are characterized by complex, layered assessments and offsets). Finally, in recognition that the termination of an offshore project bestows a complex legacy, considerable regulatory attention is devoted to shutdown and removal. The overall sequence of regulatory concerns, and the policy cycle stages that underlie them, are captured in Table 2.1.

Within the offshore policy network, perspectives differ on the nature of the policy cycle. Governmental authorities often refer to the template as evidence that state oversight of offshore petroleum activities is deliberate, comprehensive, and rigorous in balancing public interest concerns with the profitable search for strategic energy supplies. By inserting serial reviews and authorizations at key points of transition, they argue, oversight can be achieved. On the other hand, non-governmental interests in the labour and environmental sectors warn that a dangerous logic of cumulative momentum can build as an operator advances a project through the developmental sequence. The process, they argue, is oversensitized to the scale of the corporate sunk investment and tends to tilt the advantage for further approval to the proponent who has successfully met the preliminary stage requirements. The petroleum exploration and development industry holds yet another perspective. These firms are well aware of the complex challenge of offshore project completion, but their political concern is with the cumulative burdens of step-wise regulation in threatening the viability of projects. While part of this critique centres on the monetary costs of regulatory compliance, an equally important issue for business is the uncoordinated buildup of detailed regulatory requirements, by multiple authorities, both within

TABLE 2.1

Offshore regulatory and management policy cycle, by stages

	Activity	Terms	Instruments
Early exploration	Geophysical and seismic	Open ocean access, indefinite duration	Operator certificate
Late exploration	Exploration drilling and testing	Exclusive right to drill for 5-10 year stipulated term	Exploration permit/ licence; drilling approval; HSE certificates
Conversion of tenure	Shift of exploration rights/licence to discovery licence	Continuing exclusive rights to discovery on 15-year plus term	Discovery licence or qualification; commercial discovery licence
Project development	Design and installation	Compliance with policy guidelines	Development plan approval; benefits plan approval; environmental review approval
Exploitation	Extract and sell product subject to fiscal/regulatory provisions	Compliance with conservation and health, safety, and environment (HSE) regulations	Conservation regulations; royalty/ tax statutes; activity approvals
Abandonment	Shut down, secure, and/or remove offshore facilities	Decommissioning plan part of project approval; open to subsequent amendments	Decommissioning plan approval and monitoring

and between cycle stages. Firms point out, for example, the high cost of overall regulatory cycle time required for a proponent to move from exploration to production, an interval that has lengthened significantly in many basins, including the Scotian Shelf.[29] These contrasting perspectives underline the inherently contested or political character of offshore decision making. They illustrate that even as a petroleum management regime is being applied, parallel political processes may be under way to modify or entirely transform its essential terms.

Clearly, the overriding challenge for offshore state authorities is how to achieve developmental mandates. Such mandates, of course, will vary according to the political objectives of sitting governments. For example, offshore petroleum may be seen principally as a component of domestic energy self-sufficiency. If so, locating new commercial reserves and planning timely supply is a top priority. Alternatively, state policy can centre on industrial diversification through domestic investment and employment gains from a new growth sector. Different again, offshore petroleum can be approached principally on fiscal grounds. The goal is to capture new streams of government revenue through rents and taxes, regardless of final market destination. From this perspective, the emphasis falls on advancing major project development regardless of ownership or target market. All of these imperatives have figured in the Scotian Basin at various points in its forty-five-year history. Not surprisingly, each macropolitical strategy prompts the selection and ordering of a set of policy measures for its implementation.

This section focuses on identifying some of the crucial policy provisions that can set the pace of basin development. Any state seeking to manage offshore petroleum is challenged to design an enabling regime with appropriate checks and balances. Exactly where the state should exert its weight, through a combination of incentives and restrictions, is a complicated and fluid problem with few invariable rules. There are, however, some prerequisites to opening offshore continental lands for exploration.

One critical variable is the supply of permittable or leasable tracts for exploration. It depends on a series of interrelated provisions for work obligations on designated lands. A progressive leasing regime seeks to avoid speculative lock-ups without timely exploration; instead, it attempts to allow leaseholders a fair opportunity to exercise their rights while at the same time ensuring that underexplored or neglected tracts are brought back into circulation. Exclusive exploration rights are allocated by a nomination and bid process. This entails a trade-off between conveying large areas to enhance prospector interest or smaller areas that can be tested and assessed more rapidly.

Block size is closely related to the temporal duration of exploration rights. Initially, the Canadian Oil and Gas Lands Administration permits were held for six years and could be followed by up to six one-year extensions if work requirements were met. In a tight investment climate or in a modestly endowed basin, the relaxation of tenure terms (i.e., longer duration or more flexible staging) was allowed in an effort to attract new players. In 2007, for example, exploration was moribund in the Scotian Basin. In response, the CNSOPB revised the exploration rights system to offer an initial three-year licence to encourage pre-drill geoscience to be followed by a six-year drill period.[30] The goal was to facilitate relatively low-cost preliminary work without high-cost well-drilling obligations. However, if policy-makers fear that large block holders may lock up big acreage for speculative rather than active exploration purposes, they might lean toward smaller block sizes, shorter terms, and the mandatory release of significant proportions of every retained block to enable renewed public bidding on those sections. Some suggest that the vast size of the licence blocks taken up by international oil capital on the Scotian Shelf during the deepwater land rush of 1997-2001 worked against orderly exploration. These massive blocks were difficult (perhaps impossible) to assess on the basis of a one- or two-well work program. Even more damaging in such situations, a string of early failures tended to dampen the commitment of a few large operators and leave little room for others. As Michael Enachescu puts it, "one dry hole in a block degraded the whole neighbourhood."[31]

The lock-up scenario assumes a particular form in maturing basins where the largest fields have already been developed and producing licence holders may lack interest in further exploration. This scenario began to emerge in the 1990s in both the British and Norwegian sectors of the North Sea, when production appeared to have passed its peak. The policy assessment held that there was a mismatch in scale between the large corporations holding exploration rights to actively producing blocks and the small to intermediate firms interested in chasing the more modest but collectively significant reserves that remained. This mismatch led to the development of fallow fields initiatives, in which the state interest in renewed and extended exploration presented inactive licence holders with the choice of use it or lose it. In effect, a tightening of the terms for exploration license rights encourages holders to accelerate their plans or face relinquishment. This expectation was conveyed with particular force in Newfoundland during the tenure of Premier Danny Williams.

State rights administrators can also offer multiple licence types according to policy priorities. For example, the UK government decided in 2007 that new measures were needed "to ensure we ha[ve] full activity and an environment which would attract wider interest and investment in North Sea acreage." To encourage small but vigorous explorers, a promote licence was introduced at only 10 percent of the traditional cost. To encourage firms to take on the complex and expensive conditions in remote waters west of the Shetland Islands, a frontier licence was likewise announced.[32]

The perceived degree of stability in an exploration regime can become a policy variable in its own right. In Atlantic Canada, the initial regime was transformed three times in a decade – in 1976, 1981, and 1986. The first revision aimed to extend and consolidate land opportunities for new domestic corporate entrants, and the second deepened this thrust through preferential treatment of state oil companies. The third revision, however, reversed prevailing policy by downgrading the offshore priority.[33] Rapid turnover of tenure and capital incentives need not be prohibitive, particularly given high-quality assets, but it can complicate matters.

Alternative policy tools are also available. An important element of flexibility in the upstream sector is the industry practice of spreading risk through farm-ins that allows non-permit/licence holders to develop a stake in a prospect by financing a share of the project costs. In principle, this flexibility enables late entrants to buy in to a basin whose favourable acreage has already been committed. Flexibility is, however, dependent on the willingness or need of permit holders to broaden the range of investors and dilute the holders' share of future returns. Between 1980 and 1984, the National Energy Program years, Ottawa managed to elevate the value of farm-in partners with high Canadian equity content. New explorers could enter a sector where the most prospective blocks had already been tied up.

Another type of response was popular in the North Sea in the 1970s, when state-owned or national oil companies were given the legal prerogative to back in to any exploration permit or licence in which commercial oil or gas was found. During the search period itself, the private rights holders were required to carry the state actor. Once a discovery was made, however, the state corporation would pay for its 25 percent (or more) share of the producing project. In Ottawa, revisions to the Canada Oil and Gas Land Regulations were announced in May 1976 as the first step in a broader (post-OPEC) review of the prevailing tenure system. The recently established federal state oil company, Petro-Canada, was doubly privileged – it had back-in rights of up to 25 percent in existing permits and a prerogative to select up to 25 percent of the offshore lands not yet leased or recently surrendered. These rights enabled Petro-Canada to quickly assemble a land position in northern and Atlantic basins and to buy into wildcat wells on other firms' lands.

The model of the entrepreneurial upstream state oil company was not confined to the federal domain. In fact, the emerging North Sea model of the 1970s was embraced with great enthusiasm in the provinces. Newfoundland in particular adopted features of the Norwegian model, establishing a Petroleum Directorate as its policy arm and the Newfoundland and Labrador Petroleum Company as its analogue to Norway's Statoil.[34] Although some of these initiatives were blunted by a combination of slumping markets in the 1980s and legal jurisdictional constraints, the impulse did not completely disappear and indeed re-emerged in the 2000s.[35]

Nova Scotia likewise unveiled a state oil company – Nova Scotia Resources Limited – in the early 1980s. Its purpose was to catalyze new exploration efforts and share in the financial returns on behalf of the province. The National Energy Program of 1980 made it possible for provincial state oil corporations to enjoy Crown share provisions in the same manner as Petro-Canada.

Another potential set of pacing levers seeks to mobilize exploration capital for offshore exploration and production. Such levers involve fiscal measures on either the tax or expenditure sides of public accounts. Historically, the high risks and costs of prospecting have been acknowledged and compensated through measures to lower the costs of exploration capital by allowing substantial write-offs of expenses against taxable income. In Canada, the Kierans Report of 1970 demonstrated the uniquely favourable treatment these measures conferred on minerals and petroleum in comparison to other sectors.[36] Under such terms, it was possible for investors to make money in any eventuality. These measures had their intended effect: they released a cascade of exploration capital from corporate accounts and so-called drilling funds that sprang up to channel investor capital.[37]

The tax expenditure regime for petroleum exploration was refashioned in 1980 under the National Energy Program. In place of tax deductions, Ottawa adopted a system of grants conveyed directly to firms engaged in approved exploratory work. The Petroleum Incentive Program (PIP) was in place from 1982 to 1986, and its sunset period extended to the close of 1987. The shift from tax deductions to grants enabled the state to target incentives to particular classes of firms.[38] In particular, the level of PIP support increased with the level of Canadian ownership, and to encourage domestically owned firms to enter the offshore industry, it was increased for frontier activity. Depending upon the level of Canadian ownership, PIP payments varied from 25 to 80 percent of approved costs. Equally significant, PIP grants provided immediate and meaningful support to new, small, and marginal firms that lacked sufficient revenue flow to take advantage of the previous tax-deduction provisions. The PIP underwrote much of the second phase of Scotian Basin exploration.

Following its election in 1984, Brian Mulroney's Conservative government moved immediately to undo the National Energy Program. The PIP regime was terminated, and exploration incentives returned to the prior tradition of tax deductions. In any event, the collapse of oil prices in 1986 forced most upstream explorers to radically scale back exploration. Only four wells were drilled on the Scotian Shelf between 1987 and 1992. Today, the Canadian Exploration Expense allows a 100 percent deduction of eligible expenses for geological and geophysical work and well drilling. In addition, the Canadian Development Expense allows a 30 percent deduction of well drilling and completion expenses not covered by the exploration expense.[39]

When a project shifts from the exploration to the petroleum production phase, a separate calculus emerges. The decision to spend billions of dollars on the design, manufacture, and installation of production systems, with expected payouts over fifteen to forty years, is almost entirely separate from issues of the discovery phase. Proven and recoverable reserves remain central, but the capital value of in-ground assets and the gross returns associated with their sale are also important factors that hinge upon committed long-term markets and prices. These factors are connected in turn to forecasts for project capital costs and net returns, questions for which the choice of production system technologies and infrastructure options loom large. In addition, the development consortium may involve a different or expanded set of corporate sponsors. The existing market for discovered but not yet exploited hydrocarbon reserves allows these assets to change hands. Furthermore, although the reserve holders will capitalize their discoveries to fund shares of development costs, the syndication of risk opens an avenue for new entrants. Once again, the structure of opportunities available to each firm determines the priority attached to such participation.

As the process shifts from exploration to production, the powers available to state authorities are transformed. Key policy attributes include royalty structures, market-making controls, and powers of offshore project oversight. Although royalty terms may not always be project-determining on their own, they can affect the overall business calculus in significant ways, for instance, as a signal of overall policy disposition. Royalties can be structured on a continuum ranging from the concessionary to the prohibitive. The effect turns on more than just the percentage of royalty take. Royalty schedules may be tapered according to project or site to reward early entrants or to redirect industry attention from the known to the unknown. In the US Gulf, a critical factor in attracting capital to deepwater production was Washington's tiered royalty relief program. Enacted in 1995, it scaled back eligible royalty payments as the depth of operation increased. Royalty schemes may also be designed to correlate the timing of the obligation to profit taking. In the late 1990s, the Government of Nova Scotia shifted from a traditional cash flow royalty system to a profit-based royalty take. This policy has had the effect of shifting the royalty incidence into later years, when basic project costs have been paid out and net profits increase. A variation, also adopted in Nova Scotia, includes special provisions for marginal-field projects and for high-risk or first-entry projects that pioneer production in new areas. Since 1995, marginal-field provisions have become increasingly important to the maturing fields of the North Sea Basin. A very different scheme is the US Royalty in Kind Program, which allows operators to provide product in kind to strategic petroleum reserves.

It is not only through fiscal instruments that the offshore state influences the production phase of basin development. Although oil and natural gas pricing and gas infrastructure transport have been significantly deregulated in North America since 1985, state authorities retain several key market-making powers that shape commercial prospects for hydrocarbon producers. This is not to say that public policy is always determinative. It cannot, for example, defy the basic commercial realities of comparative energy source pricing or transportation expenses. However, it can intervene, decisively at times, in providing the marginal advantage that tips the calculus of project approval from negative to positive or from one destination market to another. A dramatic example is sovereign authority over strategic commodity export, particularly in the context of national energy security and long-term need. Through its regulatory agent, the National Energy Board, the Government of Canada invokes the right to judge prospective hydrocarbon exports against considerations of public convenience and necessity. The exploration and production industry in the Western Canada Sedimentary Basin has traditionally been fuelled by opportunities for long-term exports to the United States. However, the complexities of sourcing hydrocarbon supplies for eastern Canada have led to a variety of state-sanctioned market arrangements – for offshore imports, west-to-east transmission, and (in the age of offshore Atlantic discoveries) domestic East Coast supply.

In all cases, public policy measures are critical underpinnings for market, and therefore industry, development. At some points, a strict application of the fifty-year domestic reserve guarantee could override new western export deals. At others, a decision to allocate East Coast reserves to East Coast

Canadian markets would do the same in Nova Scotia. The Mulroney government's decision (as part its 1986 energy policy) to eliminate the fifty-year rule and its agreement to the cross-border energy supply provisions of the Canada–United States Free Trade Agreement of 1989 therefore had a profound influence on commercial outlets for oil and natural gas. The Government of New Brunswick's 2002 application to the National Energy Board to have Sable gas designated a principal source for westward transmission through New Brunswick to Quebec was likewise important. The same could be said for the National Energy Board's pipeline toll hearings on the Maritimes & Northeast Pipeline project in 1996. The outcome defined the commercial framework for the emerging gas transmission industry for years to come in terms laced with corporate and political bias.

A third state-policy instrument of primary importance is the project licensing procedure. Any sea-based extractive system is subject to an assessment process that deals with safety, technical quality, environmental impacts, and worker health. A host of issues are bound up in comprehensive reviews, particularly since the legislative and administrative provisions for approvals may derive from separate and uncoordinated statutes, at one or more levels of government. In some cases, the regulatory regime is tailored to offshore petroleum activities; in others, it may represent an extension of a broader policy template to new offshore activities. As a result, there is a high probability that multiple standards will be applied by multiple agencies through multiple processes. Not surprisingly, industry has resisted such incremental procedures, which tend to be expensive both in monetized compliance costs and in the time it requires to secure approvals. Consequently, offshore operators have pressed strenuously for unified or consolidated regulatory regimes in which jointly constituted panels fulfill multiple mandates through a single process. There are also calls for stipulated time frames for regulatory work to avoid procedural delays and, as a result, shorten cycle times. Since 2002, this sort of regulatory reform has been a central focus of the business-government forum known as the Atlantic Energy Roundtable.

When it comes to the decline and exit phase of offshore activity, two distinct approaches are evident. The first focuses on reducing the transactional and regulatory costs to operators. In the North Sea and Atlantic Canada, business initiatives have emerged in the past decade to promote concerted industry-government action to streamline and simplify regulatory structures to enhance competition in the basin. Significantly, both efforts coincided with the recognition that the basin had passed peak output and was experiencing a declining rate of new investment. The United Kingdom devised the PILOT initiative, and in Norway the counterpart is KonKraft. These initiatives need to be distinguished from offshore industry associations that engage in business advocacy. Unlike these associations, they are bipartite consultative initiatives to identify barriers and eliminate rigidities that stand in the way of competitive progress on the shelf and in the land supply chain. After more than a decade, these initiatives are regarded as useful ongoing mechanisms. Indeed, they offered a loose model for an initiative in the Atlantic offshore region in 2002. Known as the Atlantic Energy Roundtable, the initiative drew together offshore industry representatives and federal and provincial officials to explore ways to streamline regulation rather than enhance competitiveness (the assumption being that success in the former will advance the latter).[40]

A second approach is to plan for decommissioning at the basin rather than the project level. Project wind down involves sealing in wells and removing seabed and platform fixtures. Operators submit plans for regulatory approval. Field decommissioning, by contrast, singles out critical infrastructures, particularly those with shared-use potential, and ensures that facilities relevant to future development are maintained in serviceable order. Decommissioning applies to gathering systems, central platforms, and pipelines.

In sum, state authorities have access to a wide range of policy measures that can be applied to set the tempo and direction of offshore exploration and production. Any one of these measures represents a potential focal point in which political leverage can be exercised.

The Scotian Basin: A Developmental History

The Nova Scotia offshore area has had more than four decades of development as a petroleum region, providing a point of reference for the detailed political profiles that follow. This chapter presents the Scotian Basin as a cyclical phenomenon, with all of the complexity that this designation entails.[41] A number of themes run through the account. The first is the uncertain interplay of geology and commerce as firms face the challenges of prioritizing prospects and projects. Another is the tension between past, present, and future when it comes to gauging uncertainty and forecasting scenarios. In some respects, the pathways of basin development recall the biological metaphor of the punctuated equilibrium. This concept captures the notion of prolonged structural stability that is subject to occasional but fundamental break periods.[42] The third is the way in which key events in the offshore chronology are the product of compound and conflicting forces. The fourth and final is the danger of confusing simple chronology with causal chain.

It was Mobil Oil Canada that first took on the risk of entry to the Scotian Basin, both in Nova Scotia and Newfoundland. Not coincidentally, its parent company, Mobil Corporation, had been an offshore pioneer and leading player in the Gulf of Mexico. Mobil Canada began geophysical work on the east coast in 1959. It took out federal exploration permits in 1960 that covered 4 square kilometres in the vicinity of Sable Island. It was joined by a consortium of Shell Explorer (US) and Shell Canada, which acquired larger blocks along the Scotian Shelf in 1963-64 and on the deepwater slope in 1968-69. At that time, Shell Canada was also the lead company on British Columbia's coastal shelf, where it held major acreage and drilled fourteen dry holes between 1967 and 1969. The Canada Oil and Gas Land Regulations allowed large permit blocks of 95,000 acres (38,400 hectares). The entire basin was almost covered by 1971.[43] In the years that followed, however, rights holders began to release areas after disappointing results. Within a decade, total acreage dropped by 75 percent.[44] In the meantime, the extensive first cycle of Sable Basin exploration was completed.

Mobil Canada launched its first drill campaign from the sandy dunes of Sable Island. An Alberta rig, the *Bawden 18,* was transported to the island, where it drilled the first hole in 1967 and nine more between 1971 and 1973. Although the original Sable Island C-67 was a dry hole, Shell recorded the first gas discovery in 1969 at the Onondaga well. Two years later, in October 1971, Mobil announced its first strike, prompting Premier Gerald Regan's headline-making exclamation, "It's oil!"[45] Mobil went on to record five of the first eight oil and gas finds around Sable Island. Shell took a different approach, sponsoring thirty-six wells over the decade. Whereas Mobil sought to concentrate its efforts, Shell spread its wildcats across the shelf from east to west. Shell's success rate fell well short of Mobil's, though it did record one more significant gas discovery in what became the Primrose field. Together, however, the two firms drove a vigorous first wave of exploration drilling. Later in the decade, when the pace slowed, the newly established state oil company, Petro-Canada, joined in to advance its mandate to catalyze frontier development. Petro-Canada farmed-in to six of the eight wells drilled in 1976 and 1977.

There was no dramatic "super find" along the lines of the Forties and Brent fields in the UK North Sea or Ekofisk in the Norwegian sector.

However, a series of modest oil and gas discoveries was sufficient to maintain some momentum from already-committed firms. More important, this first exploratory phase unearthed eight significant (mainly gas) discoveries at Onondaga (1969), West Sable (1971), Primrose (1972), Thebaud (1972), Cohasset (oil, 1973), Citnalta (1974), Intrepid (1974), and Venture (1979). A ninth field was located at East Point in the Magdalene Basin in the Gulf of St. Lawrence. But by the mid-1970s the rate of wildcatting was on the wane, down from ten to twelve wells per year to fewer than five. All things considered, this first foray into the Scotian Basin failed to sustain industry expectations. The head of Shell Canada, Harry Bridges, described his firm's failure to get results from its massive 1970s campaign as "the biggest disappointment of my life."[46] Even for the successful discoverers, the initial decade was modest when measured in terms of global offshore exploration. In the Gulf of Mexico, the average time between acquiring leases and starting production was five years.[47] On the Nova Scotia shelf, more than a decade elapsed without a single commercial project being advanced.

On the other hand, there were positive developments. The ratio of discoveries to wells drilled was one in five, an excellent rate by international standards of the day. Furthermore, the Government of Canada offered substantial fiscal incentives for drilling on frontier lands, including the Scotian Basin. These incentives included a 100 percent deduction of exploration expenses against individual or corporate income and an earned depletion allowance that added a further 33 percent deduction of exploration expenses against resource-sector profits. Finally, in the 1977 budget, the Trudeau government added the frontier exploration allowance as a tax deduction of 66 percent on any expense exceeding $5 million on a single well. In Calgary, this was known as the Gallagher amendment in reference to the president of Dome Petroleum who had lobbied for additional offsets to frontier risk costs. It was said that under such a regime companies could even make money on dry holes.[48] On the East Coast, it was not possible to drill a well for less than $5 million. Not surprisingly, brokers and investment houses found it easy to capitalize drilling funds to buy into frontier wells in northern and Atlantic Canada.

In the fall of 1978, the Mobil-Texaco-PEX group spudded a well on a site 16 kilometres east of Sable Island. Known as Venture D-23, it was one of only five new holes drilled that year. There the Gulftide rig struck gas in a medium-sized fault in Jurassic and Cretaceous sandstone, giving new life to the basin. Venture was far from the first significant gas discovery in the Sable Subbasin, but four delineation wells revealed it to be larger than all

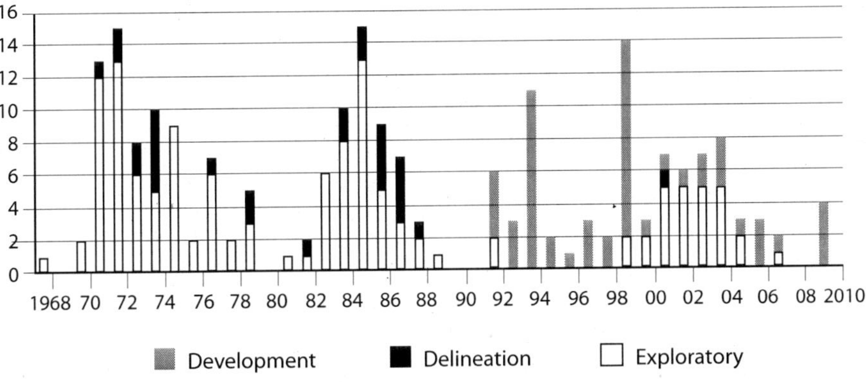

Figure 2.3 Wells drilled in Sable Basin, 1967-2009
Source: CNSOPB, Directory of Wells.

earlier finds combined. Most importantly, the discovery underlined the still unexplored potential of the region and led the way toward a new round of exploration between 1981 and 1987.

The Venture discovery coincided with a large convulsion in global petroleum exploration and production. In 1979, the Shah of Iran was toppled, and oil exports were halted as the Islamic Revolution progressed. This development fed into the second OPEC oil crisis, which saw the nominal price of oil double to approximately $40 per barrel. The Government of Canada responded with the National Energy program in October 1980, identifying frontier basins (Arctic and offshore) as critical priorities for the future security of supply. By 1981, companies undertaking offshore exploration could qualify for substantial federal subventions through the PIP. The sliding set of benefits was richest for Canadian-owned companies and, not surprisingly, the offshore corporate community took a different shape this time around. Two state-owned firms – Petro-Canada and Nova Scotia Resources Limited – played prominent roles, as did Alberta independents such as Bow Valley Industries, Husky Oil, Home Oil, Hudson Bay Oil and Gas, and Canterra. All figured as valued partners in joint ventures seeking to raise their PIP eligibility.

Figure 2.3 illustrates the cyclicality of Scotian basin drilling and the shifting makeup of the exploration community. A distinct wave occurred in each decade. Cycles in the 1970s and 1980s were classic explore-and-delineate sequences. In the 1990s, however, production wells were drilled for the Cohasset-Panuke and Sable energy projects. The fourth and final wave of the 2000s comprised a new exploration cycle, one that included the deepwater slope and production drilling for the Tier 2 fields in the Sable project. Also notable is the shifting ensemble of corporate players over time. Although Mobil and Shell kicked off the exploration campaign of the 1970s, a wider range of farm-in partners closed it out. The second cycle, which included a number of Canadian independents, was similarly heterogeneous. Although producing companies dominated the third wave, multinational majors with Gulf of Mexico experience returned for the deepwater round.

The second phase of exploration and production in the Scotian Basin proceeded in two periods. Of the twenty-seven wells that were drilled from 1980 to 1984, half were wildcats sprinkled across the shelf from Georges Bank to the Laurentian Channel, including a number of sites at the shelf-slope divide.[49] Others were concentrated in the Sable Island area and combined new exploration with known-field delineation. Four prospects adjacent to Venture were drilled, and three more discoveries were made. In 1983, activity reached an all-time high in terms of metres of rock drilled.[50] Notably, the first half of the decade coincided with the PIP regime, which provided unprecedented cash for new corporate entrants.

The latter half of the second phase followed a different pattern. From 1984 to 1988, another twenty-five wells were drilled, and four-fifths of them were located in the Sable Subbasin. Wildcatting became more cautious after the Mulroney Conservatives terminated the PIP in 1986. Attention instead centred on the delineation of the Sable discoveries, particularly new significant discoveries at Banquereau (1982); South Venture, Olympia, Arcadia, and Glenelg (1983); Uniacke, Alma, and Chebucto (1984); West Venture and West Olympia (1985); North Triumph (1986); and South Sable (1988). The final well of the second phase was drilled in 1988 and was followed by a three-year hiatus in the basin. Equally striking, the 1980s were the decade when the Sable fields assumed a larger, more modern shape. Only one significant discovery has been made since 1988. In effect, the region has been discovery deficient for more than twenty years.

Another critical step that marked progress in basin development was the announcement of the first production complex. The Venture gas project was unveiled by Mobil Canada in 1983. It called for the stand-alone development of the Venture field from two producing platforms to supply gas to a pipeline linked to onshore processing facilities. Estimated recoverable reserves of 2.5 trillion cubic feet (70 billion cubic metres) were projected for a lifespan of eighteen years. Sixteen to twenty production wells would be drilled between 1984 and 1987 to tap gas from twenty-seven potential reservoirs.[51] Mobil Canada was joined in the project by Petro-Canada, Texaco, Nova Scotia Resources Limited, and Eastcoast Energy Ltd. In addition to a development plan, the partners submitted an environmental impact statement for review in 1983. A joint federal-provincial panel approved the latter expeditiously (with conditions) in December 1983. However, the forward progress of the project was hampered by sharp declines in natural gas prices in the mid-1980s, and after an extended hiatus, the project was shelved in 1987.

Following Venture's demise, a more modest crude oil project began to take shape. Despite Premier Regan's excitement back in 1971, crude oil did not figure prominently in the discoveries of the first decade. The upstream companies shared his disappointment. In the second phase, however, Mobil Canada returned to delineate the Cohasset D-42 find of 1973, and other companies took up leases in the area. In 1986, Shell struck oil at its Panuke well, and Petro-Canada made a parallel discovery that turned out to be part of the same field. It was a modest step forward. To put the discoveries in perspective, the 1979 Hibernia discovery in Newfoundland was originally estimated to contain more than 500 million barrels of crude, whereas for Cohasset-Panuke recoverable reserves were estimated at 60 million barrels. In any event, the same depressed oil markets that delayed development at Hibernia in the 1980s also influenced Cohasset.

The three-year drilling hiatus from 1988 to 1991 was more than a temporary respite. The second phase did not end with a dramatic sense of promise similar to that offered by Venture D-23. Globally, the offshore sector had slumped from the halcyon days of the early 1980s. But in other active basins, this decline meant a dampening of rig activity, not a wholesale flight. For the Scotian Basin, the decline signalled a shift in industry investment to more prospective areas such as the US Gulf, northwest Australia, the North Sea, and offshore Brazil. This was not lost on Nova Scotia operators.

One of the catalysts for renewal was Nova Scotia Resources Limited (NSRL), the provincially owned petroleum corporation. As exploration slowed, the potential for future drill partnerships receded, and NSRL began to rethink its strategy as early as 1986. The PIP was ending, oil prices were at a decadal low, and the Venture project was fading into obscurity. Nova Scotia Resources Limited identified offshore production as a possible pathway to basin revival, and Cohasset-Panuke oil became its centrepiece. The field could generate corporate revenue that NSRL could shelter with future exploration drilling, and it could help fund NSRL's equity share in the Venture project, if revived. In July 1990, NSRL announced a joint venture with Lasmo UK, an independent producer in the North Sea. Following two years of licensing and installation, crude oil began to flow on 3 June 1992. The Cohasset-Panuke (COPAN) project triggered a third but somewhat muted wave of development well drilling between 1990 and 1994.

The symbolic importance of the COPAN initiative as Canada's first offshore oil production project was substantial. As a production system, it included two unmanned wellhead platforms, a series of fifteen production wells, and the mobile drill rig *Rowan Gorilla III.* Oil flowed to a CALM buoy connected to a floating storage offloading vessel that was itself linked to a shuttle tanker. Over seven years, the project generated 44.5 million barrels of sweet light oil (graded Nova Scotia light) from the two fields.

COPAN oil production was a bridging project in another sense. It kept engineering and regulatory agents active in the basin until momentum returned for another larger project. By the early 1990s, new concepts were being considered for developing the Sable gas fields. Rather than a standalone Venture field, the model was a multi-field plan to exploit a half-dozen significant discoveries around Sable Island and required a consortium to amalgamate the necessary reserves and to underwrite the capital costs. The initiating agent was Mobil Canada, which held rights to the Thebaud, Venture, and South Venture finds. It approached Shell Canada, which brought in three fields closer to the edge of the shelf: North Triumph, Alma, and Glenelg. The remaining rights holders brought into the development consortium were Petro-Canada, Imperial Oil, and NSRL. By 1995, the Sable offshore energy project was armed with positive findings from its resource and market studies. The business plan called for the extraction of gas and its transport via pipeline to Country Harbour, Guysborough County, where it would be processed and fed into a high-pressure trunk pipeline. The majority of the gas would be exported to New England, while smaller volumes would move by spur lines to markets in the Maritime provinces. Attention then turned to the technical design and regulatory applications for the $2-billion complex. Final sanction was given in February 1998, and the first gas flowed just before the turn of the century.

The third commercial field prospect emerged in the late 1990s at Deep Panuke, operated by PanCanadian Energy. In 1996, the company purchased Lasmo's interest in the Cohasset project and took over operation of that field for its final years. PanCanadian then began exploratory drilling below the producing field as part of a separate Abenaki carbonate play. Gas was discovered, and Deep Panuke was announced as a significant find in 2000. It was the first gas discovery in the basin in more than a decade. Following further delineation, PanCanadian decided to proceed to commercial development and filed a project description with the CNSOPB in July 2001. Nine months later, regulatory applications were formally submitted for a complex that included three platforms and a 60-centimetre pipeline to deliver gas to the Maritimes & Northeast Pipeline at Country Harbour. At this point, corporate restructuring had an impact. PanCanadian entered a corporate merger with the Alberta Energy Company, leading to the newly named EnCana Corp. In March 2003, EnCana announced the suspension of its development application pending project review. Several years later, Deep Panuke was revived with a separate design, a 2010 start-up target, lower volumes, and reliance on the Sable offshore pipeline instead of a standalone line.

Another new exploration frontier opened in the late 1990s, when the CNSOPB awarded the first exploration licences for the coastal margin. To that point, petroleum operations had always taken place far from mainland Nova Scotia. That changed when Hunt Oil acquired two blocks off the east coast of Cape Breton Island and when Corridor Resources acquired one block on the west coast. The licences triggered protest from a coalition of coastal interests, including fishers, tourist operators, and rural residents concerned about the damaging consequences of seismic and drilling work. With the agreement of federal and provincial ministers, the board declared a prohibition on petroleum activity on these properties for the duration of the public inquiry to determine whether additional conditions should be attached to the activities authorized by exploration leases.[52]

For the first time, offshore leases impinged directly on a substantial coastal constituency. The result was to politicize offshore activities in a way that had not been seen since the Georges Bank moratorium campaigns. The inquiry commissioner heard more than three weeks of heated presentations from a variety of perspectives. More scientific and stakeholder consultations followed the inquiry report. Ultimately, Corridor Resources was approved to conduct a week of seismic surveys later in 2003. However, no further activities followed, and the Corridor and Hunt licences lapsed in 2008. This revealing episode in industry-community relations, occurring far from the offshore epicentre of the outer Scotian Shelf, has not been repeated.

While attention was focused on the SOEP installation and while PanCanadian was drilling deeper on the COPAN formation, a dramatic new exploration play was building at the edge of the Scotian Shelf. This play may be described as Phase 3b. In the late bidding round of 1997, eleven blocks were posted, and seven of them were subsequently awarded the following year. Among them was Chevron EL 2359, the first deepwater lease in more than a decade. In December 1998, twenty more blocks were posted, and nineteen of them were awarded the following June (covering 2.2 million hectares). The exploration and production industry had returned to Nova Scotia in force. Not since the 1970s had so much land been under lease, but this time it was centred along the deepwater slope. In late 1999, eleven additional blocks were issued, and ten more followed in November 2000. These blocks included BP's EL 2403, which carried a then-record $97-million work obligation. The deepwater enthusiasm that was driving new investment in more southerly basins had swept north. Overall, work bids for exploration in the Scotian Basin exceeded $1 billion. A further round awarded in January 2002 brought nine more leases, including Marathon Canada's twin bids of $176 million and $193 million. Most of the deepwater slope was now taken up, from Georges Bank to the Laurentian Channel.

By 2002, the international exploration and production industry had the Scotian Basin back on its radar. Some enthusiastic forecasters were convinced that a long-deferred promise was at hand. The first offshore field was shipping gas to New England, and the deepwater slope was under exploration permit. Ziff Energy of Calgary suggested that the accepted natural gas reserve estimate of 18.5 trillion cubic feet (518 billion cubic metres) would soon be obsolete and that an ultimate resource in excess of 50 trillion cubic feet (1.4 trillion cubic metres) was a reasonable expectation. It predicted that "development of this emerging supply basin will aggressively continue throughout this decade."[53]

The first deepwater well was spudded by Marathon late in 2001. Drill complications led to the original Annapolis B-24 being abandoned and restarted as G-24. A gas discovery followed in an Early Cretaceous turbidite formation (an impure sandstone deposit). Over the next three years, five additional wells were drilled in three play types along the slope, and although gas shows were reported, no discoveries followed.[54] This negative result chilled enthusiasm among the remaining leaseholders, and more than half of the properties were surrendered without drilling. Forfeitures exceeded $100 million by 2006. The extraordinary exploration boom and bust of this period is illustrated in the licensed acreage in Map 2.2. Given the enormous costs of a deepwater well, it is clear that the absence of a major

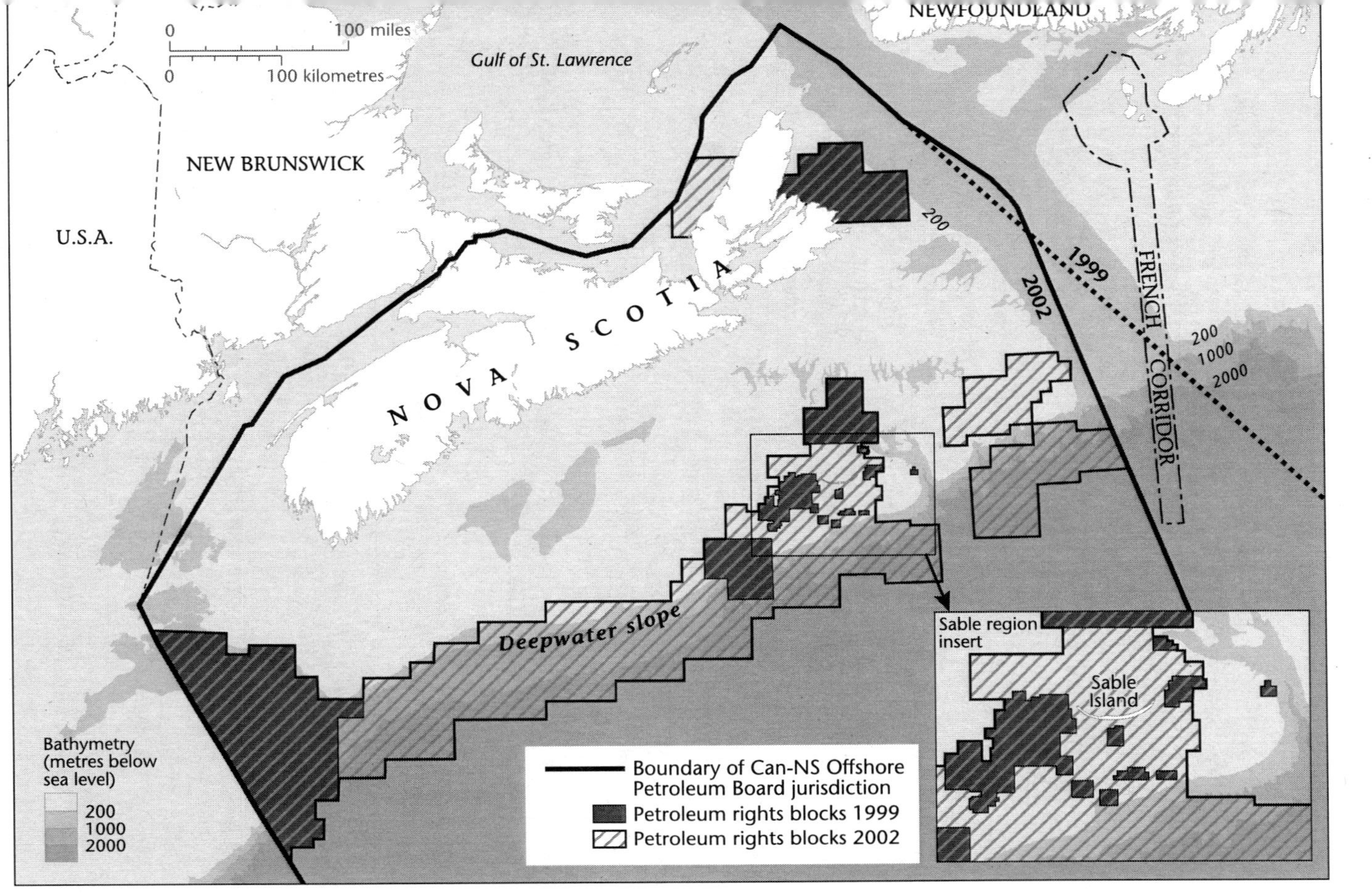

Map 2.2 Scotian Basin licence interests, 1999 and 2002

Source: CNSOPB Onshore and Offshore Regions Maps, 1999 and 2002.

gas reservoir find drove explorers back toward the more familiar and rewarding deepwaters of the Gulf and the South Atlantic. Although exploration on the Scotian Slope has barely begun – only ten holes have been drilled in only three of ten identified play types – the most recent and flashy exploration phase has come to an abrupt close. Even on the Scotian Shelf, no exploration well has been spudded since February 2006.

Since then, offshore authorities have wrestled with a new policy challenge – how to reignite industry activity and push Sable Basin development to a new level. The latter part of the millennium's first decade differed qualitatively from earlier slumps. The downturn was not simply a global contraction in response to weak markets or overcapacity: the firms withdrawing from the Nova Scotia sector hired rigs and spent their exploration budgets in basins perceived to be more promising. Only in the fall of 2008 did the world financial crisis kill the demand pressures that had pushed crude oil and natural gas to record levels. While optimists continued to point to the Sable project, Deep Panuke, and several liquefied natural gas terminal proposals as evidence of forward motion, realists recognized that the underlying engine of development was absent. The corporate community had become risk averse, and the basin had been downgraded.

Officials in the Nova Scotia Department of Energy advanced the policy response. With ministerial support, a share of the deepwater licence forfeiture revenue was allocated in 2006 for consultancy studies. Researchers assessed the competitiveness of the basin, industry perceptions, and the state of offshore geoscience. Their work, in turn, fed into a recovery strategy premised on the need to improve the attractiveness of a region widely viewed as too complex geologically and too expensive commercially and politically. The plan had four goals: stimulating new geoscience perspectives, lowering regulatory and infrastructure costs, simplifying and accelerating regulatory processes, and promoting these changes internationally.[55] Of the four, emphasis has been placed on reducing geological uncertainty. In light of the above discussion, however, it is reasonable to doubt whether anything short of a dramatic new discovery along the lines of Venture, Cohasset, or Deep Panuke will be sufficient to revive the exploration cycle.

Conclusion

A complex multivariate causality shapes field or basin development, and it is certainly evident in the history of the Scotian Basin. Elements include judgments on risk and reward, perceptions of threshold conditions or critical mass, investment opportunity costs, and knowledge of geological plays and state regulatory incentives and burdens. For example, although a lively pattern of rights bidding suggests growing corporate interest, there are limits to how long this interest can persist in the absence of significant discoveries. Similarly, the announcement of early development projects is likely to have a spillover effect in the form of renewed exploration effort, for the prospect of installed infrastructure lowers the potential capital costs and cycle times of future projects.

Factors such as these also serve to highlight the role of firm-centred interests. Generic tendencies can be discerned among exploration and production companies according to size, nationality, structure, ownership, and style. The newly formed global elite of supermajor players may focus on the largest and most promising basins in their search for elephant fields that can generate the extraordinary revenues required for profits at that level. However, the commercial horizons of other firm categories are sufficient to drive large, medium, and small basin developments elsewhere. Over the past decade, the top echelon of independent exploration and production firms has become internationalized to an impressive extent. These companies seek to balance their portfolios of holdings among basins and throughout project cycles. This strategy has created a lively market for established assets to be traded at the rights-holding, discovery, and producing stages. In addition, innovations in field development and reservoir management have enabled firms to profitably match the scale of offshore projects to their revenue and profit needs. Although supermajor enterprises may operate globally in pursuit of super-giant (billion barrel) fields and may be satisfied with the discovery of giant fields (with ultimate recovery exceeding 500 million barrels of oil equivalent), other types of firms can flourish on field projects of lesser magnitude. For example, second-tier majors and large independents may profitably develop fields with ultimate recovery of 100 million barrels of oil equivalent. Threshold size may also be achieved by consolidating modest properties. There are cases in the deepwater Gulf of Mexico in which up to a half-dozen distinct fields have been tied into central production structures from distances up to 40 kilometres. Different types of opportunities arise at the other end of the cycle. When basins pass into the mature phase, small independents and even junior companies have an opportunity to acquire proven but depreciated assets and turn respectable profits, as has happened in the British North Sea since 1995. Equally, they can develop small- and medium-sized projects as offshore market niches.

For a field or basin to be fully developed, a variety of firms will be needed. Pioneer entrants will serve as catalysts, achieving the conceptual, technological, or commercial breakthroughs to confirm the status of a region. More conservative players may stand aside and await the results of early rounds, buying in only after the categorical uncertainty of the novel play gives way to the relative uncertainty of expanding exploration. Once again, there are tactical variations, for the range of corporate participants can broaden with the appearance of new rights holders, farm-ins, or other partnerships based at the capital investment rather than operational level.

At a separate level of analysis, each firm emerges as a decision-making centre. Exploration programs are intensively analyzed and competitively assessed within firms. Ranking encompasses a range of factors that reach well beyond the scientific evidence. Geological prospectivity – a complex combination of conceptual science and on-site drill results – is a determining factor, shaping both the industry's attitude toward a basin and the calculus of corporate investment. However, prospectivity itself is a structured phenomenon with its own causes and consequences. For particular firms, corporate strategy is tied to such considerations as exploration portfolio balance, reserve assets, short-term cash flow needs, and share price on equity markets.

For a number of understandable reasons, the exploration and production industry tends to regard prospectivity as a primary datum – an objective, ground-truthed reality and an overriding determinant of business opportunities at a fixed point in time. This may not be the whole story, however. Prospectivity is also a politically and economically constructed circumstance. For states seeking to exploit offshore oil and gas, the challenge of basin development policy is to orchestrate the appropriate tools, in the necessary contexts, to promote the desired political results. At various points in the modern history of petroleum exploration, these tools have included the exclusive exploration concession, the state petroleum company, and the regulatory agent. Today, the tools are also likely to include the fiscal incentive, the industrial benefits strategy, and the smart regulatory regime. Few states are content to rely on a single policy instrument. The need to manage fields and basins throughout the full development cycle is increasingly evident. However, policy design, approval and implementation are quite separate political challenges. The following chapter takes up issues of institutional design in the Scotian Basin, beginning in the formative era of the 1970s.

PART 2

Parameters of the Offshore State

3 The Political Construction of Administrative Institutions

This chapter explores the origins and structure of the central state authority for administering Scotian Shelf petroleum: the Canada–Nova Scotia Offshore Petroleum Board (CNSOPB). It was created by intergovernmental agreement in 1986, formalized by mirror federal and provincial statutes in 1988-89, and opened for business in January 1990. Since then, the board has operated at the centre of the offshore exploration and production regime. However, this joint management model, as it has come to be known, has a longer history that is important to understanding the shape and function of the board.

To fully appreciate the board's significance, this chapter analyzes it from an institutional point of view, seeking to understand it as an organizational channel of government action created by political design. The board is treated as an institution of government, as a complex of values, rules, and procedures exercised in coordinated and consistent ways. An institution is an organized structure that shows continuity and consistency over time. Normally, this continuity requires the assemblage of certain key elements: elite leadership, expert staff, financial resources, and social recognition or legitimacy. As a result, an institution is a conduit for coordinated action insofar as it functions in deliberate and rational ways to accomplish designated goals. If politics is about the clash of rival interests and power is the capacity to prevail in situations of conflict, then much of these activities are played out within formal institutions. This analysis of the CNSOPB sets the stage for a more detailed exploration of offshore politics in the chapters that follow.

An institutional approach draws out several points. First, institutions are products of human artifice but not strictly of purposive design. It may be more helpful to see institutions as the compound products of intention and circumstance. New institutions are fashioned by political actors who may well clash over the goals being pursued and the desired results. In an evocative phrase, E.E. Schattschneider notes that "organization is itself a mobilization of bias in preparation for action."[1] This comment, directed initially at interest groups, applies also to the organization of state institutions. This chapter explores the biases inscribed in the structure and process of offshore institutions and their influence on petroleum politics. At the same time, it should be noted that institutions seldom emerge on a blank page but rather can be deeply affected by what has gone before. Not surprisingly then, the process or history of institutional formation looms large in any attempt to understand an institution's function. It also follows that institutions are dynamic and capable of evolving over time. This is certainly the case for the management authority explored here.

A second point to note is that institutions can be understood at multiple levels. An important starting point is the formal arrangements that set out, often on paper, the statutes, legal regulations, executive directives, and organizational charts of official business. Such arrangements reveal the players and the procedures that bring institutions alive and point to the patterned sets of roles that are carried out by assigned actors. Formal arrangements are important for setting limits and authorizing action. In short, they prescribe certain modes of political behaviour and proscribe others; they confer elements of stability and durability on designated fields.

There are always, of course, limits to official accounts of institutions that make it unwise to accept them at face value. Indeed, the behaviour of an institution may be at sharp variance with its promise, and key goals may be latent (hidden or dormant) in the structure. Also, operational tensions often exist within a structure that struggles with multiple mandates, diverse objectives, or other complications. These tensions also tend to be reflected in institutional behaviour. In the case of the CNSOPB, the textbook history presented by institutional architects and participants needs to be addressed, but so too do the more elusive underlying operational dynamics.

Looking beyond the descriptive level, modern institutional analysis advances a set of tools to better understand formal structures. It asks, what are the underlying values associated with prescribed measures and the underlying logics associated with institutional operations? Archer and colleagues put forward several key questions in this vein: "What is an institution's logic? Is it consistent or contested? How are logics connected to rules and roles? How do institutions interact in the policy process?"[2]

The CNSOPB is a particularly complicated example of a resource management authority. Whereas most of Canada's petroleum provinces vest the administration of Crown-owned resources in a single department of natural resources or energy, the offshore board is a joint creation of two sovereign governments. As a result, it was cast from a new and original template. The board succeeded in resolving several difficult federal-provincial political tensions, though it created a new series of problems in the process, including a complicated pattern of accountability. The board members are appointed by senior governments not only to exercise delegated legal powers but also to follow policy directions from above. Furthermore, joint management boards answer to not one but two ministerial masters, who sit at separate cabinet tables and may be elected by different political parties. Finally, it is important to recognize that an offshore board such as the CNSOPB is not the sole state agency with important policy and regulatory responsibilities offshore. In fact, the "offshore state" for the Scotian Basin includes more than a dozen departments and agencies from the federal, provincial, and municipal levels. The relationship between the board and these other institutions needs to be spelled out.

The following institutional logics are explored: proprietary ownership (to hold and use natural materials); constitutional jurisdiction (to legislate); administrative and regulatory function; joint delegation of authority (to a third agency); and coordinate action (within an assigned policy sector and beyond it). This chapter also examines policy values, including the reduction of petroleum investment risk, the orderly allocation of legal rights to explore and exploit, the balance of fiscal proceeds among sovereign and non-sovereign interests, the maximization of domestic economic benefits flowing from offshore commercial development, and the protection of marine environmental conditions throughout these processes.

Constitutional Primacy: Who Owns? Who Legislates?

Although the first East Coast offshore exploration well was drilled from an artificial island in Charlottetown Harbour in 1943, the history of the modern Atlantic industry dates from 1959, when Mobil Canada filed for rights to seabed acreage in the Sable Island area. Given the uncertain status of offshore jurisdiction, Mobil took out mineral rights from Nova Scotia (the only seabed instrument available in the province at the time) and petroleum rights from Ottawa.[3] After years of seismic work, the company drilled its first exploratory well on Sable Island in 1967. These early rights-seeking strategies underscored a central problem for the offshore petroleum industry in Canada – the uncertainty of constitutional jurisdiction. The only way for a prospective explorer to fully secure its legal position in the 1960s was to hold rights with dual authorities. For petroleum capital, the jurisdictional issue was an annoying and expensive legal ambiguity; for governments, it was a primary issue of jurisdictional power.

A parallel conflict had already played out in the United States. In the 1930s, the state of Louisiana established a Mineral Board with legal powers to lease offshore lands. However, in 1945 President Truman issued proclamations that claimed federal jurisdiction to the same resource. From 1947 to 1950, when Texas joined Louisiana in postwar leasing and the industry pushed farther into offshore waters, the question found its way to the US Supreme Court in the Tidelands cases. The result was a full legal victory for Washington.[4] However, the issue resurfaced during the 1952 presidential election, and the Republican winner, Dwight Eisenhower, was quite partial to the states' rights position. Congress passed the Submerged Lands Act in 1953, which assigned state ownership to a three-mile coastal belt. The companion Outer Continental Shelf Lands Act opened the way for the federal Department of the Interior to assume the central role in petroleum management of the broader shelf beyond the three-mile line. The first federal leases were sold in 1954.[5]

Australia faced these same jurisdictional issues not long after but resolved them in a different fashion. By 1963, exploration firms had acquired offshore permits from a number of states, including Victoria, Tasmania, South Australia, and Western Australia. In these years, the offshore petroleum framework was simply an extension of state mining law on land. Although the Commonwealth government signed the 1958 Convention on the Continental Shelf, Canberra did not deal squarely with the issue until offshore exploration was well under way. The vehicle was the conference table rather than the courtroom. Because the postwar period had seen several successful Commonwealth-state collaborations on cross-jurisdictional resources such as water and hydroelectricity, the governments launched a multi-year process of intergovernmental consultation that culminated in the Australian Offshore Petroleum Agreement of October 1967 and subsequent legislation.[6] By agreeing to enact a common mining code through mirror legislation for state waters (the three-mile territorial sea) and Commonwealth waters (the balance of the continental shelf), a seamless approach was forged. Furthermore, a unified administration was created by establishing a designated authority for each state appointed by the state government and responsible for applying all statutes and policies. The legislation was a substantial achievement, as Cullen notes, for it created "a national uniform offshore mining regime, a secure titles system, a revenue-sharing arrangement and a state-based day-to-day administration."[7]

Thus, by the time Canadian authorities began to grapple with offshore jurisdiction, there were at least two prior patterns of resolution, and each eventually proved to have an influence. Not surprisingly, each level of government in Canada staked out a case for Crown ownership. According to the coastal provinces, their claims over seabed and subsoil resources lay in sovereign and proprietorial rights that predated Confederation. For its part, Ottawa invoked sovereign authority to both the three-mile territorial sea and the wider continental shelf under the 1958 Geneva Convention. (The wider continental shelf was defined as the seabed adjacent to the coast that fell outside the territorial sea to a depth of 200 metres or, beyond that, as deep as resource exploitation was possible.) In 1965, the federal government, seeking a ruling on ownership and jurisdiction off the coast of British Columbia, put a reference question before the Supreme Court of Canada. Two years later, the Court issued its opinion in *Reference re Offshore Mineral Rights of British Columbia.* In a sweeping decision, the Court found that property rights and legislative power to both the territorial sea and the continental shelf lay with the federal government.[8] Although there would be further court challenges in subsequent decades, this judicial ruling dramatically elevated Ottawa's political position in the offshore resource stakes. Yet, having won a victory even more sweeping than that of Washington in the Tidewater cases, Ottawa proceeded to conciliate the provinces in a manner that partly reflected the US example but was also informed by developments in Australia.

From Crown Ownership to Joint Management

Even before the BC litigation was resolved, the Atlantic provinces had pressed the federal government for expanded offshore jurisdiction. The joint statement that flowed from a meeting of Atlantic premiers in September 1964 asserted "provincial ownership and control of submarine minerals" underlying both territorial waters and the Nova Scotia and Newfoundland "banks." The premiers also called on Ottawa to define offshore sectoral boundaries and to alter provincial boundaries accordingly.[9] The following month, the Atlantic premiers restated their claim to proprietary rights at a federal-provincial First Ministers Conference.

Following the Supreme Court's decision in the BC reference case of November 1967, a new path toward political accommodation emerged. Ottawa offered to negotiate an offshore settlement based on federal-provincial revenue sharing from offshore mineral exploitation but under a system of federal administration. Prime Minister Trudeau outlined this proposal publicly in December 1968. A year later, in an effort to overcome what was perceived to be the premiers' uncertainty about whether to act en bloc or individually, Trudeau guaranteed that all provinces would receive the most favoured terms in the event that agreements were negotiated incrementally. Nonetheless, in 1972 the five eastern premiers rejected Ottawa's proposal and reasserted their claims to ownership.[10]

Ottawa's 1968 offer did, however, introduce a new policy paradigm. By its terms, the dispute over ownership would be set aside, and the fiscal benefits from petroleum and mineral exploitation would be shared between jurisdictions. Moreover, a single administrative or management authority would oversee exploitation. Although the particular terms remained open to discussion, these new features were central to all major agreements in future decades. Five years later, in 1977, this federal approach to offshore management resurfaced in a memorandum of understanding signed by Ottawa and the three Maritime premiers. (Newfoundland had left the group of five in 1972, when it began reviewing its offshore petroleum strategy in light of developments in the North Sea. Quebec's position had also changed after the election of the Parti Québécois in 1976.)

The 1977 Memorandum of Understanding

The centrepiece of the February 1977 memorandum of understanding on the "Administration and Management of Mineral Resources Offshore of the Maritime Provinces" was a proposed joint authority to administer mineral resources seaward of a 5-kilometre (3-mile) coastal belt and extending outward to the limit of the continental shelf jurisdiction. The joint authority would be known as the Maritime Offshore Resources Board and would be made up of three federal appointees and one member from each Maritime province. The board would exercise management powers delegated by federal and provincial governments. It would issue resource exploration and exploitation rights, set their terms, optimize regional economic benefits, advise senior governments on resource policy and legislation, and receive and distribute resource revenues.[11]

According to the memorandum of understanding, a federal agency would be designated to administer offshore resources on the board's behalf, and Ottawa would assume all operational costs. The revenue pool flowing from offshore activities – including royalties, fees, and bonuses but not export, income, or commodity taxes – would be split between Ottawa (25 percent) and the province (75 percent) in the offshore area. Landward of the five-kilometre line, each province would receive 100 percent of the stipulated revenues, and Nova Scotia would also enjoy 100 percent of revenues within a coastal band to be fixed around Sable Island.[12]

The 1977 memorandum of understanding also called for a formal intergovernmental agreement to be drawn up to formalize the arrangement and joint federal-provincial legislative action. However, the newly elected Conservative government of Nova Scotia, led by John Buchanan, opted to withdraw from the agreement in September 1978. Among the reasons given were flawed revenue terms, an asymmetrical board structure that left Nova Scotia (a prime offshore partner) with only one of six voting seats, and the designation of the federal minister as the tie-breaking authority.[13] Nova Scotia's departure hastened the collapse of the entire memorandum of understanding edifice.

Despite this failure, a new policy debate had begun, one centred on the concept of negotiated joint control of offshore exploitation. With the intractable issue of Crown ownership set to the side, attention shifted to maximizing regional resource benefits – in fiscal, investment, and employment terms. Expectations also shifted toward accelerating exploration and development by means of an effective petroleum exploitation regime. (At the time, there was little offshore policy or regulatory sophistication at either level of government). The next decade saw a flurry of variations on these basic principles. Some, like the 1977 template, were strikingly asymmetrical in the alignment of federal and provincial interests. On the other hand, the Canada–Nova Scotia Agreement of 1982, concluded by the Trudeau Liberals and the Buchanan Conservatives, shifted the tilt some distance toward a balance. However it was left to the Canada-Newfoundland Atlantic Accord of 1985 and the Canada–Nova Scotia Offshore Petroleum Accord of 1986 to achieve more symmetrical and lasting versions. These accords continue to apply today. They also served as the basis for a possible Pacific Accord, which was discussed by British Columbia and Canada from 1986 to 1989 without resolution.

Because it was never implemented, the 1977 memorandum of understanding must be assessed as an expression of intent rather than an actual offshore management regime. Its conceptual features, as argued above, marked a significant new trajectory in offshore politics. However, it is the accords, boards, and development projects of the 1980s and 1990s that require more careful attention, for they forced the Government of Canada to make significant concessions.

Striking a Federal-Provincial Offshore Equilibrium

Although it was separated from the 1977 memorandum of understanding by only a few short years, the accord era belongs to a new and different phase of petro politics marked by a number of intense and closely punctuated watersheds. The first was the discovery of the Venture natural gas field near Sable Island in June 1979 and the follow-up Hibernia oil strike off Newfoundland in August. Both came at the end of a prolonged if inconclusive period of offshore exploration. Although several dozen discoveries had been made among the hundred-plus wells that were drilled during the decade, a big commercial discovery proved elusive until Mobil Canada announced major gas flows at three levels of its Venture D-23 well. This discovery, combined with the proximate markets and straightforward transportation features of the Scotian Shelf, brought new momentum to the natural gas play.[14]

Second, and almost simultaneous with the Venture strike, was the OPEC oil price shock triggered by the Iranian Revolution. While its complex ramifications shaped global business conditions for years to come, the two-fold increase in oil prices had a dramatic influence on Canada's East Coast.[15] Higher oil prices transformed the economics of Canada's so-called frontier basins in ways that brought new interest in exploration and a far more positive calculus of risk and return.

Finally, the dramatic petroleum price spike forced Canadian governments at all levels to rethink their energy policies. In Nova Scotia, this reevaluation began with a conference held in Halifax in January 1980 titled "The Opportunities and the Challenge."[16] Six months later, the province released a new strategic plan, outlining wholesale revisions to legislation, regulation, and management.[17] The central thrust of the plan was the affirmation of full provincial control over offshore mineral resources. To this end, the province enacted four new statutes during the fall of 1980 legislative session (though they were not immediately proclaimed). In effect, the Buchanan Conservatives took whole pages out of Newfoundland premier Brian Peckford's offshore political playbook.[18]

Not to be outdone, the Government of Canada unleashed its historic National Energy Program (NEP) in late October 1980. Since its influence extends throughout the entire decade of offshore politics in the 1980s, only a brief description is offered here. Not only did Ottawa restate its historical claim to the offshore continental shelves as Canada lands, but it also signalled its intent to ask the Supreme Court to hear a reference on the East Coast. The government outlined a comprehensive system of exploration incentives (both grant- and tax-based) to heighten frontier activity, but it afforded a privileged role to Canadian-owned enterprises and reserved a 25 percent federal Crown interest in every exploration right.[19] The NEP also repeated Ottawa's offer to Nova Scotia and Newfoundland (advanced earlier in the year at the first minister's constitutional talks) to provide 100 percent of "provincial-type resource revenues" to the adjacent province, subject to some form of equalization cap, along with "a substantial voice" in policy matters of social, environmental, or economic import.[20]

Since Nova Scotia and Newfoundland had already outlined offshore development strategies of their own, there was obvious concern for the displacement effects of the NEP. At the same time, the elevated priority of continental shelf exploration offered definite opportunities, as evidenced by the substantial new federal fiscal outlays. In short, it was a period of extraordinary policy flux and political uncertainty in which a constellation of offshore interests struggled to calibrate their interests. Notably, the institutional context remained as opaque and rudimentary as it had been fifteen years earlier.

The Canada–Nova Scotia Agreement on Offshore Oil and Gas Resource Management and Revenue Sharing

For Canada as a whole, the new era of constitutional deal making originated in the sovereignty struggle in Quebec. The Parti Québécois presented its first sovereignty referendum in May 1980. Trudeau Liberals in Ottawa promised a program of renewed federalism if Quebecers reaffirmed their tie to the Canadian union.[21] However, the federal-provincial diplomacy of the next few years, which culminated in the Constitution Act, 1982, required a broader base of provincial support. In the Atlantic provinces, attention focused more on regional resource issues pertaining to fisheries and offshore petroleum, particularly jurisdictional transfers. Here lay the price of East Coast support for Ottawa's broader agenda.

Atlantic premiers had already had their appetites whetted in 1979. The election of the federal Progressive Conservatives brought Prime Minister Joe Clark's offer to treat seabed resources the same as land-based resources

– that is, as provincial Crown assets under section 109 of the Constitution.[22] However, the early demise of that government, before any formal measures had been taken, and the return of the Liberals in 1980 signalled that the opportunity had been lost.

For the Government of Nova Scotia, Trudeau's NEP was a mixed bag of goods. Exploration incentives triggered a sustained drilling boom on frontier lands, including the Scotian Shelf. Halifax was confirmed as the first city of East Coast exploration. However, Ottawa's blunt claim of jurisdiction over Canada lands – with new rights, royalty, and tax provisions – relegated the provincial state to the margins. Moreover, even though Premier John Buchanan enacted his own package of Crown rights statutes in 1980, the likelihood of it being sustained in a judicial challenge seemed remote.

Ultimately, it was these considerations that led Nova Scotia back to the negotiating table. Always more the tactician than the strategist, Buchanan recognized a window of opportunity in 1981. In neighbouring Newfoundland, Premier Brian Peckford was railing against Ottawa, refusing offshore truck and trade amidst grumbled threats of new court challenges. (If any province had a case to meet the Supreme Court's standards for pre-Confederation ocean claims, it was the late-joining Colony of Newfoundland). In the meantime, the continuing prospect of jurisdictional gridlock was causing East Coast petroleum operators to look elsewhere. For its part, Ottawa was eager for at least one regional victory to vindicate the promise of the NEP, which was increasingly being maligned by both industry and petroleum-producing provinces. In a striking reversal of form, Buchanan abandoned the political rhetoric of Nova Scotia sovereignty and broke ranks with his neighbour. By negotiating the March 1982 bilateral agreement with Ottawa, Nova Scotia stole a march on Newfoundland. It hoped to shift attention in the oil patch from Hibernia to Venture and to consolidate the Scotian Shelf as a world-class basin.

The concept of policy learning refers to the ability to engage in reflective analysis of past experience to generate remedies for errors or problems.[23] A notable amount of policy learning is evident in the 1977-1982 deliberations. Negotiators definitely learned from earlier experience. For instance, no memorandum of intentions was released prior to the formal agreement of 1982. Not only did this tactic short-circuit the possibility of a public debate in principle, but it also sped the way toward enacting the authorizing statutes.

Equally revealing, the 1982 agreement contained a detailed set of offshore development policy objectives, described as a "framework for oil and gas resource management decisions." In effect, these objectives provided the new offshore board and administration with a rounded policy mandate. For example, the two governments affirmed their desire to "maintain a significant degree of initiative and policy control" and to "promote actively economic and social objectives rather than simply respond to industry's proposals."[24] Furthermore, the issuing of land rights, review of development plans, approval of production systems, and control of field production rates were described as pacing elements to achieve desired results. While corporate investment, contracting, and employment plans for "Canada benefits" were identified as crucial determinants of licensing at all phases, "optimal benefits for Nova Scotia" were singled out for particular emphasis. Overall, the policy objectives set out in Schedule II covered eleven pages of text.

Another pressing challenge was inserting the Government of Nova Scotia, its interests and its programs, into what was then overwhelmingly a federal regulatory regime. Because the key offshore statutes – the Canada Oil and Gas Act and the Oil and Gas Production and Conservation Act – flowed out of Trudeau's NEP, it was the Government of Canada that established the powerful new frontier agency known as the Canada Oil and Gas Lands Administration (COGLA). Such measures echoed one of Buchanan's complaints when he abandoned the earlier memorandum of understanding among the Maritime provinces. Accordingly, one of the central roles of the newly established Canada–Nova Scotia Offshore Oil and Gas Board was to direct the activities of the COGLA in the Nova Scotia offshore area.

Furthermore, the 1982 Canada–Nova Scotia agreement contained a number of innovative provisions, the most substantial of which was the establishment, outside of board activities, of a separate Executive Committee on Economic and Social Objectives. With federal and Nova Scotia co-chairs, the committee was charged with formulating the policy objectives mentioned previously. In addition, the committee was responsible for administering two new funds – one for education and training and the other for research and development. Both were to be financed by additional levies on offshore rights holders, an arrangement that triggered much consternation in the industry. Another non-board item was the creation of a $200-million Offshore Development Fund to support new infrastructure. Financed on loan by the Government of Canada, the fund was to be repaid over a decade following the start of offshore oil or gas production. A third element was elaborate offshore revenue-sharing rules, while a fourth was the establishment of several special committees: a Fisheries Advisory Committee, to develop links between the fishing and petroleum industries, and an Environmental Coordinating Committee, to facilitate joint federal-provincial assessments and reviews.

Finally, the Government of Nova Scotia achieved special leverage in the policy deliberations of the 1982 Canada–Nova Scotia Offshore Oil and Gas Board. As noted earlier, one of John Buchanan's most trenchant critiques of the 1977 memorandum of understanding was its flawed representative base. Nova Scotia would have had just one vote in six on the management board that controlled Scotian Shelf resources, and in the event of a deadlock, the federal minister would serve as the tiebreaker.[25] The 1982 agreement altered the numerical ratio somewhat by creating a board of three federal and two provincial members. It also stipulated an innovative set of decision-making rules on key matters such as calls for exploration proposals, signing exploration agreements, approving Canada Benefit plans, granting production leases, and authorizing production systems.[26]

The key element in the arrangement was a suspension right to be exercised only by the two Nova Scotia members when they found themselves caught in a three-to-two minority position upheld by the federal minister. Invoked by the members giving notice to the minister, the suspension right would delay execution of the decision by a period varying (by subject) from three to twelve months. The agreement stipulated that all board members were to be civil servants who operated according to ministerial instructions. The purpose of the suspension right, therefore, was to flag a situation of fundamental intergovernmental disagreement and freeze events for a sufficient time to negotiate a solution. In the event that no solution was possible, the minister's decision would be executed. The innovative elements in the arrangement were the designation of a special tier of fundamental decisions subject to the suspension right, the acknowledgment of asymmetrical representation, and the creation of informal channels to reconsider and resolve problems. Variations on these themes were embedded in all future offshore accords.

To better illustrate the institutional contours of the 1982 agreement, Figure 3.1 sets out the key agents and processes. The Canada–Nova Scotia Offshore Oil and Gas Board's structure is represented by the central block. The ministerial parties to which it reports are also shown, together with the non-board arrangements specified by the agreement. The figure captures the institutional structure of the Scotian Shelf between 1982 and 1989.

The final key issue, perhaps the most central to the province of Nova Scotia, was provisions for federal and provincial Crown receipts of offshore petroleum revenue. It is revealing that this is the longest section of the entire

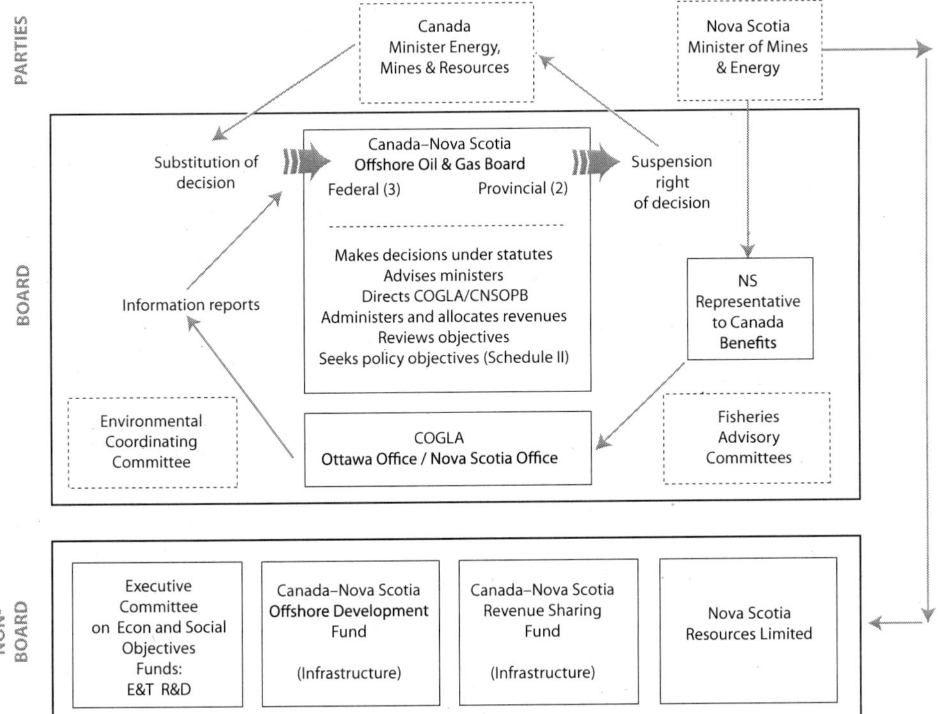

Figure 3.1 Institutional arrangements of the 1982 Canada–Nova Scotia Agreement on Offshore Oil and Gas Resource Management and Revenue Sharing

agreement, covering fifteen pages and attached schedules. It is on this issue that long-standing provincial claims to offshore Crown title resurfaced most dramatically. Perhaps inevitably, the Atlantic provinces viewed their offshore petroleum jurisdiction through the lens of the Alberta experience, where the fortunes of geology and the ensuing industrial base not only made the province an economic leader but brought a fiscal windfall to the government in Edmonton.

For Nova Scotia and Newfoundland, the key to defending their perceived birthright has been securing the equivalent of onshore Crown title terms to the offshore region. The 1977 memorandum of understanding offered little in this regard. Beyond the 5-kilometre coastal belt, the flow of petroleum revenues would be split 75/25 in favour of the province. Inside that line (where the prospects for oil- and gas-bearing sediments were lower but coastal minerals was higher) the province would receive 100 percent. The Buchanan government also complained that the formula excluded corporate income taxes paid on offshore product and contended that if Ottawa's share was fully accounted in this way, then the split would be 33/66 in the federal government's favour.[27]

Against this backdrop, the 1982 agreement included several improvements. It began by guaranteeing Nova Scotia the full flow of revenues as if the resource were located on land. This referred to the entire cluster of offshore revenues, including royalties, bonus and license fee remissions, and revenues equivalent to provincial corporate and retail sales taxes on the offshore product at the prevailing Nova Scotia rate. At a higher level, however, the agreement threatened to conflict with another crucial fiscal program for federal-provincial equalization. As a result, the offshore revenue terms were qualified. The deal applied only so long as Nova Scotia's per capita fiscal capacity (PCFC), calculated according to a defined formula, did not exceed 110 percent of Canada's average PCFC (with a Nova Scotia unemployment adjustor added in). If the flow of offshore revenues proved insufficient to bring the province to the national average, then further proceeds from a separate petroleum and gas revenue tax would be included. If, however, Nova Scotia began to exceed the national average by more than 110 percent, then its share of the additional offshore revenues would decline, in stages, until it fell to nil at 130 percent.

In effect, the 1982 arrangement tied the province's share of the resource revenue cluster to its relative economic performance as reflected in the federal-provincial equalization formula. So long as Nova Scotia tax flows fell below the national average, full revenues would be enjoyed. However, if petroleum prosperity lifted the province into the fiscal elite, the share would be curtailed. The implications of this provision are explored in greater detail in Chapter 8.

The Mulroney Revision and the Atlantic Accord

Less than three years into the era of the joint Canada–Nova Scotia board, the institutional coordinates began to change, largely because of the election of Brian Mulroney's Conservatives in the fall of 1984 and their commitment to reversing central elements of the National Energy Program. Even before his victory, Mulroney had signed a statement of intent with Premier Brian Peckford of Newfoundland, pledging that Newfoundland would be the "principal beneficiary of the wealth of the oil and gas off its shore, consistent with a strong and united Canada."[28] (Parallel language in the 1982 agreement described Nova Scotia as a major beneficiary.)[29] Having spent the past two years pursuing a judicial recognition of Newfoundland's ownership and jurisdiction to the continental shelf without success, Peckford was now open to negotiated measures.[30] The result was the Canada-Newfoundland Atlantic Accord of February 1985.

Since Nova Scotia was not a party to the deal, it stood to be affected only in a collateral fashion. The 1982 agreement had included a "most favoured province" commitment that guaranteed that Nova Scotia could accept any agreement concluded with another province prior to the beginning of 1985. Although the deadline had passed, Nova Scotia's claim to enhanced provisions in subsequent offshore arrangements had both moral and realpolitik force. While the Atlantic Accord contained a number of such clauses, it was not the radical departure that Canada and Newfoundland claimed. Indeed, in many respects the clauses embodied incremental though significant adjustments on the 1982 template. On a jurisdictional continuum ranging from full provincial control to full federal control, the Atlantic Accord nudged arrangements a step beyond the federal-leaning 1982 agreement to a mid- or balanced point on the scale.[31]

Several significant new elements stood to affect Nova Scotia. First, the composition of the Canada-Newfoundland Offshore Petroleum Board (CNOPB) reflected parity between federal and provincial appointments. Each side selected three members, and the chairman was jointly selected as the seventh.[32] Also in contrast to the Nova Scotia agreement, the board members were not civil servants, and they "were not to act as nominees of the government that appointed them."[33] This arrangement represented a more genuine form of delegation to an independent regulatory and administrative board. Second, the board's own staff, directed by a chief executive officer and funded jointly by the two senior governments, would administer its offshore responsibilities.[34] The newly established board and agency assumed many of the core functions previously handled by the Canadian Oil and Gas Lands Administration and the Provincial Petroleum Directorate. Evidently, this new offshore board was positioned more symmetrically between the sponsoring governments.

Third, the Atlantic Accord provided a more succinct delineation of the powers reserved to Canada (on Canadian ownership, federal taxes, and laws of general application) and to Newfoundland (on royalties, provincial taxes, and laws of general application). The CNOPB was left to handle "all other decisions related to the regulation and management of petroleum-related activities in the offshore area."[35] Within this general remit, however, a subset of fundamental powers was designated: powers pertaining to rights issuance and the approval of offshore development plans and extraordinary powers such as directing interest holders to drill, to start, increase, or suspend production, or to cancel rights altogether. On such matters, the board would transmit its decision to both governments for confirmation or denial.[36] In effect, the senior governments agreed to bracket out certain political or policy-sensitive matters for final control. Notably, the lines of review ran directly to responsible ministers and cabinets.

In the event that the parties could not agree on fundamental decisions, the determining role would turn on whether "national [energy] self-sufficiency and security of supply" had been attained. These criteria should be understood in the context of the National Energy Program, whose goal was to achieve "security of supply and ultimate independence from the world oil market."[37] Until this occurred, the federal energy minister would have final approval on fundamental decisions; after such time, the power would pass to the provincial minister. There was an exception, however. Approval of the mode of development or production system would rest with the provincial minister but would be subject to a federal override if the minister's decision unreasonably delayed the attainment of self-sufficiency and security. (*Self-sufficiency* being defined as the capacity of Canadian hydrocarbon production to satisfy domestic refined product requirements in a calendar year. *Security of supply* being anticipation of self-sufficiency for the ensuing five years.) Evidently, these criteria could themselves become the point of political contention between the parties. Should conflict occur, an external three-person arbitration panel would be constituted to make a final ruling.[38]

Fourth, the Atlantic Accord enhanced the policy-initiating roles of the senior governments. Acting jointly, the two ministers could issue policy directives – on matters pertaining to fundamental decisions, public reviews, Canada and Newfoundland benefits, and policy studies – to which the board must respond. The public review directive, for example, has since been used to commission an inquiry into possible terms to be attached to exploration in licensed blocks off the coast of Cape Breton Island. In addition, ministers must approve the board's plan for annual exploration and development at the start of each calendar year. Fifth, the terms on revenue sharing covered the same set of taxes as in 1982. Equalization offsets were also set out in a separate and simpler formula but one not different in principle.

The Atlantic Accord, signed by Mulroney and Peckford on 11 February 1985, called for parallel federal and provincial legislation to be introduced within one year. The Legislature of Newfoundland approved the Canada-Newfoundland Atlantic Accord Implementation (Newfoundland) Act in 1986, while the Parliament of Canada took slightly longer to pass the Canada-Newfoundland Atlantic Accord Implementation Act in 1987.

Reworking the Canada–Nova Scotia Regime

After the Atlantic Accord was announced, there was no surprise when Ottawa and Nova Scotia entered discussions to revise their 1982 deal. A number of considerations shaped the parameters of the review. It is useful to treat each offshore agreement as a political bargain that reflects both the interests of the principals and the balance of power between them. In the rapidly shifting petroleum politics of the 1980s, a three-year interval was a long time. Accordingly, each successive bargain was a major challenge to deliver. First, the principle of most-favoured province ensured that Nova Scotia would enjoy the enhanced terms of the Atlantic Accord. Second, the province needed to maintain advantageous terms not reflected in the Atlantic Accord. Third, Nova Scotia was anticipating negotiations on a major offshore project – Venture gas – that was in the advanced stages of regulatory review.

Not surprisingly, work on the new deal took considerable time. Eighteen months passed before the Canada–Nova Scotia Offshore Petroleum Resources Accord was signed on 26 August 1986. During this time, the Mulroney government had reversed the thrust of the National Energy Program by enacting the Canada Petroleum Resources Act. The global oil market had experienced a striking reversal when prices collapsed in the first half of 1986. Finally, the corporate sponsors of the Venture project had withdrawn their applications in the face of the new economics. Thus, it was a considerably altered energy world that federal and Nova Scotia officials faced when they sat down at the negotiating table.

The accord is described in its Preface as "a unified administrative and fiscal regime for petroleum resources in the offshore area ... founded on the same basis of parity and fairness as exists between the federal Government and other petroleum-producing provinces of Canada."[39] Just as the Newfoundland agreement had drawn many of its central provisions from the 1982 agreement, the second Nova Scotia agreement reflected elements first introduced in 1985 Atlantic Accord. As Table 3.1 shows, the objectives of the two accords are broadly parallel. They affirm the two parties' interest in developing the petroleum resource and identify the aims of achieving national security of supply and the province as principal beneficiary. There

TABLE 3.1

Objectives as specified in the Atlantic and Canada-Nova Scotia accords

Atlantic Accord	Canada–Nova Scotia Offshore Accord
To provide for the development of oil and gas resources offshore Newfoundland for the benefit of Canada as a whole and Newfoundland and Labrador in particular.	To achieve the early development of Petroleum Resources in the Offshore Area for the benefit of Canada as a whole and Nova Scotia in particular.
To protect, preserve and advance the attainment of national self-sufficiency and security of supply.	To protect, preserve and advance the attainment of national security of supply.
To recognize the right of Newfoundland and Labrador to be the principal beneficiary of the oil and gas resources off its shores, consistent with the requirement for a strong and united Canada.	To recognize the right of Nova Scotia to be the principal beneficiary of the Petroleum Resources in the Offshore Area, consistent with the requirement of a strong and united Canada.
To recognize the equality of both governments in the management of the resource, and to ensure that the pace and manner of development optimize the social and economic benefits to Canada as a whole and Newfoundland and Labrador in particular.	To give effect to the equality of both governments in the management of the Petroleum Resources and to ensure that the pace and manner of development optimize the employment and industrial benefits to Canada as a whole and to Nova Scotia in particular.
To provide that the Government of Newfoundland and Labrador can establish and collect resource revenues as if these resources were on land, within the province.	To provide the Government of Nova Scotia with responsibility for, control of and revenues from provincial-type fiscal instruments as if these resources were on the land portion of the province.
To provide for a stable and fair offshore management regime for industry.	To ensure the continuance of a stable offshore administrative regime for the industry consistent, insofar as is appropriate, with regimes established for other offshore areas in Canada.

►

◄ TABLE 3.1

Atlantic Accord	Canada–Nova Scotia Offshore Accord
To provide for a stable and permanent arrangement for the management of the offshore adjacent to Newfoundland by enacting the relevant provisions of the Accord in legislation of the Parliament of Canada and the legislature of Newfoundland and Labrador and by providing that the Accord may only be amended by the mutual consent of both governments.	To ensure that Nova Scotia will receive financial benefits equivalent to those it would have achieved had it exercised its crown share option.
To promote within the system of joint management, insofar as is appropriate, consistency with the management regimes established for other offshore areas in Canada.	

Source: Atlantic Accord, 1985, s. 2; *Canada–Nova Scotia Offshore Petroleum Resources Accord,* 1986, s. 1.

is also a commitment to optimize economic benefits to both Canada and Nova Scotia and to treat offshore resource revenues in the same way as those from provincial lands.

In addition, the principle of equitable board representation was finally achieved. The new CNSOPB consisted of five members (rather than Newfoundland's seven) – two federal and two provincial appointees plus a jointly appointed chair. At least two of the four members would be non-civil servants and, in fact, all four became non-officials by 1997. Over twenty years of operation, the board was chaired by three individuals. Before taking up the position, Fred Weir (1990-96) worked with Mobil Oil, Glen Yungblut (1997-2004) was a federal petroleum engineer, and Diana Dalton (2005-11) was a lawyer with offshore experience, including being an adviser on the 1982 Canada–Nova Scotia agreement. The federal and provincial nominated membership has circulated more frequently, but multi-year service has likewise been common. The federal government selected Calgary oilmen Don Axford (1990-95), John Currie (1997-2003), and Douglas Gregory (2007, as alternate) as well as Fundy Mobile Gear fisherman leader Brian

Giroux (2002-8) and petroleum engineer Mary Jane Snook (2004-8). Nova Scotia appointed Lunenburg businessman Peter Kinley (1995-2001), marine lawyer Edgar Gold (1997-2003), accountant Michael Casey (2001-5), and retired civil servant William Hogg (2003-9).

The Atlantic Accord's template for board powers, including fundamental decision procedures, was adopted as well. The board also employed its own professional staff to administer its legal responsibilities. So far as revenue sharing was concerned, the province's receipt of full offshore revenues, accompanied by equalization offset provisions, was confirmed in language identical to the Atlantic Accord.

The industrial and employment benefits terms were likewise revised. Benefit plans still had to accompany exploration and development applications, but they were now placed under the jurisdiction of the CNSOPB. As in Newfoundland, a system of joint consultation linked federal and provincial agencies to the board's benefits regime. This meant that the 1982 machinery of the dual-chair Executive Committee on Economic and Social Objectives, together with the twin funds for education and training and research and development (which were so troubling to industry), disappeared. The Atlantic Accord had avoided the arrangement by folding corporate responsibilities for education and training and research and development into the generic benefits-regulating process. The politics of benefit regulation is explored in greater detail in Chapter 7.

A number of more specific provisions also underwent significant modification. For example, the $200-million Offshore Development Fund was converted from a loan to a grant when Ottawa waived the repayment of the sizeable transfer. In addition, Canada agreed to provide $25 million to Nova Scotia Resources Limited to cover half the costs of drilling and development wells to further early offshore development (in effect, a last-gasp gesture for a flattened exploration sector). The federal government also pledged to compensate the province for any loss of "Crown share" opportunities spelled out in the earlier agreement but since nullified by the Mulroney government.

Parliament assented to the enabling statute on 21 July 1988; however, the legislation did not come into force for almost a year and a half, or late December 1989. For its part, the Nova Scotia Legislature enacted the Canada–Nova Scotia Offshore Petroleum Resource Accord Implementation (Nova Scotia) Act in 1987. Thus the new era of symmetrical joint offshore petroleum regulation began in January 1990.

The three-year period between the signing of the 1986 accord and the onset of CNSOPB operations was interesting in another sense. During this time, the geopolitical dialectic of successive joint offshore management institutions took more turns. In the West, provincial and territorial governments with claims to the continental shelf had closely followed the new petroleum arrangements on the East Coast. Both Yukon and Northwest Territories were pushing Ottawa, across a broad front, for the political devolution of provincial-style powers.[40] Not surprisingly, the Crown resource title figured strongly among them. The constitutional status of the northern territories differs critically from the provinces, and the prospect of one or more northern accords to deal with joint energy management (onshore and offshore) moved slowly forward in these years.[41] Ultimately, Canada and Yukon reached an agreement, but negotiations are ongoing in Northwest Territories.

Further west, British Columbia also faced a complicated offshore gridlock, and there was obvious interest in the emerging institutions of joint petroleum management. Yet, despite a number of physical, legal, and commercial parallels to the East Coast, the so-called Pacific Accord negotiations proved to be far more politically problematic and ultimately resulted in a non-decision. Although developments on the West Coast are strictly beyond the concerns of this study, specific political failures in offshore institution building can offer lessons for the industry as a whole.

A Pacific Coast Counterpart?

The history of petroleum exploration and production on the western continental shelf is similar to East Coast developments in many respects but departs significantly in others. The first seismic exploration work took place in the 1950s. By 1961, federal and provincial authorities both claimed jurisdiction: Ottawa through the Canada Oil and Gas Lands Regulations and British Columbia by declaring a Crown reserve over seabed resources to the east of a line running from Haida Gwaii to Vancouver Island.[42] In addition, the province imposed a moratorium on exploration drilling in waters north of Vancouver Island. Shell Canada Inc. was the lead industry player. It took out federal exploration permits in 1961 and did mapping, magnetometer, and seismic work on its holdings. When the provincial moratorium was lifted in 1966, Shell drilled fourteen wells over the next three seasons.[43] It was during this time that the Supreme Court of Canada issued a reference decision that found the Pacific continental shelf (specifically, the lands of the seabed and subsoil, in both the territorial sea and the continental shelf) to fall under federal jurisdiction.

During the 1970s, the two governments traded moratorium announcements. British Columbia re-imposed a moratorium on exploration in the Juan de Fuca and Georgia straits in 1970. Whereas the prior closures had sprung largely from jurisdictional uncertainties and the province's willingness to freeze exploration pending clarification, the new moratoriums were influenced by environmental considerations. In 1972 Ottawa banned petroleum tankers from sailing along the BC Coast, a measure that was later extended to drilling in the offshore area.[44] The ban ruled out exploration activity, and the province returned to the courts with a new reference case. The case involved a proprietorial claim to the seabed and subsoil of four coastal straits – Juan de Fuca, Georgia, Johnstone, and Queen Charlotte – located between the Mainland and Vancouver Island. The province's claim was upheld by both the Provincial Court of Appeal (1976) and the Supreme Court of Canada (1984). The finding was that subsea property in the straits (the so-called inshore-offshore) lay with the provincial Crown. However, for other areas, including the open ocean side of Vancouver Island and coastal waters to its north, the 1967 reference findings continued to apply in Canada's favour.[45] Significantly, the 1984 reference case did not address the more northerly offshore region with the strongest geological prospects, the Queen Charlotte Basin under the Hecate Strait. Nonetheless, it became clear that in legal terms, both British Columbia and Canada have a role in offshore resource jurisdiction.

Since the northern offshore region remains subject to rival federal and provincial legal titles, its status would have to be resolved should the moratoriums ever be lifted.[46] An alternative to further litigation would be to negotiate an offshore accord and joint management structure along East Coast lines.

The prospect of lifting the moratoriums has arisen twice since the 1970s. The first incident occurred during the energy boom of the early 1980s, when Chevron and Petro-Canada submitted environmental studies aimed at activating their rights. A joint federal-provincial environmental assessment panel was struck in 1983 and reported three years later that exploration could resume subject to extensive conditions. One of these conditions was a strong and effective regulatory regime designed specifically to meet the West Coast's needs.[47] This qualified green light prompted the two governments to begin talks on a Pacific Accord in 1987. The points of departure were the 1985 and 1986 deals between Canada and Newfoundland and Canada and Nova Scotia. By 1988, draft terms had been partially completed. As in the East, the draft accord granted full offshore royalty revenues to

British Columbia. Outstanding issues were the tie-in to land claim settlements and the particular form of joint management structures to be adopted.[48] A tactical pause in negotiations was prolonged in March 1989, however, when the oil tanker *Exxon Valdez* ran aground and spilled millions of gallons of crude oil into Prince William Sound. Extraordinary coastal and marine degradation in Alaska rekindled public opposition to offshore exploration that had exploded after the Santa Barbara offshore blowout of 1968. British Columbia announced a five-year extension of the moratorium, while Ottawa pledged to approve no more offshore work until British Columbia agreed. The moratorium remains in effect, and BP's Macondo blowout in the Gulf of Mexico in 2010 will likely reinforce the decision.

Not surprisingly, public records associated with a failed policy negotiation that took place behind closed doors are hard to find. But it is clear that political circumstances on the West Coast made the option of a joint management board particularly timely. In British Columbia more than other regions, the legal claims to the offshore resource were complex, and both levels of government were armed with favourable court findings. By setting aside the questions of title and jurisdiction, as the accord model allowed, at least one major impediment to development could be neutralized. In addition, prospective operators had faced the potentially paralyzing predicament of separate and rival authorities for far longer than their counterparts in the East. The simplicity of a single-source administrator and regulator of exploration and development work, embodied in a Canada–British Columbia Offshore Management Board, offered evident advantages.

Yet there were complications in the new region that distinguished it from the East. First, governments had to take into consideration the legal and political status of Aboriginal claims. When the Pacific Accord talks began in 1987, the Canadian Charter of Rights and Freedoms had entered its fourth year. Section 35 affirmed the constitutional standing of all existing Aboriginal and treaty rights and titles. The absence of treaties in British Columbia meant that almost all Crown lands potentially had unextinguished title, and Ottawa was already negotiating with several tribal groups. However, the status of Aboriginal claims to seabed resources had not yet been tested either politically or judicially. Nonetheless, the Supreme Court of Canada was feeling its way forward under the Charter, and the parameters of Aboriginal rights were fluid, to say the least. With the *Guerin* judgment of 1984, the court introduced the doctrines of the Crown's fiduciary duty to protect Aboriginal interests and the *sui generis* character of Aboriginal title. During the years when the Pacific Accord was under discussion, specific

Aboriginal rights had yet to be resolved in the high court, but the possibility, indeed the likelihood, of an offshore activity or title right could not be ignored. At least four First Nations are in a strong position to assert rights to marine resources in the Hecate Strait–Queen Charlotte Sound area: Tsimshian, Heiltsuk, Haida, and Kwakwa̱ka̱'wakw.[49]

The second factor that limited the prospect of a joint offshore regime in British Columbia was environmental. The accord or board model was appropriate only if a political consensus on petroleum development existed in principle. In the economically challenged Atlantic region, which was reliant on imported oil and equalization transfers, the principle was seldom challenged, even though the precise terms proved elusive. Things were different in west coast waters, which were characterized by intensive ocean use, unstable geological formations with the potential for earthquakes, and recent memories of offshore blowouts and spills in California and Alaska. The policy tool of the licence moratorium, one of the most dreaded words in the vocabulary of offshore petroleum explorers, had run north from California to British Columbia in the intervening years. The West Coast is in the vanguard of Canada's environmental movement. Extensively organized, generously funded, and embedded in public consciousness, the West Coast movement is deeply skeptical about the cost-benefit balance of offshore petroleum. In sum, First Nations and environmental movement separately presented formidable obstacles. Together, they were politically prohibitive.

This is not to say that the terms cannot change. Elected in 2001, Gordon Campbell's Liberal government declared its desire to have offshore gas fuelling British Columbia by the year 2010. It took a series of steps to revisit and presumably reframe the case for a moratorium, and events in recent years suggest a strategy of step-wise policy change. Independent expert reviews were commissioned to assess the risks and the remedies.[50] Offshore oil was presented as an economic lifeline to the province's northwestern heartland. Public debate accelerated,[51] and the provincial government set out a transition strategy.[52] The signs, however, still point to a prolonged period of political adjustment before attention can return to a Pacific Accord and a prospective (possibly tri-party?) joint or co-management regime.

The Offshore Board as Political Institution: Underlying Values and Logics

The federal-provincial board has become a central institution for modern resource management on the Atlantic continental shelf. It is possible to speak of past, present, and future incarnations of this model. At present, however, the best measurements are the Newfoundland and Nova Scotia boards. It is clear that the formative years for these political innovations were the 1980s, when a window of opportunity allowed for considerable innovation. That window may or may not remain open today; however, the institutions forged to meet the challenges of the time remain intact and continue to shape offshore policy and activity.

Resource Title and Jurisdiction

It is important to distinguish between relations of property ownership and relations of jurisdiction. For reasons that are not hard to understand, the two have occasionally been so closely bound together that they have been conflated. A proprietorial claim of Crown ownership of seabed minerals, either federal or provincial, is itself a jurisdictional claim in the Canadian constitutional scheme. With ownership comes the opportunity to control extraction and the financial terms that accompany it. The ambiguities of such claims flow in part from the historically limited exercise of state sovereignty beyond the low-water mark of international and common law. The 1958 UN Convention on the Continental Shelf extended state prospects while also posing sharp problems within federal systems as to who had jurisdiction over seabed resources. This issue sparked a string of constitutional litigation in Canada, beginning with the reference case on BC offshore minerals and continuing with the East and West Coast cases in the 1980s. Given sufficient disputes and decisions, jurisdiction over the entire continental shelf might eventually have been clarified, possibly to the advantage of Ottawa. However, the process was overtaken by an alternative dispute settlement process rooted in intergovernmental bargaining. The goal of this bargaining was to set aside the issue of ownership and focus on developing a single-agency administration or management board with joint federal and provincial sponsors and federal and provincial legislation.

At the core of bargaining in the 1980s was a political equation that linked title to the resource, the authority to manage or regulate it, and the receipt of revenue flows that followed. Unlike Newfoundland and British Columbia, Nova Scotia chose not to legally test its proprietary claim, preferring instead to achieve a managerial and financial advantage first affirmed in the 1982 Canada–Nova Scotia agreement. Despite its asymmetries, this agreement served as a template against which future offshore bargains would be adjusted. Other policy questions and relationships later emerged within the joint management mandate, for instance, workplace safety, environmental protection, and employment and industrial benefits (to name the most prominent). However, the political bargain on which the entire edifice rested was title–management–revenues. Each term in this equation was challenged over the next quarter century, and each challenge carried the potential to pull down the entire structure.

Serving Two Masters

The joint boards sprang to life at the behest of the federal and provincial governments. In effect, the authority to manage the petroleum resource was delegated by the two legislatures to a new hybrid creation. However, delegated authority is a two-way street, and channels of political accountability were necessary. The normal trappings of administrative responsibility were spelled out in the legislation. The senior governments would appoint board members for stipulated terms of office. The board would issue an annual report, and its financial accounts would be audited in the conventional manner. A chief executive officer would direct agency operations and support board deliberations. Disguised within these terms, however, was a potentially difficult challenge – connecting the board to its creators. The relationship between the board and the two governments was triangular, but the shape of the arrangement was far from equilateral. The problem arises in large part from the fact that the offshore boards, as decision-making bodies, enjoy less than exhaustive jurisdiction. As the terms of the accords and the legislation make clear, the federal and provincial governments have delegated a limited range of powers to the board and staff to be exercised on behalf of the twin Crowns. At the same time, the Crowns retain other powers to exercise in separate domains beyond the remit and mandate of the board. This division of labour is fundamental to understanding the workings of the board, and it highlights the critical role of the federal and provincial ministers (and energy departments) as conduits to a wider state authority. Obviously, this implies effective coordination. The designated federal and provincial ministers can issue directives to the board, and boards can offer policy advice to ministers.

Cases in which the ministers and governments may disagree are a greater problem. Possible deadlocks were anticipated at the design stage. For example, if the two governments cannot agree on the appointment of a board chair, they are to name a member each to a three-person external arbitration panel. Should they fail to agree on a choice, the provincial chief justice will select the arbitration panel chair. An arbitration panel with similar appointment provisions would likewise deal with disputes over the geographic boundaries of designated offshore areas.

Most importantly, the two levels of government took potential disagreements into consideration in their treatment of fundamental decisions of the offshore board, those matters that primarily affect the pace and mode of exploration, the pace of production, or the mode of development. Fundamental decisions include the issuing and cancelling of rights; extraordinary directions to interest holders to drill, cease drilling, or avoid waste; and the approval of development plans. On such matters, board decisions are not final until both governments consent. Although the expectation is that the two governments will agree on the disposition of fundamental decisions within one month, a decision rule is stipulated for cases of continued disagreement. Until national self-sufficiency and security of supply is reached, the federal energy minister's decision will carry the day; after that point, final say rests with the provincial minister. A special kind of interest advocacy is likely to arise between the senior governments and non-governmental groups on matters regarding fundamental decisions. Awareness of the secondary vetting process makes it possible for affected parties to lobby federal provincial ministers and their departments directly, depending on their desire to confirm or overturn board decisions.

Multiple Constituencies

A larger question is whether various interests have adequate representation to the board. There is an understandable tendency to assume that the board is closely oriented toward an industrial clientele in petroleum exploration and production. These clients are, after all, the developers who seek the licences and certificates and who spend the money under the board's regulatory ambit. It was in part to assuage their anxieties and to reduce the scale of political risk that the accords were advanced in the first place. It would be wrong, however, to exaggerate this group's importance. Although the exploration and production industry may well figure as a core clientele that enjoys privileged access, it is far from being the exclusive clientele of offshore petroleum management.

The accords and the statutory instruments that flow from them acknowledge a significantly wider range of actors. By establishing a Fisheries Advisory Committee, the 1982 Canada–Nova Scotia agreement recognized inevitable tensions between industries and the need for special channels of adjudication and compensation. Similarly, the research and development and education and training committees underline expectations in the coastal provinces that employment and manufacturing benefits would be monitored and championed in favour of workers and firms. Similar provisions can be seen in the case of environmental protection. The Environmental Studies Research Fund, funded by a levy on offshore operators, was established to facilitate inquiries into emerging environmental impact issues.

By providing parallel and dedicated sites to consider such matters, it appears that the agreement's designers assumed that board members and staff would primarily administer the offshore licensing regime. However, the role of principal beneficiary extended well beyond royalty flows. By 1986, the approval of benefits plans and environmental impact strategies had become an integral part of the licensing process. Various interests from all stages in the offshore supply chain, many of which were non-petroleum in nature, intervened to shape policy and gain from its application.

The offshore agency's deliberations also required periodic consultations with the broader public that could take many forms. Section 44 of the Canada–Nova Scotia Offshore Petroleum Resources Implementation Act empowered the board to undertake a public review of any of its powers or operations deemed in the public interest. In addition, federal and provincial ministers could issue directives to the board to undertake public reviews. In 1996, for instance, a panel was appointed to consider the future of the Georges Bank moratorium on oil and gas activities.[53] In 2001, the board was asked to research and report on conditions to attach to any licences issued in the new drilling area off the shore of Cape Breton Island. The act further stipulated that when potential petroleum field developments were being proposed, the proponent was obliged to prepare and make available the development plan, environmental and socio-economic impact assessments, and preliminary benefits plans.

Complex Decision Rules

Once the organizational parameters of the joint petroleum board model had been settled in the 1980s, there was a variety of roles and functions that had to fit together for it to work. On the surface, the petroleum board was a variation on the common Canadian practice of allocating and regulating rights to a resource through Crown title. Given the involvement of both levels of government, however, this convention was difficult to implement. As discussed, it required that the policy content of a normally unified field be segmented according to board and non-board domains. Furthermore, within the board's domain, primary policy or administrative initiatives were assigned to the CNSOPB; however, in the case of fundamental decisions, final approval authority (with tie-breaking provisions) was assigned to federal and provincial ministers. This arrangement has been aptly described as "an inspired [and] elaborate series of trumping powers."[54]

In actual operation, these vetting provisions are not often used. Yet their symbolic significance, achieved in part through the opacity of the details, is to affirm the coordinate and equal importance of the federal and provincial positions. The board's managerial mandate remains intact, but the provisions for selective review reflect the need for ultimate ministerial direction. The financial provisions for offshore royalties and fees are similarly complex. On the surface, the province receives full receipts as the principal beneficiary. However, the federal government's insistence (applied equally to other royalty-collecting provinces) that these receipts be factored into the national revenue equalization regime requires a series of caveats and contingency rules.

Durability and Adaptability

Institutions must adapt to survive. Durability is the capacity to persist through time in the face of external challenges. As such, it measures end results. Adaptability is the capacity to adjust to changing conditions. It is a functional process whose results may well determine durability.

Durability derives in part from formative arrangements. The Canada–Nova Scotia Offshore Petroleum Resources Accord is a bilateral agreement between sovereign authorities, and the exacting conditions of its creation may provide added stability. Furthermore, the offshore regime is embedded in legislation that reflects the initial political consensus. In other words, undoing an offshore management regime requires far more than a cabinet order or ministerial directive. Of course, the regime can be reassessed if necessary. The two parties will review the accord every five years, and it can be opened by notice of either party in the interim. In actual fact, the Canada–Nova Scotia accord has never been amended. The legislation, however, has been modified, mostly to align it with changes in external petroleum law. On the other hand, the accord includes a provision (article 42) to enable its principles to be constitutionally entrenched "upon the achievement of such support as may be required." Entrenchment would presumably fall under section 43 of the Constitution Act, 1982, which allows an amendment that applies to one or more but not all provinces to be achieved by motion of the relevant federal and provincial legislatures. To date, this has not been proposed.

This is not to imply that the parties lack concerns about the offshore regime as it stands. In 1994, the parties commissioned a confidential review by two board members. The review proposals ranged from designating a new federal technical regulator to replace the board, devolving provincial concerns such as industrial benefits back to Nova Scotia (i.e., dividing erstwhile board functions between jurisdictions), and maintaining the status quo (industry strongly favoured the single-regulator model). It is likely that the driving force in this process was the Nova Scotia government. Both governments of the day (Jean Chrétien's federal Liberals and John Savage's provincial Liberals) took office in 1993, and neither had strong ties to the 1986 accord regime. However, the province experienced greater constraints under the CNSOPB, for its departments had lost control over both benefit plans and development plans when the board became active in 1990. In any event, it was the federal government that defended the accord regime when the question went to the ministers. In the absence of a consensus for change, and with the oil and gas industry pressing for certainty, the status quo prevailed.[55]

In fact, certain parts of the accord regime have been institutionalized further through measures to protect them from the effects of subsequent treaty measures. The most significant case involves the industrial benefits (employment and procurement) provisions as a required criterion for rights issuance and licensing. The Canada-US free trade agreements of 1989 and 1993 made provisions to grandfather both East Coast petroleum accords, protecting the latter from trade challenges of business discrimination on the basis of nationality. Absent these provisions, it seems likely that the Canada and Nova Scotia benefit clauses would have been open to challenge for violating US procurement opportunities.

Part of the explanation for durability is adaptability, an enduring theme in the chapters that follow. The circumstances that help shape institutions seldom last indefinitely. For example, the federal energy strategy of 1980 was a thing of the past by 1985. The booming commodity prices of 1979-80 had collapsed into a slump by 1986. And the window for federal-provincial constitutional bargaining, which helped advance the early joint management negotiations, had closed with the passing of the 1982 Constitution Act. Institutions may come under pressure as founding circumstances fade, and the prospects for adaptation are then tested. How far can new realities be accommodated within existing institutions? Can the key actors – the ministers, board members, technical staff, and associated interests – find a basis for adapting to new circumstances? Or are they immobilized by incompatible visions and strategies to the point of institutional decline? A lack of exploration drilling can be overcome by fashioning new incentives, recruiting new rights holders, or focusing on bringing established commercial fields into production.

Between 1980 and 2000, policy coordinates shifted along with their underlying regulatory philosophies. At the beginning of accord negotiations, offshore industry regulation was essentially prescriptive. Whether the policy object was environmental protection, platform workplace safety, or procurement and employment benefits, the regulatory paradigm assumed that statutory bodies should fulfill their mandates by formulating and issuing (or prescribing) detailed rules that licensees and permit holders would be obliged to follow. The result was an ever-expanding accumulation of directives. It was not unusual, however, for rule-making procedures to lag behind scientific and technological changes and for the increasing volume of regulations to be both redundant and contradictory. Not surprisingly, these practices came under increasing attack from neoliberals and market-oriented advocates. By the late 1990s, an alternative doctrine of performance-based regulation had emerged among a broad group of interests that included offshore authorities. Advocates of this doctrine sought to rationalize the rule-making process and make it more flexible and cost efficient. Statutory bodies concentrated on identifying preferred outcomes while allowing licensees and permit holders to select the particular mechanisms of compliance.[56]

Offshore Petroleum and the Offshore State

In many respects, it seems that the offshore accord system has a high degree of sector autonomy. In fact, however, the sector in question is confined to seabed resources that are only a part of the offshore domain. Understandably, the driving policy priority of the 1980s was to establish a new petroleum regime that would clear away obstacles for investment, discovery, and exploitation. Elaborate institutional provisions to ensure internal coherence demonstrate that governance was not neglected at the formative stage. However, as time passed and as development progressed, the interests of the offshore state expanded and were shaped by a range of external imperatives.

The board's offshore petroleum mandate is far from exhaustive. The accord system anticipates and acknowledges this limitation to a degree. Article 40 of the 1986 Accord provides that memoranda of understanding can be struck with "those departments and agencies of the Parties [Canada and Nova Scotia] having continuing responsibilities in the offshore area, with a view to ensuring effective coordination and minimum duplication." This provision nods in the direction of the broader federal and provincial state presence that preceded the board structure and continues in effect. However, it suggests also that administrative liaison alone is sufficient to ensure the required coordination. The accord's designers therefore failed to grasp the extent to which petroleum development is embedded within a broader offshore state. The progressive discovery of this wider context and the constraints that it imposes, both politically and administratively, is a key theme in subsequent chapters. Yet this encounter continued to be shaped by the cast of formative arrangements of the 1980s.

There are at least two dimensions here. First, how far did the accord go toward establishing a stand-alone petroleum regime? This outcome was likely achieved to the greatest extent in the field of rights allocation and licensing. Put simply, for any matter involving upstream petroleum activity on and under the water, the CNSOPB would be a central but not exclusive presence. For example, the regulation of safety conditions on drill rigs and offshore platforms fell largely under provincial health and safety laws and the regulation of Nova Scotia officials. In addition, before a major production project could be approved for construction and operation, Environment Canada was charged with ensuring that the terms of the federal Environmental Assessment Review Policy and, after 1997, the Canadian Environmental Assessment Act were met. Should a pipeline be necessary to transport offshore oil or gas to the mainland for processing or transit (much less export), the National Energy Board had a statutory role to play in certifying a public interest before issuing permits. When it came to calculating the net allocation of offshore royalties and provincial taxes, the federal Department of Finance enjoyed control over certain fiscal levers, including federal-provincial equalization grants. Each case involved deliberations that fell far beyond the operating scope of the offshore petroleum board. It is likely at this level that the provision for interagency memoranda of understanding was intended.

Second, how does the offshore petroleum regime fit within the structure of offshore governance writ large? In the earliest years of East Coast exploration, the two might well have been viewed as one domain in operational terms. However, a number of wider constitutional, legislative, and policy developments altered this situation. The variety and breadth of new offshore mandates asserted by non-petroleum agencies is striking. It is worth recalling that Canada significantly extended its offshore jurisdictional reach in 1977, when it asserted the 200-mile economic exclusion zone. This development led to a dramatic reorientation of the fisheries management mandate of the Department of Fisheries and Oceans, and it changed the character of the Atlantic ground fishery.[57] In a different political context, the Constitution Act, 1982, includes provisions that entrench existing Aboriginal and treaty rights in the Constitution. This act opened the way for new judicial challenges to the Crown's title to resources and the constitutionality of traditional management regimes. Offshore Crown title was not spared. During the 1990s, the Department of Fisheries and Oceans once again made inroads into offshore programming through the Oceans Act of 1997 and subsequent initiatives to integrate the planning of large ocean areas and marine protected areas. The recognition of a new "ocean public" was part of these policies. In the memorable phrase of Cynthia Lamson, "the sea has many voices."[58]

Such factors raise questions about the levels of coherence and capacity associated with the petroleum regime and the offshore state. Clearly, the board's mandate does not exhaust the state's offshore powers. Also, to the extent that delivery of the board's mandate is circumscribed by external agents, the need for coordination and alignment is a major challenge. This case recalls the literature on strong and weak state forms. A strong state agency need not be the exclusive decision-making centre in its field, but it does require the capacity to plan and deliver coordinated measures and sufficient autonomy to protect its core mandate. In many respects, formative negotiations for joint offshore management sought to achieve these goals, thereby avoiding a situation of dual authorities answering to separate cabinets, legislatures, and publics. How far these aspirations were realized is explored in the chapters that follow.

Conclusion

Novel and intriguing institutions of joint offshore petroleum management emerged on the East Coast during the 1980s and continue today. They, along with the formal instruments that authorized and shaped their structures, were devised through political negotiations at the federal and provincial levels in response to deep-seated political differences over offshore ownership and jurisdiction. In such a turbulent decade – when global, national, and regional conditions in the energy sector seemed to be in constant flux – the new offshore arrangements unfolded in a series of dialectical compromises. Each arrangement was formalized by an intergovernmental agreement and fleshed out by a parallel statutory instrument. In each case, the result was a series of norms, rules, and procedures through which the Crown right to offshore petroleum would be administered, regulated, and allocated to producers.

The formal structure assumed its modern form in 1990, when the terms of the 1986 Canada–Nova Scotia Offshore Petroleum Resources Accord came into force. This regime has now surpassed its twentieth year of operation on the Scotian Shelf, and its performance is the subject of several of the chapters that follow. It is worth noting that, far from being static, this legal-administrative edifice has been capable of continuing evolution and growth. It has always been open to formal legislative amendment, which has occurred a number of times. Yet formal amendment of the accord, which requires the joint consent of the sponsoring parties plus legislative amendments at the provincial and federal levels, is an exacting and even cumbersome process. This mechanism was never likely to provide a sufficiently flexible or responsive means of ongoing adjustment. On the other hand, there were moments when the joint management model seemed to fall out of favour with senior authorities. For example, Chrétien's Liberal government – particularly Ann McLellan, minister of Natural Resources Canada – considered rescinding the structure altogether. In 1995, the parties to the accord initiated an overall review of the offshore regulatory mandate that led, ultimately, to its reaffirmation. To abandon the board structure would likely reignite tensions of earlier times, on a variety of political fronts. However imperfect, the joint management model has provided a workable vessel for coordinated collective action.

Another avenue of flexibility lies in the stipulated channels of ministerial policy directives (to the board) and board policy advice (to ministers). The most obvious signals of this intent are the formal directives and reports authorized in the accords. However, another dimension of implicit communication and policy learning is the behaviour of the sponsoring governments on fundamental decisions. How often, and on what matters, were board decisions suspended, vetoed, confirmed, or substituted? The broader policy orientations of federal and provincial departments are also of note. The federal government's administrative reorganization of 1993 established Natural Resources Canada as the new federal department in charge of offshore petroleum. Not surprisingly, the department has articulated a philosophy distinct from that of the Department of Energy, Mines and Resources, which rode the National Energy Program tiger after 1980. In Nova Scotia, the Conservative government of John Hamm launched a comprehensive review of energy policy in 2000 that culminated in a new strategy that has significantly altered the province's orientation to offshore areas.

Central to any process of administrative and regulatory growth is program implementation, a multilayered process that includes professional staffing, systems design, board-staff interactions, decision making, and execution. In many respects, the CNSOPB displays striking continuity in this regard. Although the turnover of board members has been almost continual, the resilience of senior management is equally striking – many key figures have served for a decade or more. The board began with a modest staff complement that seldom exceeded a dozen personnel. However, it expanded to more than double that size after 1995 in response to the massive Sable offshore energy project application and renewed interest in exploration on both the Scotian Shelf and deepwater slope. Only weeks after the board's office opened in 1990, the Cohasset-Panuke oil project application was received. Major projects have driven the learning process ever since.

It is important to appreciate the many ways in which the board's relationship with broader state structures has impinged on offshore management. This influence comes in part through the enforcement of laws of general application to the ocean sector. As a result, federal agencies responsible for marine fisheries, ocean environments, and marine transport and provincial agencies responsible for coastal resources, the environment, and health and safety continue to interact with the petroleum administration. The accord acknowledged such issues by stipulating a process for developing memoranda of understanding "with those departments and agencies having continued responsibilities in the offshore area, with a view to ensuring maximum coordination and minimum duplication" (article 40). There are grounds to question how effectively this has worked. Interdepartmental diplomacy is a notoriously difficult problem for public administration, one that often leads to slow results. Furthermore, statutes, in contrast to the collaborative ethic, often assign clear responsibility to lead ministers and officials.

Finally, there is the matter of political clientele outside of state circles. Power in the field of offshore petroleum exploration and production is best understood as an assemblage of linked policy networks in which an array of organized interests – oil operators, industrial suppliers and workers, fishers, conservationists, marine transporters, coastal communities, Aboriginal peoples, and others – interact in regular and structured ways. Such efforts are sometimes channelled through formal advisory channels; at other times, through dedicated public forums and consultations. The petroleum industry mounted a major initiative in 2001 to comprehensively rationalize an offshore regulatory regime whose languor and redundancy threatened the goals of prompt and efficient exploitation. A number of community and conservation interests have simultaneously criticized the absence of meaningful public input into the board's over-bureaucratic procedures and called for more widespread use of the public-hearing provisions in section 44 of the Canada–Nova Scotia Offshore Petroleum Resources Implementation Act. These developments underscore potential political tensions in petroleum sector management and broader oceans governance.

The CNSOPB in Action: Regulatory Politics in Multiple Dimensions

Even though the Canada–Nova Scotia Offshore Petroleum Board (CNSOPB) forms only part of the overall administrative and political apparatus for offshore petroleum, it is a major part. To foster an appreciation for the key issues and decisions adjudicated within its domain, this chapter explores how activities are organized and executed at the board's administrative level. Quite apart from the formal institutional provisions discussed earlier, the operational practices of an agency (what Sproule-Jones calls rules in use) play a major role in shaping its identity.[1] This chapter examines the board's internal bureaucratic structure and culture and the way that it manages both internal and external interfaces. The previous chapter's focus on intergovernmental relations and the joint management board arrangement, while essential to an understanding of the institutional-legal foundation of offshore rights management, is incomplete without a discussion of operational programs and decision processes. Equally important, by focusing on rules in use, this chapter offers insights into operational changes that have occurred at the ground level over time.

Precursor programs – including an offshore bureaucratic structure designed and propelled by Ottawa – were in place in the 1970s, well before the board made its appearance. In fact, the regime underwent nearly continual transformation for a decade prior to the offshore board's establishment. The 1982 agreement and the 1986 accord certainly made a difference – reaffirming certain program thrusts and initiating new ones. But at the

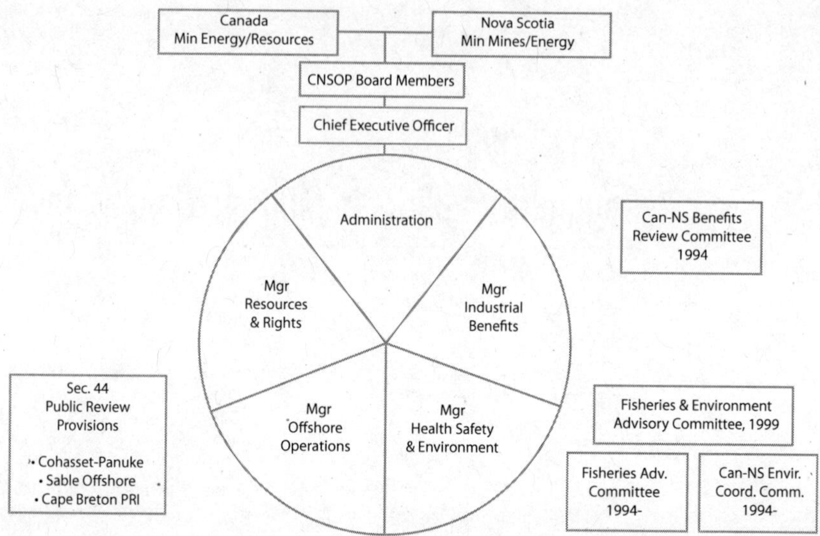

Figure 4.1 Functional relations of the Canada–Nova Scotia Offshore Petroleum Board

administrative level, many of the principal policy drivers of the 1980s lay outside of the board, and in this respect there is a danger in overstating the board's initial novelty. It was only in the 1990s that the CNSOPB became a unified assemblage of board and staff members in a single organization. Its golden age was the dynamic period between 1995 and 2005, when it dealt actively with projects in all phases of the offshore petroleum cycle. Toward this end, personnel were assembled with four principal functions. A resources and rights group handled the legal rights to explore and appropriate. The offshore operations group dealt with the licensing of exploratory and extractive activities. A third group handled matters bearing on environment, health, and safety, while the fourth approved industrial benefits and linkages. An administrative support group looked after records and databases, and the entire bureaucracy was overseen by a full-time chief executive officer, the first of whom, J.E. Dickie, was appointed in 1986. The general administrative structure is mapped out in Figure 4.1.

The initial staff complement in 1990, consisting largely of transfers from the Canadian Oil and Gas Lands Administration (COGLA), numbered about fifteen persons. As activities expanded and new projects such as Cohasset-Panuke and Sable emerged, the workload expanded, and the board grew to thirty-three members by the year 2000. A decade later, the complement had increased again to a total of forty. Not surprisingly, the professional backgrounds of members tilted predominantly toward petroleum sciences – approximately half were geophysicists, petroleum engineers, and technicians. Another third brought legal and regulatory skills to the board or advised on the environment, health, and safety, and the balance were administrative personnel. From 2000 to 2010, staff growth was due principally to the expansion of the board's data and information management function.[2]

These findings present the joint management phenomenon in a different light. Each of the four functions is surveyed below, and major policy shifts are duly noted. This chapter also offers an extended case study of the Cohasset-Panuke oil complex, the first offshore production project in the Scotian Basin. If every institution is at least in part a product of accumulated experience, Cohasset-Panuke imprinted a variety of early lessons on the CNSOPB.

The path-dependent character of institutional growth has been alluded to in earlier chapters and is strikingly evident in the workings of the board. To fully understand the board's character, a broad arc of management policies over more than forty years is considered. Veterans of the early era of East Coast offshore management (1960-73) would find something that is familiar in contemporary practices, particularly rights administration and the oversight of offshore operations. However, in other areas, including environmental oversight and industrial benefits administration, they would have no point of reference. Even in the rights and operations fields, first-generation bureaucrats departed before an extraordinary fifteen years of policy turbulence that began with the first OPEC crisis, included several iterations of Liberal national energy policy, and closed with the Mulroney government's return to a market-based oil and gas regime after 1985. Seismic shifts in petroleum markets propelled most if not all of these policy initiatives.

The basic elements of Crown petroleum management are common to most offshore lands jurisdictions. First, how does the Crown allocate the legal rights for exploration and development to prospective exploiters? Second, how does it regulate the extractive activities of these corporate agents as they pursue profit on the water? Third, in light of the particular sensitivities of marine settings, should the state regulatory regime pay special attention to environmental protection and, if so, how? Finally, can the rights and regulations system for upstream operators be used as a fulcrum to forge linkages with onshore supply chains and labour markets? The answers to these questions animated the politics of offshore basins from the

Gulf of Mexico to the North Sea to the Scotian Basin, and there was some policy cross-fertilization between them. In Atlantic Canada, elements of a North American model, relying on market-driven auctions and tax-based policy incentives, have been prominent on the rights and operations side. At the same time, the North Sea model, which favours negotiated concession rights and policy-oriented state petroleum companies, also had moments of influence in Ottawa and Halifax, particularly on industrial benefits policy.

Crown Rights Administration

The two senior governments delegate jurisdiction to the board for the management of the subsea petroleum resource, an area running from the Nova Scotia low-water mark to the outer edge of the continental margin and from the Canada-US maritime border in the west to the Nova Scotia–Newfoundland offshore boundary in the east. In addition to the Scotian Basin, the area includes subsea lands to the midpoints of the Bay of Fundy (with New Brunswick), Northumberland Strait (with Prince Edward Island), the Gulf of St. Lawrence (with Quebec), and the Cabot Strait (with Newfoundland). The board's jurisdiction is illustrated in Map 2.1. A major part of this mandate is the administration of Crown property rights, in effect, acting as landlord for offshore oil and gas deposits. In this role, the board executes the terms of several statutes, including the Canadian Petroleum Resources Act of 1986.

The present system of dispensing exploration rights to private developers is a nomination-and-bid process. The offshore seabed is set out in a grid-like system of spatially numbered blocks. Following seismic work, companies nominate the blocks of interest that they would like to pursue. At its discretion (normally once or twice annually), the board issues a call for bids on specified blocks, and firms respond by outlining proposed activities and expenditure levels. Following the board's appraisal, the results are announced in the award of exploration licences to the highest bidders. The initial term lasts for five years, after which a second four-year phase can be authorized if the initial work obligations (well drilling and additional seismic exploration) have been met.

In the event of a major find, the initial exclusive exploration right can be transformed into a longer-term stake by applying to the board for a significant discovery licence. A significant discovery is defined as "the first well on a geological feature that demonstrates by flow testing the existence of hydrocarbons [with] ... a potential for sustained production."[3] The significant discovery licence may be transformed by subsequent application into a declaration of commercial discovery. The declaration signifies that the discovery "has been demonstrated to contain petroleum reserves that justify the investment of capital and effort to bring the discovery to production."[4] The declaration of commercial discovery is also a significant pacing measure. Legislation empowers the board to set a time frame for commercial development, after which the licensee faces a reduction in the size of interest.

The final major step on the road to hydrocarbon development is an application for a production licence, which gives the holder the exclusive right to develop, produce, and hold title to the petroleum, subject to stipulated terms.[5] A production licence carries a twenty-five-year term with automatic extensions if production is still under way. The CNSOPB granted its first production licence to Lasmo/Nova Scotia Resources Limited's Cohasset-Panuke project in April 1991.

Over the more than forty-year history of Scotian Basin petroleum, the legislative and administrative framework has shifted several times. In the 1960s, Canada Lands included both the territorial North and the offshore regions. The enabling statute was the venerable Public Lands Grants Act and Territorial Lands Act, and the subordinate regulations were the Canada Oil and Gas Land Regulations. Until 1966, their administrative vehicle was the federal Department of Northern Affairs and National Resources. The federal resource tenure was then split along geographical lines: Indian Affairs and Northern Development assumed the lead role in the territorial North, while Energy, Mines and Resources took over east and west coast offshore lands. Administrative responsibilities were vested in Energy, Mines and Resource's Resource Management Branch. Centred in Ottawa but with regional offices in Halifax and St. John's, this staff group handled petroleum rights permits, geological analysis, environmental assessment, and offshore activity monitoring.[6]

Following the 1973 OPEC crisis and the first comprehensive rewriting of federal petroleum policy, the federal energy minister announced a new priority for offshore oil and gas exploration in May 1976.[7] The legislation was introduced but never enacted; however, significant policy changes were made the following year by Order-in-Council. Exploration permits were replaced by exploration licences that could cover larger spatial areas on terms subject to ministerial discretion. In addition, the newly established state oil company, Petro-Canada, gained the right to acquire a working interest of 25 percent in properties with low levels of Canadian ownership. Petro-Canada also gained a preferential right to acquire up to 25 percent of Crown reserve lands (i.e., those not under permit). These terms marked a major shift in federal offshore policy that was part of the broader politicization of energy during the 1970s.[8] The new land provisions sought to attract new entrants into exploration and greater involvement by Canadian-owned firms as both offshore investors and operators.

The October 1980 release of the Trudeau government's National Energy Program (NEP) marked a further transformation. The Canadianization provisions of 1977 were extended and deepened. Virtually all of the coordinates of federal upstream oil and gas were affected, and comprehensive legislative changes occupied most of 1981. As far as land rights were concerned, the new Canada Oil and Gas Act required all exploration permits to be renegotiated into exploration agreements, a massive task that touched all members of the offshore corporate community. To handle the federal side of negotiations, Ottawa created a new agency known as the Canada Oil and Gas Lands Administration (COGLA), which quickly became a bête noire to offshore petroleum capital (particularly the foreign-owned faction). Rather than retreating, however, the industry found the new NEP's fiscal incentives so rich that dealing with this new and powerful bureaucracy was unavoidable. As an offshore land bureaucracy, the COGLA presided over the rise and fall of the second major cycle of Scotian Shelf exploration during the 1980s.

Following the 1982 Canada–Nova Scotia Agreement on Offshore Oil and Gas Resource Management and Revenue Sharing, the COGLA fitted readily into its mandate. Not only was the administration's chief administrator designated the board chairman, but the two key federal statutes were also adopted by Nova Scotia as mirror legislation. Although the board began meeting in April 1982, the enabling legislation for the agreement was not in place for two more years, leaving unanswered the question of whether the board could fully exercise its power of "directing the activities of COGLA in respect to the offshore region."[9] In any event, the COGLA continued to function as the bureaucratic power in the Scotian Basin. Although it shared the information-providing and policy-advising roles with the Nova Scotia Department of Mines and Energy, the relationship was, inevitably, asymmetrical. By 1986, when the Canada–Nova Scotia Offshore Petroleum Resources Accord was signed, the Mulroney government had eliminated much of the agency's legislative mandate. Although the agency remained the designated Crown authority for the 1986 Canadian Petroleum Resources Act, the accord provided that the new board would have its own administrative staff to support its new "management responsibility for all matters directly related to offshore petroleum resource activity."[10] When the CNSOPB opened its doors in January 1990, it was in the process of assembling an initial staff group of fifteen members, assuming the role formerly played by the now-defunct COGLA.

The rights allocation rules administered by the new board's Rights and Resources staff had reverted (by the terms of the Canadian Petroleum Resources Act) to a version of the nomination and bid system. As was the case before 1976, companies nominated lands that were formally announced in annual or biannual calls for proposals.[11] This system remains in place today. In addition, the Rights and Resources section plays an important role in assessing exploratory results and in collecting exploration fees and royalties on producing properties.

Regulating Petroleum Operations

It is one thing to apportion legal rights to offshore petroleum lands but quite another to monitor their exercise and application. Whereas rights are about tenure and property rules, operations are about regulating activities. If rights administration is dominated by petroleum geologists with expertise in traps, faults, and sedimentary formations, then operations is staffed predominantly with petroleum engineers whose professional focus is scoping reservoirs and devising extractive and processing systems and strategies for field depletion. The government's task is to monitor and authorize such schemes. As the inaugural chairman put it, the board serves as "the "window to the offshore" for all users and persons interested in offshore-related matters."[12] Not only do regulators track all offshore actions: the basic regulatory premise is that no significant offshore activities may be conducted without an authorization issued by the board. It is incumbent on the operator to apply for all necessary authorizations and supporting materials. This process begins with geophysical sensing work and continues through exploratory drilling, the installation of extractive systems, production flows and, finally, the decommissioning of terminated facilities. Since the common denominator is the application of complex technologies, a series of policy priorities emerged to deal with matters of resource conservation and extractive efficiency.

When East Coast exploration commenced in the 1960s, the prevailing operational rules were the Canada Oil and Gas Drilling and Production Regulations of June 1961. Given the still-limited state of offshore activities, however, the regulations' application was largely confined to licensing geophysical surveys and exploratory drilling. The pace accelerated toward the end of the decade with the enactment in 1969 of a new statute modelled on Alberta legislation (which was based on the Texas Conservation Act).[13]

Applied initially to the northern territories, the federal Oil and Gas Production and Conservation Act was extended to the Atlantic offshore area in June 1970. The legislation aimed to ensure efficient production and marketing through regulations on optimal drilling and spacing, unitization, and pooling practices. It addressed a range of field conservation practices and made waste (defined in terms of extractive inefficiency) an offence. Furthermore, a chief conservation officer was designated the federal official in charge. Other sections of the act made provisions for offshore work safety and pollution prevention.

The 1982 Canada–Nova Scotia agreement reaffirmed the centrality of the Oil and Gas Production and Conservation Act. As a reflection of the dual executive control of the board, the agreement required Nova Scotia to enact mirror legislation. Further provisions and procedures were spelled out in the Nova Scotia Offshore Area Petroleum Production and Conservation Regulations and the Drilling Regulations.

Throughout the several decades that these regulations provided the backbone of offshore operational oversight, industry practice evolved markedly. The techniques of exploration and production brought continual innovation: improved seismic imaging and modelling, larger and stronger offshore rigs, more sophisticated well-monitoring systems, and the capability to work in deeper water and to install more elaborate seabed gathering systems. These techniques were pioneered as the North Sea basin moved into production after 1975, the Gulf of Mexico revived after 1990, and other prospects were developed around the world. State regulators responded to the surge of expanded activities offshore by adjusting their own practices. To a great extent, the Scotian Basin was insulated from these pressures by the extended hiatus of 1987-93. The result was that the CNSOPB and other offshore regulatory agents ended the century with a legal regime that was struggling to catch up with international practice.

The level of industry concern with this predicament was evident in the convening of the Atlantic Energy Roundtable in 2002. The growing interest in regulatory regime change was driven by at least three distinct trends rooted in the 1990s. The first was resurgent industry interest in the Scotian Shelf, which began in 1997. The second vector was the effect (or, to some, burden) of extending the Canadian Environmental Assessment Agency provisions to the Nova Scotia offshore area in 2001. A third vector was the new drive by the global offshore industry, especially in maturing basins, to reduce cost structures, including the twin paths of business-cost reductions and state regulatory change. For example, in the North Sea, the United

Kingdom Offshore Operators Association launched its Cost Reduction Initiative for a New Economy (CRINE) campaign in 1993. The follow-up business-government PILOT collaboration emerged in 1998, in light of "the urgent need to reduce the cost base of activity," and set out a ten-year time frame to achieve its goals.[14]

On the Atlantic coast, a parallel process kicked off in November 2002, when a high-level business-government conference convened in Halifax under the name of the Atlantic Canada Energy Roundtable. The catalyst was the Canadian Association of Petroleum Producers, which had designated regulatory efficiency and effectiveness as a national public policy concern. More immediate driving pressures were the disappointing results of early drilling on the deepwater continental shelf and the regulatory "time out" taken by leading operator EnCana, which suspended its Deep Panuke project application early in 2003.

One of the leading work themes was broad-spectrum regulatory renewal based on streamlined processes and performance-based criteria.[15] Discussions culminated in 2009 in the unveiling of a wholesale revision to drilling and production regulations. The revisions addressed the high level of duplication in the accumulated rules, the rigidity of their prescriptive standards and reporting requirements, and the lack of recognition for the role of management systems models as a corporate-led response to compliance.[16] The new consolidated regulations were the product of three years of deliberation by federal state regulators, including the two Atlantic offshore boards and the National Energy Board (for northern Canada).[17] The result was the merger of hitherto separate drilling and production regulations into a single format. Even more significant was the preference for goal-oriented regulations that left to companies the choice of means to achieve them. This policy would allow firms to ride the crest of new technologies and practices without the drag of time-consuming prescriptions. Under the old regime, firms routinely applied to regulators for "exemptions or equivalencies that stem from outdated or non-applicable prescriptive requirements."[18] The adjustments that this entailed could now be internalized within the firm, in part by the expanded use of management system practices already employed in other global basins. This distinct type of regulatory practice suggests a new type of regulatory logic has emerged.

Returning to the Board processes of operational regulation, once an explorer judges a significant discovery to be commercially viable, a detailed series of work authorizations and approvals follow. Some of the leading permit or approval points administered by the CNSOPB are itemized in

Table 4.1. Before any particular applications are made, however, an operator is required to hold several qualifying certificates, including an operating licence from the board. Although issuing the licence is relatively straightforward, an operating licence may be suspended for a contravention or default of any subsequent undertakings, leading to the interruption of all activities. The second is the benefits plan, which sets out commitments for Canada- and Nova Scotia-based contracting of goods and services and employment. The third is an approved safety plan, which demonstrates a systematic approach to offshore safety management in all activities and includes an emergency response plan and, where applicable, an oil spill response plan. The fourth is an environmental impact statement (including an environmental protection plan), which typically applies to activities before the approval of a comprehensive development application. The impact statement documents substances to be discharged, while the protection plan addresses plans for the handling, monitoring, and mitigation of effects. The fifth is a certificate of fitness, issued by an accredited certification authority, for all production, drilling, diving, and accommodation installations. Finally, a proof of financial responsibility certificate indicates possession of insurance, credit, or other guarantees that cover the costs of compensation and restoration arising from the work.

As it moves toward commercial development and before any onshore or offshore fabrication begins, an offshore project as a whole requires review at the design stage. The proponent submits a comprehensive development plan and a benefits plan that require approval by the CNSOPB. Even prior to this, the proponent's comprehensive study report must be examined by joint federal and provincial agencies (including public panel hearings) and approved on environmental grounds.

Before and after the overall project review, a series of approvals are required for activities at each stage in the exploration and production cycle. For example, an exploration program on any licence area cannot proceed before a drilling program authorization is issued to cover seismic, drilling, and diving activities. Each rig requires authorization before it can commence operations. Each proposed well also requires an authority to drill a well on a particular site.

Other provisions apply to operational safety. The loss of the Ocean Ranger semi-submersible rig off Newfoundland in 1982 and the explosion on the Piper Alpha platform in the North Sea in 1988 prompted fundamental overhauls of offshore safety systems. The CNSOPB's enabling legislation was amended in 1992 to require a series of inspections and certifications.

TABLE 4.1

Major CNSOPB regulatory instruments, by stage in cycle

1. Pre-requirements for applications for work authorization
   - Operating licence
   - Benefits plan
   - Safety plan and emergency response plan
   - Environmental impact statement and an environmental protection plan
   - Certificate of fitness from a certifying authority
   - Proof of financial responsibility

2. Key work authorizations at the exploration stage
   - Drilling program approval
   - Authority to drill a well
   - Diving program authorization
   - Canadian Environmental Assessment Agency (CEAA) permit (2001-)

3. Key work authorizations at the project development stage
   - Development plan approval
   - Benefits plan approval
   - Comprehensive study report (CEAA) approval (2001-)

4. Key work authorizations at the development/installation stage
   - Development program authorizations

5. Key work authorizations at the production stage
   - Data acquisition program
   - Flow system approval
   - Formation flow test
   - Flaring or venting of gas approval
   - Production operations authorizations
   - Well operations program approval

6. Key work authorizations at the decommissioning stage
   - Decommissioning work authorization
   - Approval of any deviations from decommissioning commitments included in an approved development plan

Source: Adapted from Atlantic Canada Petroleum Institute, *Offshore Oil and Gas Approvals in Atlantic Canada* (Halifax: Atlantic Canada Petroleum Institute, 2001).

Regulating Environmental Impacts

As a policy field, offshore environmental regulation is both old and new. It has roots in the history of land-based production, when the primary concerns were for petroleum conservation and extractive efficiency. This included contingency planning for blowouts and spills. However, the offshore petroleum environment only emerged as a central object of policy much later.

Not surprisingly, the environmental dimensions of offshore drilling centre on marine pollution, which can generally be divided into two categories: the routine and the catastrophic. Routine matters include dealing with the effects of the normal operations of drilling, production, and transport. Offshore rigs are marine vessels; as such, their bilge and ballast have often been subject to the same lax regulation as transport ships. As drill and production platforms, however, offshore rigs are point source polluters so long as they are fixed in place. Consequently regulations cover the use of platform fuels and fluids such as drill muds that are used to lubricate drill stems and casings. After-use muds are generally released into the sea and include the crushed rock cuttings from the well hole. Another category of produced materials that is also released is formation water from the reservoirs. A variety of maintenance and cleanup materials can enter the water as deck wash, and accidental spills of fuels and cargo can also occur during transfer to and from vessels.

Catastrophic forms of offshore pollution include blowouts while drilling or producing. A blowout is an uncontrolled high-pressure flow of fluids or gas from an underground formation into the seawater or the air. Normal drilling practices include controlling blowouts by installing steel pipe casings in the hole and pumping in mud to offset pressure. In addition, a blowout preventer is installed on the seabed to shut in the well if pressure control is lost. Although blowouts occur in only a small fraction of wells, the scale of disruptions combined with the lingering evidence of impacts place them front and centre as a public concern. The January 1969 Santa Barbara blowout at Union Oil's Platform A proved to be a pivotal event in the emergence of the North American environmental movement.[19] Estimates of the oil spilled ranged from 1 to 3 million gallons over a year-long period. Media coverage of damaged birds and polluted California beaches within sight of a major city rendered the blowout the benchmark for extreme offshore despoliation. Not only did the disaster attest to the risk of offshore operations and symbolize the inadequacy of existing regulations, it also led directly to state government opposition to continental shelf drilling on both US seaboards and extended closures that continue today.

Yet even the Santa Barbara blowout pales in comparison to BP's Macondo blowout in the Gulf of Mexico in April 2010. Operating in mile-deep water at a location forty miles offshore, the drill operators lost control of the well while attempting to exit and close the hole. The seabed blowout preventer then failed to close the drill pipe, and a massive gas escape ignited on the surface, destroying the Deepwater Horizon platform, killing eleven crew members, and injuring seventeen others. For almost three months, crude oil escaped into gulf waters, inflicting environmental damages that are still not fully appreciated. Multiple investigations into both the causes and consequences are under way, but the efficacy of deepwater regulation and compliance will lie at the heart of them. Attention will centre on whether the project design had been adequately reviewed by the Minerals Management Service before and after licensing; whether the Macondo licence holder, rig operator, and contractors followed accepted procedures and exercised diligence; and whether commercial pressures led to breaches of legally approved practice. The policy consequences stand to be profound. The regulatory regime will be overhauled, and the Minerals Management Service will be restructured and re-mandated. The Macondo blowout will have deeper and longer term policy consequences for the future of performance-based regulation.

On Canadian frontier lands, the first blowouts occurred in the high Arctic. In the 1960s, Panarctic Oils made two gas discoveries in its first eight wildcats wells, and both blew out. With memories of Santa Barbara still fresh, the Drake Point well on Melville Island blew out gas and water in July 1969. After initial containment, it blew out the following month and almost a year passed before a relief well shut it in. A blowout on King Christian Island in October 1970 caught fire and burned for ninety-one days while a relief well was drilled.[20] Because they were natural gas formations, the pollution was airborne only; however, the implications of lengthy oil well blowouts was evident.

The Sable Subbasin has experienced two offshore natural gas blowouts. The Uniacke G-72 well blew out in February 1984. Gas and condensates escaped for nine days before they were brought under control. More prolonged, West Venture N-91 blew out in September 1984 when it encountered high formation pressures. It began as a surface (i.e., seabed) blowout, but when the well was shut, it then blew out through the well casing underground. Rising natural gas "charged" a shallower rock zone, complicating the task of finding a safe site for a relief well. In the end, the blowout required nine months to be brought under control.

As might be expected, the protocols on the acceptability of discharges have evolved markedly over time. Prior to the 1970s, there was little formal environmental policy for upstream petroleum. Regulations for drilling included requirements for blowout preventers and well logging, but these requirements were long-standing engineering standards. It is important to bear in mind the political context. Environment Canada was established in 1971, and its initial mandate was limited.[21] Indeed, the environmental assessment of oil and gas plans was vested elsewhere, in the petroleum-development branches of Indian and Northern Affairs Development and Energy, Mines and Resources. In a telling policy decision, the federal cabinet accepted a 1973 recommendation from Indian and Northern Affairs to approve Arctic frontier exploration in principle while accepting existing federal regulations and expertise as "adequate to ensure reasonable and effective safeguards and contingency plans for the protection of Canada's arctic marine and coastal environments."[22] That this recommendation came several years after the Drake Point and King Christian events underscores the depth of the pro-development ethic in the Trudeau government. Equally revealing was the reaction of Jack Davis, minister of the environment, that the cabinet decision had been taken "without enough time to do proper environmental assessment work."[23]

Over the past forty years, there have been four waves of offshore environmental regulation. The first, as described above, emerged out of the resource conservation tradition. It required applicants to submit plans or measures to deal with oil spill contingencies, which would be vetted by Crown officials. A 1981 amendment to the Oil and Gas Production and Conservation Act added a section on oil spills that covered both discharges and debris and imposed responsibility for notification and cleanup on the operator. Offshore operators were required to maintain records and report meteorological conditions on site. Over time, however, the offshore environmental challenge came to be defined not simply as one of well control but also of interaction between petroleum operations and a wider marine setting, particularly ocean fisheries. The 1982 Canada–Nova Scotia agreement moved forcefully in this direction, declaring that "the offshore environment, including the rich fisheries, are enduring aspects of the offshore resource heritage which will not be sacrificed for shorter term offshore oil and gas considerations" and calling for proponents to "meet stringent baseline environmental requirements, and to demonstrate that the development options being considered are fully consistent with environmental values."[24] By 1985, the COGLA had issued guidelines on one of the most sensitive routine discharge matters, drilling muds. The concerns ranged from industrial contaminants to benthic disturbances caused by used-mud plumes being released into the water and settling on the seabed. Over time, federal authorities encouraged firms to minimize their reliance on oil-based muds and to adopt water-based muds (or synthetics) whenever possible. Another emerging concern was the release of used muds containing solid rock cuttings that might themselves carry pollutants.

The next stage involved the Crown delineating more detailed criteria and provisions to be met by operators. These criteria are often described as prescriptive standards because of their intent to set thresholds for applicants to reach. Under a series of regulations issued between 1992 and 1995, operators were required to submit environmental protection plans for exploratory drilling programs. The plans extended to routine discharges as well as extreme events. In 1996, the National Energy Board collaborated with the Nova Scotia and Newfoundland petroleum boards to produce a set of offshore waste treatment guidelines that set out the minimum standards acceptable for operational treatment and disposal. A revised set of guidelines was issued in 2002.[25] A separate set of guidelines for chemical usage was framed in a similar way.

The third phase of environmental oversight began in the late 1990s, when the board began to consider broader categories of environmental assessment such as the subbasin or region. The phase began with a generic study of seismic exploration on the Scotian Shelf in 1998, which was followed by a study of exploratory drilling.[26] The aim was to identify features and impacts common to all instances of an activity to inform assessment in advance and allow particular activity-based applications to concentrate on unique features. In effect, the value to the board of advance scanning was combined with the value to applicants of more focussed impact submissions. The board then moved on to strategic environmental assessments. Once again, the aim was to tackle area-wide environmental impacts prior to particular projects. First recognized by the federal cabinet in 1990, the assessments were adopted by several offshore regulators (including the United Kingdom) in the early 2000s.[27] The CNSOPB has commissioned three subbasin strategic environmental assessments to explore the environmental impacts associated with opening new areas for bidding. The assessments covered the Eastern Sable Bank, the Laurentian Subbasin, and the Misaine Bank.[28] The goal was the twin gains of advance scanning and simplified site-based studies for applicants. The adoption of strategic environmental assessments went some way toward meeting criticism that project and site-specific reviews fail to capture cumulative impacts that build as the number of projects increases. Importantly, the assessments also injected environmental sensitivity into the earlier stages of the policy process.

One geographic region that would have benefitted from a strategic environmental assessment was the in-shore coastal margin.[29] Significantly, the board had been caught unprepared to deal with a controversy over environmental impacts of shallow-water coastal exploration. In 1997-98, the board issued calls for nominations in three shallow water blocks to the east and west of Cape Breton Island. A variety of community interests pointed out significant environmental vulnerabilities – the shellfish industry and an area that had been used as a marine munitions dump following the Second World War.[30] Protest escalated after the board issued exploration licences to the parcels in question. Ultimately, federal and provincial ministers directed the CNSOPB to freeze the applications while a public inquiry was held under section 44 of the offshore act. This episode highlighted the flaws of activity-based regulation from an environmental point of view, and it likely pushed the board toward accepting the merits of strategic environmental assessments.

The fourth phase originated outside of the CNSOPB's orbit entirely. Thus far, the focus has been on environmental measures advanced by the offshore regulatory agency. Significant as they are, they do not capture the entire picture. Other agencies also play a role, including Fisheries and Oceans and the National Energy Board. However, the most important parallel regime is that of Environment Canada, in which the Canadian Environmental Assessment Agency (CEAA) has asserted an ever more prominent role. The CEAA's extension into offshore areas in the 2000s created a situation in which exploration and production interests now face two simultaneous regulatory templates. It offers a graphic illustration of the unintended consequences that can follow from generalized national policy mandates.

When the Canadian Environmental Assessment Act was proclaimed in 1995, it put environmental assessment on a new footing. All designated federal authorities were required to self-assess and identify any projects that would qualify for review by virtue of federal policy initiative, funding, regulation, or land interest. The act spells out provisions for various levels of review – screening, comprehensive, and public panel. The lead agency for petroleum projects was the National Energy Board, which exercised extensive regulatory powers under the Canada Oil and Gas Operations Act. The effect was to make exploration, production, and decommissioning projects subject to the CEAA. However, the Atlantic offshore area fell outside the mandate of the National Energy Board, and the two (Nova Scotia and Newfoundland) joint boards held jurisdiction over it. Since the CNSOPB's implementation statute was not listed as a trigger for the CEAA, only extraction licence applications (that is, permissions to produce) were subject to the act's provisions. In effect, the intergovernmental character of the two accords resulted in their being grandfathered when the CEAA era began in 1995. From the perspective of federal environmental agencies, however, where the legislation was championed as a cutting edge renewal of an aging regime, the offshore anomaly never sat well. In 2001, the CNSOPB was designated as a federal authority under the act, and legislative amendments in 2003 brought major changes to the status of the offshore area. The result was that "in all parts of Canada where offshore oil and gas activity is permitted, authorizations for exploration projects, the de-commissioning of projects, and the approval of physical activities relating to the production of oil or gas, will be subject to a prior federal EA [environmental assessment] process."[31]

Industry attempts to have seismic activity exempted from the list of reviewable activities were unsuccessful. A further issue of even greater consequence involved the designated level of environmental assessment scrutiny. The Canadian Environmental Assessment Act set the bar high by bringing exploratory drilling under the comprehensive study list, a category that also contained larger development projects. The industry favoured screening study on the grounds that wildcatting was a standardized activity whose generic impacts were well understood and that such impacts were temporary in duration and more limited in physical scale. Environment Canada did not give ground, but in the end a compromise allowed new exploratory wells sited in study areas already subject to a full review (e.g., the Sable gas project area) to be grandfathered. In the future, as the scope of exploration progresses across the continental shelf, only the first exploratory well in any new area (never before drilled) will require a comprehensive assessment. It is ironic that Environment Canada, having been largely fenced out of offshore jurisdiction in the early 1970s, turned the tables on the offshore industry regulators after several decades of subordination. Nevertheless, the burden of being the first corporate explorationist, responsible for the comprehensive assessment in a newly opened subbasin, would be heavy.

Regulating Industrial and Employment Benefits

The fourth major functional area of the CNSOPB's administration is industrial and employment benefits, the Crown requirement that offshore rights holders and project operators achieve significant levels of domestic participation in their contracting and workforce activities. The East Coast's regulatory regime in this area was strongly influenced by host state policies in the North Sea Basin. In the 1970s, both the United Kingdom and Norway fashioned regulatory schemes to maximize domestic participation and benefits from petroleum exploitation in their sectors. These schemes were prompted by concerns that normal business practices in the highly internationalized industry would bypass host state economies in favour of established patterns of supply and contracting based in the US Gulf Coast.

Another program vector within Canada fed into this policy thrust by combining elements of federal state procurement or purchasing policy with recognition of energy megaprojects as the next generation of big investment. Government of Canada procurement included the practice of requiring firms pursuing large contracts to make advance commitments to Canadian manufacture as part of their contract bids. Known as offsets, these provisions were integral to bid adjudication. In effect, the benefits approach adapted this same policy to the offshore arena. Even before the 1982 Canada–Nova Scotia joint management agreement, Ottawa intended to link major energy project approvals with domestic sources and employment. Appointed in 1978, the Major Projects Task Force brought together almost eighty business and labour leaders to "identify, discuss and make recommendations on the nature of potential industrial and regional benefits that could arise from major capital projects to the year 2000."[32] Among other matters, the task force advised the government to institute a procurement preference in favour of Canadian firms. Following receipt of the 1981 report, the federal government established a new monitoring agency within the Department of Regional and Industrial Expansion.

Although a number of national styles of benefits regimes emerged, the basic approach was to require operators to make explicit commitments to domestic sourcing as part of their business plans. Formal approval of such benefits plans, at both the exploration and project development phases, became a key gate-keeping step. In the absence of an approved benefits plan, an offshore firm could not obtain the desired work approvals or certificates. On the Scotian Shelf, these instruments were stipulated in the 1982 Canada–Nova Scotia agreement and confirmed in the 1986 Canada–Nova Scotia accord. They were authorized by statute in the Canada Oil and Gas Act (1982) and maintained in the Canadian Petroleum Resources Act (1986). As the offshore accord put it, a key policy objective was "full and fair opportunity" for domestic Canadian participation, with "first consideration" going to Nova Scotia goods and services that were competitive in terms of "fair market price, quality and delivery."[33]

Administrative responsibilities were assigned initially to the Benefits Branch of the COGLA. Throughout the 1980s, policies were worked out, and the COGLA Industrial Benefit Guidelines of 1986 spelled out the rules of that time. In 1990, the newly staffed Benefits Section of the CNSOPB assumed this role, though the 1986 Industrial Benefits Guidelines continued to apply.

It is generally recognized that the greatest share of offshore investment takes place at the field development stage (as much as 80 percent of total spending). However, for basins such as the Scotian Shelf that are still rooted in the early phases of the development cycle, the initial benefits focus was on exploration spending, and each corporate exploration program required an approved benefits plan. The same was true of the commercial stages, in which the applicant's benefits plan was adjudicated at the same level as the project development plan. A number of techniques were available, including board review of approved bidder lists, of supplier development plans, and of the terms of major tenders awarded. Following approval, the regulators were equipped with a number of tools for monitoring commitments, including audits. Not surprisingly, the offshore industry took an active role in influencing these matters. In general, operators preferred to rely on market instruments and information-sharing networks for tendering, while minimizing the scope and detail of regulatory pre-screening and monitoring. The politics of industrial benefits is explored in greater detail in subsequent chapters.

As with many of the board's staff functions, the fiscal year 1989-90 was a transitional period for benefits administration. An attenuated COGLA continued to provide technical support until the CNSOPB recruited its initial staff complement. Initially, the benefits function was located with legal services in a section headed by the chief administrator. In 1995, the Canada–Nova Scotia Benefits Review Committee was created. It was an inter-jurisdictional working group with representation from multiple departments, including Natural Resources Canada and the Nova Scotia Petroleum Directorate. Its technical advisory role to the board increased significantly once the Sable offshore energy project benefits application was filed in June 1996.

Although the mechanisms of industrial benefits regulation might have change over the years, the underlying policy principle has never been seriously questioned. Significantly, the Mulroney government was willing to accept this part of the regulatory map even as the bulk of the National Energy Program was dismantled in a flurry of price deregulation, fiscal changes, and market-based rights allocation. Retention was due in no small measure to the pro-benefits position of the Nova Scotia government in the Buchanan years. Shore-based supply chains and employment were two of the province's strongest priorities. From its office in Halifax, the Onshore/Offshore Trade Association of Nova Scotia served as a clearinghouse for Scotian Basin procurement and viewed the benefits deal as a business charter. Under the terms of the 1982 agreement, the province had representation in the COGLA's benefits machinery, and it never wavered from the ambition of confirming Halifax as the Atlantic offshore hub (as the next Aberdeen or Stavanger).

Regulating the Cohasset-Panuke Project

Thus far, the description of legal and administrative procedures has painted a comprehensive picture of the board's instruments of intervention. However, it cannot capture the dynamic and subtle qualities of their application to a particular project. This section examines the board's multiple roles in asserting the Crown's interest on the first fields to produce on the Scotian Shelf – the Cohasset and Panuke light oilfield development. It follows this initiative from cradle to grave, from initial exploration and discovery, through project engineering and design, to construction, operation, and termination.

The COPAN project, as it came to be known, was an intimate part of the CNSOPB's opening decade. It was almost the first item of business facing the new board when it convened in January 1990. Moreover, given the hiatus in exploratory effort from 1987 to 1996, the board devoted by far the greatest share of its effort to handling the succession of cycle stages in the COPAN fields. Although the project's scale was quite modest in relation to its counterparts in the Gulf of Mexico or North Sea, it was an invaluable prototype on which the board and the sponsoring governments could cut their regulatory teeth. As the board put it, "many refinements have been made to the regulatory process as a result of experiences with the Cohasset project."[34] The techniques of administrative discretion exercised by the regulatory authority within its statutory framework are particularly notable.

The project's story begins prior to the basin-altering Venture gas discovery of 1979. In those days, the responsibility for Crown rights administration lay with the Department of Energy, Mines and Resources. In the summer of 1973, Mobil Canada and partners drilled the exploratory well Cohasset D-42 from the semi-submersible *Sedco J* at a site located 48 kilometres southwest of Sable Island in about 40 metres of water. Drilled to a depth of 4,400 metres, the well encountered a significant show of light crude oil before it was plugged and suspended. Five years later, in the summer of 1978, the Mobil partners returned to drill two exploratory wells from the jackup rig *Gulftide*. The first was Cohasset P-42, in about 35 metres of water. Drilled to a depth of almost 2,600 metres, it proved dry and was plugged and abandoned. The rig then moved slightly west to drill Cohasset L-97, this time to 4,800 metres, with similar results. Not only were the Cohasset wells not promising, there were few other oil strikes in the opening decade. Most first-generation finds were natural gas, and the Sable Subbasin came to be regarded principally as a natural gas play.

COPAN's history resumed in the mid-1980s, when offshore exploration was encouraged by the rich federal incentives of the Petroleum Incentive Program. Canadian-owned companies or syndicates could receive grants covering up to 80 percent of their approved frontier exploration expenses. For Nova Scotia, much of the action was concentrated in a rectangle centred on Sable Island. The first joint offshore board was now functioning, and the duties of rights administration fell to the COGLA. Under the terms of the 1981 Canada Oil and Gas Act, all existing exploration permits had to be renegotiated into exploration agreements, a new tenure that created larger blocks and provided for a Crown share on any commercial development. This accentuated the normal turnover of exploration rights, and when attention turned again to the Cohasset sites, in the winter of 1985-86, the lead operator was Petro-Canada, in partnership with Mobil. Cohasset A-52, a delineation well positioned close to the original hole, was drilled from the *Rowan Gorilla I*, a jackup platform. When oil flowed to 1,220 cubic metres per day, the COGLA reported that "it demonstrated the potential for oil development."[35]

During the late summer of 1986, another group, this time led by Shell Canada, drilled Panuke B-90 from the semi-submersible *Vinland* at a location some 13 kilometres west of Cohasset. Once again, oil was discovered, and it flowed to 969 cubic metres per day before the hole was plugged. These results led Petro-Canada to return the following summer to drill Panuke F-99, a successful delineation well that confirmed the zone as oil-bearing.

By the end of 1987, Petro-Canada was reported to be studying production alternatives and facilities design for the Cohasset field.[36] However, its plans coincided with the oil market slump, and all Sable Shelf activities came to a screeching halt. These were years of deep torpor for the Atlantic offshore industry. Among the few players choosing to maintain a foothold was Nova Scotia Resources Limited (NSRL), the provincial Crown enterprise whose history is explored intensively in a later chapter. In contrast to the international majors, NSRL was a junior explorer whose business strategy followed a different trajectory. It sponsored a 1988 study on the economics of small-field development that recommended joint development of the two fields.

This study brought NSRL into contact with Lasmo plc (formerly known as London and Scottish Marine Oil), an established operator in the British North Sea. Together, they purchased the rights to the Cohasset (255) and Panuke (299-300) significant discovery areas in 1989. They also took up other exploration rights on recently surrendered lands around Cohasset (EA 352) and Panuke (EL 2100) in 1989 and 1990, respectively, and performed additional seismic work. The subsidiary firm Lasmo Nova Scotia Ltd. opened its Halifax office in November 1989, while work continued on design plans and regulatory documents for the proposed production system.[37] In two short years, this fifty-fifty partnership emerged as the lead player on the Scotian Shelf, bucking international trends. The pairing of NSRL with Lasmo combined Canadian content with proven production experience. In advancing its mandate to spark offshore petroleum development, NSRL was seeking commercial income against which to charge its exploration expenses. As the operating partner, Lasmo could draw on a track record in field development.

The COPAN preliminary development application was submitted on 20 December 1989 and offered the first official outline of the project.[38] It estimated a commercial reserve of 35-million barrels of sweet light crude oil (later marketed as Scotia Light), which would be extracted from the two fields over five to six years. Each season would last about seven months before a winter shutdown. The initial estimates were $160 million in capital investment to install the facilities and $405 million to operate them over the life of the fields. The design originally called for simultaneous production from the two fields, which would be linked by about 10 kilometres of sub-sea flow lines and a power cable weighted by hundreds of concrete mattresses. At each field, oil and produced water would be separated (in a 3:4 ratio), and the water would be re-injected to maintain formation pressure. At Cohasset, a converted jackup platform would be positioned to control the overall system of five production wells and two produced-water injection wells. At Panuke, an unmanned platform would anchor three production wells and one injection well. At Cohasset, the flow line continued several kilometres beyond the platform and then rose to the surface to pass through a CALM buoy and on to a floating storage and offloading tanker moored to the buoy.[39] A shuttle tanker would periodically ship the crude to markets in the United States.

The COPAN filing was expected in government circles. Yet it arrived at a sensitive moment, when the terms of the 1986 accord were just coming fully into force with the creation of the new CNSOPB. During the transitional year of 1990, while the board was assembling its staff complement, it was agreed that the COGLA (whose jurisdiction was now narrowed to the federal northlands) would provide professional support.

The regulatory responsibilities for appraising a commercial development were certainly more complex than those for exploration licensing or well activities. Indeed, they required a negotiated division of activities on the state side. The CNSOPB had two key legal instruments. The first was a decision on the development plan that covered the proponents' overall production system; the second was a decision on the benefits plan that covered the terms of project contracting, manufacture, and employment.[40] Consent for both plans was required before any further action could be taken. In practice, the COGLA's staff advised the board on geological issues and reservoir depletion, while consultants were hired to evaluate the well and topside structures and to assess the project's marine aspects, including the CALM buoy and tanker configurations. Since these approvals had the status of fundamental decisions under the board's governance, the results were forwarded first to the federal and provincial ministers for confirmation (which followed).

A separate process applied to environmental and socio-economic review. The board used the section 44 provisions on public hearings in its enabling statute to establish the COPAN Environmental and Socio-Economic Public Review Commission. A single commissioner, retired banker J.R. (Pat) Ellis, was appointed to appraise the environmental and socio-economic dimensions of the preliminary development plan through public hearings. Working with the preliminary development plan, Ellis convened a series of informal public meetings to kick off a ninety-day consultation period, which began in March 1990.[41] The consultations culminated with four days of formal public meetings in late June, at Port Hawkesbury, Liverpool, and Halifax. A month later, on 24 July 1990, Commissioner Ellis submitted his report to the board.

The commissioner's central conclusion was that "from an environmental point of view, the project can proceed without serious environmental impacts if the recommendations put forward are adopted."[42] Ellis advised against the use of oil-based drilling muds, accepted the proposed loading of hydrocarbons in formation-produced waters, and found that even a large spill of light COPAN crude would have an insignificant environmental impact. He called for meaningful negotiations with fishing interests on three key matters: the enforcement of a safety exclusion zone around the platforms, compensation for attributable damages to fishing gear, and environmental monitoring activities. On the macro-economic side, Ellis concluded that surplus capacity in the offshore business and labour sectors would prevent any local inflationary effects.

It was at this point that the proponents submitted the final versions of their development and benefits plans to the Board. These plans were described as being "substantially similar" to the preliminary versions.[43] Notable here is the condensed time frame that applied to the multi-track analysis and review. From January to July 1990, the state agencies advising the board in its technical assessments, the consultants advising the commissioner, and the interested public were working with a still-tentative set of plans.

These factors help to capture the real business and political expectations that were part of the CNSOPB's final deliberations. Both senior governments, along with the board itself, were keen to restore some momentum to a moribund offshore play. Less than a month after the partners' final filings, and a mere two weeks after receipt of the commissioner's report, the board announced its conditional approval for the project on 8 August 1990. (The detailed CNSOPB decisions on the COPAN development and benefits plan reports were released the following month.)

From this point, events moved swiftly on the design, construction, and installation fronts. When the 1991 season opened, the first three Panuke development wells were drilled. The steel jacket frames for the two offshore platforms were assembled in Halifax, as were the topside modules. On 1 April, the board issued production licence PL 2901 for Cohasset and PL 2902 for Panuke. By the summer of 1991, the *Rowan Gorilla III* was in port

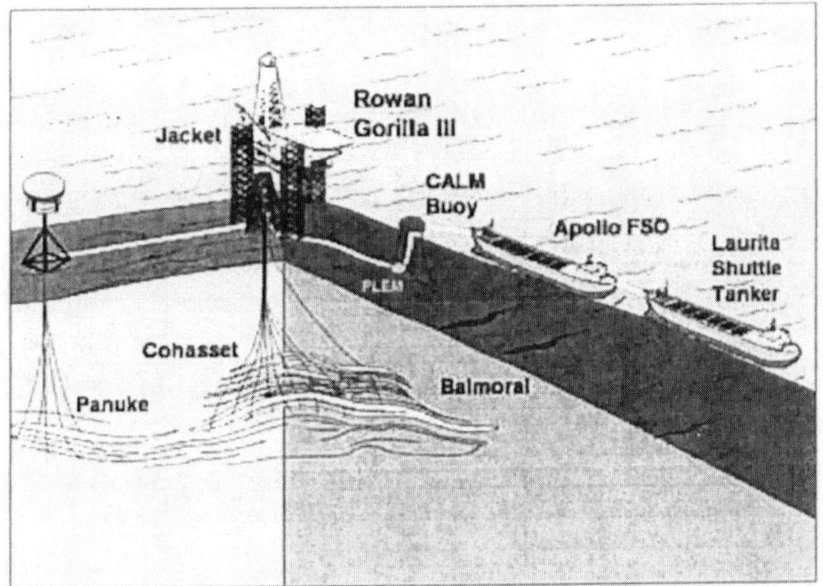

Figure 4.2 Schematic of the Cohasset-Panuke project
Source: CNSOPB, *Application to Amend the Cohasset Development Plan: Decision Report* (Halifax: CNSOPB, 2004), 6.

for modifications for its new role as field platform. In the autumn, the jackets were anchored on their respective sites, the flow lines were laid between the two fields, and the CALM buoy was installed. By November, the *RG III* was onsite at Panuke for additional production well drilling.[44] As previously noted, each significant offshore work activity required step-by-step applications and authorizations at the board. The process culminated in an application for production operations authorizations immediately prior to start-up (targeted for June 1992). The full scale of the COPAN project is presented in Figure 4.2.

A complex relationship links any overall development plan to the particular work authorizations that follow. In the COPAN case, this is highlighted by Lasmo and NSRL's submission of revised comprehensive plans at the end of February 1992. Their submission was prompted partly by geological analysis and partly by financial considerations. The estimate of recoverable oil was raised by one-third to 47.7 million barrels. The revised plans pointed toward additional production wells in both fields and a higher daily production rate of 40,000 barrels per day. The project's lifespan did not change, however, since the plan was switched from seasonal to year-round production. These modifications were also linked to a new sequence of development. The proponents sought permission to drain the fields sequentially rather than simultaneously and to commence production in 1992 at Panuke rather than Cohasset. These changes were prompted at least in part by estimates of escalating capital and operating costs, a continuing theme over the life of the project. By 1992, the capital expenditure had more than doubled to $356 million. The COPAN benefits plan had similar problems. In this case, there were two revisions, one associated with the revised development plan of 1992 (approved within two months) and another submitted in the fall of 1993. By this time, the COPAN project was in its second year of production.

With all field installations in place by May 1992, and the terms of the work authorizations met, the board was ready for Lasmo's request to authorize production operations. The authorization was issued on 3 June 1992, and oil began to flow two days later. During the initial six-and-a-half-month season, which closed in mid-December, 3.6 million barrels of light crude were loaded and shipped. Like most producing projects, COPAN's reservoir depletion strategy evolved almost constantly over its seven-and-a-half-year life. There was the question of how to balance extraction from the two fields and Balmoral, which bordered Cohasset. Oil flowed only from Panuke during the first year, but Cohasset led the way from 1993 to 1996. Panuke was out of action for several years at mid-decade but resumed in 1997. Although it was expected that Cohasset operations would be abandoned that year, they were extended to final oil in December 1999. The challenge of utilizing multiple production wells in each field and the need to drill additional wells as time passed also had to be dealt with. The Rowan rig moved from Cohasset to Panuke in 1997 for this reason. Following a final production peak in 1998, the overall volumes went into terminal decline.

During the life of the COPAN project, the board monitored operations continually, assessing applications for activities ranging from well drilling to reservoir depletion. In 1996, a major structural recertification was done, and the certificate of fitness was reissued. Throughout the active phase, the partners submitted annual benefits reports to the board. When PanCanadian purchased Lasmo Nova Scotia Ltd.'s equity stake in the winter of 1995-96, a board ruling was necessary as well.

In fact, the entry of PanCanadian served to dramatically transform the COPAN licence area in another way. By 1998, it was an active exploration area once again. Between 1996 and 2001, PanCanadian applied for approval of a spate of new wells to drill a play that lay below the Panuke oilfield. Geological interest in the Abenaki carbonate bank dated from the 1970s, when Shell Canada had drilled several wildcats without result.[45] Several geological models later, PanCanadian struck a major gas formation with its PP-3C discovery well. Five additional delineation wells were drilled by 2003, by which time Deep Panuke had been declared a significant commercial discovery, and a development plan was in the hands of state regulators. To date, Deep Panuke continues to be the only Jurassic-aged carbonate discovery in the Scotian Basin.

The final phase of the COPAN story began in December 1999, when the wells were shut permanently. The original COPAN development plan application was required to address decommissioning issues. It specified the field facilities and wells below the seabed that needed to be sealed and dismantled, the platforms and floating equipment (much of it leased) that needed to be moved out, the wellhead jackets to be severed at the foundations, and the subsea flow lines to be retrieved.[46] By granting approval, the board accepted this approach and added only the requirement that Lasmo and NSRL submit an acceptable plan to ensure that sufficient funds were available to carry the plan out.

The abandonment terms of the 1990 development plan serve as a reminder of just how rudimentary disposal practices were at that time. The board referred to slowly emerging practices in the US Gulf of Mexico as an ongoing benchmark and pointed out that specific approvals would need to be given for each phase in any disposal strategy. Tellingly, the board noted that the proponents had not yet indicated whether the wellhead jackets (i.e., the largest fixed structures) would be scrapped on land or at sea. At the time, an industry accustomed to a twenty- to thirty-year field life had not yet confronted the logistics of dismantlement. By the new millennium, all that had changed. In 1995, the North Sea industry was wracked by controversy when Shell and the UK government tried and failed to scuttle the giant Brent Spar storage buoy in deepwater. Broad public protests orchestrated by Greenpeace ensured that decommissioning would henceforth be subject to far more intensive scrutiny. By the early 2000s, only the largest North Sea production platforms (over 10,000 tonnes) could be abandoned *in situ.* (The Cohasset and Panuke jackets weighed 1,900 and 1,600 tonnes, respectively.)

Back in Nova Scotia, the COPAN decommissioning proposal lay dormant during the production life of the fields. It gained new life, however, when the decade ended and the closure question loomed. By then, the field operator, PanCanadian Petroleum, had filed a two-phase decommissioning plan. The first was carried out in 2000 after the cease of production and involved cold-phase operations. The mobile components were removed, the wells were closed in, and the flow lines were flushed and sealed. The board then permitted EnCana Resources (the successor firm to PanCanadian) to suspend the second phase on the grounds that the fixed structures may be reusable in EnCana's planned Deep Panuke development in the same vicinity.[47] The following year, EnCana chose not to use the COPAN structures, and the board requested a phase-two plan. In 2003, the firm began to prepare the platforms for removal. It also applied to the CNSOPB for a significant alteration to the original disposal plan. EnCana argued that "on the basis of safety ... and environmental impact, partial sub-sea removal is the preferred method."[48] It argued that the risks to workers combined with the environmental site disruptions associated with excavating the now sand-buried flow lines exceeded the impacts of leaving the lines in place. EnCana planned to remove all seabed equipment that could cause a snagging hazard to fishers or others.

This application triggered a very different review from that of 1989-90. Because it was now a designated authority under the Canadian Environmental Assessment Act, the board's legal power of approval on EnCana's request triggered a screening-level impact assessment under the act. In the spring of 2004, EnCana submitted its environmental assessment document, and the board responded with its own scoping document. The two scenarios – complete and partial subsea removal – were evaluated together. Ultimately, the board was joined by Environment Canada and Fisheries and Oceans to assess the Phase 2 variance request. The application was circulated to stakeholders, and public input was solicited. The board found that, given the proposed mitigation measures, "neither partial nor total decommissioning proposals is likely to cause significant adverse environmental effects."[49] In this light, the board approved the partial option. Since this was a fundamental decision under the joint management regime, the board's ruling was conveyed to federal and provincial ministers who, in effect, confirmed it.

In 2005, five years after field production had ceased, the Phase 2 seabed work was performed. The following year, a site survey confirmed that the flow lines were buried and no protuberances remained.

What does this tell us? The time separating initial development project approval and Phase 2 decommissioning work was fifteen years, a significant passage of time on the Scotian Shelf. Not only did COPAN field production start and finish, but considerable changes had also occurred in project ownership, decommissioning strategies, legal regimes and, especially, the discipline of environmental regulation. EnCana was both the inheritor of the COPAN legacy obligations and the first corporation to move into Scotian Basin decommissioning. The distance travelled is evident in the contrast between the cursory environmental review process followed by Commissioner Ellis in 1990 and the legislation-governed review process followed by the board in 2004. The outcomes of the Phase 2 variance application can also be viewed as a first step toward the formalization of more elaborate decommissioning procedures. Although it is not the case that developers must be strictly held to end-of-project plans formulated years or even decades earlier, they must justify new practices being imported into the basin.

Conclusion

A close examination of the legal powers and policy levers conferred on offshore regulators reveals a fascinating story of change over time. Long before the CNSOPB came on the scene, Crown authorities were grappling with the challenges of simultaneously promoting and channelling upstream petroleum operations. Over four decades, the range of available offshore administrative measures expanded and evolved. In the early years, the template was drawn from land-based oil and gas exploration with little acknowledgment and few adaptations to the special conditions of the continental shelf. This changed over time.

The driving forces of policy change were episodic rather than continuous, partly for commercial reasons. The urgency accorded to offshore exploration and production varied with market conditions. Only a few firms with offshore experience or ambition were willing to take the risks of early entry in the 1960s and 1970s. Their gamble seemed to pay off when international supply-and-demand conditions pushed prices to heights that were inconceivable before 1973. Indeed, each time global market conditions made the higher-cost thresholds of frontier exploration viable, firms large and small rushed to offshore prospects.

State policy has also ebbed and flowed, but according to a separate calculus. At different times, the imperatives of domestic self-sufficiency, export promotion, price control, frontier Crown lands promotion, enhanced rent collection, maximizing industrial and employment linkages, and protecting workplace safety and environmental security have driven offshore intervention.

By mapping offshore program delivery, this chapter presents the modern joint management regime in a new light. By the time the 1982 oil and gas agreement was signed, the federal administrative template had evolved through several phases, aptly illustrated by the changing legislative base. These changes are evident, for example, in the rights allocation system, which evolved from an industry-driven process into one in which the Crown's preferences could shape where and how exploration took place and who controlled it. Another significant example is schemes for overseeing operational practices. From a rudimentary template borrowed from terrestrial agencies preoccupied with field resource conservation, these practices evolved in a more complex direction by incorporating social and political priorities. A case in point is the rise of the industrial benefits program. Another is more comprehensive engagement with offshore environmental issues.

The 1982 Canada–Nova Scotia agreement reinforced these tendencies, but it also redirected some of them. A different thrust is evident, in setting aside the Crown ownership dispute, reconciling the royalty and revenue tensions, and devising a workable mechanism for dual ministerial responsibility. But as innovative as the 1982 deal was in macropolitical terms, it did not address the challenges of offshore rights or operational administration. In part, this oversight was inevitable. In a petroleum world wracked by upheaval, the agreement was framed to reassure resource capital, to remove political uncertainty, and to reduce political risk factors. The goal was to accelerate offshore exploration and production, not curb it. As a result, the Ottawa regime emerged as the point of reference, and the provincial government acknowledged this reality by enacting mirror legislation. In a sense, the deal was locked in by federal-provincial consent and the creation of a powerful new federal agency – the COGLA – to implement it. Four years later, shifting electoral and federal-provincial fortunes opened a window for review. Negotiations on the 1986 Canada–Nova Scotia accord offered an opportunity to reaffirm or redirect the offshore regime. Once again, negotiations occurred during a time of flux. The Mulroney Conservatives dismantled the National Energy Program during a severe petroleum market slump, and the COGLA was, by then, on the back foot. The administration had less work to do as exploration died and the Venture gas proposal lapsed.

In the hiatus of the late 1980s, the offshore administration was consolidated during the shift to the CNSOPB's bureaucracy. If the early 1990s were a period of orientation and learning, with the COPAN oil project in many ways matching the scale of an embryonic board institution, then the late

1990s were halcyon years. The board's staff doubled in size and was challenged to manage, simultaneously, a producing oilfield, a vastly scaled-up natural gas production proposal, and a sudden exploration rush into a new deepwater subbasin. These challenges coincided with more environmental responsibility and more responsibility in terms of regulating industrial benefits. In sum, it is important to distinguish political form from function. Despite the superficial continuity of intergovernmental accords and enabling legislation, the administrative template of 2000 stood in striking contrast to its 1980 (much less 1970) counterpart.

This chapter demonstrates the extensive range of statutory controls exercised by the board as it regulates offshore petroleum operations, beginning with the package of requirements (licences, plan preparations, and certifications) that must be achieved before commencing any operations and continuing with the more particular activity-based authorities and approvals attached to the respective stages of the development cycle. Significantly, these activities are formalized in law and in bureaucratic rules, both areas of technical speciality that are dominated by professional advisors.

Ultimately, however, decisions are made in the name of the CNSOPB, following deliberations by the appointed members of that body. The question naturally arises, how does politics – the activities of rival groups seeking to extend or defend their interests by securing preferred outputs on questions of government policy – surface in these quarters? This chapter identifies a series of critical processes. In one, government officials work to flesh out their legal mandates by stipulating the criteria and procedures that will guide their deliberations. In another, the officials (staff and board members) deliberate on formal applications by operators seeking to locate and extract commercial product. Some of these matters are comprehensive in scope while others are highly specific. Some sequences are resolved almost as soon as they arise, while others follow multi-year trajectories that last decades or more. Depending upon the context of what went before, some of the decision points seem almost mundane, the perfunctory unfolding of normal procedures as applicants conform to necessary standards. Other decision points are clearly more open-ended and consequential, for they constitute defining moments in the cycle. Offshore politics is far more likely to be revealed at such watersheds, when longer-lasting agendas are set. Notably, these break points are distributed across a period of almost twenty years that began well before commercial production and ended well after its closure.

Theorists of business-government bargaining note that the terms of advantage can shift from one party to the other during the life of a project or deal, a process encapsulated in the term *obsolescing bargain.*[50] In essence, the opening advantage lies with proponents. As the providers of capital taking the risk, they have the prerogative to determine the contours of the proposed enterprise. Should the regulatory strictures be excessively prohibitive, the proponents will withdraw or migrate to a more accommodative jurisdiction. Consequently, it is in the proponent's interest to prolong the negotiations, particularly the moment of irreversible commitment, as long as it is possible to win additional advantage. However, there comes a point in every negotiation when the proponent is inextricably committed to a set of terms. At this point, the model suggests that when a project is effectively locked in, the host state will become less reactive and less dependent. In fact, over time, the state can begin to alter the terms of the bargain, which has in effect become less than sacrosanct. The state can assert sovereign power over regulation and, if necessary, invoke changing conditions as grounds for policy change. The project owner, having sunk significant amounts of capital that is no longer open to flight, becomes a subordinate partner. The CNSOPB has been involved in several obsolescing bargains, and the COPAN case study reveals the mechanisms in fine detail.

5 The Provincial State and the Entrepreneurial Impulse: NSRL

Although the Government of Nova Scotia was a partner in the Canada–Nova Scotia Offshore Petroleum Board (CNSOPB), it also played a role as an autonomous political actor in offshore exploration and production, from its beginnings in the 1960s to today. This chapter reveals a complicated pattern of executive and administrative interplay, shifting political vectors, and policy challenges as provincial politics intersected with offshore capital. After outlining the contours of the provincial state's role in this policy sector, the chapter focuses on an intriguing policy experiment in petroleum entrepreneurship – Nova Scotia Resources Limited (NSRL) – the state enterprise that became the government's chosen instrument for direct business participation in the offshore industries. Established in 1981, the story of NSRL is a telling tale in Scotian Basin politics and fills an essential part of the offshore chronology.

Ultimately, NSRL's history is one of political and policy failure. The ambitions that prompted its creation, at the high-water mark of the global energy boom, were not, in the end, realized. This failure was not for lack of effort or enterprise, however. The company struggled to transcend the political ambivalence that was inscribed in its formative structures. Along the way, it played a significant part in events ranging from National Energy Program frontier exploration and the Cohasset-Panuke oil production project to the Venture and Sable natural gas projects and the Deep Panuke field discoveries. Ironically, today, when the issue of petroleum state equity vehicles is being raised again forcefully in the neighbouring province of Newfoundland, the NSRL story takes on a different meaning. However, to fully understand the role of Nova Scotia Resources Limited, it must be situated within the wider context of the provincial state.

The Nova Scotia State and Its Shifting Capacities

The Nova Scotia provincial state exercises a presence offshore that extends well beyond the joint board's mandate. The province preceded the CNSOPB as a rights-issuing and project-regulating authority, and it continued to exercise a series of important roles throughout the era of the board. Nova Scotia Resources Limited is one such case, but there are others. To provide a fuller understanding of the province's involvement with offshore petroleum, this section surveys its activities in the round.

A striking feature of the provincial state is the continuing evolution of its structures and functions since the 1960s. On reflection, this should not be entirely surprising. This evolution derives in part from the unfulfilled character of the Scotian Shelf as a resource endowment. The shelf has not conclusively demonstrated its long-term commercial value. Consequently, it has not been elevated to a central, much less hegemonic, role in Nova Scotia's political economy. In turn, certain variables are absent: the advocacy of a powerful business bloc; the emergence of a dominant bureaucratic champion; and, perhaps most critically, an acceptance by political executives of offshore petroleum's central structural importance to provincial well-being. This is not to say that there have not been moments of high political commitment; however, by these terms, Scotian Basin petroleum remains an "almost" resource, and the uncertainty has prompted periodic reviews, recalibrations, and reversals.

Each government and premier since 1970 has framed a distinctive view of the resource, the province's interest in it, and the policies required to realize its goals. In the Gerald Regan years (1970-78), the central question was Crown title and the extent of Nova Scotia's claim. During the Conservative era dominated by John Buchanan (1978-90), title was set aside, and the twin accords articulated new priorities for royalty payments and industrial benefits. Liberal John Savage (1993-97) concentrated on galvanizing a long-expected natural gas project from the Sable fields, and his successor, Russell MacLellan (1997-99), shifted attention to pipeline politics, both on the export line to the United States and onshore gas distribution in Nova Scotia. Conservative John Hamm (1999-2006) inherited legacies from several predecessors but made the fiscal question – the "Campaign for Fairness" – his central motif, an approach continued under his successor Rodney MacDonald (2006-9). It remains to be seen what signature themes will emerge for Darrell Dexter's NDP government, elected in June 2009.

Regardless of its political priorities, the provincial government acted through a set of institutions that evolved over time. From the outset, the Premier's Office was central to the equation. Its prominence derived in part from the marquee character of the new energy resource and in part from its offshore location. The provincial premier was destined to take the lead in the formative years, particularly given the fact of intergovernmental rivalry. Moreover, it was Regan and Buchanan who spoke for Nova Scotia at First Ministers' Conferences at which offshore jurisdiction was raised, and it was their names that appeared on the offshore agreements of 1977, 1982, and 1986. Beyond this, individual premiers decided how closely to identify with offshore issues. Buchanan, MacLellan, and Hamm made the fight for principal beneficiary status a major part of their political personalities. Indeed, Buchanan, who led the province through four terms, was so closely involved that he seemed to function as his own petroleum minister.

In performance terms, a continuing tentativeness, manifest in repeated cyclical shifts from expectation to disappointment, has resulted in institutional adjustments among multiple departments and agencies. The bureaucratic locus for offshore petroleum policy has rotated across the decades. In the 1960s, the lead player was the Department of Attorney General, and the Department of Mines played a lesser role. From the beginning of federal-provincial jurisdictional discussions in 1964, constitutional lawyers played a central role in shaping Nova Scotia's position and developing the necessary statutory instruments. The unresolved nature of the negotiations kept the file active, episodically, until the 1986 accord and the 1989 enabling legislation were in place. In terms of offshore operations, exploration firms such as Mobil and Shell dealt with the Petroleum Rights Office within the Department of Mines. It should be noted, however, that petroleum was dwarfed in importance by the coal and industrial mineral sections of the department in the opening phase.

In the late 1970s, as the provincial state aspired to a more coordinated energy perspective, the Department of Mines and Energy assumed a more prominent policy role. The decade was a time of complicated cross-currents – higher oil prices, the continued importance of coal, rising electricity costs, and the catalytic effect of the 1979 Venture gas discovery all demanded attention. The result was a new offshore title and management strategy in 1980, the threat of constitutional litigation if necessary, and a spate of new statutes enacted but not yet proclaimed.

John Buchanan's Conservative governments are not usually regarded as highly technocratic or forward-looking in terms of policy making. However, the first two governments (1978-81 and 1981-84) did focus on offshore petroleum as a developmental fulcrum. Indeed, Buchanan drew heavily on a positive vision of Nova Scotia's oil and gas future in his first re-election campaign. In 1981, the Conservative slogan was "The Future is Now," and the premier asked the electorate to furnish him with a strong majority position from which to negotiate in Ottawa. Once he achieved a majority, Buchanan became an indefatigable cheerleader for the emerging industry. The premier was joined by two of his closest ministerial colleagues, Joel Matheson, minister of finance and (later) mines and energy, and Rollie Thornhill, minister of development. Within the government, the three men became known as the "O-team" since the promise of prosperity from offshore petroleum was so frequently invoked in their public comments.

At the time, Nova Scotia was aggressively staking out its jurisdiction in offshore areas. The Department of Mines and Energy released policy papers defending provincial jurisdiction, asserting its prime beneficiary status, and exploring the possibility of gas pipeline links to central Canadian markets. The Justice Department prepared the terms for a possible judicial challenge to Ottawa, and the Department of Development built networks of prospective business suppliers to offshore companies and focused on devising measures to maximize industrial linkages. Finally, the Nova Scotia Resources Limited was activated in 1981 as an entrepreneurial vehicle for the upstream sector.

Suddenly in the autumn 1981, however, the premier reversed field and launched negotiations with the Government of Canada on a possible bilateral management regime. This policy was confirmed the following March with the announcement of the 1982 Canada–Nova Scotia Agreement on Offshore Oil and Gas Resource Management and Revenue Sharing. The agreement resulted in several follow-on measures for the Scotian Basin. Anxious to vindicate the agreement, Ottawa dispensed generous exploration incentives under the National Energy Program. It also approved a flexible Offshore Development Fund of some $200 million to support provincial infrastructure linked to basin exploitation.[1] There were also important fiscal agreements on the treatment of provincial offshore revenue gains under the national equalization program and industrial benefit review terms linked to exploration and development permits.

The 1982 agreement and the 1986 accord altered the shape of the province's administrative initiative more than it altered the content. The Nova Scotia members of the first CNSOPB were civil service delegates who operated under provincial instructions. The Department of Mines and Energy gave up its direct role in rights administration to the board and its administrative agent, the Canadian Oil and Gas Lands Administration (COGLA). The department did, however, continue to have jurisdiction over land-based petroleum deposits. For its part, the Department of Development retained a prominent role in the definition and application of benefits policy, in concert with the COGLA.

Between 1985 and 1990, the Sable Basin went cold and with it, offshore politics. Interest in exploration slumped after the Mulroney government phased out frontier-drilling incentives. The world oil price slid precipitously in 1986, and the Venture gas project was frozen. The O-team was silent on the offshore bonanza to come. Even more remarkably, Buchanan intervened personally in 1987 to impose a ten-year moratorium on drilling on existing leases in the Georges Bank Subbasin.[2] His actions were in response to a movement to defend the fishery in western Nova Scotia that had sprung up in response to Texaco Canada's plan for two exploratory wells. In the process, the premier reversed Matheson's earlier support for Texaco. Thus, offshore petroleum played a far different role for Buchanan during the 1988 election than it had in 1981. In less than three years, Buchanan would retire and be appointed to the Senate of Canada.

The next bureaucratic realignment in the Government of Nova Scotia came in the autumn of 1991, when the Departments of Mines and Energy and Lands and Forests were merged to create a new Department of Natural Resources. In effect, the mineral and petroleum responsibilities of the former were added as a new branch to the Crown land and forest responsibilities of the latter. The CNSOPB reported to the minister of natural resources, and the petroleum section provided policy advice to the minister.

In comparative terms, the early 1990s were lean years for the Scotian Basin. The Cohasset-Panuke project began operations in 1992, but exploration had entirely dried up. It was not until mid-decade that the Sable gas partners revived an interest in developing their commercial finds. In response, the Liberal government of John Savage upgraded the Oil and Gas Office (symbolically at least) to the Petroleum Development Agency.

Although it was now headed by a chief operating officer rather than a branch director, the agency still functioned as one of four branches within the Department of Natural Resources and reported to the deputy-minister.[3] However, its mandate now emphasized the coordination of provincial measures to increase offshore activity, with particular attention to be paid to the emerging Sable offshore energy project and connecting pipelines. One of the agency's defining contributions, developed in concert with the Department of Finance, was the Sable offshore energy project royalty deal of May 1996, which was pivotal in opening the way for corporate approval. The agency also assumed responsibility in 1997 for the in-province gas distribution strategy.

Late that same year, the agency was renamed the Nova Scotia Petroleum Directorate. This time, it was lifted out of the Department of Natural Resources to function as a separate agency that would report to Premier Russell MacLellan and serve as the "government's focal point in the development of the province's oil and gas resources."[4] Responsibilities were allocated among four divisions: pipelines and gas distribution, royalties and resource assessment, benefits and training, and communications and policy.

With the arrival of the Hamm Conservative government in the summer of 1999, the Nova Scotia Petroleum Directorate was realigned with the economic development portfolio. The new cabinet's priorities reflected the changing policy context. With Sable gas production under way and a projected twenty-year lifespan, the first priority was to secure the province's royalty flow against equalization clawbacks. Premier Hamm spent much of the next six years pressing Ottawa for fair fiscal treatment, a campaign in which he relied heavily upon the Department of Finance for technical support. Another hallmark measure was the energy policy strategy review of 2000-2. The review looked beyond petroleum, even though offshore prospects (and the new deepwater exploration boom) remained central points of reference. Part of the outcome was the consolidation of the directorate and the residual petroleum elements of the Department of Natural Resources into a new Department of Energy in June 2002.

Although the new department's constituent parts were almost all prior parts of the provincial state, there was a new emphasis on coordination. Many of the new issues could not be contained within the traditional administrative silos. The question of the distribution of provincial gas spilled over into municipal taxation and even highway maintenance programs. The Cape Breton offshore licensing dispute recalled the Georges Bank moratorium campaign and involved a plethora of terrestrial interests. The Nova

Scotia–Newfoundland boundary arbitration (on the eastern end of the Scotian Shelf) required the province to marshal evidence and arguments from all corners of its experience with offshore petroleum. Finally, the offshore regulatory review initiative required sustained deliberations with federal and industry actors, and the Department of Energy served as the lead provincial voice.

When John Hamm stepped down in 2006, he left his successor, Rodney MacDonald, with something of a poisoned chalice. The campaign for fairness had not been resolved, and Scotian Shelf exploration was once again becalmed. In addition, the Sable energy producer had seriously shortened its reserve estimates and project life. Overall, the industry had become risk averse, and the basin had been downgraded in comparative terms. However, the Department of Energy began to demonstrate some intriguing policy responses.

Over the next three years, the department formulated a renewal plan of some originality. First, the cabinet allocated more than $5 million from offshore licence forfeits to two new associations for technological and environmental research and to consultant studies on the competitive status of the basin and options for its promotion. Ultimately, this research fed into the October 2008 Offshore Renewal Plan. In geoscience, new models of hydrocarbon sources would be developed using "play fairway analysis" techniques. In policy, a number of modest but collectively significant adjustments were launched that involved common access infrastructure, easier data dissemination, and exploration licensing incentives. Under regulation, a number of symbolically friendly measures were announced that favoured the expansion of performance-based and flexible goal-oriented legal rules.[5] Although none of these measures constituted game-changing strokes, they were in direct contrast to the passive resignation with which some offshore authorities greet the slowdown in exploration and production.

Although more limited in scope, the mandates of other ministries were also integral to Nova Scotia's offshore petroleum profile. The department charged with industrial development gained leverage through the promotion of offshore-onshore business linkages (see Chapter 7). The agreements of the 1980s mandated the regulation of industrial benefits, by which firms with exploration and production licences were expected to source capital and operational acquisitions within the province and region to a maximal extent. To assist offshore exploration and production firms, the provincial Department of Development, as it was known in the Buchanan years, published an annual directory of resident businesses that were available for offshore tendering. The department worked closely with the COGLA and later with the Benefits Section of the CNSOPB to promote and monitor procurement performance.

The Department of Finance was another bureaucratic player. As Chapter 8 explains, questions of offshore royalty payments were central to Nova Scotia's budgetary position. Furthermore, once oil and natural gas began to flow, a complex dispute emerged over the interplay between offshore royalties and federal-provincial equalization payments. These highly technical but politically consequential matters were an ongoing brief for the Finance Department and were finally settled by Premier MacDonald's 2006 fiscal accord with Ottawa.

The Department of Environment and Labour also formed part of Nova Scotia's offshore state. Of the several provincial statutes and mandates that were extended from land to sea in the 1980s, none was more significant than regulation of the environment. The environment section of the CNSOPB largely handled exploration activities such as seismic surveying and drilling. However, the building of offshore structures, whether fixed production platforms or pipelines, was another matter, for provincial statutes came into play. As a result, the Department of Environment and Labour has had a direct role in the scrutiny of production proposals for the Cohasset-Panuke oil field, the Venture gas field, the Sable project, and the Deep Panuke gas project.

The provincial utility regulator is a final agency of note. Long known as the Public Utilities Board, its mandate was expanded in 1997 to include onshore oil and gas pipelines and the licensing of intra-provincial natural gas distribution systems. Since then, it has been known as the Utilities and Review Board (UARB). The utilities board, whose traditional mandate involved the electric power sector, was brought into onshore pipeline regulation by the terms of the 1980 Gas Utilities Act. However, it was not until the construction of the Sable offshore energy project that the utilities board was obliged to exercise positive powers. As an arms-length board, it was expected to adjudicate licence applications in a non-partisan manner. However, as Chapter 9 reveals, the board also functioned within detailed policy directives issued by the broader government through cabinet.

It is evident that the provincial state's responses to offshore petroleum concerns can be tracked in different ways. The discussion in this chapter is organized according to the range of organizational players and by landmark policy interventions. The account of the organizational players reveals that the administrative lead shifted over time. The analysis of landmark interventions brings to light a series of policy agendas, including the 1977 memorandum of understanding, the 1980 offshore vision, the 1982 and 1986 agreements, the 1996 Sable royalty regime, the 2001 Energy Strategy, the 2006 fiscal accord, and the 2008 Offshore Renewal Plan. After an initial phase of provincially driven action, the 1982 agreement split offshore petroleum into two political domains – the upstream offshore licensing domain and the residual petroleum operations sector. As the latter became progressively more significant, the opportunities for provincial policy leadership expanded. Provincial assertiveness was due to the growing differentiation of basin cycle demands as well as the state's changing orientation to development over four decades. A final complication was that the province's priorities increasingly failed to mesh with those of Ottawa after 1985. The federal government, managing a continental energy supply system, did not share the sense of developmental urgency that Nova Scotia held for its offshore basin.

The provincial state for offshore governance was a complex ensemble. It was into this configuration that Nova Scotia Resources Limited was inserted in 1981. Its story, which spans the intermediate decades of offshore petroleum activity, offers revealing insights into the limits of provincial policy ambition and political will.

State Enterprise and State Capacities

One of the new policy instruments to emerge in the wake of the first OPEC oil boom was the state-owned petroleum company. In the developing world, the state firm had a particular profile: it had assets acquired by nationalization, it often enjoyed a monopoly or near-monopoly, it was closely aligned with the state petroleum bureaucracy and the ruling elite, and it generated massive surpluses almost immediately. By contrast, the oil-endowed OECD nations (such as Norway, the United Kingdom, Canada, and the United States) tended to stand apart from OPEC. The state petro-corporation became a common fixture in many of these nations, and while it invariably enjoyed certain politically defined advantages, it operated in a competitive market environment. As a result, the world of state oil included not only PetroMexico and the Nigerian National Oil Company but also Norway's Statoil and the British National Oil Company.

Each of these instruments had its institutional particularities, often rooted in the policy traditions and industry structures of the host state. Canada followed the trend, but it developed a surprising array of state enterprises at both the national and provincial levels. The best known is Petro-Canada, which was established in 1973 to open a window on the upstream exploration and production industry but was later restructured by takeovers into an integrated oil and gas major. The petroleum-producing provinces followed suit the same year. Conservative premier Peter Lougheed established the Alberta Energy Company, New Democrat Allan Blakeney founded SaskOil, and New Democrat Dave Barrett created the BC Petroleum Company. The oil-consuming provinces were not excluded either. Quebec was the first jurisdiction to directly enter the industry in 1970 with the Société québécoise d'initiatives pétrolières (Soquip). In Ontario, Conservative Bill Davis established his province's presence in the industry through the creation of Ontario Energy Corporation in 1975. Newfoundland's Brian Peckford announced the Newfoundland and Labrador Petroleum Corporation as part of his comprehensive 1977 offshore energy development plan.

Clearly, the state-owned petro-corporation was an idea whose time came in the 1970s. However, these institutions had diverse circumstances, mandates, and forms.[6] Ottawa's initial plan for Petro-Canada was to catalyze frontier exploration and provide a window on the industry. Alberta Energy Company was a vehicle for petroleum diversification, while the BC Petroleum Company was principally a marketing instrument and rent collector for provincial Crown gas. Saskoil was charged with integrated operations, as was the revamped (post-1976) Petro-Canada. Ontario Energy Corporation combined "window" and "rent-collecting" roles, while Soquip focused on exploration in the Gulf of St. Lawrence and the Newfoundland and Labrador Petroleum Corporation focused on the East Coast. Some of these vehicles were classic Crown corporations (Petro-Canada, Soquip, SaskOil, BC Petroleum Company, and the Newfoundland and Labrador Petroleum Corporation), while others were mixed, public-private equity ventures (Alberta Energy Company and the Ontario Energy Corporation).

It was into this world of state petroleum ventures that Nova Scotia stepped in 1979, when the newly elected Conservative premier John Buchanan authorized the creation of Nova Scotia Resources Limited. Set up under the provincial Business Corporations Act, NSRL was initially a shell company with three issued shares. The firm began with none of the political or legal fanfare that was common to the practice. In fact, it is doubtful whether the provincial political class, much less the public, was widely aware of the company in its early years. Ambivalence was an accurate reflection of the prevailing policy culture of the Buchanan era, which was derivative rather than original in impulse, closed rather than open in policy development. It is not for nothing that the years between 1978 and 1990 are so closely associated with the politics of patronage and clientelism. Indeed, Buchanan was renowned for perfecting the art of the issueless election and for refusing to debate public affairs during campaigns. Instead, he chose to wrap himself in the tartan and promote an avuncular, "down home" political personality.[7]

In recent decades, a prolonged debate in policy science has centred on the role of states in societies and explored many interesting themes, including the prospects for state autonomy in the face of capital, resistance by labour or interest groups, the continuum from "strong" to "weak" states in the management of market societies, and the changing role of the modern state in the face of globalizing economic and cultural pressures. In early studies, states were frequently grasped in aggregate – as coherent institutional wholes directed by political elites. Later, however, states were disaggregated – by policy area and institutional sub-unit – to grasp striking variations in decision making and power at intermediate levels. On this plane, intervening variables such as bureaucratic organization, knowledge epistemes, network relations, and even political ideology come into play.

The theoretical questions of state autonomy, strengths, and weaknesses are all relevant to the Nova Scotia case. Over its two decades of existence, NSRL was both an instrument and a measure of political purpose. On the one hand, NSRL is a familiar Canadian policy tool – a state-owned petroleum enterprise; on the other hand, it is also a particular instance of this type. Nova Scotia Resources Limited was created by a small provincial state that lacked a history of oil and gas exploitation but was acting in response to an exploration boom on the adjacent continental shelf and the prospect of Maritime regional development. The company operated within a wider complex of petroleum (and energy) policy measures, which both facilitated and constrained its performance. In addition, the overarching commercial and political coordinates shifted significantly over the three decades. Since the company's lifespan coincided with the intensification of globalizing forces, it offers an intriguing case study.

In this exploration of NSRL, the term *state capacity* refers simply to the ability to get things done. In a classic definition, Skocpol describes capacity as "the ability of a state to implement official goals, especially over the actual or potential opposition of powerful groups, or in the face of recalcitrant socio-economic circumstances."[8] This definition highlights several key attributes: the definition of goals, the mobilization to fulfill them, encounters with resistance, and the eventual attainment of preferred outcomes.

Capacities, however, are far from being homogeneous or standardized units that can be easily measured Rather, they are varied, nuanced, situationally grounded, and process-related. It is useful to think of each state actor as an embodiment of multiple attributes that, when combined and in interplay with the broader environment, determine the parameters of an agency's achievement. John Ikenberry points to a series of relevant considerations, including internal state structure and leadership, levels of expertise located inside and outside the state, access to key resources (both legal and fiscal), the ability to capture wider political forces through alliance and coalition, and nimbleness in reconfiguring policy mandates in response to changing opportunity structures.[9]

Offshore Diplomacy, 1978-83

The origins of NSRL cannot be understood apart from the province's broader approach to offshore petroleum during Buchanan's first five years in office. Politically, *offshore* is a flexible and diffuse adjective. It can be used in reference to a marine environment, a sub-ground mineral treasure house, a potential economic-growth pole, an ambiguous constitutional jurisdiction, or a part of the Bluenose heritage stretching back to the eighteenth century. All of these domains figure, in varying configurations, in contemporary politics.

One of the first major decisions of the Buchanan government was to repudiate the 1977 Maritime Provinces Offshore Mineral Resources Agreement. By its terms, Ottawa and the three Maritime provinces had agreed to set aside ownership claims and manage offshore minerals through a joint board. The federal government would receive 25 percent of revenues and the province the remainder.[10] Newfoundland was highly critical of this arrangement, and Premier Brian Peckford aggressively asserted full provincial ownership over its continental shelf lands. In eastern Canada, the most promising petroleum-bearing lands were on the Scotian Shelf and the Grand Banks, areas that had attracted considerable attention after 1966.

Although more than 125 holes were drilled, the first decade of offshore exploration had not brought dramatic commercial discoveries to Atlantic Canada.[11] All of this changed in May 1979, when Mobil Canada announced major natural gas flows at three levels of its Venture D-23 well. The discovery brought new momentum to the Sable Island area that carried over for years to come. Three months later, Mobil reported a second major discovery on Newfoundland's Grand Banks, with the discovery of crude oil at Hibernia. In September, Joe Clark's federal Conservative government confirmed its intention to allocate full offshore jurisdiction to the Atlantic provinces. Thus, by the close of Buchanan's first year in office, the coordinates of a new petroleum strategy were in place.

Unlike Newfoundland, whose legislative and management structures were largely settled, Nova Scotia was caught almost completely unprepared. The Government of Nova Scotia sponsored a seminar early in 1980. Four hundred business, labour, and government representatives received a primer from fourteen keynote experts on "the opportunities and the challenge" of offshore petroleum. The jurisdictional vacuum was acknowledged, and the need for a provincial regulatory regime, a central planning agency, business contracting, and labour-training measures were underscored.[12]

Within six months, the Nova Scotia legislature had enacted a package of four statutes to fill the void. Modelled closely on developments in Newfoundland, the package's centrepiece was the Petroleum Resources Act.[13] Asserting Nova Scotia ownership, the act covered exploration and production licensing, royalties, and provincial participation terms for business contracting and employment. Other bills covered the regulation of oil and gas production, the licensing of pipelines, and the regulation of gas utility pricing.[14] Armed with these legal provisions, Halifax went on the political offensive.

The defeat of the Clark Conservatives brought an end to Ottawa's offer of full provincial jurisdiction over offshore minerals. Indeed, Pierre Trudeau's return to power in February 1980 reset the parameters of diplomacy. The Buchanan government was forced to turn advocate once again. In July, the Government of Nova Scotia put its case to the public in the discussion paper *Offshore Oil and Gas: A Chance for Nova Scotians*. No doubt anticipating future court challenges, the Buchanan government set out an aggressive legal case for provincial control, dismissing the Supreme Court of Canada's reference case on BC's offshore area on the grounds that the pre-Confederation circumstances of the two regions had been different. The provincial government offered two possible avenues of settlement: formal constitutional amendment to confer offshore jurisdiction or the extension of provincial boundaries to encompass the continental shelf.[15]

Despite clear differences on the question of Crown ownership, the federal Liberal energy policy was not entirely antagonistic to East Coast interests. The October 1980 National Energy Program, with its goals of energy self-sufficiency and frontier supplies, brought the richest set of fiscal incentives in history. Firms with high levels of Canadian ownership qualified for Petroleum Incentive Program grants of up to 80 percent of approved offshore exploration costs.[16] These grants, coupled with record-high crude oil prices of $40 a barrel and beyond, accelerated the second East Coast drilling boom that had begun with the Venture and Hibernia discoveries in 1979. To confirm Halifax's role as an incipient energy centre, the first Canadian Offshore Resource Exposition (CORE) took place in October 1981. It soon became an annual fixture.

Buchanan was quick to sense the partisan potential of these developments. Only three years into his first term, the premier called a snap election. One of the few themes of the Conservative campaign was the need for a popular mandate to prevail over Ottawa and protect the offshore bonanza for Nova Scotians. This rhetoric, which Brian O'Neill aptly describes as the "Sable Elixir," was used repeatedly by Tory ministers in these years.[17] Armed with a modestly expanded legislative majority, Buchanan took his case to Ottawa in November 1981.

The contrast between Buchanan's pragmatism and Peckford's purism was fully evident. Once it became clear in the wider constitutional discussions that sole provincial offshore jurisdiction was not negotiable, the two province's strategies diverged. Recognizing a confluence of opportunities, Buchanan chose to cut a deal with Ottawa. The energy industry warned that jurisdictional clarity was a prerequisite for commercial development and that Sable was approaching threshold commercial volumes. Ottawa was anxious for a frontier exploration success story to legitimize the National Energy Program. In addition, there was concern within the Government of Nova Scotia that Halifax trump St. John's as the East Coast energy metropole. With the Petroleum Resources Act (still not proclaimed) in his back pocket for leverage, Buchanan entered negotiations with the federal energy minister, Marc Lalonde. The result, was the Canada–Nova Scotia Agreement on Offshore Oil and Gas Resource Management and Revenue Sharing, which was signed on 2 March 1982. At St. John's, Peckford took a different tack, preparing to send a reference case to the provincial Supreme Court to test Newfoundland's offshore jurisdiction. This initiated a three-year period of litigation between Newfoundland and Canada. The court found against the province, and the case was followed by a reference to the Supreme Court of Canada, which ended in a similar result.[18]

In the short term, Buchanan's ploy worked perfectly. Eased by the Petroleum Incentive Program and the 1982 agreement's industrial benefits regime, offshore exploration surged on the Scotian Shelf, while onshore fabrication and servicing businesses thrived in Halifax Harbour. Anxious to realize the National Energy Program's goals on frontier lands, Lalonde joined Premier Buchanan in August 1982 to announce the first in a series of new exploration agreements for the shelf. Petro-Canada took a lead role, along with Bow Valley Industries and Husky Oil. Soon, a dozen wells were on the drawing board, and the drill seasons of 1982 and 1983 saw new Canadian-made platforms join those leased from interests in the Gulf of Mexico and the North Sea.

Enter Nova Scotia Resources Limited

Nova Scotia Resources Limited was activated in 1981 when its three authorized shares were transferred to the Government of Nova Scotia. An Order-in-Council of 26 May 1981 conferred Crown corporation status on the firm. The cabinet approved a mandate "to propose, negotiate and manage investment by the province of Nova Scotia in mineral, petroleum and energy resource and related projects, usually in partnership with the private sector."[19] A number of reporting channels were established between company and government: the company was required to issue an annual report, the government would be the guarantor of corporate borrowings, the company would submit annual operational budgets and board of directors' minutes to the minister of mines and energy (later natural resources), and there would be an independent audit of annual financial statements.[20]

The company clearly had a diversified mandate, one that extended to different resources and projects. As a conduit for public investment, NSRL was expected to play a strategic role, but to what end: rent collection through business operating profits? window on the industry through exploration farm-ins? leverage over project design through joint venturing? The absence of an enabling statute, and the legislative debate and public scrutiny that would accompany it, proved politically costly to NSRL. Such questions were left unresolved because of the closed character of the policy process and the absence of inaugural publicity. The premier avoided discussing specifics, claiming that "we incorporated NSRL so that when we were ready to implement our policies in energy development and mineral development in this province, we would have the vehicle ready to protect and look after the interests of the people of Nova Scotia, using that corporation as a vehicle."[21] The consequence was to vest extraordinary discretion in the officers (directors and management) of the firm.

On 12 June 1981, the government named Peter Outhit, a Halifax lawyer, president and CEO. It was left to Outhit to expand upon the company's role. In November he assured the Truro Rotary Club that NSRL would not be a political tool.[22] This charge had been provoked in part by the appointment of several well-known Tory lawyers to the board, including Buchanan's principal secretary. The following summer, Outhit told an audience of German investors, "We intend to be present in every link in the chain of production through to the market. Those links include the pipeline, gas processing and liquids extraction facilities, liquids storage and probably the petrochemical complex based on either the dry gas or the abundant natural gas liquids from the Sable area."[23] Yet, despite such apparent ambitions, NSRL's corporate footprint was always modest. The staff complement seldom exceeded a half-dozen people, and technical and commercial services were brought in on contract as required. The board of directors tended to fluctuate between eight and ten members and was closely linked to the public service. In 1982-83, it consisted of four provincial civil servants at the deputy-minister level, along with Outhit and three outside business representatives. This pattern persisted, even as the personnel changed, until 1994, when a fully private-sector board was appointed.

For the 1981-82 fiscal year, the provincial government provided working capital up to $525,000. It was the only direct infusion of public funds from the province over the life of the firm, a fact that had multiple consequences for NSRL's bottom line. The company had four potential sources of working capital: it could be seeded by transfers from the shareholder provincial government, it could borrow on the commercial debt market, it could capitalize on direct incentive grants for exploration on Canada Lands, or it could earn revenue from production activities. Cut off from the first source by Buchanan's policy, NSRL's strategic direction was determined by the need to pursue alternative forms of working capital.

In corporate scale, NSRL resembled a small junior exploration company, of which Calgary hosted several hundred. Even so, the initial $525,000 did little more than cover the initial salaries of the core staff. Consequently, NSRL borrowed the capital required to negotiate a way into new exploration projects. Known in the industry as farm-ins, these deals allow companies lacking land rights to finance drilling operations on lands under licence to others, thereby earning a share of any future product (and revenue) from the property. As a 100 percent Canadian-owned company, NSRL was a potentially valued partner to offshore rights holders during the National Energy Program era because the level of exploration incentive grants rose in proportion to the overall level of Canadian ownership. Nevertheless, the scale of these drilling projects imposed major capital demands on participants. At approximately $350,000 per day, an offshore rig could cost $50 million to drill a well to full depth, test, and cap it. Yet the combination of Petroleum Incentive Program and tax incentives could reduce the real cost to an 80 percent Canadian-owned company to $3.5 million.[24]

Corporate goodwill was also an intangible but no less real consideration. Certainly, there was no harm in involving the state firm in exploration syndicates that may return to the joint regulator in future years for approval of development schemes.

Finally, NSRL was presented with investment opportunities because of the "Crown share" provisions of the National Energy Program, the 1982 Canada–Nova Scotia agreement, and Ottawa's 1981 Canada Oil and Gas Act. The Crown share enabled the federal Crown to assume a 25 percent interest in any project that was converted into the production phase. The policy also enabled the provincial Crown to exercise an option on half of the federal Crown share. In 1983, NSRL openly speculated that its stake in the Venture gas group could rise to 18.25 percent.[25] A parallel and equally significant provision covered pipeline or other transport conveyance systems established to bring oil or gas onshore. The provincial Crown could take up to a 50 percent position in any transport company, an option that NSRL exercised in May 1983 when it co-founded Sable Gas Systems Ltd. as a fifty-fifty partnership with TransCanada Pipelines Ltd.[26] (This project faded along with Venture gas in 1987.)

Shelf Exploration and the Petroleum Incentive Program

For Nova Scotia's offshore area, the National Energy Program triggered a renewed and intensified wave of exploration activities. The so-called first round of Scotian Shelf exploration began in 1967, when the initial hole was drilled on Sable Island. Over the following dozen years, seventy-one wells were drilled on the shelf (accounting for 53 percent of all East Coast holes over this time).[27] The late 1970s, however, saw a sharp decline in the number of wells spudded. However, the frontier lands priorities of the National Energy Program, together with the lucrative new incentive grants, brought revived industry interest to the Nova Scotia region. When the second round of exploration was launched in 1981, NSRL was an eager participant.

During the duration of the Petroleum Incentive Program (PIP) (1981-86), NSRL borrowed, invested in farm-ins, and recouped a significant share of total exploration expenses via the grants. The parent firm established a subsidiary, Nova Scotia Resources (Ventures) Limited, to undertake these operations and to serve as its PIP recipient. The first significant business opportunities arose only days after the signing of the 1982 agreement. Premier Buchanan announced the program, which was a joint venture with Hudson's Bay Oil and Gas and Inco Energy Resources. This farm-in, acquired at no cost to NSRL, covered a 20 percent interest in 593,000 acres of exploration rights in the east Sable area, 32 kilometres northeast of the Venture discovery wells.[28]

Nova Scotia Resources (Ventures) Limited was one of the first Crown corporations to establish a 100 percent Canadian ownership rating under Ottawa's National Energy Program.[29] As such, it was a useful potential partner in drill programs that aimed for the highest (80 percent) level of PIP support.

At the same time, NSRL won the provincial government's backing for a $52-million loan, which was used in April 1982 to purchase a 10 percent working interest in 1.12 million acres of exploration rights held by the British Columbia Resources Investment Corporation. As it turned out, it was the most important transaction in the company's history. At the time, however, the deal was debated in surprisingly partisan terms. Two weeks before the closing of the loan – when it became evident that the minister of mines and energy, Ron Barkhouse, did not know the identity of the lender – the Opposition complained about the apparently loose nature of provincial government oversight.[30] Outhit argued forcefully for NSRL's role as the province's "window on the industry." As he put it, "by becoming part of the risk-taking, you learn the business, gain the technical knowledge and also help influence decisions in a manner that places more benefits in Nova Scotia."[31]

No doubt Outhit had the Venture gas project in mind. The company's 10 percent share of Mobil's permit area around Sable Island carried over to all gas discovered on those lands. This share quickly became the centrepiece of NSRL's holdings and the most likely avenue for company growth and profit. Indeed, the rise and fall of the Venture project's fortunes was a dominant motif of the company's story in the 1980s.

The pages of NSRL's annual reports detail its many exploration partnerships of the 1981-86 period. Overall, the industry drilled thirty-three wells on the shelf, three-quarters of which pushed to depths below 5,000 metres. Nova Scotia Resources Limited was involved in twenty-four of these holes, and an impressive two-thirds of them contained hydrocarbons. By 1987, the company could respond to skeptics with tangible results. It owned 6.3 percent of the total Sable gas reserves, along with 25 to 40 percent of the Cohasset-Panuke oil reserves.

Planning for Production: The Venture Gas Project

During its initial operating era, the NSRL's most significant earning opportunity was the commercial exploitation of Sable Island gas. As mentioned,

NSRL gained a 10 percent share of gas reserves by purchasing an interest in Mobil Oil Canada's Sable exploration permit in 1982. At least three separate fields had been confirmed by this time, and three more would be found in subsequent years. In the 1982 drill season, NSRL participated in a series of delineation wells that extended the size of the reservoirs and advanced the proven reserve estimates toward commercial thresholds. The most prominent of these, the Venture field, lent its name to the broader commercial project. By 1983, the Venture gas project's partnership agreement had been finalized, and predevelopment work was under way.

The dimensions of this plan were ambitious. Decisions had to be made about the sequence of offshore field developments, the underwater gathering systems and pipeline routings, and the configurations of platform facilities. Onshore, partners had to determine the landing point, gas-processing and separation facilities, and pipelines for dry gas and for natural gas liquids. Since the lion's share of the product was intended for export to the United States, interprovincial and international export licences and tariff approvals were involved. On the US side, gas import and pipeline certificates were also needed.

The terms of the Mobil Oil exploration agreement required the Venture development plan to be submitted by January 1984. The plan anticipated that engineering and design work would be finalized over the next several years. Project planning would parallel the multidimensional regulatory proceedings to assess environmental impact, socio-economic impact, and natural gas export and import. The initial timeline estimated that regulatory decisions would be complete by 1987, construction would follow during the next two years, and production would commence in 1989. At that point, NSRL would realize its first long-term business revenue.

The story of the Venture project is a fascinating case in its own right, but its interface with NSRL is of special interest. In 1983, even before the Venture plan was filed, the company struck a fifty-fifty partnership agreement with TransCanada Pipelines Ltd. to form Sable Gas Systems Ltd. It proposed to build the offshore pipeline from the Sable area wells to Guysborough County. That same year, federal and provincial authorities struck a joint environmental assessment panel (under the authority of the 1982 agreement) to set guidelines for the anticipated Venture project public review.[32] Perhaps inevitably, the initial project timetable proved overly optimistic, and slippage was apparent by 1984. A North American gas supply bubble complicated the New England gas purchase negotiations; over a year elapsed before contracts were finalized. For its part, NSRL agreed to supply

85 million cubic feet (2.4 million cubic metres) per day over twenty years to the New England Supply Corporation and a much smaller portion to Canada's Maritime markets.[33] Once the tentative long-term export sales contracts were agreed upon with US clients, the partner companies filed concurrent export applications with the National Energy Board in July 1985. This action was followed by the sharp global oil slump of early 1986. By year's end, the Venture project was effectively becalmed. The 1986-87 annual report noted, in restrained language, that "most new pre-development work ... was deferred pending price recovery."[34] As it turned out, the Sable area development was not revived until the mid-1990s – under new sponsors.

Crisis and Corporate Strategy, 1985-86

The Venture gas project was only one aspect of NSRL's business that was overtaken by the economic and political changes of the mid-1980s. The company's first six years had been framed by a business strategy based on five objectives: owning an interest in every significant discovery, being accepted by industry as a valuable partner, initiating desirable resource investments, acquiring key technical information, and developing its own operating expertise.[35] As indicated, these aspirations were largely met on a provisional basis. However, the underpinnings of the strategy were eroding rapidly by 1986.

This began with the unwinding of the National Energy Program following the election of Mulroney's Conservatives. Their comprehensive reworking of energy programs was designed, in close consultation with the Calgary oil sector, in 1985. It included new pricing agreements with producing provinces, a jurisdictional settlement with Newfoundland (which rebounded to Nova Scotia), and a shift from grant to tax incentives for future exploration. As far as the East Coast frontier was concerned, key legislative changes were contained in the Canada Petroleum Resources Act (1986), which included a new competitive bidding system for exploration rights, a new licensing regime to convert exploration discoveries to production licences, the elimination of the 25 percent Crown share provision at the production level, an exploration tax credit to replace PIP grants, and a new royalty scheme that reduced these payments in the early (cost-recovery) years of production. Overall, the turn toward market instruments in rights issuance and land management "served to make the resource management regimes on the east coast much more similar to those in the western provinces."[36]

Another significant shift involved petroleum economics. During the first quarter of 1986, global oil prices plummeted by 60 percent to an average of $15 a barrel. The price decrease was caused by the OPEC decision to recover its declining market share by lowering posted prices. The effect was to undercut the commercial viability of all high-cost production facilities and prospective fields. Not surprisingly, the major East Coast exploration firms scaled back their offshore commitments, postponing or cancelling drill plans as part of parent company budget constraints. Most firms chose to restrict spending to the minimal level necessary to maintain permits in good standing.

Phase 2: From Explorer to Operator

The compound effect of such radical policy and price shifts was to undercut NSRL in the very flush of its initial success. The termination of the National Energy Program and the accompanying redesign of the exploration regime on East Coast lands prompted NSRL to rethink its underlying strategy in 1986. Despite participation in more than a dozen wells the previous year, commercial finds were slower to materialize and, more critically, the sudden retrenchment in exploration spending could only lengthen this hiatus. Nor was there an early prospect of commercial production. With declining prices and an oversupply of natural gas (together with the slower than expected confirmation of threshold reserves), the Venture consortium suspended its regulatory applications as the year progressed. The suspension represented a significant blow to NSRL's initial strategy because the original timeline had anticipated that Venture gas would begin to flow in 1989. The contrast between the annual reports of 1985-86 and 1986-87 tells the tale. Whereas the former notes ongoing preparatory work on the Venture project (export applications had been filed with the National Energy Board in 1985), the latter confirms the deferral of Venture work and the continuing flat exploration profile.

Recognizing that Venture production prospects were fading into the distance, NSRL's board approved a new business strategy in 1987 that called for stimulating and achieving early offshore production, securing the early drilling of key oil and gas structures, diversifying cash flows, and retiring all corporate borrowings within a reasonable time frame[37]

The realization of early oil production from the Cohasset and Panuke fields was central to this plan. The two fields became the company's new commercial centrepiece, though on a far lesser scale than Venture gas.

However, the business logic of a bridging project was similar. Offshore oil would provide NSRL with operating revenue that could be sheltered by exploration spending. It could also generate prospective equity for NSRL's stake in Venture gas, when it was eventually revived. The longer-term Venture project would then earn the funds needed to pay down NSRL's mounting debt. In the interim, NSRL planned a number of tactical measures to bolster its balance sheet.

The second wave of exploration on the Scotian Shelf was in its twilight by the late 1980s, a casualty of depressed oil markets and federal fiscal change. Although the PIP ended formally in March 1986, as part of the Mulroney government's legislative unwinding of the National Energy Program, there were bridging provisions that enabled NSRL to continue to show the exploration flag. The PIP's grandfather period extended up to a year to allow companies to wind down projects that had already been approved and committed. Responding to a vigorous provincial lobby, the federal government also agreed to a vastly scaled back transitional program of direct grant support to cash-poor exploration firms such as NSRL. The Offshore Drilling Fund, spelled out in the new Canada–Nova Scotia Offshore Petroleum Resources Accord of August 1986, earmarked $25 million for NSRL. In addition, Mulroney's new exploration tax credit (which applied to expenses in excess of $5 million per well) allowed non-taxpaying companies to claim 40 percent of the credit in cash.[38] Overall, NSRL was able to claim $109 million from Ottawa in exploration support in the 1987-1992 period.[39] However, the company was obliged to assume a far larger share of the cost of the few available holes. For the dry hole Como P-21, for example, NSRL was obliged to put up half the capital for a less than one-third interest.

The second significant business dimension of the drilling game was that it was a source of tax-deductible expenses. Like any petroleum venture, Nova Scotia Resources (Ventures) Limited accumulated these expenses in a tax pool, from which it could draw when properties began to generate corporate income. In the interim, these potential deductions could be capitalized against future earnings. In the subsidiary's case, the total tax pool reached $457 million by the end of 1995. Approximately half of this amount was based on exploration ventures between 1981 and 1988, while the balance was drawn from the Cohasset oil project.[40]

The late 1980s also saw NSRL move in a new direction – involvement in petroleum production in western Canada. With the need to generate production income growing more urgent, NSRL's board endorsed the move toward an established petroleum basin. This shift resulted in a program of investments, in the fall of 1987, in working properties in the three most westerly provinces. These investments, it was hoped, would generate income that could be sheltered by amortizing the tax pools and provide a positive cash flow. Another subsidiary, Venwest Resources Limited, was incorporated for this purpose, and a Calgary oilfield management company was contracted to manage the properties. Venwest bought, held, and sold properties in its effort to maximize income. At its peak, in 1988, the portfolio numbered eighty-nine properties. One of its holdings included a 9.9 percent interest in Direct Energy Marketing Limited, a marketing company that bought and sold natural gas.[41]

The Cohasset-Panuke Oil Project

One of NSRL's successful farm-ins was the oil discovery at the Panuke B-90 well in 1986. Although it was a modest reserve in comparison to the Newfoundland finds at Hibernia and Terra Nova, it was judged commercial in scale. Initial estimates of Cohasset were for a 50-million-barrel reserve of non-sulphurous light crude with an expected life of six years. As a result, Nova Scotia Resources (Ventures) Limited announced a joint venture agreement with Lasmo Nova Scotia Ltd. on 12 July 1990. Two months later, the Canada–Nova Scotia Offshore Petroleum Board approved the Cohasset-Panuke development plan, and preparations commenced. With Lasmo Nova Scotia designated the operator in the fifty-fifty partnership, a two-year preparatory period followed. The jack-up platform *Rowan Gorilla III* was installed as a production platform at Cohasset, and the crude was channelled through a CALM link to a storage tanker. Production began on 3 June 1992. (The Cohasset-Panuke complex is described in detail in Chapter 4.)

It soon became clear that the production costs at Cohasset would run dramatically over the level budgeted in 1990. From an initial total investment of $705 million ($225 million capital, $480 million operating), costs soared to $1.05 billion (a 48 percent increase) by 1995. Inevitably, costs increases turned the projected profit into a gaping loss and created sharp tensions among the partners. There were allegations that management errors at Lasmo were responsible for the debacle.

These allegations coincided with a change in senior management at NSRL. Calgary oilman James I. Livingston was appointed president and CEO in April 1993. Not surprisingly, one of his first priorities was to remedy the Cohasset problem. With the threat of legal action in the background, Lasmo agreed in August 1993 to a redistribution of the assets of the partnership by way of a negotiated settlement.[42] Nova Scotia Resources Limited was assigned a full 100 percent interest in the adjacent Balmoral field plus full rights to the residual Cohasset reserves once Lasmo declared the field uneconomic. (The partnership called for discontinuation of production once the daily flow fell to the level of 10,000 to 15,000 barrels per day.) The company also gained ownership of all Panuke project equipment for a nominal dollar, though it was required to assume liability for all subsequent operations (Lasmo's share of liability was capped at the transition point).

Marginal Field Management on the Scotian Shelf

The Cohasset renegotiation prefigured a broader shift in NSRL's business strategy. The company proposed to focus on operating small oil fields, such as the projects that were expected to follow Cohasset, to generate a revenue stream on the Scotian Shelf. This strategy emerged after Livingstone's appointment as a solution to the intractable cash-flow problem. Since large multinational consortia were interested only in huge commercial prospects that paid out over the long term, the small marginal fields were being neglected. A firm that mastered the art of small-field (five- to ten-year) operations could fill a significant gap in the East Coast offshore industry. In fact, NSRL was familiar with several such fields, including the Balmoral field. Nova Scotia Resources Limited was convinced that such fields could turn a profit, subject to a reduced scale of service contract rates and the use of less expensive equipment.

Approved by NSRL's board, the plan was presented in the summer of 1993 to Don Downe, the newly appointed minister of natural resources. Politically, the timing was delicate. John Savage's Liberals had been elected only a month earlier, and his government was only beginning to discover the deficit crisis bequeathed by its Conservative predecessors. Once the scale of the $600-million deficit became clear, massive program and job cuts and wage controls followed.[43] Not surprisingly, high-risk offshore entrepreneurship was an awkward fit with the new fiscal realities.

The cabinet did, however, approve NSRL's new business plan on 23 July 1993, subject to favourable vetting by an independent consultant (this was confirmed in September). Yet, as the government's first year unfolded, a deeper set of political doubts emerged. In March 1994, the government announced a new board of directors. The cabinet then instructed NSRL to prepare a new, more comprehensive five-year business plan to canvas a variety of options. The plan was complete within six months. After reviewing options ranging from closure to privatization to a small-oil strategy, the board concluded that the latter still offered the best prospects.

Another thread in Livingstone's revenue-generating offensive was the monetization of NSRL's tax pools, tax deductions "earned" by drilling ventures but unclaimed by the company because of its lack of taxable income. At the time, the Income Tax Act permitted the transfer of these deductions, for a commercial return, to petroleum companies that could utilize them. At mid-decade, NSRL had $457 million in deductions available, roughly half arising from drilling ventures and the balance from the Cohasset-Panuke project. Various avenues were available to utilize the allowances. For example, they had been used to completely shelter NSRL's western Canadian production revenues. In 1994, under Livingstone's direction, NSRL began negotiations with PanCanadian Petroleum, one of the leading Calgary independent oil firms. The plan was to establish a joint exploration company through which NSRL deductions could be transferred to PanCanadian. Nova Scotia Resources Limited would sell shares and issue debentures to PanCanadian and the joint corporation would continue for five years, at which time NSRL would buy back the shares and debentures. It soon became clear that this business tactic ran well outside of the Liberal government's comfort zone. When the minister of natural resources, Don Downe, was informed of this plan in the summer of 1994, he directed that the negotiations be suspended, pending the preparation of the new business plan.

At the cabinet table, however, NSRL's long-term prospects were still an open question, and an alternate strategy of divestiture was actively discussed. As NSRL's management and board vigorously relaunched the firm, the question of provincial government support – symbolic, financial, and political – was key. Moreover, the Liberals came to power as confirmed skeptics about the value of NSRL, having spent more than a decade excoriating it as a flawed experiment by the Buchanan government. With tax pools and marginal oil ventures on the drawing board, a political decision clearly loomed. Throughout the fall of 1994, the ministerial skeptics prevailed. On its own initiative, the Savage cabinet commissioned a separate report on the valuation of NSRL assets (as part of the divestment debate). The result, conducted and written by Rothschild Canada Ltd., was released in March 1995. By then, however, the Savage government had decided on its course of action. On 27 February, the NSRL's board was terminated, and a new board consisting entirely of provincial civil servants was installed. Hours later,

Livingstone and two senior managers were dismissed (litigation and settlements followed). The cabinet then announced its decision to divest NSRL, and Rothschild Canada was engaged in June to advise on the process.

The period was one of sustained tension, much of it centred on the question of managerial and directorial autonomy. Together with the majority of the previous board, Livingstone defined his job in business terms. (Prior to accepting the job offer, Livingstone had the executive search firm KPMG meet with both Conservative and Liberal party leaders to determine their expectations of the president's role. Livingstone stated that he "was given a personal guarantee by both of them, through KPMG, that there would be no political interference in the running of NSRL.")[44] In 1994, the reconstituted board became an epicentre for conflicting agendas and roles, which were manifested in policy differences between Livingstone and Bob MacKay, the board chairman and civil servant. In legislative testimony, Livingstone characterized the conflict as a contest over control of the company. The politically attuned MacKay was perceived as having the ear of cabinet, which rejected several key board recommendations on the sale of tax pools to PanCanadian and on the approval of the five-year business plan. Following his dismissal, Livingstone launched legal action against the province, the minister, the chair of the board, and the company for $1.4 million. During the discovery phase of the trial, in September 1995, the Government of Nova Scotia offered a settlement of $500,000 (two-thirds more than his contract required), and the case was closed. Livingstone returned to Calgary, where he established the junior oil company K2 Energy.

Divestment: The Long Goodbye, 1995-2003

It could be argued that nothing captured the life-long contradictions of NSRL so well as the manner of its death. If the government hoped for a quick and clean exit from the oil business, it was surprisingly naive. In fact, the process absorbed the energies of three successive premiers: John Savage, Russell MacLellan, and John Hamm. Initially, the scene was clouded by the fallout from the firings of February 1995 and complaints from the Opposition (regardless of party). However, it was the combination of grossly insufficient equity and excessive debt capitalization (both long-standing burdens) that rendered the company unsustainable in its prevailing form. The cabinet's decision to sell was driven more by the need to avoid future outlays than it was to remove current debt.

The most marketable assets were the western Canadian oil and gas properties, which were sold during the latter years of the Savage government.

When MacLellan succeeded Savage in 1997, he suspended the sale process and described the province's Sable offshore interest as a strategic interest to be held and strengthened. It proved to be a short-lived hiatus, however. The Conservative Party's electoral victory two years later reopened the question, and on 12 June 2000 the Hamm government directed NSRL's board to put the company's assets back on the market. Significantly, this decision took place during a period of record (to that point) natural gas markets in North America, a period when spot prices exceeded $6 per thousand cubic feet. Seventeen expressions of interest were received in 2000, and after a period of confidential review, six binding offers came forward. Three of these offers were short-listed, and NSRL selected the highest bid, received from a group that included Emera Inc., the Pengrowth Energy Trust, and PanCanadian Petroleum.

On 6 February 2001, the Government of Nova Scotia accepted the board's advice, and an agreement of sale was signed. By its terms, Emera (the privately owned Nova Scotia power utility) would purchase the company's share of Sable Offshore Energy Inc.'s infrastructure assets for $90 million and gas reserves for $265 million. The latter would be sold to Pengrowth. PanCanadian would pay $65 million for the remaining shares in NSRL, including its production leases for Panuke and Cohasset and sixteen significant discovery licences outside of the Sable offshore energy project.

The road to final approval was complicated through several "rights of first refusal" provisions on the part of the deal with Sable Offshore Energy Inc. The first option (agreed to in the dying days of the MacLellan government in 1999) allowed either ExxonMobil or Shell Canada to match the Emera-Pengrowth sale price on NSRL's Sable holdings and acquire those assets instead. The two multinationals waived this right in March 2001. A second right of refusal, this one based on the Sable Offshore Energy Project's partnership agreement, allowed any or all of the four partners to purchase specific portions of the holdings (as distinct from the package as a whole) at stipulated sale prices. The option was invoked in June 2001 for the subsea gas-gathering line, the Goldboro gas plant, and the natural gas liquids pipeline and fractionation plant at Point Tupper. As a result, the original deal was fractured to include a wider set of purchasers, a development that raised doubts about the attractiveness of the price of residual components of Emera-Pengrowth-PanCanadian interests.

Two more years elapsed before the asset sales were finalized. During this time, Pengrowth dropped out of its $265-million deal for NSRL's Sable gas deposits in December 2001. Sable Offshore Energy Inc.'s partners decided to resell their first refusal acquisitions to Pengrowth (bought for $40 million and resold for $57 million) and to Emera (bought for $40 million and resold for $50 million). For its part, PanCanadian backed out of the significant discovery licence purchase deal ($65 million), as did Pengrowth Energy, which held the alternate options for the licences. Both cited as rationales the burden of certain contract provisions that obliged NSRL to help finance transportation of future gas product from the licences. A subsequent deal to sell eleven of the licences to Endless Energy, a Calgary junior firm, collapsed when Endless' financing fell apart. In 2003, Pengrowth came back into the picture, purchasing all but one of the significant discovery licence properties for the far lesser price of $5.6 million. At the conclusion of this complicated and confusing three-year juggle, provincial treasurer Neil LeBlanc claimed a victory of sorts by trumpeting the $400-million gross return eventually realized on NSRL's assets. This return amounted to almost half of the NSRL's accumulated debt, which the province was forced to write off in the lead up to the asset sales.

Conclusion

Nova Scotia Resources Limited was one of a subset of state petroleum instruments established in Canada during the high-rent OPEC years. From the start, however, the Crown firm was conditioned by institutional and fiscal shortcomings. The company emerged late in the history of provincial oil enterprises, and it emerged in a province with no significant petroleum industry experience. Therefore, the policy impulse that drove it was derivative and hypothetical. The conditions for strong policy capacity were a decisive public launch, a firm legislative base, a clearly endorsed mandate, and strong evidence of political executive support and ownership. None of these conditions was present when NSRL was created. The company was designed by stealth, its launch went unnoticed, and no place was allotted for it in the province's petroleum development strategy of the early 1980s.

The history of NSRL divides rather neatly into three consecutive periods. The first, from 1982 to 1988, corresponded with the petroleum boom years and the frontier bonanza of Ottawa's National Energy Program. Favoured by multiple policy premiums as a Canadian and Crown-owned enterprise, NSRL parlayed a minimal equity stake into loans, grants, and interests in a series of petroleum discoveries. Even more important, the anticipation of early production from the Venture gas project pointed toward a long-term income stream that would secure the firm for decades to come. The sharp and sudden price collapse of 1986 put paid to that strategy, though it took several years for the full implications to become clear.

During the second period, from 1988 to 1995, corporate officials displayed a high degree of tactical agility. Recognizing the new business reality of soft prices and gas-supply surpluses, they fashioned plans for short-term income relief, monetization of tax credits and the acquisition of western Canadian producing properties. The plan's new centrepiece, however, was the Cohasset-Panuke oil project, in which NSRL stepped up from farm-in partner to operator. Cohasset served as a modest (relative to Sable) but profitable bridging operation while world petroleum conditions stabilized. In partnership with Lasmo Nova Scotia Ltd., the revenue stream began to flow in 1992. However, the formidable capital costs associated with developing Cohasset-Panuke, and NSRL's significantly greater exposure in this venture, dramatically increased its debt load. By the time this project reached the production phase, the provincial government was also wrestling with a fiscal crisis every bit as pressing, a situation that altered the policy context irretrievably.

The final eight-year period from 1995 to 2003 covered the long and fitful campaign to unwind Nova Scotia's Crown petroleum enterprise. Alternating between boldness and caution, optimism and farce, the campaign revealed the tightly wound constraints in which NSRL and its multinational partners operated. With its entrepreneurial impulse deadened by the harsh realities of commercial risk, debt, and failure, the Government of Nova Scotia was willing to cut its losses and recoup fifty-cent dollars on its petroleum account. The confidence of the early 1980s, during which the state served as a catalyst for offshore exploration and secured the Crown's share, had no place in the neoliberal 1990s. If and when exploration in the Scotian Shelf was renewed, private capital would drive the process. The divestiture process illustrated how dramatically the terms of offshore policy bargaining had changed over two decades.

The travails of NSRL were inevitably bound up with the very concept of a provincially owned upstream petroleum enterprise. Given the politically volatile provenance of NSRL, it was not likely that the government would soon revive the concept in a different form. However, the option remained, and the institutional instrument of the state enterprise could be utilized again. It is therefore significant that the province of Newfoundland has moved aggressively in recent years to assume equity positions in offshore developments. In the 2007 Energy Plan, Premier Danny Williams announced the creation of Nalcor Energy. This company began with provincial state holdings in the electric power-generating and power-transmitting business, but it also includes an oil and gas division. The latter holds the provincial equity positions that the government has taken in the Hebron, White Rose, and Hibernia South field developments. Although Nalcor emerged in a context of offshore investment that is presently absent in Nova Scotia, its existence underlines the continuing relevance of this policy option.

Whether the ambiguous legacy of NSRL will affect Nova Scotia's future policy mix remains to be seen. In the interim, the provincial government chose to rely on a series of alternative policy mechanisms.

PART 3

Case Studies in the Offshore Petroleum Chain

6 Corridor Politics: Sable Gas Project Development

Although it was not the first hydrocarbon field development on the Scotian Shelf, the Sable offshore energy project is the most important in the basin to date. Based on two generations of natural gas reservoir discoveries in the 1970s and 1980s, it signified a commercial coming of age for Nova Scotia's offshore industry. The Sable project represented much more than an exploitable gas field with a projected twenty-five-year life, however: its associated infrastructure of subsea pipelines and onshore plants signalled the potential for profitable next-generation projects and provided a catalyst for further exploration on the shelf. Furthermore, the regulatory and fiscal arrangements that senior levels of government fashioned for the Sable project established a governance template that would carry over to future projects. Finally, the export-dependent commercial logic of the project, which committed the predominant share of the natural gas for sale to the New England states, indicated that Nova Scotia's offshore resource was going to follow the pattern of earlier generations of Canadian hydrocarbon trading.

Given its anchor status in basin development, a rounded understanding of the politics of the Sable project is central to this study. This chapter explores the project's history in the 1990s – as a case study in modern petroleum capitalism and its relationship to the state. Its story – from preliminary concept and project design to product sales agreements, regulatory compliances, facilities construction, and eventual operation – comprised a series of critical decision points that involved a rotating set of corporate and sovereign interests. The internal dynamics of major offshore projects are seldom subjected to the extended analysis that they deserve. More typically, the commercial integrity of major projects is assumed or acknowledged at the margin. Terms such as *commercial viability, return on investment,* and *public-interest dimension* are invoked almost casually in attributions of motive or outcome and without any apparent sense of the complex transactional arrangements that created such attributes and determined the viability of major projects.

It is important to understand the constellation of forces that render major offshore energy projects viable, particularly in the case of initiating projects such as Sable Offshore, projects that provide the fulcrum for exploiting new resource endowments. These cases reveal the interdependency of enterprise, industry, and state institutions, which intersect on multiple levels and generate a continuous stream of interstitial pressures. As Brian Galligan puts it, in the context of a different resource and geopolitical setting, "state and corporations are variously related as sovereign and subject, benefactor and client, parasite and host and as partners of necessity and convenience. Working such a multifaceted relationship is a major part of both business and government."[1]

In the pages that follow, the Sable project is explored through a series of discrete stages, each of which reveals an essential dimension of the overall political economy. The first stage begins with the emergence of a core business enterprise and its circumstances, sponsors, and structure. The second stage is the period of pre-development strategy, when the operational parameters of the project are explored and the basic institutional features are agreed upon. The third stage is the interface between enterprise and state, particularly at the regulatory nexus where statutory powers are exercised and facilitating measures may be extended. The fourth stage is the technical design and physical construction of the project, which culminates in first production. Finally, the fifth stage is the period of business operation, when the ongoing challenges of doing business (including the second-order consequences of the prior stages) must be managed.

It should be noted that this model seldom if ever unfolds in reality in a linear series of discrete and sequential steps. Rather, the stages tend to be characterized by a dialectical interplay as events in multiple streams spill over, feed back, reinforce, or contradict the emerging tendencies in others.[2] Indeed, the ultimate shape of a major project – in design, operation, and performance – can be viewed profitably as a distillation of political and economic contests throughout the project's life.

The Core Corporate Enterprises

To unlock the black box of the Sable project, it is necessary to reconstruct a decade-long history. In the process, a framework of increasing complexity is built to illustrate not only the milestones of project evolution but also the underlying politics of critical decisions along the way. This history begins with the constitution of two central corporate enterprises. The first was established to extract, process, and bring to land natural gas from several of the most promising fields. This firm was known until 1997 as the Sable Offshore Energy Project (SOEP) and thereafter as Sable Offshore Energy Inc. (SOEI). The second firm – the Maritimes & Northeast Pipeline (MNP) – was formed to transport gas across land to markets in Maritime Canada and the New England states. Since the first firm is essentially an upstream gas production business, while the latter is a midstream gas transmission business, they operate in quite different industries. However, they are at the same time interdependent and complementary, for neither could operate profitably without some version of the other.

The particular nature of this relationship, and its evolution over time, is a driving force of the project's politics. There is a tendency in studies of business politics to treat the corporate players as organizationally complete and autonomous, as having clear and rounded public policy agendas that are pursued with discipline and determination. Although this tendency is understandable in light of the institutional coherence displayed by companies, it ignores the circumstances in which every business enterprise originates and becomes organized. Closer examination of these formative years reveals firms as coalitions of business interests that must be united and sustained if commercial purposes are to be successfully achieved. In this sense, each firm has internal politics that provide a key analytic starting point.[3] Who is providing the firm with capital? What range of product lines constitutes the firm's business? How much competition or concentration is there among rivals, and what crucial business and political strategies are being pursued? Corporate politics is underscored further by the range of roles assigned to the Sable project in the contractual and commercial literature. The firm is described variously as the proponent, the vendor, the contractor, the operator, and the licensee.

Sable Offshore Energy Project

In the petroleum business, the road to production normally begins with the discovery of significant reservoirs of oil and gas. Although they are generally subject to certain statutory terms of access, the corporate rights holders are in a dominant position to determine if and when the natural resource will be exploited. As a result, upstream investment is typically triggered by corporate initiative. Because most hydrocarbon producers aspire to a portfolio of projects, the projects' selection, priority, and timing are assigned by a comparative analysis of risk and reward that unfolds through a continuing process rather than at a single point in time. It begins when sponsors launch preliminary appraisals, continues through several stages of design and planning, faces a moment of ultimate decision making when the formal corporate sanction is given, and continues to evolve during the construction and operational phases. Over its lifespan, a project can be treated as a continuously negotiated agreement.

Throughout the project's life cycle, each corporate rights holder follows a strategy that springs from its organizational interests. For example, some junior explorers may specialize in wildcat drilling in speculative plays in the hope that success will translate into major stakes in the ensuing development syndicates. Others may concentrate on neglected opportunities in heavily explored structures that may be profitable for a small- or medium-sized company though of little interest to giant firms. Companies of all sizes exploit opportunities to farm-in to an ongoing exploration program whose sponsors are seeking to spread the risk, or accelerate the pace, of exploration on a property. It should be noted that assets in the ground are themselves tradable on commercial markets; consequently, the initial discoverer is not always part of the ultimate extractive venture.

As was previously outlined, a series of natural gas and crude oil strikes were made in the shallow waters of the central Scotian Shelf between 1969 and 1983. Shell Canada made the first gas discovery with its Onondaga well. For Mobil Oil Canada, the highlights included the Thebaud gas discovery of 1972, the discovery of the Cohasset oil field the following year, and the Venture strike in 1979. The latter formed the basis of Mobil's Venture gas project proposal of 1982.[4] This proposal led to a formal development application, a gas export application, and the negotiation of gas supply contracts. However, the Venture project was suspended in 1986 in the face of collapsing international petroleum prices. As further gas discoveries were recorded, the operators converted their legal rights from exploration permits to significant discovery licences, which allowed them to hold position until commercial exploitation was viable.

In the first decade of exploration in the Scotian Shelf in the 1970s, lead companies operated independently on large tracts of land. By the end of this phase, more than 3 trillion cubic feet (84 billion cubic metres) of reserves had been booked in the Sable Subbasin, the area surrounding Sable Island in waters ranging from 20-70 metres.[5]

The second exploration phase was spurred by the National Energy Program. Because Canadian-owned firms were eligible for exploration grants up to 80 percent, the phase was dominated by drilling consortia that linked the foreign-owned majors with the Canadian independents.[6] Among the second-wave gas discoveries were South Venture, Glenelg, Alma, and North Triumph, and the lead explorers were the multinational subsidiaries Mobil Canada and Shell Canada. Because of their foreign ownership levels, however, the companies operated in consortia with Canadian partners to access the 20-cent exploration dollars facilitated by the Petroleum Incentive Program. The partners included the rapidly expanding federal state enterprise Petro-Canada and the Nova Scotia provincial state enterprise Nova Scotia Resources Limited, as well as private independents such as Husky/Bow Valley and Canterra. By the time forty wells had been drilled, the total gas reserves approached 7 trillion cubic feet (196 billion cubic metres).[7] By 1985, however, the National Energy Program was being unwound, a development that undercut the second exploration wave. The 1986 petroleum price slump completed the job.

The shift from exploratory work to field development and production represented a qualitative step change in corporate commitment. Once again, there was an opportunity for intercorporate alliances to spread risk, attract capital, and broaden the asset base. In the petroleum business, joint ventures offer a means for discrete enterprises to associate for limited purposes under the terms of a governing contract known as a joint venture operating agreement. Such opportunities may also be open to state agencies under the terms of subsurface rights-granting regimes. During the 1980s, for example, the Canada Oil and Gas Act and the Canada–Nova Scotia Offshore Petroleum Resources Accord included provisions for a public sector back-in to petroleum projects on Canada Lands such as the Scotian Shelf.[8] This back-in could be exercised during the transition from discovery to production, as public authorities were authorized to acquire an ownership stake in the venture (either funded up front or carried by the private partners until it could be paid out of product flow). This is how Petro-Canada and Nova Scotia Resources Limited took up equity stakes in the Sable offshore energy project. In sum, the range of corporate interests that may be combined in joint ventures is impressively diverse, and each partnership can be explored according to both the constituents and terms of the association.

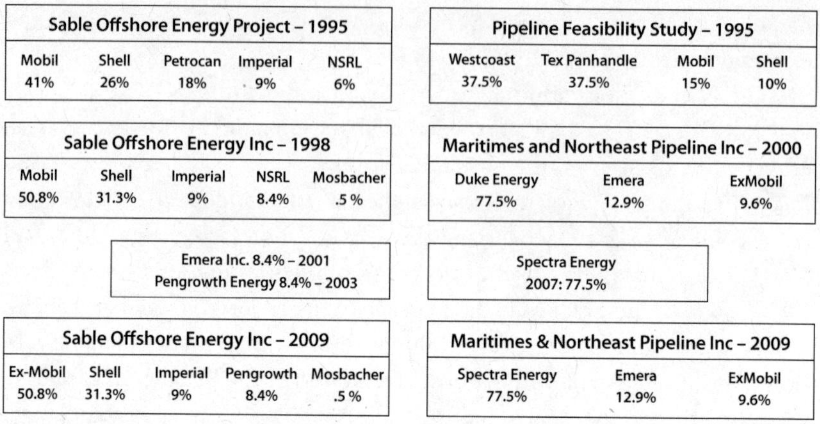

Sable Offshore Energy Project – 1995				
Mobil 41%	Shell 26%	Petrocan 18%	Imperial 9%	NSRL 6%

Pipeline Feasibility Study – 1995			
Westcoast 37.5%	Tex Panhandle 37.5%	Mobil 15%	Shell 10%

Sable Offshore Energy Inc – 1998				
Mobil 50.8%	Shell 31.3%	Imperial 9%	NSRL 8.4%	Mosbacher .5 %

Maritimes and Northeast Pipeline Inc – 2000		
Duke Energy 77.5%	Emera 12.9%	ExMobil 9.6%

Emera Inc. 8.4% – 2001
Pengrowth Energy 8.4% – 2003

Spectra Energy
2007: 77.5%

Sable Offshore Energy Inc – 2009				
Ex-Mobil 50.8%	Shell 31.3%	Imperial 9%	Pengrowth 8.4%	Mosbacher .5 %

Maritimes & Northeast Pipeline Inc – 2009		
Spectra Energy 77.5%	Emera 12.9%	ExMobil 9.6%

Figure 6.1 Equity base of the Sable Offshore Energy Project and Maritimes & Northeast Pipeline

Outside firms with critical experience or expertise may also be recruited into the sponsoring syndicate as it progresses toward the operating stage. This offer may extend to firms in separate industries that are linked in the value chain, as when a pipeline transmission carrier assumes an equity share of the production enterprise or when a petroleum producer takes a position in the pipeline firm. The latter situation occurred in the mid-1990s when Mobil Canada assumed a 25 percent ownership in the MNP. Nor is it uncommon for major hydrocarbon consumers to take on equity roles in upstream ventures. After the turn of the century, Nova Scotia Power, a prospective natural gas buyer, purchased part of Nova Scotia Resources Limited's stake in SOEI to add to the half of Mobil Canada's stake in MNP that it already held. The changing equity ownership of the project's two anchor firms is presented in Figure 6.1.

In any event, project sponsors faced several threshold tests related to recoverable volumes, sunk capital investment, and prospective markets when they took the first steps toward hydrocarbon extraction. When gas demand and market conditions began to recover from the late 1980s slump, the exploitation of the Sable discoveries re-emerged as a possibility. Of particular significance were burgeoning consumer demand for natural gas in the East Coast states, the electricity-generating industry's shift toward gas inputs, and the newly deregulated market for gas sales in both Canada and the United States.[9] The Scotian Shelf enjoyed significant locational advantages for servicing the New England market, if the necessary infrastructure could be installed.

In such situations, the presence of initiating agents is always critical. Initiating agents are willing to take long-term risks and invest the time, capital, and prestige to kick-start a development prospect. Mobil Canada assumed the catalyst role in 1993 by launching an internal review of the commerciality of its Sable holdings. Based on favourable findings, Mobil approached Shell Canada and other rights holders with an aim to consolidate their major Sable discoveries to achieve threshold reserves for development.[10] The result was an agreement to pool the companies' fields into the jointly operated SOEP. Mobil Canada brought its Thebaud, Venture, and South Venture fields (those closest to Sable Island) into the SOEP, while Shell Canada brought North Triumph, Alma, and Glenelg. The latter were located south and west of Sable Island, closer to the edge of the shelf. The agreement opened the way for a proposal for a series of jointly sponsored and phased pre-development studies. The prevailing gas reserve numbers suggested that almost all the confirmed significant discoveries around Sable Island would need to be aggregated to achieve the threshold volumes and the revenue return the project required.

The following year, Petro-Canada, Imperial Oil, and Nova Scotia Resources Limited joined in a memorandum of understanding that designated Mobil and Shell as joint operators for the production team as a whole. The companies also agreed to pool the partner-operated fields in any joint venture that followed. Based upon reserves and capital commitments, the initial shares in the development phase were as follows: Mobil, 41 percent; Shell Canada, 26 percent; Petro-Canada, 18 percent; Imperial Oil, 9 percent; and Nova Scotia Resources Limited, 6 percent. In 1996, Petro-Canada exited the consortium by agreeing to an asset swap with Mobil. It traded its interest in the Sable fields and project for Mobil's petroleum properties in western Canada.[11] Another shuffle took place in 2001, when Nova Scotia Resources Limited was wound down by the provincial government, and its share was assumed by Emera Inc. (the parent firm of Nova Scotia Power). The share was sold to Pengrowth Energy Trust in 2003.

The 1994 memorandum of understanding authorized the expenditure of $1 million for several years of Phase 1 studies. It called for the scoping of three key issues – resource potential, development options, and market potential – to be completed by mid-1995.

With positive findings reported for Phase 1, the second phase began in June 1995. The new work program covered technical studies, government consultations, and regional public consultations, this time at a budgeted cost of approximately $5 million. By this point, the broad outlines of the

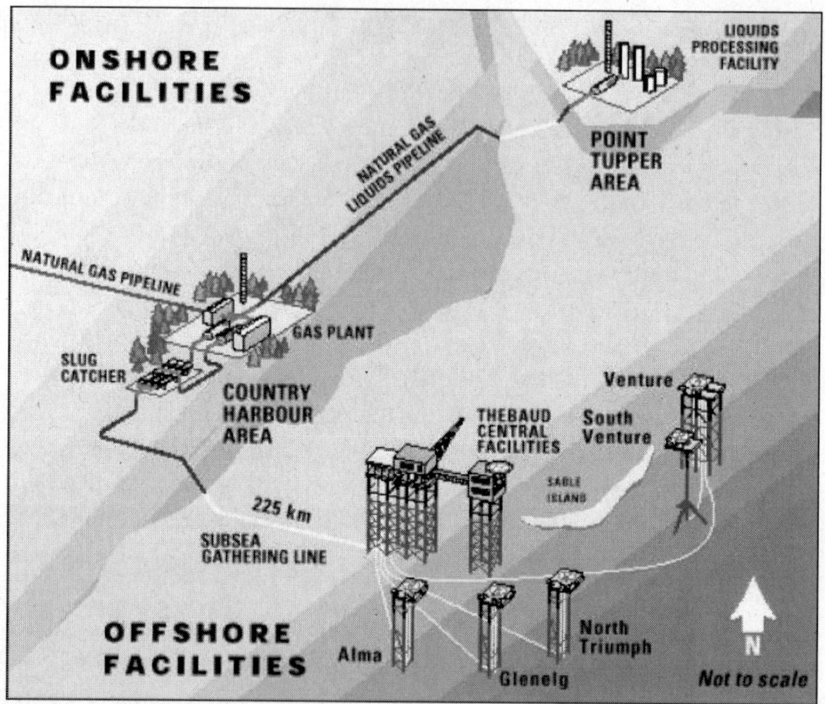

Figure 6.2 Schematics of the Sable Offshore Energy Project and Maritimes & Northeast Pipeline
Source: Joint Public Review Panel, *Report: Sable Gas Projects* (Halifax: Environment Canada and Nova Scotia Environment and Labour, 1997), 15.

project were evident (see Figure 6.2). The project would draw on six gas fields to be developed in several phases and would produce approximately 400 million cubic feet (11 million metres) of gas per day. Extraction would require some thirty wells that would feed into 180 kilometres of interfield gathering lines that would lead to the Thebaud processing platform, where water and gas condensates would be removed. The gas would then move through a 225-kilometres trunk gas line to a site at Country Harbour in Guysborough County. At the main onshore gas plant, the heavier hydrocarbons, including propane and butane, would be separated from the methane natural gas, which would be piped onward as fuel. The natural gas liquids distilled at Country Harbour would then move through a separate, smaller-diameter pipeline to Point Tupper on Cape Breton Island, where a fractionation plant would separate the butane, propane, and other (light-oil) condensate liquids for commercial sale.[12] Overall, the Sable project carried an estimated $2-billion capital cost, making it the largest construction project in Nova Scotia's history.

Maritimes & Northeast Pipeline Inc.

In a parallel process, a second consortium was established in 1995 to explore different modes of transporting energy to markets. The consortium was led by two established pipeline operators, Westcoast Energy Inc. of Vancouver and Panhandle Eastern Corporation of Houston. The two lead partners assumed equal shares totalling 75 percent, while Mobil and Shell assumed 15 percent and 10 percent, respectively, creating an incipient interfirm and interindustry alliance. The pipeline study was budgeted for $3 million.

Not surprisingly, the planned capacity of the onshore gas transmission system closely matched that of the offshore system.[13] Immediately beyond the Country Harbour gas treatment plant, a custody transfer metering station monitored the flow of gas into a MNP trunk pipeline measuring 76 centimetres in diameter. The pipeline's route ran along a 1,365 kilometre right-of-way, through the provinces of Nova Scotia and New Brunswick and the state of Maine. At intervals of approximately 40 kilometres, mainline valves controlled the flow of gas. The line terminated at Dracut, Massachusetts, north of Boston, where it connected with a trunk pipeline network that brought supplies from the Gulf of Mexico, Appalachia, and the Midwest. On the Canadian section of the MNP's mainline, a series of spur lines or laterals of smaller diameter were planned to take gas to larger urban markets. The number of laterals was subject to negotiation during the preparatory phase, but it ultimately included Halifax (30 centimetre, 130 kilometres), Saint John (40 centimetre, 115 kilometres), Moncton (20 centimetre, 12 kilometres), and Point Tupper (20 centimetre, 63 kilometres).

The technical challenges of onshore pipelining had long been mastered in North America, which experienced a quantum jump in installed transmission capacity during the 1990s. However, the commercial imperatives of any new pipeline venture were anything but secure. As the first gas infrastructure provider to the Sable geological province, MNP faced the challenge of designing its facilities for the SOEP's supplies while also positioning itself as a dominant player as the basin matured. The initial pipeline needed to be profitable as a stand-alone venture over twenty to twenty-five years, while at the same time setting the foundations for what its sponsors clearly anticipated to be a long-term supply channel to an energy-hungry region. This tension permeated the trunk pipeline venture from project design and financing to contracting and regulatory approval.

The conceptual foundation of the MNP was the transmission of the SOEP's natural gas for sale in the New England states. Allied to the goal was supplying gas to the Canadian domestic market in the Maritimes (a long-standing Government of Nova Scotia policy precondition and also an expectation of the New Brunswick government). Since natural gas was a new fuel source to the Maritime region, estimates of the MNP's market potential were really part of a wider estimate of regional consumers' acceptance of the new fuel source. Moreover, some of the critical business decisions lay beyond the transmission company's control, since the local gas-distribution business – the so-called city-gate business – had yet to be established when pipeline project planning began in 1995. (The politics of local distribution is explored in greater detail in Chapter 9.)

The evolving structure of the natural gas transmission business was also significant. The Westcoast-Panhandle venture needed to be framed within the new partly deregulated world of the late 1990s. In earlier days, long-distance pipeline operators purchased gas from producers at source and re-sold it to consumers at terminus. As effective monopolists, these operators were subject to extensive state regulation on tolls and prices, which were monitored to ensure safe and reliable standards of service and acceptable rates of return.[14] The new regulatory philosophy, by contrast, treated pipeline companies as transmission service providers to any available supplier of natural gas, enabling the latter to retain ownership of their product and sell it directly to consumers in competitive market circumstances.[15] For MNP, this meant that its overall profitability would turn on key factors such as throughput volumes and tolling rates (price for service).

In 1995 and 1996, the Westcoast-Panhandle team prepared the scenarios that formed the basis of its MNP project description, which was unveiled in October 1996 in its application to the National Energy Board. By this time, MNP had made considerable progress in consolidating its commercial relations. The result was a tiered set of commercial agreements, of varying degrees of finality, to ship gas. Negotiations began formally in the spring of 1996, when MNP invited requests for service from prospective customers. Not surprisingly, there was no shortage of interest. By 1997, this interest had translated into precedent agreements covering a daily volume of 440 million British thermal units for export and another 90 million British thermal units of domestic Maritime traffic. Although these agreements were subject to certain conditions – including regulatory approvals, acceptable shipper supply arrangements, and shipper satisfaction with approved rates – they would be finalized into firm service agreements once the conditions were met.

The Maritimes & Northeast Pipeline enjoyed a further level of security from the twenty-year backstop precedent agreement that it signed for the offshore gas of Mobil Natural Gas Inc. and Imperial Oil Resources Ltd. This committed all of the Sable project's throughput not already covered by firm service agreements to MNP up to a maximum of 440 million British thermal units per day.[16] In effect, this agreement made MNP the sole carrier of the Sable project's product. It also raised questions about the tightness of the intercorporate alliance between the SOEP and MNP and, perhaps, its legitimacy in the new era of competitive shipping.[17] This alliance would be tested by bids from rival transmission interests at the regulatory phase.

The final decision on installed pipeline capacity remained open to adjustment while sales contracting continued. The project description indicated a designed capacity of 650 million cubic feet (18 million cubic metres) per day, though it was anticipated that initial operations would start below this level and would rise to intended volumes over time. In the long run, MNP recognized that further development of the Sable Subbasin, and the Scotian Shelf in general, would offer opportunities for expansion. (Sable Offshore Energy Project informed the joint panel that it estimated there was an additional 2.3 trillion cubic feet (64 billion cubic metres) of proven gas in the sixteen significant discovery licences located outside of the project fields.)[18] Not only was there room for expanded throughput in the proposed pipeline, but there was also the option of looping the line or laying additional pipe in parallel paths along the right-of-way.

Although the scale of the Sable project was clearly framed by the anticipated production volumes, the downstream allocation was always destined to raise political sensitivities. On one level, there was the inevitable pull between long-distance transmission and local distribution. This tension set MNP as the trunk gas carrier against a separate set of firms buying and delivering gas in local Maritime markets. Separate regulators presided over federal trunk line firms and tolls and provincial distributor firms and tolls. On another level, tensions surfaced on the question of domestic and export allocative shares. The domestic portion was itself a function of the number of lateral lines planned, the urban markets served in Nova Scotia and New Brunswick, and the balance between provinces. Building a lateral line as part of the main trunk line, with its capital costs folded into the mainline rate base, served to dramatically enhance the prospects of early service and lower domestic delivery costs.

The combined commercial and political character of these constraints became evident once the project came under regulatory review in 1996-97. The prospect emerged for a full-blown battle over key project parameters that would end either in prolonged deadlock or regulatory resolution. In response, the two project sponsors and the two host provinces began private discussions on tolling matters in 1997. The rationale was to hammer out a mutually acceptable plan in a closed forum, thereby pre-empting some of the most politically sensitive debates before they could take hold in an adversarial way in the public domain. The result was a deal known as the Joint Position on Tolling and Laterals, announced on 19 June 1997.[19]

The structure of the MNP's pipeline tolls was central to the dispute. The two basic options were a toll by distance, in which the charge for moving a given volume of natural gas varied by distance travelled, or the postage stamp toll, in which the charge would be the same for delivery anywhere within the MNP's network. From the outset, tolling emerged as a central point of contest. In Nova Scotia, for example, both government and user industries expected that the principal beneficiary status for offshore development should include proximity advantages in natural gas access. Not surprisingly, toll by distance was strongly supported. At the same time, the adoption of a postage stamp toll throughout the MNP's system would create a broader Maritime community of users enjoying equal terms of access, a frequent practice in regulated utility industries. The province of New Brunswick, which would host a longer share of the pipeline than Nova Scotia, asserted its own beneficiary claims. Unwilling to be relegated to second place, it championed the postage stamp toll that MNP itself favoured. At the regulatory panel hearings in 1997, voices were raised on both sides of the issue.

It was in this context that the four parties endorsed the postage stamp toll structure in a joint position statement. It was, however, a more nuanced compromise than the announcement suggested. Within the deal, MNP agreed to discount firm service tolls in the Maritimes in its initial operating years.[20] For Nova Scotia, this discount amounted to 10 percent for the first eight years and 4 percent for an additional two years. In New Brunswick, the discount was 4 percent for the first three years.

The second part of the joint position statement dealt with lateral pipelines, which would run from the main trunk line to selected Maritime city gates. The MNP had proposed to build laterals to Halifax and Saint John that would coincide with the completion of the mainline and be subject to market interest. There was pressure, however, to increase the number of laterals to include, at the least, Cape Breton Island and northern New Brunswick. According to the joint position statement, MNP had committed to develop work plans for these laterals as demand reached an economic threshold. There was also provision by which either provincial government could release MNP from this term if the province preferred a different owner or operator for the lateral. Finally, MNP agreed to make available, for local distribution, 10 billion British thermal units for each province (approximately 10 million cubic feet per day or 280,000 cubic metres per day) for the initial three years of operation.

The significance of this tolling bargain depends upon the point of departure. The company won dual provincial endorsement for its basic system proposal on all regulatory and federal Order-in-Council decisions. In return, it committed to providing gas-price discounts and setting aside a guaranteed reserve for the initial operating years. The question of laterals was divided into two phases. Beyond Halifax and Saint John, pre-installation of laterals would not be required, and thus upfront capital costs were reduced. Along with one guaranteed lateral, New Brunswick achieved parity with Nova Scotia both in general tolling and in early gas-supply guarantees. Nova Scotia won preferential toll discounts over the initial decade of gas delivery. Both provinces gained the option of promoting additional laterals in the years ahead.

Within weeks of the announcement, however, the foundations of the joint position were put into question. Nova Scotia's new Liberal leader, Russell MacLellan, declared that the province required better terms. The declaration posed an interesting problem for the regulatory panel, whose public hearings on SOEP-MNP operations had already closed. When the new premier tried to submit an altered position on tolling, the panel declined to reopen proceedings and released its report on October 1997.[21]

During the fall, it became increasingly evident that MacLellan was determined to improve gas-delivery terms for Nova Scotia, even to the point of refusing key statutory consents. The only available path for settlement was further bilateral agreement. At the eleventh hour, on 10 December 1997, a memorandum of understanding was announced between SOEP, MNP, the Nova Scotia government, and Nova Scotia Power. Central to the deal was an enriched price advantage for Nova Scotia gas users, which was delivered "in the spirit of the [1986] Accord."[22] A new Nova Scotia Gas Market Development Fund was also established by the project's producers, with a fixed sum to be paid by SOEP over ten years to promote use of gas in the province. In effect, the fund offered an indirect subsidy to gas prices, enhancing the consumer discount to the equivalent of 20 percent over the initial decade. In addition, a second lateral – to the Strait of Canso area and terminating at Point Tupper – was to be built by MNP. Nova Scotia Power could also buy an equity stake in MNP. Finally, to allow domestic liquids processing to develop, SOEP would limit natural gas liquids sales contracts to a maximum of two years.

This episode graphically reveals the transitory character of even the most fundamental political bargains. MacLellan arrived in power with no obligation to uphold the work of his predecessors and every reason to carve out a personal signature on a critical, one-time project. The case also highlights the time-sensitive character of decision streams. The six-month period that extended from June to December 1997 was critical for resolving many key questions that had been years in the making. However, the bid for last-minute leverage was relational. If too many parties chose to block or renege on commitments, there was a strong chance that the entire edifice would have collapsed. However, if most of the crucial terms were resolved positively, the prospect for redefining limited items was increased.

The Regulatory Context and State Policy

The shift of focus from the first to the second phase of pre-development review reveals how the technical and commercial dimensions of a project can blend into the governmental dimensions. The relationship between the two dimensions is a complicated and paradoxical one. It is only at the point when a project shows preliminary operational viability that it is possible and necessary to address the interface with the sovereign powers. Yet, because the terms of the state policy framework are themselves a substantial part of the prospective operational environment, their ultimate substance co-determines much of the project's viability. Consequently, corporate sponsors will push to negotiate and resolve government expectations as promptly and conclusively as possible, thereby creating a bargaining situation in which each party has an interest in extracting firm commitments from the other while disclosing as little as possible and minimizing its own fixed commitments.

During the policy-scoping period, which began in June 1995, the SOEP team commissioned baseline studies and hired professional consultants to generate the data and plans needed to meet state regulatory requirements.

Sable Offshore Energy Project also opened channels to a variety of federal and provincial departments and agencies with statutory responsibilities. The offshore industry often deplores the sheer weight and scope of both legislative and administrative hurdles, which they present as uncoordinated, repetitive, and expensive to meet. Yet this very heterogeneity may provide flexibility at the formative stages. These structures and sequences can be adroitly managed by the applicant to build agency-specific understandings and alliances, along with a cumulative momentum toward settlement. In addition, by launching into campaigns with municipal authorities and affected communities, SOEP acknowledged that local public opinion was a significant political arena. Coalitions can mobilize both in favour and in opposition, and community relations are a mandated element in modern megaproject politics.

In the political environment of 1995, there were several types of pressing policy issues. One, of course, involved the determination of threshold volumes of the natural gas resource within commercially viable reservoirs, which was determined within the corporate confines of the Sable consortium. A second concerned the fiscal terms of Crown royalty arrangements that would apply to this prototype offshore development. This second question obviously exerts a parallel influence on the commercial viability of a venture, and it was handled within the closed negotiating setting of the provincial state. Statutory authority in this case is derived from the Offshore Petroleum Royalties Act. Proclaimed in 1990, it authorizes agreements to be made with licence holders, subject to the terms of the Offshore Petroleum Royalties Regulations of June 1999.[23] To this end, SOEP and the Nova Scotia Department of Finance began talks in 1996 with the aim of concluding a mutually satisfactory royalty and tax agreement. There can be no doubt that the Savage Liberal government wanted the Sable project to proceed, to kick-start further offshore investment. In the end, the parties agreed to a form of royalty scheme based initially on gross profits and with sliding terms throughout the life of the project that would bring in net profits over time.[24] This profits tax in effect enabled the partners to recover their capital costs relatively rapidly over the first years then pay greater shares of the profits to Nova Scotia over the life of the project. A version of the agreement was announced in May 1996, and a revised version followed in July 1999.[25] Because the Sable project was the first major gas project, and therefore deemed of particular risk, the government later decided to fence it in by developing a separate generic royalty schedule for future projects. However, given that the generic version now includes multiple variations – the base case, the high-risk (i.e., non-Sable Shelf) case, and the small-oil case – project specific negotiations will apply to each new venture.[26]

Progress on royalty terms opened the way for SOEP to trigger state regulatory proceedings by filing two key documents with the Canada–Nova Scotia Offshore Petroleum Board. The first was the multivolume "Sable Offshore Energy Project Development Plan," which covered all pertinent aspects of the sea-to-shore operation. Its companion was the "Industrial Benefits Plan," which detailed SOEP's commitments for provincial and regional contracting and employment. After the filing occurred on 30 May 1996, the project shifted into the third phase. An equally pivotal filing was the MNP's application to the National Energy Board in October 1996 for a certificate of public convenience and necessity authorizing land-based pipeline construction and gas export. Only after the approvals were granted could the consortium sanction the project and begin construction.

These core licence applications triggered another wave of reviews centred on environmental and socio-economic impacts that involved several federal and provincial agencies. Under the Canadian Environmental Assessment Act, any major project under federal jurisdiction was subject to environmental-impact screening. This stipulation applied to both the SOEP's offshore works and the MNP's onshore works (the latter because of the export dimension). Furthermore, the Nova Scotia Environment Act set out comparable responsibilities and required separate provincial permits. Finally, the CNSOPB Accord Implementation Act required a socio-economic review of the offshore proposal. In contrast to the royalties question, all of these licensing questions would be adjudicated within open and contestable public hearings.

A striking feature of the regulatory process is the sheer number of agencies involved. A major proponent such as SOEP or MNP faces a panoply of regulatory oversights before construction, much less operations, can commence. From June 1995 to June 1996, the corporate proponents conveyed to government officials their urgent concerns about the uncoordinated, duplicative, and overall burdensome weight of the statutory requirements, which imposed costs both financial and temporal. It was made clear that these hurdles threatened project viability at a basic level. Extended discussions took place, not only between the consortia and state officials but also among state officials from various jurisdictions and agencies.

In an effort to meet this concern, and to rationalize a potentially byzantine tangle of separate panels, hearings, and reports, the federal and provincial governments agreed to a coordinated and harmonized procedure for the environmental reviews. This agreement was formalized in the intergovernmental and interagency Agreement for a Joint Panel Review of the Sable Gas Project, which was released in July 1996. The joint panel brought together three federal, two provincial, and one joint agency: the National Energy Board, the Canadian Environmental Assessment Agency, and Natural Resources Canada; the Department of Environment and the Department of Natural Resources; and the Canada–Nova Scotia Offshore Petroleum Board.[27] To conduct the necessary review, the agreement established a five-person panel that combined two National Energy Board members with three members nominated by various permutations of responsible ministers. A series of public hearings was authorized to collect evidence pertinent to the assessments, and the Canadian Environmental Assessment Agency provided limited public funding for selected intervenors. The joint panel was instructed to present its findings to all six parties to the agreement. It then fell to responsible ministers to take statutory decisions.

The members of the panel were announced in August 1996. Although the five appointees would sit and deliberate together, their statutory responsibilities and reporting relationships were varied. As a group, the panellists combined a range of professional backgrounds and management experiences. The chair, Robert Fournier, was an oceanographer and senior administrator at Dalhousie University. Jessie Davies was a professor of environmental planning from the University of New Brunswick, and John Sears was a retired professor of business and a senior administrator from St. Francis Xavier University. The final two members, Kenneth Vollman and Anita Côté-Verhaaf, an engineer and an economist, respectively, also sat on the National Energy Board.

The basis for their review was the Sable project description. In the autumn of 1996, public scoping meetings were held. The project's documents were disseminated, and limited amounts of public funding were made available through the Canadian Environmental Assessment Agency. It was reported that more than nine thousand people had been contacted by May 1997. For almost two months in the spring and summer of that year, the public hearings convened in several locations throughout Nova Scotia and New Brunswick. Then, in October 1997, the joint panel issued its report.[28] Overall, it found that the project could proceed without significant adverse environment effects, provided that a series of specified conditions were met. In a separate report, John Sears dealt with the socio-economic impacts of the project and reached similar conclusions.[29]

November and December 1997 were decision months for the federal and provincial ministers. Each was obliged to consider the joint panel advice before exercising statutory responsibilities in relation to the environmental impacts of the Sable project. By the end of December, all consents and certificates had been issued, and the regulatory path was clear. From this point forward, government agencies shifted from an adjudicatory mode to a new surveillance mode. During the construction and operational phases, their role centred on inspection and monitoring.

As significant as these outcomes proved to be, some of the most revealing politics surfaced during the review process itself. One of these episodes raised fundamental questions about the scope of environmental review and the ability of the process to take into consideration wider political questions about project planning. Given that environmental review is largely a reaction to business project initiatives, it was inevitable that the proponents, SOEP and MNP, would be at the centre of the review. Indeed, it was their project proposals that formed the basis of environmental review. The complicating question that surfaced, however, was whether the review process could allow the submission of alternative proposals once the initial proponents had filed. This question arose when separate consortia announced rival proposals, one of which involved Tatham Offshore Inc. However, the more consequential question was the Sable TransCanada project, which linked the Trans Québec and Maritime Pipeline (owned by Gaz Metropolitain of Montreal) and TransCanada Pipelines (owner of the giant west-to-east Canada transmission line). This second rival could be described as the domestic gas alternative, for these firms sought to deliver Sable gas into Quebec (and New Brunswick) markets. The proposed 50- to 60-centimetre pipe would run 1,080 kilometres from Goldboro to Bernières, Quebec, where it would join the existing trunk system from the west. Part of the proposed throughput of 400 million cubic feet (11 million cubic metres) per day would be exported to New England by existing or planned connections at the New York and Vermont borders. In effect, the scheme sought to reverse the domestic and export destination market proportions of the Sable gas supply.

To accomplish this, Sable TransCanada sought to use the National Energy Board as a legal fulcrum. In March 1997, it notified the board of its intentions by filing intervenor evidence in the Maritimes & Northeast hearing. This filing was accompanied by a request that the National Energy Board hearing be adjourned until the Trans Québec and Maritime Pipeline could file its own formal application and allow the board to hold comparative regulatory hearings.[30] Soon after, the three-person National Energy Board panel embedded in the joint review announced that no adjournment would be granted and that the Trans Québec and Maritime Pipeline's request for a delay would be addressed at the close of the public hearings.[31] When this came, there were a number of legal issues that involved weighing two arguments: first, that the board should pause the review under the discretion conferred on it by the "public convenience and necessity" standard to enable a comparative environmental hearing, and second, that procedural fairness to a declared and bona fide applicant (i.e., MNP) dictated prompt adjudication. The National Energy Board panel concluded that "delay in the issuance of our decision in respect to the SOEP and M&NPP applications would be commercially prejudicial to the proponents of those projects. The ... cases have been heard and the proponents ... are entitled to a decision from this Board."[32] The Sable TransCanada option, which recalled Nova Scotia's 1980 offshore planning scenario, was not simply a victim of timing. It had developed outside of the privileged SOEP-MNP dyad and could succeed only to the extent that it could sever this prior affinity.

By the fall of 1997, momentum was clearly building in favour of project approval. What remained to be determined were the conditions of approval and, therefore, the scope of the alterations that needed to be made. The joint public review panel, which was clearly the epicentre of state oversight, was integral to this process. Perhaps an unintended consequence of consolidating the regulatory proceeding was to make the process less flexible than it might otherwise be. Not enough is known about the interactions and influence of small-group panels over the year or more of deliberations. However, the logic of a common submission, public hearing, and report may have impeded selected members from factoring out their concerns by means of dissents or minority reports. At the same time, the lists of conditions that accompanied approval may be read as the product of these same joint deliberations.

Project Design and Construction: Contract Alliances

Throughout the period of state regulatory reviews, activities continued to move forward on other fronts. For example, the SOEP's partners undertook new three-dimensional seismic surveys in 1996 and 1997 to better understand the precise shape of the gas fields. These surveys served to update earlier seismic data that were ten to twenty years old. Although the deposition of the resource would not have changed, the tools available for its delineation certainly had. Most significantly, three-dimensional seismic imaging had all but replaced the more traditional two-dimensional technology of earlier times. By the mid-1990s, advances in acoustic recording, especially in data storage and computation, had made it an indispensable exploratory tool for planning field development. On the strength of the new surveys, the aggregate project reserves were raised to 3.5 trillion cubic feet (98 million cubic metres).

Another area that saw dramatic progress was engineering design and construction planning. On projects of this scale, preliminary work begins well before the sponsors face their ultimate "go or no go" decision. The initial stage of detailed project planning is known as front-end engineering design (FEED). After a competitive process that extended through 1995 and early 1996, the FEED contract was awarded in July 1996 to a joint venture that included Monenco AGRA of Calgary and Brown & Root (Halliburton Canada), whose parent was based in Houston. This $9-million contract covered work up to formal sanction of construction (in this case, the eighteen months until February 1998).[33]

The partners had already made a key decision – reflected in the FEED contract – to organize their infrastructure program as a project alliance rather than relying on a traditional contracting structure.[34] The alliance model was a relatively recent industry development that had emerged from the North Sea experience. The pioneer was British Petroleum, a major operator who concluded that the costs of conventional contracting, in both money and time, had become unsustainable by the early 1990s.[35] This new business arrangement was adopted broadly by North Sea firms involved in the mid-1990s program Cost Reduction in the New Economy (CRINE).

In the traditional model, the principal firm hires a general contractor to supervise the overall project from start to finish. This firm in turn hires a plethora of subcontractors to provide specialized services. In British Petroleum's experience, the arrangement was highly adversarial, for each constituent secured its role through competitive bidding and then made claims for unanticipated modifications to hike the tender price. Furthermore, it was a master-servant relationship that required principals and general contractors to maintain continuous oversight and resulting in frequent quarrels between contracting agents.

The alliance model, by contrast, sought to overcome this dichotomy by drawing all of the key providers (principal, general, and subcontractors) into a single structure based on trust and co-operation among all.[36] The infrastructure project is managed by a board composed of representatives from all parties. Rewards and risks are shared according to an alliance agreement, and conflict is resolved internally, with a no-dispute clause preventing the costly tradition of lawyers and courts. The obligations of all parties and the works to be delivered are spelled out by contract. In effect, all parties are committed to completing the project on or before time and on or under budget, with provisions to share any such benefits. Organizationally, an alliance involves a new structure in which staff from a variety of contractors come together for the duration of the project and work under the direction of the project's board. Since their parents stand to realize maximum gains from completion on budget, the staff members sink their differences in an effort to get the job done.

For the Sable project, the alliance was designed to select a corporate partner for each major phase of the infrastructure work. Seven major partners were sought in 1997 for a combination of offshore and onshore work. Offshore, these elements included platform jacket and topside fabrication, interfield gathering lines, and the field-to-shore pipeline. Negotiations were planned to culminate in late 1997 with the signing of the Sable Facilities Alliance Agreement. For a variety of reasons, the agreement was postponed several times. In the dying days (and hours) of December 1997, the formal owner sanction was still not finalized. Yet, rather than allowing the finely negotiated structure to dissolve at the end-of-year deadline, the partners felt sufficiently confident to take the risk of continuing beyond year end. Later, on 8 January 1998, the contracts were confirmed, and the first sod was turned. Finally, on 11 February 1998, the official sanction was announced.[37]

There were seven major areas of alliance within the overall construction plan. The first was the overall contract for engineering and construction management. Then came alliance leaders for each major functional area: fabrication of offshore platform jackets (foundation and leg structures), fabrication of offshore platform topsides (modules sitting atop the jackets); transportation and heavy lift services (for platform installation); the subsea pipeline system (connecting the fields and delivering to shore); and onshore construction (the Goldboro plant, the liquids pipeline to Point Tupper, and the fractionation plant at Point Tupper) (see Table 6.1).

Throughout 1998 and 1999, the procurement alliance was the epicentre of the Sable project's activities. The owners' interests were handled by a team headed by staff from Mobil Oil Canada and Shell Canada. John Brannan from Mobil was project manager, and the Combined Operations Committee brought together owners and contractors regularly to share progress reports. During the construction phase, the committee met each morning to talk with managers onsite. Broadly speaking, the first fifteen

TABLE 6.1

Sable offshore infrastructure alliances

Tier 1 alliances	
Front-end engineering design	Agra Monenco/Brown & Root Joint Venture (B&RJV)
Offshore well drilling	Rowan Inc./Santa Fe Drilling Co. (Can.)
Platform jackets	MM Industries/B&RJV yard (Dartmouth, NS) Peter Kiewit & Sons Co. (Houston, TX)
Platform topsides	MM Brown & Root Kvaerner Oil & Gas Ltd. (Teeside, UK)
Offshore pipelines	Allseas Canada Ltd.
Offshore transportation and installation	Saipem UK Ltd./Daewoo (S. Korea)
Onshore plants and pipelines	BBA Joint Venture BMS Offshore/Black & MacDonald Brown & Root Agra Monenco Elsag Bailey (Can.) Ltd
Tier 2 alliances	
Alma jacket and topsides	
South Venture jacket and topsides (2002)	Irving Shipbuilding Ltd. (NS)
Thebaud compression platform and facilities – ECPI	Saipem/Daewoo

Sources: Sable Offshore Energy Inc., "Milestones," press release, http://www.soep.com; SOEP benefits plan application, 1996.

months centred on design and construction, while the final eight months were taken up with the actual installation. The intensive phase of offshore work began in the spring of 1999, when jacket installations commenced. In addition, the twin (gas lateral and gas liquids) pipelines were completed in June and were followed in the summer with topside lifting and pipe laying. In August, the Thebaud processing plant was installed. By September, the North Triumph and Venture topsides were also in place, and the sea-to-shore pipeline was completed. The Country Harbour gas plant was undergoing tests, and the MNP pipeline was complete in October. The autumn was devoted to testing and final commissioning (after which the facilities were turned over to SOEI).

On 18 December 1999, the first gas arrived at the Thebaud platform. Not long after, it moved on to the Country Harbour (Goldboro) plant. On 4 January 2000, the sales meter turned for the first time, with a target rate of 400 million cubic feet (11 million cubic metres) per day by month's end. At the time, it was stated that "Sable's wells are some of the best producers in Canadian history" at 50 to 100 million cubic feet per day.[38] Tier I of the Sable venture was operational.

Almost immediately, attention shifted to planning for Tier 2, which had an estimated capital cost of $1 billion or half of Tier 1. In January 2001, SOEI announced the start of FEED studies for the Alma field, and the partners agreed to proceed with it a year later. Construction and installation began in 2003. On 2 December 2003, first gas flowed from the Alma field at 120 million cubic feet (3 million cubic metres) per day, along with 3,000 barrels of condensates. The next field, South Venture, was about a year behind. By December 2002, the fabrication contract for the South Venture topside had been placed with Irving Shipbuilding. Installation followed, and first gas flowed in 2004.

It was during these years that ExxonMobil assumed the formal role of SOEI operator (from Mobil Oil Canada).

Production, 2000-2010

The month of December 1999 is rightly seen as a watershed for both Sable Offshore Energy and MNP. Both enterprises shifted from being construction projects to operating companies. However, this distinction is misleading if it is taken at face value. Although the flow of gas and the revenue stream was vital to both SOEI and MNP, the Sable project was far from complete. The offshore Tier 1 facilities were in place, and the onshore trunk pipeline was operational, with a decade's worth of natural gas online. Yet the three Tier 2 fields were just entering the design and construction phase, and it was from them that the next source of supply would come. In short, the construction and production phases of the project were interconnected throughout the entire projected lifespan, which was scheduled to end in 2025.

Changes such as shifts in ownership, alignment, and resources also continued to occur within the core enterprises and reflected, in part, the dynamic character of energy markets in the late 1990s. Prices had recovered from a decade-long slump, and deregulated gas markets offered significant new (if rapidly changing) opportunities for a new source of supply. Yet the distinction between the operating project and its constituent investors continued to be key. The fortunes of the latter can shift suddenly and force changes for reasons quite separate from the project itself. Takeovers, mergers, strategic redirection, investor needs, and other factors can also be expected to intervene.

Finally, both SOEI and the MNP stood to be affected by new developments on the shelf. For example, PanCanadian Petroleum's Deep Panuke discovery pointed to the next prospective field development. Optimism likewise surged along with the boom in new exploration rights awarded in 1999-2000 and as drilling commenced on the deepwater slope in 2001. Almost immediately after gas service commenced, MNP grappled with expansion contingencies. It also faced new rivals such as the El Paso "Blue Atlantic" proposal for a subsea gas pipeline directly from the Scotian Shelf to New York and New Jersey (which was later abandoned as deepwater prospects faded). A prospective new sector also emerged in 2002 in the form of liquefied natural gas terminals in Nova Scotia to import and process overseas gas for the MNP's transmission system. The business and political contexts were far from settled when natural gas began to flow at the turn of the millennium.

Sable Offshore Energy Inc.

Even as Tier 1 production proceeded, preparations were under way for Tier 2 development. The first of the second-stage fields, Shell's Alma property, was in design by 2001. Construction continued the following year, and subsea well development and installation of the platform jacket (April) and topsides (September) was completed in 2003. Installation of the fifth field, South Venture, was scheduled for 2004.

One of the most significant changes in project parameters involved the scale of the gas reserves. According to the 1996 development project application, the six-field reserves were estimated at 4.6 trillion cubic feet (129 billion cubic metres). Of this, a volume of 3 trillion cubic feet (84 billion cubic metres) was expected to be recovered as sales gas over the life of the project. By the spring of 2004 (i.e., just under four and a half years into production), the cumulative project production was 718 billion cubic feet (20 billion cubic metres). This was 30 percent of the volume outlined in the application. It was drawn unevenly from the fields developed: 30 percent from Thebaud, 35 percent from Venture, 24 percent from North Triumph, and 2 percent from the newly opened Alma field.

The original configuration of the Sable project has been significantly transformed over the production years. First, as field development has proceeded, the anticipated natural gas reserves have not been proven up. Although the initial project forecast was 3 trillion cubic feet (84 billion cubic metres) of recoverable gas, the gas formation structures have been found to be more complex than initially thought and more expensive to develop. In recent years, both ExxonMobil and Shell have reduced their reserve estimates as a result of new seismic data, drill results, and production performance. For Shell, this reformulation coincided with a profound and damaging restatement of its global reserve holdings, including the Scotian Shelf. In a series of announcements that ended in 2004, Shell Canada downgraded its estimates for recoverable Sable reserves from 3.3 to 1.4 trillion cubic feet (92 billion cubic metres to 39 billion cubic metres).[39] In 2007, this estimate was revised marginally upward to 1.5 trillion cubic feet (42 billion cubic metres).[40] The recalibration was related to the significant decision, also announced in January 2004, that the Glenelg field was not economically viable. As a result, the scope of the Tier 2 expansion was confined to Alma (online in late 2003) and South Venture (online in 2004) alone. In a gap-filling effort, Shell returned to the site of its 1970s Onondaga discovery (in the middle of the Tier 2 field area) to drill for deep formation gas. However, after sinking a $90 million well, the results were declared insufficient for testing. More generally, these events led to the Sable fields, and perhaps the shallow water Scotian Basin in general, being perceived as a difficult and complex geology in which to operate.

Sharp declines in reserve estimates brought a number of major changes to the project. First, the project's life was cut dramatically from twenty-five to fifteen years based on forecast rates.[41] For many years, the possibility of additional reserves being incorporated into an enlarged SOEI consortium had remained alive, since there are additional significant discovery licences in the Sable Island area. However, the possibility faded in July 2010, when ExxonMobil announced that it had decided against extending the project.[42] Another possible restructuring might have involved the Pan Canadian/EnCana discovery at Deep Panuke, a major commercial field of some 1 trillion cubic feet (28 billion cubic metres). Although it was initially envisaged as a stand-alone project in the development plan application of 2002, the application was subsequently withdrawn. An alternative scenario that attracted some speculation at the time had EnCana gas flowing through the Thebaud platform complex and into the SOEI's offshore pipe system. A further scenario, also unrealized, had EnCana sell its Deep Panuke rights to

ExxonMobil or another partner in the Sable project. In fact, under the present development plan, Deep Panuke gas will be processed on site before moving to land.

Second, the reserve downgrades accelerated the SOEI's plans for installing compression facilities at its gas fields, a process that involved the addition of a new platform at the Thebaud site. Although pressures within the reservoir formations were sufficient to drive the flow of natural gas in the Tier 1 phase, their projected (and now accelerated) decline could be compensated for by mechanical compression. In 2003, SOEI operator ExxonMobil placed the engineering, procurement, construction, and installation contract for this work with Saipem-Daewoo. Installation took place in 2006 in an effort to extend the life of the Sable project to 2015.

Other significant corporate changes occurred at the ownership level. The proportion of the partners' stakes evolved over time. While Mobil Oil Canada and Shell Canada retained the largest shares, Petro-Canada departed during the development phase. In addition, the global merger of Exxon and Mobil brought the Sable project into the portfolio of the world's largest supermajor. The Sable project stood to be affected in two respects. The first involved its fit with the new corporate strategy. Whereas Mobil Oil Canada, which had lead holdings in both the Nova Scotia and Newfoundland sectors, had been a vigorous participant in Atlantic offshore exploration from the outset, ExxonMobil operated on a higher scale in the search for worldwide investments. Unless the Scotian Shelf (particularly the deepwater slope) demonstrated such potential, Exxon's interest in a standalone gas field of modest proportions was open to question. This uncertainty was underlined when ExxonMobil assumed operator status for SOEI in 2002. The second was the shift in exploration and production culture that underlay corporate decision making. Mobil had demonstrated a historical affinity for the East Coast continental shelf that was absent from Exxon.

Another significant change in the consortium involved Nova Scotia Resources Limited (NSRL). A founding partner on the basis of its field discoveries during the National Energy Program's exploration wave, NSRL was also a provincial state enterprise whose fit with 1990s energy policy was increasingly tenuous. As seen in earlier chapters, NSRL had long suffered under the twin burdens of weak access to capital and low political legitimacy in Halifax. After 1993, this weakness was magnified by the Nova Scotia government's acute fiscal crisis, in which ballooning deficits were met by deep and systemic expenditure cuts. Within the Liberal government of Premier John Savage, there was a strong commitment to catalyzing the

Sable project. However, there was also deep cynicism about NSRL's contribution to this process. Consequently, the sale of the company's stake in SOEI, as part of its overall wind down, came as little surprise. After a series of interfirm manoeuvrings (detailed earlier), Nova Scotia electricity supplier Emera Energy emerged with NSRL's 8.4 percent share of Sable's onshore assets but sold them to Pengrowth Energy Trust in 2003.

Maritimes & Northeast Pipeline Ltd.

With key Canadian regulatory approvals secure, MNP also conferred a project sanction in 1998. The initial phase was partly one of construction planning, particularly contracting materials, assemblers, and skilled workers. The phase also involved negotiating consents for rights of way along the projected route through Nova Scotia, New Brunswick, and Maine. As seen above, the first gas passed into the MNP in early January 2000.

It was not long after transmission commenced that corporate control of MNP shifted hands. This shift was influenced by the rise of Duke Energy as a major presence in the deregulated era of North American pipelines. In 1997, Duke Energy took a share of the MNP project through its merger with the Texas Eastern Corp. Five years later, this stake was doubled to more than a 75 percent share when Duke tookover Westcoast Transmission for US$8.8 billion. The remaining interests were held by Emera Energy (12.9 percent) and ExxonMobil (9.6 percent).

The MNP had been designed with expansion possibilities in mind. The original system was built without compression stations, since the formation gas pressures (together with the Goldboro plant) were sufficient to drive the product. Consequently, the throughput of the original line could be expanded significantly with the installation of compressor stations. For example, MNP estimated in 2002 that the installation of four compressors would more than double capacity to over 1 billion cubic feet (28 million cubic metres) per day. Another option was to loop the line by installing a parallel pipeline within the right of way. Both options depended, of course, on the pace of new discoveries and the development of major new fields.

At the turn of the millennium, MNP was entitled to be optimistic. Record acreage had recently been taken out for exploration in the Sable Shelf, and PanCanadian Petroleum announced plans for its Deep Panuke project. The project was based on a property that had been acquired from NSRL in 1996. By drilling far deeper than the established oil reservoirs, PanCanadian found recoverable gas reserves estimated at 1 trillion cubic feet (28 billion cubic metres) or more, marking the second significant supply source in the Sable

Basin. PanCanadian's development plan, submitted to the Canada–Nova Scotia Offshore Petroleum Board in 2001, proposed to process the gas offshore and pipe it in to connect with the MNP near Goldboro. With an estimated ten-year supply, the project was forecast to begin as early as 2008. On this basis, PanCanadian, which became part of EnCana through the PanCanadian-Alberta Energy Corporation merger in the fall of 2001, signed a conditional firm service agreement with MNP. The latter in turn filed an application with the National Energy Board to upgrade its mainline and install compressor stations to cope with the added volume. The doubling of the MNP's capacity would reduce tolls for existing shippers by one-third.[43] On March 2002, the board gave its consent.

Only months later, however, the expansion project came to a halt when EnCana announced that it was withdrawing its development plan or, in the terminology of the day, taking a time out for further review. In 2006, the company resubmitted, and a project-development process commenced. Deep Panuke's "go-stop-go" sequence offers a salutary example of just how sensitive the supporting conditions for major offshore developments can be.

Conclusion

The Sable project provides compelling evidence of how a major offshore production project unfolds as a series of stages. These stages can be described in terms of activity or function: petroleum discovery and delineation, commercial analysis and technical engineering, construction of the productive system, and actual operations. However, these functional categories fail to grasp the active and negotiated nature of business. Events do not simply happen but rather must be set in motion by agents who can initiate, block, or alter the direction of motion. In this sense, action unfolds through a sequence of key windows for forward action and results. Forward progress is a matter of creating opportunities and reacting to obstacles.

The Sable project's history has a half-dozen watershed events whose outcomes dictated the ultimate course. Each watershed was political in nature, setting terms of advantage or disadvantage both within the firms and outside of them. Decisions were framed and confirmed in different venues where process variables are influential. Perhaps the first key event was the apprehension of shifting market prospects as the long petroleum slump began to lift in the 1990s. The prospects for North American natural gas were much improved as the electric power sector shifted sharply toward the new fuel. The second key event was the need to overcome the limitations of separate corporate holdings by means of a consortium. To realize the threshold gas volumes required for a greenfield project, significant discovery licence holders needed to act in concert. Sable Offshore Energy Project emerged as the vehicle for this co-operation as was signified by the partners' memorandum of understanding in 1994. It is notable that changing priorities within the constituent firms required periodic transactions among the partners to maintain the integrity of the enterprise. A third critical moment was the confirmation of final sales markets in both Maritime Canada and the northeast United States. The allied firm MNP came into play, concluding sales agreements at threshold volumes or greater. A fourth closely related event was gaining regulatory consent in 1997 from the National Energy Board to ship and sell Sable gas outside of Canada.

In the midst of these market-making negotiations, a separate issue emerged that had the potential to derail MNP's business strategy. Gas carriers and Maritime provincial governments came into conflict over the share of natural gas to be allotted to the region, the shipping tariff structure, and the extent to which mainline tolls would cross-subsidize the installation of lateral delivery lines to Maritime markets. The so-called joint-tolling issue needed to be resolved before the export issue could be addressed.

The fifth watershed event was the decision by federal and provincial state authorities to mount a joint regulatory panel on the Sable project. At the time, this experiment in stacked proceedings was innovative in nature and avoided duplication by crafting a composite panel to advise one joint, three federal, and two provincial agencies. Although its remit centred on environmental impacts, the approval in principle from the joint panel served to legitimize the project and opened the way for ministers and agencies to concentrate on particular conditions of compliance. A sixth key moment that attracted less public attention than most of the others was the 1996 royalties agreement between SOEP and the Government of Nova Scotia. This agreement was a product of the Savage Liberal government. In addition to clearing the way for the Sable project, it created the basic template around which future royalty agreements would be framed.

This chapter's findings also raise questions about the notion of a resource-extraction project. Despite a necessary organizational coherence, this type of project cannot be treated as a unitary structure. Any such enterprise evolves through a series of discrete stages, and its shape and purpose are open to change as time unfolds. From an initial concept, the project progresses to a formal proposal or series of proposals and undergoes adjustment in response to the external pressures of finance, commerce, and sovereign regulation. The project assumes concrete form as a built extractive system and is modified further during its operational life. For the Sable project, the exploration and production firms that made commercial discoveries on the shelf – most notably Mobil Canada and Shell Canada – were the key movers of the early decades. Mobil advanced the Venture gas project on its own terms. By the 1990s, the interfirm consortium had emerged as the most promising form of enterprise, and the Sable project was born. Sable Offshore Energy Project in turn negotiated a cross-firm project alliance with MNP as a means of internalizing necessary business parameters. Together, the two companies' momentum was sufficient to gain intergovernmental support and to repel alternative development schemes such as Sable TransCanada. Indeed, SOEP's ultimate triumph put transnational capital in a dominant political position in Nova Scotia's petroleum politics.

Finally, there are questions about short- and long-term appraisals of the project. In the former, the successful design and installation of the project at the specified scale stands as a significant commercial achievement. The Sable project was, as already noted, the largest construction project in Nova Scotia's history, and it fuelled the provincial economy for the better part of a decade. The dual-phase installation plan extended the macroeconomic impact from 1995 to 2005. In addition, state regulatory proceedings and decisions were also triggered by development, benefits, environmental impact, and gas export applications in 1996. Particularly intensive was the period from 1996 to 1998, when deliberations by a host of federal and provincial agencies took place. At the centre of this process was the joint review panel, although other regulatory provisions also played out. On one level, the facilities-planning and state regulatory reviews were sufficiently complex to establish brief but intensive political subfields. Here, the impact of time constraints was evident, as was the need for compromises and trade-offs to maintain forward momentum, avoid deadlocks, and protect the core properties of the prospective enterprise while satisfying emergent demands.

In the longer term, however, some striking alterations occurred. The Sable project's initial operating horizon was set at twenty-five years. Following the start-up of the Tier 1 fields and the geo-commercial reappraisal, however, recoverable reserve estimates were slashed by half. The project's life was shortened to as little as twelve to fifteen years, and one of the Tier 2 fields, Glenelg, was abandoned for commercial purposes. Whether the Sable project would have received project sanction in 1997, on the basis of the revised resource estimates, is doubtful.

The fiscal planning of the Government of Nova Scotia was equally influenced by the project's shorter lifespan. The Savage Liberal government had put construction at the top of its policy priorities, along with the negotiation of a tax and royalty regime for the project. The most significant incentive was loading the royalty payments into the middle and late phases of the project's operating life, enabling the company to recover capital costs and reach a profit position early. Such arrangements were common in the petroleum sector, and they fell well within accepted Crown-operator relations. Indeed, the political trade-off for the province was that the deferred royalty payouts would be compensated for by the macro-economic stimulus associated with installing critical infrastructure and renewed exploration. Ultimately, however, the project served as a critical bridge between exploration cycles, bringing economic vitality to the basin and making a strategic investment for the future.

7 The Politics of Backward Linkage: Industrial Benefits

For understandable reasons, modern petroleum politics pits capital against the state in distributional struggles over revenues, royalties and, in the case of state oil companies, shares of the commodity markets. This reality applies to offshore petroleum regions as much as onshore areas, but offshore operations bring added complications of jurisdiction and physical environments. Since the 1960s in Canada, these complications have fed an ongoing political struggle that encompasses three oceans, six provinces, three territories, the federal state, and a range of industries and subindustries. The political permutations are, as a result, intriguing and revealing.

One issue that can get lost in the process is the promotion of links between host economy and emerging offshore sector.[1] Industrial, regional, or local benefits are the focus of this chapter. In the early 1980s, the topic of industrial benefits needed little introduction. As the National Energy Program flared across the political horizon, state interest in the strategic management of industrial benefits was strong. For a time, megaproject management was considered Ottawa's de facto industrial policy.

Perhaps the durability of the benefits issue in frontier energy policy is more surprising. The issue both preceded and survived the epoch of the National Energy Program. Indeed, it remains a pressing and contested issue today. Benefits policy rests upon a distinct set of policy instruments. Consequently, it offers strong opportunities for policy diffusion and learning, for each new offshore jurisdiction crafted a regulatory configuration at least in part by reference to those that had gone before. The logic and dynamics of the offshore benefits question run parallel in many ways to secondary industry strategy, thereby offering a comparative point of reference. Yet, at the same time, there are significant differences in institutional tradition and regulatory culture. Furthermore, the political involvement of petro-capital is complex, for far more is involved than the Seven Sisters and the state oil companies of OPEC. Despite the near hegemonic tradition of petroleum capital in terrestrial environments, offshore hydrocarbon activity was, as we have seen, a distinct industry.

This chapter tackles several aspects of offshore benefits policy. First, it explores how the benefits question emerged as a core policy dimension of Nova Scotia offshore petroleum management. Second, it outlines the surprisingly complicated structure of offshore petroleum capital and its implications for the design and implementation of a benefits regime. Third, it traces the genealogy of offshore benefits regulation in Canada from 1981 onward. Fourth, it raises questions about the pattern of benefits politics on Canada's Scotian Shelf and the contemporary state of play. Two case studies are developed to illustrate the trajectories of change. Finally, the chapter argues that a new phase of benefits politics has begun, for the regulatory paradigm is more open to challenge than it has been in two decades.

The Offshore Industry's Structure and the Sable Basin

The offshore exploration or production platform is one of the icons of modern global industry. Like the communications satellite, the nuclear reactor, or the automated assembly plant, the offshore platform is an assemblage of advanced technologies that involves myriad parts and processes that are designed, fabricated, and operated to accomplish tasks of impressive difficulty.[2] However, an icon can be both expressive and misleading. The offshore industry is an elaborately layered business structure in which only the most visible elements – for instance, the topside rig carrying the name of the corporate operator – are clearly labelled.

These iconic images highlight the commercial core of offshore petroleum development: the drilling, pumping, and transport of crude oil, natural gas, and associated liquids. Missing, however, is the terrestrial umbilical cord that makes production possible. The strategic gains of local or regional business contractors are contingent on recognizing the links between firms, products, and services throughout the offshore manufacturing and service value chain. Michael Jenkin defines the offshore supply industry as "all those firms engaged in a support role for offshore hydrocarbon exploration and production, be it in the form of services or manufactured products."[3]

As seen earlier, there are a variety of discrete business stages – exploration, discovery, development and production, and decommission – that make up the life cycle of an offshore project. Furthermore, there are distinct enterprise structures of differing scope and scale, beginning with permit or licence holders – such as ExxonMobil, EnCana, or the Sable consortium – who have secured the legal rights and committed the capital to explore or develop tracts of subsea petroleum-bearing sediments. In addition, the geology and exploration divisions of upstream oil firms play a crucial role in determining prospective plays, including reconnaissance work in the form of geophysical, magnetic, and seismic surveys performed by air or sea. Since these companies seldom if ever undertake all of the necessary activities internally, they are commonly tendered by contract to specialized technical firms. In cases where the evidence is sufficiently promising to merit further investigation, permittees move to exploration drilling, by which holes are sunk at designated locations to test for hydrocarbon deposits.

At this stage, specialized offshore platforms are either purchased or hired to undertake the drilling and analysis of data. Here again, a set of specialized service firms, capable of operating facilities worth hundreds of millions of dollars and employing crews exceeding one hundred workers, are hired for individual projects, entire seasons, or multi-year campaigns. Over time, the market oscillates between periods of tight rig supply, when costs skyrocket and bottlenecks proliferate, and periods when exploration wanes and whole fleets are idle. In cases where exploration drilling confirms fields with commercially exploitable reserves, permit holders and other bidders have the opportunity to convert their rights to longer-term development leases. At this point, plans are designed for petroleum production systems, which include subsea wells, seabed control facilities and gathering lines, production platforms, and pipeline or ship-based transport and storage facilities. One supply study identified twenty-nine major categories of equipment required for one production platform. As Jenkin observes, bearing in mind that an average field involves two or more platforms, several hundred firms are often linked in the fabrication and operation of key development facilities.[4]

In offshore industry and regulatory circles, an accepted rule of thumb is that the exploration-activity phase should represent less than 20 percent of the monetary value of all offshore expenditures involved in field development. In contrast, the development of production systems, including the costs associated with decommissioning at project termination, should account for the far larger proportion. This rule highlights a central reality of offshore industrial benefits programming – the leverage attainable during exploration activities is only a fraction of the leverage available at the development stage. A successful transition from the first phase to the second is critical for the expansion of offshore-onshore linkages.

At the exploration stage, the operating or permit-holding company normally plays an active role in managing the overall activity through its exploration arm but contracts onsite work to rig and service firms. At the development stage, however, the operator hires general engineering and fabrication contractors to deliver large modules or finished systems. These general contractors consequently represent a separate level of enterprise. A third level includes the specialized firms, large and small, who provide goods and services through seismic programs, exploratory drilling, platform construction, and production system installation.

Although industrial diversification is normally measured by the number of specialized offshore service firms established, general contractors and major subcontractors have long been recognized as critical connectors. Their standing procurement preferences and business allies tend to represent a default option even when the firms enter new petroleum provinces. Initial experience in the North Sea showed an overwhelming Gulf of Mexico enterprise nexus, for US rights holders relied on familiar US goods and service suppliers. State benefits policies aim to break these default connections and to fashion new local and regional networks. In Scotland, the political problem was sometimes described as the "de-Dallasification" of Aberdeen. Although their strategic approaches differed, both the United Kingdom and Norway developed systematic approaches to offshore benefits as their basin was developed in the 1970s.[5]

Evidently, the task of maximizing linkages is not a simple one. For offshore operators, contracting with local firms is relatively straightforward when it comes to off-the-shelf services such as office support, maintenance, and catering. Other procurement fields are more restrictive, requiring the adaptation of existing expertise to marine applications such as offshore sea transport, stand-by rig support, and helicopters. Another supply cluster involves proprietorial services, which are often dominated by subsidiaries of global offshore service firms. Examples include advanced seismic work, well log analysis, and specialty drilling operations (deepwater or directional). Firms such as Schlumberger and Halliburton carved out niches in this way. The production-systems stage is dominated by the coordinating design, engineering, and fabrication firms mentioned above. Not surprisingly, a variety of policy instruments have figured in state efforts to indigenize offshore enterprise.

Thus far, the process has been conceptualized at the project level – such as the Sable or Deep Panuke gas projects on the Scotian Shelf. However, it is when patterns become cumulative – that is, when multiple projects emerge from a single subbasin such as Sable – that the economic impacts are magnified, extending prospector interest throughout an entire basin and enhancing the possibility for cumulative investment and growth. A thriving petroleum basin will include multiple plays at various stages of maturity, the *ne plus ultra* for offshore jurisdictions. However, the political and technical challenges of benefits programming tend to cluster in the earlier transitional phases of industry development.

Genealogy of Industrial Benefits Policy

The notion of offshore industrial benefits as an object of public policy has a durable history that illuminates two major contextual constraints. The first, which derives from petroleum industry practices, reveals the potential path of cross-national policy diffusion, while the second, which derives from Canadian industrial policy practices, reveals the national and regional tradition of state intervention in business practices.

It was in the decades immediately following the Second World War that the western Canadian sedimentary basin emerged as a world scale-petroleum play. The Leduc discovery of 1947 kicked off an extraordinary period of exploration, development, and production, and a fully elaborated industry complex emerged at Calgary. Subsequent discoveries transformed the city from an agriculture and transportation hub into an oil town. The scale of the resource, combined with its commercial potential, led to an industry structure in which foreign-owned majors were joined by domestic independents, junior explorers, and a full range of specialized service firms. It was market-driven growth, however, and state fiscal and trade policies were critical facilitators.[6]

Between 1945 and 1970, financing and managing major industrial projects were uncontested corporate prerogatives. The Keynesian shelf of public works played an important role in counter-cyclical stabilization, and state guarantees for private infrastructure (such as the TransCanada Pipeline) also figured in the mix. However, the notion of systematic state regulation to leverage domestic business opportunities out of private petroleum projects was certainly not. In isolated cases, authorities would perhaps attempt to use moral suasion to encourage domestic sourcing, as when powerful federal minister C.D. Howe had Imperial Oil maximize Canadian industrial involvement, "wherever feasible," in the construction of the Interprovincial Pipeline running from Alberta to Ontario.[7]

A generation later, Judd Buchanan, the minister of northern affairs, was working from the same repertoire. In 1975, he wrote to the corporate sponsors of Arctic energy projects to request their best efforts on domestic contracting. The federal cabinet of the day also established an Advisory Committee on Industrial Benefits – an administrative body drawn from the Departments of Northern Affairs, Energy, and Industry – to signal Ottawa's ongoing interest.[8]

On a separate policy track, however, a different paradigm had emerged. In the field of secondary manufacturing, economic nationalists had succeeded in raising structural questions about the impact of foreign ownership. Task force inquiries led by Mel Watkins and Herb Gray served to redefine the public interest in corporate performance. This interest centred on the role of regulation in altering the structural tendencies of multinational enterprises. Key performance criteria included research and development, export orientation, and equity issuing. This logic underlay the establishment of the Foreign Investment Review Agency in 1973 as a mechanism to alter the prevailing foreign enterprise strategies. A key policy instrument was the negotiated process by which foreign-owned or -controlled corporate applicants set out business plans for future performance, to secure federal state approval for proposed takeovers or major new investments in Canada. In this way, a new policy vocabulary found its way into industrial policy: one of Canadian ownership rules, corporate undertakings, and performance audits.

This logic extended beyond foreign investment, most famously in the National Energy Program of October 1980. The Canadian ownership goals are well documented.[9] Equally significant, however, were the policy objectives for industrial supply and service. A key statute in this area was the Canada Oil and Gas Act of 1981, which required ministerial approval for an industrial benefits plan before any exploration or development permits could be issued. In framing these measures, Ottawa was directly influenced by the experience of the UK Offshore Supply Office, which had used memorandums of understanding to negotiate domestic sourcing in North Sea operations. Indeed, the key passage of the Canada Oil and Gas Act stipulated that Canadian firms must have "a full and fair opportunity to participate on a competitive basis in the supply of goods and services used in that work program."[10] Anticipating the passage of this act, the Office of Industrial and Regional Benefits was established in the Department of Industry in the summer of 1981 to assume the benefits-monitoring mandate. It is important to note that these provisions were prime targets of the Reagan administration's attack on both the National Energy Program and the Foreign Investment Review Agency.[11]

Capital and the Offshore Industry

The political representation of industries is never simple or predictable, and the petroleum sector offers a strong case in point. Each phase of extraction and production has the potential to create a stand-alone industry composed of specialist firms, ranging from land rights acquisition, seismic work, and exploratory drilling to field development and production, transport, refining, and petro-chemical manufacturing. At the same time, processes of horizontal and vertical integration have created ever-larger firms with backward and forward linkages that span many or all of the subindustries just sketched. Furthermore, geopolitics tend to shape the patterns of petroleum sector representation, reflecting not only the spatial distribution of the resource but also the jurisdictional distribution of state authority. In Canada, the most visible producer associations arose regionally, after the Turner Valley oil strike of 1914, and then nationally, to represent the integrated major firms, the independent producers, and the well drill contractors.[12]

Where, then, is the offshore interest in this complex and diversified industry? It was in the early 1960s that certain Calgary-based firms began to show interest in the potential of the continental shelf on three oceans. Mobil Canada led the rights-taking initiative on the East Coast, while Dome Petroleum pioneered Arctic exploration and Shell and Chevron set the pace on the Pacific. Perhaps not surprisingly, these firms approached the offshore frontiers as extensions of the land-based industry. One significant point of contrast, however, was the preponderance of foreign-owned oil majors over independents in the offshore sector. This dominance reflected the majors' prior experience in the rapidly developing Gulf of Mexico play (begun in 1947) and in the emerging North Sea play (begun in the 1960s), as well as their greater capacity for carrying the initial risk and meeting the significantly higher cost structures of offshore operations.

Perhaps inevitably, offshore concerns were of pressing importance to only a segment of the upstream industry in Canada. As far as political representation was concerned, several organizational strategies were available. A specialized offshore association had emerged at an early date in the United

States, when pioneer firms moved into the Gulf of Mexico after the Second World War. The first well was drilled in 1947, and oil production came two years later.[13] Exploration began in shallow inshore waters, and once first-generation technologies were mastered, it spread rapidly: almost six thousand wells were drilled between 1954 and 1964. Exploration then expanded, as new technologies allowed, into depths of up to a hundred metres in the 1960s and 1970s. As mentioned earlier, the Offshore Operators Committee was formed in 1950 to speak for the offshore upstream segment of the industry. By its own account, over the past half-century the organization "has evolved into the Oil and Gas industry's principal representative regarding regulation of offshore exploration, development and producing operations in the Gulf of Mexico." In particular, the organization focuses on "direct participation in the rulemaking process which various governmental bodies follow in establishing regulations."[14] In 2002, the committee included seventy operating companies and twenty-five service companies. Many if not most of these organizations maintained parallel memberships in the American Petroleum Institute (the omnibus voice of integrated oil) and more than a dozen more specialized industry associations.

A similar organizational strategy had been pursued in Canada. The land-based industry had its first collective expression in the Alberta Oil Operators Association, which was established in 1927. Twenty-five years later, it merged with the Saskatchewan Operators Association to form the Canadian Petroleum Association (CPA). Within a well-developed committee or divisional structure, member firms could caucus to manage province-by-province or functional issues.[15] Although the CPA and the Independent Petroleum Association of Canada enjoyed similar membership numbers by the 1970s, the companies securing acreage on the East Coast continental shelf were largely foreign-owned majors. As a result, they would be familiar with the American practice of separate offshore representation.

Canadian analogues to the US Offshore Operators Committee appeared in two frontier regional associations. Once again, the timing coincided with the start of offshore drilling, a period when the first exploratory well was sunk on the East Coast in 1966 and the first in the Arctic in 1971. The permit holders banded together in regional clusters in the early 1970s. Those in the federal northlands formed the Arctic Petroleum Operators Association, while those on the Atlantic continental shelf formed the Eastcoast Petroleum Operators Association. In the latter case, the costs of collective action were met by a pro-rated assessment on the acreage held by member companies;

in the former, some of the staff costs (and benefits) were underwritten by the broader petroleum constituency.[16]

In 1983, the eastern association opted to merge with the CPA. In effect, the regional bloc entered intact and was renamed the Offshore Operators Division. It was led by a board of directors that met almost monthly to oversee an annual budget, it was supported by a single staff officer, and it spoke officially through the executive committee of the board. After the merger with the CPA, the division's board continued to exercise significant autonomy on regional and sectoral policy matters while partaking in the broader industry activities of the parent group. Several years later, in 1985-86, the Arctic Petroleum Operators Association followed suit. The offshore group was renamed the Frontier Division of the CPA, in which business was conducted through two parallel regional arms that shared a staff officer. This structure acknowledged the member firms' shared experience under Canada Lands legislation and the Canadian Oil and Gas Lands Administration while at the same time conceding that the East Coast regulatory boards and basins presented unique elements not found in the Arctic. In fact, the Canadian Petroleum Association went further by opening regional offices in Halifax and St. John's by 1983.

Other substantial industry interests, rooted in the marine world beyond oil and gas, were also important. Indeed, petroleum was a relative latecomer to business in the oceans sector, preceded by such major industry groupings as shipbuilding, marine transport, cable and communications, and commercial fishing, to name only the most prominent. Although the ocean was traditionally treated as open space in which separate core industries pursued independent operations, the situation changed in the 1970s, when ocean industries began to be recognized in government circles as a strategic growth sector.[17] The federal government's industrial strategy exercise of 1977, often known as the Tier One/Tier Two process, authorized consultations in twenty-two designated sectors, including ocean industries.[18]

Another possibility was an umbrella group comprising marine-oriented firms and sectors in the business not of petroleum extraction per se but rather of selling specialized goods and services to the offshore petroleum operators. In Nova Scotia, the Offshore Trades Association of Nova Scotia (now known as the Offshore/Onshore Technologies Association of Nova Scotia) was created in 1982. In March of that year, the Canada–Nova Scotia Agreement on Offshore Oil and Gas Resource Management and Revenue Sharing was finalized, putting aside the legal dispute over federal and provincial Crown ownership and stipulating a new joint offshore management regime to encourage early and extensive development. The agreement included an estimated $2.5 billion in tax breaks and grants aimed at catalyzing new investment.

In August, a delegation of Nova Scotia business people visited Aberdeen, Scotland, to better understand the potential for offshore-related industry. According to the umbrella association, "The group saw tremendous potential, but they also learned that the oil and gas industry is a truly global business with plenty of natural barriers to entry."[19] Before they returned, it was resolved to "put together an association aimed at pooling information and talent, and advancing the interests of Nova Scotia companies ... We wanted to be able to say very clearly what we felt were the best policies for Nova Scotia industry."[20]

From the outset, the Offshore Trades Association combined advocacy ("to support the maximization of Atlantic Canadian participation in the supply of both goods and services"), market intelligence on business opportunities ("meetings with industry leaders" and "information bulletins"), and member networking (with one another and with the lead offshore operators). The original thirty members grew to two hundred within a few years. Although the offshore supply-and-service sector waxed and waned along with the offshore business cycle, the association had over five hundred members by 2004 and described itself as Canada's largest oil and gas industry association.

Umbrella groups for ocean-sector firms fit closely with another federal policy vector of support for technology-intensive ocean industries. The Science Council of Canada identified ocean industries as a potential field in which Canada could gain comparative advantage. The Tier One committee described ocean industries as "those establishments that manufacture equipment or provide services for all commercial and scientific activities in the oceans."[21] Although still small in scale (an estimated 160 companies, of which 40 core firms depended on ocean activities for a majority of revenues in 1978), the pattern of growth was impressive. Sales grew from $5 million to $200 million between 1969 and 1976, and a ten-fold factor of future growth was projected. However, the offshore petroleum sector was seen as the driving force of greatest commercial significance. In its report, the Sector Task Force on the Canadian Ocean Industry advanced a series of proposals centred on an improved tax structure for equity, duties, and capital investment; joint industry-government investment in strategic research and development; the establishment of a national trade association; and mandatory Canadian-content rules for offshore contracting.[22]

Then, in 1981, Canada and Nova Scotia finalized the Ocean Industry Development Subsidiary Agreement under the general economic development agreement. Running for five years, it injected $35 million on a two-to-one federal-provincial contributory basis. The federal portion supported capital assistance, marketing, an ocean promotional office, and trade association funding. The Nova Scotia portion centred on development of the Woodside Ocean Industrial Park at the Dartmouth waterfront.[23]

Obviously, both the federal task force and the subsidiary agreement increased the policy visibility and the political legitimacy of ocean interests as commercial industry. A series of government departments were charged with sector responsibilities, and both governments welcomed the organized industry as a political interlocutor. A variety of policy instruments emerged. Some, on the supply side, sought to shape capital availability, market awareness, site availability, and infrastructure. However, it was on the demand side, the realm of legislated benefits reporting and review, that the most critical policy instruments emerged.

Industrial Benefits: Objectives and Tools

As far as the state policy makers were concerned, the 1980 National Energy Policy set the broad thrust of industrial benefits policy. However, the promotion of domestic industrial linkages was fleshed out through separate policies. The first of these was the Major Projects Task Force Report of 1981, chaired by oilman Robert Blair and labour leader Shirley Carr.[24] The report's emphasis on maximizing the Canadian supply-and-service component in dozens of upcoming energy megaprojects (defined then as capital projects worth more than $100 million) was rapidly incorporated into federal policy.

In fact, the Office of Industrial and Regional Benefits was established in the Department of Industry in the summer of 1981 to develop guidelines, reporting procedures, and monitoring mechanisms that could be linked to regulatory oversight. The guidelines set out the project sponsors' responsibilities in a number of areas: disclosing their corporate manpower and procurement policies, identifying capable and competitive Canadian suppliers to participate in bidding, disclosing pertinent procurement plans in advance, ensuring the inclusion of Canadian firms on bidders' lists, providing debriefings in cases of failed bids, and reporting to the Office of Industrial and Regional Benefits to demonstrate compliance with Ottawa's procurement objectives.[25] However, the task force's proposal that major project proponents be encouraged (the position of business) or required (the position of labour) to pay a Canada procurement premium of up to 3 percent on total project costs was not incorporated into federal policy. Nonetheless, the practice of formal reporting and scrutiny of major corporate purchases was firmly established.

The targeted benefits framework for the Nova Scotia offshore area was, however, defined in other circles. The new federal Crown offshore rights regime was based on the Canada Oil and Gas Act, proclaimed in March 1982. Its statutory powers were vested in the powerful new agency known as the Canada Oil and Gas Lands Administration (COGLA). One of its six operating units, the Canada Benefits Branch, exercised powers of approval and monitoring for all major offshore activities on the Scotian Shelf. In effect, it assumed the offshore petroleum responsibilities of the Office of Industrial and Regional Benefits and borrowed extensively from its methods. The Benefits Branch "advise[d] operators on the means whereby Canadians can be assured full and fair access on a competitive basis to the industrial and employment benefits" and "adjudicate[d] the plans submitted by the operator prior to the commencement of the work program."[26] These duties involved horizontal input from a variety of federal and provincial agencies.

The COGLA proceeded to define a three-part template for benefits reporting and assessment, beginning with estimates of expected domestic industrial sourcing over a planning period and proposals on how the expected levels could be enhanced (the so-called supplier development and succession plans). Particular attention was to be paid to the applicant's contributions to technology transfer and research and development in Canada. The second part dealt with employment benefits, including hiring Canadians, enhanced training opportunities, and affirmative action. The third part covered social benefits, calling for community and business impact studies, community consultation programs, and plans for regional or local expenditures (local hiring, infrastructure measures, and so on). By 1984, corporate rights holders were filing benefits reports that indicated a Canada benefits procurement value of 50 to 75 percent.[27] Figure 7.1 captures the cumulative picture over the first benefits regulation cycle from 1981 to 1990.

Nor did the provincial state ignore the issue of industrial benefits. Despite more than a decade of exploratory activity in the 1970s, the Government of Nova Scotia only began to stake out an aggressive jurisdiction in 1980. It began from a standing start: a major public conference that year asked, not entirely rhetorically, What's out there?[28] Modelled partly on the Peckford initiatives in neighbouring Newfoundland, a series of bills was passed, though not proclaimed, that asserted full provincial subsea jurisdiction to

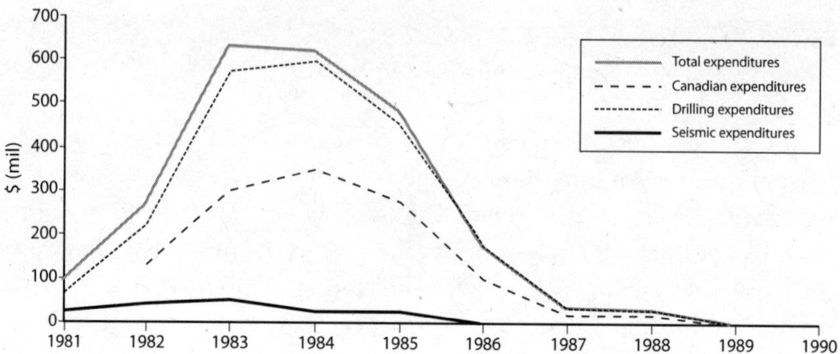

Figure 7.1 Offshore petroleum expenditures, Scotian Shelf, 1981-90
Source: Canada Oil and Gas Lands Administration, annual reports, 1981-90.

the continental shelf to a 200-mile limit. A cabinet secretariat was struck soon after, under the leadership of the Department of Mines and Energy, to draw together the six most affected ministers and departments.[29] By 1981, this body had morphed into the Industrial Benefits Office, and the East Coast's first Canadian Offshore Resources Exposition (an offshore industry trade fair) took place in Halifax. Several consultants were engaged to scope out the economic potential of offshore energy projects, and the Buchanan Conservative government assumed the mantle of local benefits overseer.[30]

As both governments extended their reach, the prospect of a Newfoundland-style jurisdictional tangle was a real possibility. However, the first Canada–Nova Scotia agreement on offshore energy was announced on 2 March 1982. By setting aside the issue of Crown ownership in favour of a new joint regulatory regime, the plan was to reassure the explorationists and seize the investment lead in the Atlantic offshore sweepstakes. Indeed, one of the agreement's key sections addressed the newly defined target of "optimum *Nova Scotia* and Canada benefits" (i.e., regional as well as national benefits). More specifically, "the parties shall give first consideration to services provided from within Nova Scotia and to goods manufactured in Nova Scotia, but only if such goods and services are competitive in terms of fair market price, quality and delivery."[31] Schedule II elaborated on potential industrial benefits by category: development of locally based supply-and-service companies; improvement in capabilities of all sizes of Canadian engineering and construction firms; building of vessels, rigs, and platforms and the fabrication of components; manufacture of equipment with broad applications; and the downstream utilization of hydrocarbons.

Significantly, the new regulatory board was designed to draw technical input from both the COGLA and the provincial Industrial Benefits Office. Furthermore, a Canada–Nova Scotia Executive Committee on Economic and Social Benefits was authorized by the agreement. Consisting of federal and provincial officials, it was charged with advising ministers on benefits objectives, along with the process and specific initiatives needed to achieve these goals. Finally, Ottawa advanced an offshore infrastructure fund worth $200 million to enable the province to prepare for the expected wave of manufacture, transport, and supply.[32]

The centrepiece of the industrial benefits policy was linking exploration and development rights to acceptable procurement plans. By design, this scheme went beyond the strict moral suasion of earlier years, since regulatory approvals hinged in part on the ministers' approval of benefit plans. Failure to file a plan would trigger a denial, and failure to file a sufficiently comprehensive and credible plan could trigger delays and eventual denial. At the same time, the process of the new benefits regime suggested a desire by state authorities for flexible discussion and negotiation over time. No formal targets or quotas were stipulated. Plans of varied durations were filed and approved but were subject to revision by applicants. Integral to corporate offshore citizenship was a commitment not only to filling procurement needs at least cost but also to revising internal procurement codes and enlisting the best efforts of major suppliers to help indigenous firms fill supply gaps and move up the value chain. Corporate experience in the renegotiation of exploration rights after 1982 drove this lesson home. By the following year, Voyer contends, offshore operators took the requirements of the new benefits regime seriously.[33] Another important issue – the matter of procurement audits – lurked on the horizon as well. Effective performance audits were widely viewed as the key to successful benefits programs in the UK and Norwegian sectors of the North Sea, and they would be equally critical in Canada.

The result was that rights holders and operators were now required to disaggregate industrial (and employment) reporting not only for Canada but also for Nova Scotia benefits. Furthermore, the agreement's executive committee announced plans for two new funds. The funds would be financed by industry contributions for the purpose of stimulating new activities in two fields already monitored by the COGLA: research and development and education and training.

As far as the province was concerned, the 1982 agreement established its coordinate status with Ottawa in some respects and additional leverage in others. The Industrial Benefits Office joined with the COGLA to appraise benefit plans (any contract exceeding $50,000 was reviewable), and joint ministerial approval was required. For infrastructure, the Offshore Development Fund (formally an advance on future offshore royalties) sweetened the deal. And several new rentier charges were levied on the offshore operators. The agreement may be described as a provincial echo of federal energy policy.

Power Struggles over Industrial Benefits: Two Episodes

The assertion of rival business strategies lies at the heart of the political encounter over industrial benefits. For international offshore operators, the quest for competitive advantage (both intrafirm and interfirm) was primary, though it was leavened by a willingness to adapt, at least at the margin, to the host state's rules. For Canadian independents such as Bow Valley Industries who were riding the crest of the National Energy Program, regional sourcing came relatively easily.[34] For host states such as Canada and Nova Scotia, the maximization of industrial and employment benefits was integral to offshore access and activity. Not surprisingly, these differences led to a deep and sustained contest for policy initiative and for control of the shifting terms of bargaining advantage. But the parameters, modalities, and costs were all politically negotiable. Two brief cases are presented below to illustrate these dynamics: the struggle over the initial policy fix in the early 1980s and the more recent (post-2000) industry effort to reopen the paradigm.

The Benefits Paradigm: Foundation and Challenge, 1982-86

By early 1983, the scale and shape of a new federal-provincial offshore benefits regime was becoming clear to the petroleum industry, and the contours were politically alarming. Both the CPA and the Eastcoast Petroleum Operators Association struck Canadian Industrial Benefits Committees, working groups that could engage with offshore authorities and their political masters.

The frontline issues were rapidly flagged, and they centred on the proactive strategic ambitions of state industrial overseers. The trio of the Office of Industrial Regional Benefits, the Industrial Benefits Office, and the COGLA Benefits Branch was aggressively developing standards and monitoring procedures to measure compliance with measures for "full and fair opportunity" contracting and the development of regional suppliers. Furthermore, the state agencies proposed a series of new compliance tools, one of which was designated-item planning, by which offshore operators would be directed to concentrate regional procurement at particular levels and sectors. Another involved the COGLA monitoring measures during the bidding process, including review of bid lists and a proposed forty-eight-hour delay between the company's choice of major tender acceptance and the formal announcement. Such proposals inserted the state into the heart of the contracting process by allowing the benefits bureaucracy to review and confirm the winning choice. Still another element required rights holders to prepare, as a signpost to regional offshore enterprise planning, five-year, forward-oriented procurement targets.[35]

Beginning in 1982, legislation obliged corporate rights holders to renegotiate their offshore land rights with COGLA and convert them into exploration agreements. Since the submission and acceptance of benefits plans was a requirement for conversion, the companies complied. At the same time, however, the CPA protested against these new burdens, pressing both ministers and COGLA officials for extensive revisions to benefits reporting. Between 1983 and 1985, these talks were fitful and inconclusive. Overhanging the regulation of exploration activities was the far more significant prize of the Venture development project for Sable natural gas, under review from 1983 to 1986.

As an alternative to the dirigiste COGLA regime, the CPA proposed its own strategy to develop indigenous supply capability.[36] Industry and government would agree upon a short list of goods and services not presently available in Canada or present only in low market share. Following review by third-party experts, a priority list would be confirmed. The government would then offer development assistance, and the oil industry would offer technical assistance for packaging bids in accessible ways. Progress could then be monitored over a multi-year period.[37] A variation on this proposal was established, on industry's initiative, in the form of the Canadian Market Opportunities Program. Enlisting a membership of supplier trade associations and government agencies, it operated until 1987. The program had three major components. The up-to-speed initiative, which pushed oil companies to develop domestic procurement policies, had considerable success. The market-opportunities initiative aimed to forecast offshore-purchasing scenarios to 1990 and emphasized eleven particularly promising product groups. Finally, the communications initiative organized meetings with prospective suppliers in six cities throughout the country.[38]

The path of the benefits talks was altered significantly by the election of the Mulroney Conservatives in 1984. By early 1985, Ottawa's most visible instruments of economic nationalism (the Foreign Investment Review Agency and the National Energy Program) were being dismantled. In May, the CPA offered federal ministers a comprehensive proposal for the revision of the Canada Oil and Gas Act. On industrial benefits, the message was succinct: "The principles of competitive bidding and best value should be upheld. Exhaustive Canada benefits statements should not be required and the current reporting requirements need to be greatly reduced and simplified."[39] The COGLA was sensitive to the Mulroney government's new conciliatory spirit, and the agency opened talks with industry to design a new reporting framework. It offered to reduce the designated item list to three items (rigs, supply vessels, and engineering and technical contracts). While the CPA insisted that the government withdraw from any involvement in bid awards, state authorities were willing only to modify procedures. The industry pressed Nova Scotia to rescind the proposed special education and training and research and development funds, but it ended up participating in both programs when they began in 1986. On the matter of future benefits guidelines, the CPA urged the COGLA to codify its performance expectations so that companies could internalize these goals in their procurement policies. These policies could then become the basis of achieving benefits gains, instead of the COGLA's prevailing focus on detailed content reporting, monitoring, and comparison. In the fall of 1985, the CPA indicated its continuing dissatisfaction with the draft guidelines.

The COGLA's revised framework, released in the spring of 1986, included three parts. The first, a statement of principles and procedures, clarified government expectations. The second and third were formats for benefits plan submissions and benefits reporting requirements.[40] They remained in effect until further revision eight years later. In policy terms, these guidelines are best seen as a compromise. Even with a more conciliatory federal regime, government ministers and officials were unwilling to fully vacate the field of benefits-report monitoring, which had links to permit and licence approval. Given political pressure from the supplier constituencies, particularly in shipbuilding, the CPA's proposals for codes of conduct and best-effort procurement pledges were insufficient. In addition, the two Atlantic provinces exercised significant leverage. For them, industrial and employment benefits were litmus test policies. The Buchanan Conservatives campaigned extravagantly in the provincial elections of 1981 and 1984, promising to extract maximum benefits from offshore investments and thereby staking their political careers to the full and fair opportunity regime.

In any event, the ink was barely dry on the 1986 guidelines when conditions changed. The offshore exploration campaign was already faltering by mid-decade in the shadow of the federal Petroleum Incentive Program's grant phase-out. Then the abrupt global oil price collapse of 1986 forced the withdrawal of the Venture proposal and a freeze on exploration work. For the short term, at least, benefits monitoring was rendered moot, and the benefits lobby receded. Exploration licence holders allowed their rights to lapse, and no new exploration wells were spudded between 1989 and 1997. Only the Cohasset-Panuke development, the modest oil-field production project announced in 1990 and started two years later, kept the flame alive until the mid-1990s.

When activity resumed following the 1996 proposal by the Sable offshore energy gas consortium, the focus in terms of benefits shifted from exploration activities to production projects. By then, the Canada–Nova Scotia Offshore Petroleum Board had assumed the industrial benefits mandate.[41] (Since the mirror legislation required to authorize the Board was not enacted until the close of 1989, the COGLA continued to administer benefits along with the Government of Nova Scotia until the board opened its doors in January 1990.) The 1986 guidelines were revised in 1994 and continue to shape industrial benefits plans.

Pressures for Regulatory Reform, 2002-

In November 2002, a high-level business-government conference was convened in Halifax under the name of the Atlantic Canada Energy Roundtable. The catalyst was the Canadian Association of Petroleum Producers, whose board had designated "regulatory efficiency and effectiveness" as a national public policy concern. The conference brought together senior leaders and staff from four federal departments (Industry, Fisheries and Ocean, Natural Resources, and Atlantic Canada Opportunities Agency); energy ministers from Nova Scotia, New Brunswick, and Newfoundland; and CEOs from twenty-five leading petroleum companies. The industry premise was succinctly stated by Gerald Protti of EnCana, asserting that "the Atlantic Canada regulatory framework is dated and inefficient; this increases costs and cycle times."[42] Of particular concern was the new burden imposed by the Canadian Environmental Assessment Agency. Government representatives were certainly willing to enter the dialogue, since Ottawa had embraced the discourse of smart regulation in its fall throne speech, and the offshore provinces recognized that the exploration bubble of the late 1990s had deflated, if not burst. Thus, this inaugural roundtable meeting was propelled by a confluence of commercial and political concerns.

The conference's structure is one of its most notable features. First, it drew representatives from the most senior levels of organizations. As a result, their endorsement of a set of policy themes and agreement to review the results in one year's time ensured not only that the consultations would occur but also that tangible progress would be made. Second, with guidance from discussion papers from the Canadian Association of Petroleum Producers (CAPP) and the Atlantic Provinces Economic Council, among others, two leading themes were identified for future work by mid-level and technical officials. The Regulatory Issues Steering Committee was charged with tackling broad-spectrum regulatory renewal according to streamlined, performance-based guidelines. The Industrial Opportunities Task Force was charged with fostering a competitive contracting environment in which current international project procurement practices would form the basis for a new benefits regime and pave the way for an export-oriented Atlantic supplier base.[43]

Speaking for large East Coast petroleum operators (and perhaps also for large general contractors who delivered major project facilities), the CAPP put the case succinctly. In terms of state policy to maximize regional supply and service opportunities, the legislative base was sound, and "the intent of the Accord is being realized." However, the administrative regime for implementing industrial benefits was flawed, for "operators and contractors must still participate in an administratively burdensome approach to contract awards and benefits reporting."[44] By any measure, the prevailing regime imposed temporal and monetary costs on operators without altering contract award decisions.

The CAPP's explanatory model is a version of the rising tide argument. It contends that the level of Atlantic regional benefits will be proportional to the overall scale of offshore activity available for tender. This scale will change qualitatively once the East Coast play evolves from project-based to basin-wide development. Even more significantly, CAPP suggests that the Atlantic offshore supply community will achieve a maximum boost from the capacity to enter international bid lists for work on the export stage. This is the case for an alternative benefits-reporting model, one that reflects "global procurement practices," including international standardization, safety, and quality management systems and certification and the practices of delivery and work guarantees to contractors.

The conference's benefits initiative was delegated to three working groups. The supplier development subcommittee addressed current performance, forecasts of future opportunities, and estimates of optimal regional capture. The result was a new initiative in operator-supplier meetings: to provide briefs on forecast activity and procurement needs. Modelled on the "Share Fair" initiative of the UK oil industry during the 2002 slump, the CAPP convened the first of these overview session in the spring of 2004, aiming to provide suppliers with early notification of project plans to enable longer lead times on bidding.[45]

Other working groups dealt with strategies for research and development growth within the region and new techniques and practices for monitoring and measuring industrial benefits. In the latter case, for example, the industry has long been critical of the Canada–Nova Scotia Offshore Petroleum Board's template, which uses Canadian value-added in procurement as a key criterion for assessment. Industry argued that this calculation tends to understate the real business impacts of offshore contracts:

> Take for example the case of a supply boat built in Halifax, based in Halifax, and managed by a Halifax company. Despite these factors, when this boat works on a Nova Scotia offshore project, the benefits accounting process assesses much of the value as foreign. The reason is that the steel, engines and machinery are all built or fabricated somewhere else ... thus, in the strict world of CNSOPB benefits accounting, few activities (other than those services that are almost entirely labour) are calculated to have a high Nova Scotia content, nor are they likely to in the near future.[46]

Alternatively, industry favours a system of cash-flow valuation and head-count employment.

Not all business interests accept that overregulation is the defining issue in contemporary offshore procurement. The Offshore/Onshore Technologies Association of Nova Scotia, for example, while participating in the conferences and supporting effective program structures, insists that full and fair opportunity remain the basis of benefits regulation. The association argues that market-driven procurement will jeopardize much of the gains of the past two decades. For example, the association has drawn attention to the tendency of major operators to bunch tenders at so high a level of aggregation as to disadvantage or exclude local participants.

Regional Benefits, 1990-2009

Not surprisingly, the political push and pull on industrial linkages operates at the multiple levels of framework policy, regulatory licensing, and operational auditing. This section considers the scale of major project expenditures, and pays particular attention to the Cohasset-Panuke, Sable Offshore, Maritimes & Northeast Pipeline (MNP), and Deep Panuke ventures. It also considers changes in benefits administration that have emerged in recent years as Deep Panuke has firmed up, particularly the provincial government's introduction of the Offshore Strategic Energy Agreement.

Beginning in the mid-1990s, the level of contracting and purchasing once again began to accelerate. The combination of the Sable Offshore project, the MNP's trunk pipeline and laterals, and surging offshore exploration brought an unprecedented benefits boom, a few dimensions of which are captured in Table 7.1. Construction expenditures dwarfed operational expenditures on offshore complexes. Also notable is the relatively high level of Nova Scotia purchases on the construction of the Cohasset-Panuke project compared to the projects that followed.

Another complication that arose in the 1990s was the relationship between two forms of Nova Scotia benefits: expenditure and employment commitments and Crown royalty payments. Simply put, it became evident that a simple state maximization strategy on both fronts could be counterproductive. The emerging royalty regime permitted project operators to earn back their capital costs, together with a designated return on capital, before royalty charges ramped up. Consequently, the level of capital and operating expenses (with the expected Nova Scotia benefits) directly affected the timing and scale of royalty returns. Wade Locke asks starkly: "Is there a royalty/benefits trade off?"[47] The question is pertinent given that the net returns to the provincial treasury and to provincial GDP (two separate flows) are not entirely commensurate. Depending on the benefits and royalty levels attained, it could be that optimal returns may favour one or the other. Certainly, provincial officials in Nova Scotia as well as Newfoundland confronted this issue.

There is evidence that the provincial government felt confined by its original role within the Canada–Nova Scotia Offshore Petroleum Board's benefits regime. An opportunity to rethink these relationships came with the Nova Scotia Energy Strategy consultation that followed the turn of the century. In the ensuing 2001 strategy statement, the province announced the introduction of the Offshore Strategic Energy Agreement (OSEA). Agreements would be negotiated between the province and a prospective project

TABLE 7.1

Economic impacts of Nova Scotia offshore projects, 1990-2000

	Cohasset-Panuke		Sable		MNP trunk		MNP laterals		Exploration	
	Expected	Actual	Expected	Actual	Expected	Actual	Expected	Actual	Expected	Actual
Development expenditure ($ million)										
Total	160	498	1,600	2,282	544	743	75	93	–	280
Nova Scotia	60	184	547	712	–	183	42	53	–	93
GDP	34	212	590	773	98	231	52	67	–	81
Employment person-years	1,280	3,080	11,100	14,460	810	2,270	985	820	–	1,300
Operations expenditure ($ million)										
Total	71	110	64	133	–	–	–	–	–	–
Nova Scotia	23	43	47	67	–	–	–	–	–	–
GDP	14	50	50	81	–	–	–	–	–	–
Employment person-years	340	700	1,030	1,670	–	–	–	–	–	–

Source: Gardiner Pinfold Consulting Economists, *Economic Impact of Offshore Oil and Gas Development in Nova Scotia, 1990-2000* (Halifax, 2002), 25.

sponsor prior to the submission of project applications. Although the government signalled its preference for an OSEA on all future ventures, negotiations remained voluntary. As to the prospective terms, "an OSEA will place particular emphasis on proposals that create opportunities for Nova Scotian firms to export or expand to other sectors. The agreement would also give consideration to how the design of the project (e.g., offshore vs. onshore gas processing) contributes to achieving the province's gas objectives."[48]

The OSEA, then, figured as a policy measure that met several goals. First, it inserted the provincial government's interests at an earlier stage of the benefits-planning process compared to the traditional CNSOPB set-up. This would afford greater leverage over project planning and detailed choices before a formal benefits plan saw the light of day. Second, it offered a significant new potential benefit to offshore proponents, for the successful negotiation of an OSEA would win provincial government support at subsequent regulatory proceedings. Third, it provided a mechanism to bridge the two great Nova Scotia Crown concerns: benefits and royalties. Both subjects could be addressed in an OSEA, and detailed terms could be modelled and trade-offs considered.

The results became clear when the agreement between the Government of Nova Scotia and EnCana was released in June 2006. The OSEA for the Deep Panuke project began by invoking the principles of the Canada–Nova Scotia Offshore Petroleum Resources Accord of 1986 and by aligning the agreement with those goals. Its content was balanced between industrial benefits and royalty terms. EnCana underlined its commitment "to providing opportunities for Nova Scotia and Canadian companies through employment, procurement and contracting on an internationally competitive basis, with full and fair opportunity for Nova Scotians, and first consideration to Nova Scotians where competitive on a best value basis."[49] It went on to set out specific commitments in particular subindustry categories to a total of 1.35 million person hours, half of which were in Nova Scotia. This goal would be attained within three months of the flow of first gas from Deep Panuke, and EnCana reserved the right to substitute equivalent person hours to meet designated targets. Significantly, the denominator for these undertakings was in labour time rather than in dollar value, recalling the industry's preferences voiced during the roundtable discussions. The royalty terms were also addressed in detail, and PanCanadian's original terms of agreement from 2001 were modified in the process. EnCana agreed to pay a royalty equivalent to 0.5 percent of gross revenue for the life of the project, which was designated as high-risk. On the government's side, it agreed to support Deep Panuke at regulatory proceedings and, provided that the application met with approval at the board level, not to withhold approval of the development plan.

The full significance of OSEA measures will become clear only with time. Certainly, the province believes that it has established greater leverage over the timing and terms of key offshore projects. For its part, EnCana has endorsed the approach. Speaking to the Offshore/Onshore Technologies Association of Nova Scotia in 2007, Gerald Protti described the OSEA as "an important step. OSEAs are really agreements that provide operators and government with certainty on development scenarios. I can assure you that without this agreement, we would not have moved forward to regulatory application."[50]

Conclusion

The story of industrial benefits on the Scotian Shelf is politically revealing in several respects. The notion that local enterprise and employment should be a prominent consideration in offshore investment emerged in a particular Canadian context. Its historical roots lie in recognition that energy megaproject construction involves high potential multipliers for upstream and downstream activities. A role for local enterprise was not, however, automatic, and indeed there were powerful counterpressures in the form of prior procurement alliances among established firms. The benefits maximizing perspective emerged in an era of Canadian economic nationalism, when federal regulators screened direct foreign investment and required negotiated undertakings for future performance in Canada. In 1980, benefits were coupled to a nationalistic energy policy and formed part of federal licensing policy on Canada lands.

In emerging petroleum jurisdictions such as Nova Scotia, an industrial benefits regime fit readily with the hard-fought goal of principal beneficiary status. As a result, the Government of Nova Scotia became an ally to Ottawa in this policy field. Indeed, as the Government of Canada began to shift back toward market-driven instruments after 1984, it was the province that defended the continued centrality of benefits regulation, and it was the accords that provided the ongoing legal backstop. After 1990, the administration of industrial benefits fell to the staff of the Canada–Nova Scotia Offshore Petroleum Board, where it remains today.

Although the government's ambition to realize a Dallas (or even a Galveston) north has not yet been fulfilled, the failure has not been due to an absence of policy. A planning process was not only stipulated for offshore procurement benefits, it was also tied closely to regulatory controls to command the petroleum industry's full-time attention. The extended political interplay of the 1980s (underwritten by the fiscal support of the Petroleum Incentive Program) certainly led to an offshore supply constituency of significant scale. Although no muscular regulator emerged on the scale of the UK Offshore Supply Office after 1975, the bureaucracy represented by the Office of Industrial and Regional Benefits, the Industrial Benefits Office, and the COGLA did withstand significant pressure from the oil industry, even in the Mulroney era. Resilience was due in large part to the Government of Nova Scotia's legislated foothold and its refusal to surrender the role won under the 1982 agreement. The government also benefitted from the expanding voice of the offshore supply constituency. How this continuing confrontation would have been resolved in the absence of the 1986 price crash, and the attendant slump in offshore activity, is difficult to determine. What is clear is that the industrial benefits paradigm was still alive when the industry revived and has been a central factor in development-plan assessment in subsequent projects.

Over the decades, the structure of offshore supply and service has evolved. Emphasis on exploration in the 1980s gave way to the production-project contracting in the 1990s and 2000s. The traditional arrangement of principal and subcontractors was expanded to include large project alliances. In recent years, the emergence of the Atlantic Energy Roundtable has called the foundations of the offshore benefits paradigm into question. By demonstrating a capacity to commission research and generate policy proposals for consideration in business-government forums, the roundtable goes well beyond the conventional consultative mechanism. Working parties reported annually to a senior body of ministerial and corporate leaders, demonstrating the roundtable's potential to fashion a new bargain of the type that has eluded joint bodies such as the Canada–Nova Scotia Offshore Petroleum Board to date. In 2001, the Government of Nova Scotia took a major step toward altering the political balance by introducing the OSEA. The OSEA is one of several examples (along with royalty flexibility, equalization offsets, and exploration incentives for basin renewal) in which Nova Scotia has taken the initiative at the margins of the joint regime.

The downturn after 2005 brought nervous times to the offshore supply and service constituency. The seismic- and exploratory-drilling subsectors went flat. The fabrication of production structures for Tiers 1 and 2 of the Sable project was completed, and Tier 3 has been ruled out. The Deep

Panuke facilities appear to be the only project on the horizon. For many industrial supply firms, the immediate future may depend upon their capacity to leverage success in Nova Scotia into business in other basins.

8 The Politics of Fiscal Entitlement: Offshore Revenues

Political communities are constituted on a variety of scales, and this chapter explores that of terrestrial Nova Scotia. How did the provincial political community (as distinct from its national or local counterparts) assert an interest in offshore petroleum? It could be argued that the provincial state is the natural (perhaps inevitable) instrument of the provincial community. This is undoubtedly true in a formal sense. But, as previous chapters have shown, there are many prospective policy sectors and political venues that touch on offshore petroleum. One derives from constitutional jurisdiction, in which it is held that provincial Crown title to offshore resources, together with the fiscal proceeds from their extraction and utilization, belongs to the people of Nova Scotia. Others argue that, as the closest landmass to the resources of the continental shelf, terrestrial Nova Scotia is more exposed to development impacts than any other community. The provincial economy risks overheating as activities accelerate, and it is the provincial infrastructure that will bear the burdens of use and depletion. Consequently, Nova Scotia is entitled to maximize its industrial, employment, and consumption links to petroleum exploitation. In sum, Nova Scotia citizens have shared interests as taxpayers, consumers, and residents, and it falls to the Government of Nova Scotia to assert these collective interests and defend their integrity.

This chapter explores the political conflicts that have arisen between the federal and provincial states over offshore revenues. Since the 1970s, fiscal allocations have emerged as one of the most prominent areas for the assertion of an offshore provincial interest. How have the public accounts been shaped by offshore petroleum activity? As far as Nova Scotia is concerned, the intergovernmental transfer scheme known as equalization lies at the heart of this issue. The province has depended on equalization for up to one-quarter of all provincial revenues, making it a crucial part of modern public finance. The prospect of provincial petroleum revenues, however, has threatened to diminish Nova Scotia's equalization returns. This has made the equalization formula a target of political controversy in which its inhibiting (rather than its facilitating) impact is stressed.

Over the course of this transition, the character of the issue itself has changed. Like most aspects of federal-provincial finance, equalization is a complex program that tends to be handled within the technical confines of finance departments. It is often said that only a handful of public servants in the entire country fully understands the workings of such programs. However, the problem of Atlantic offshore petroleum revenues has transformed the issue in significant part into a populist cause, which was always a latent possibility since Crown title by definition involves public ownership and benefit. Because the offshore petroleum agreements deal explicitly with royalty and revenue matters and declare the province the prime beneficiary in principle, this tensile thread runs as a theme over three decades of offshore politics. However, the issue exploded into public debate after 2000, when revenue splitting became the most visible and tangible grievance of Nova Scotians.

Equalization in Brief

The basic impulse of the equalization program is deceptively simple. In a federation in which provincial units vary widely in their fiscal or revenue-raising capacity, the national government underwrites a transfer scheme to lift per capita tax yields in deficient provinces to a national norm. Without prejudice to how the funds are spent, equalization seeks to provide all governments with "sufficient revenues to provide reasonably comparable levels of public services at reasonably comparable levels of taxation."[1]

Established in 1957, the equalization program has undergone continuing modifications over more than half a century, principally by revising the terms of the equalization formula that determines the levels of annual unconditional transfers. To confront the details is to enter a bewildering world of comparative public finance, a world of have and have-not provinces, revenue categories and representative tax bases, national average standards and five-province standards, and floors, offsets, and generic solutions.

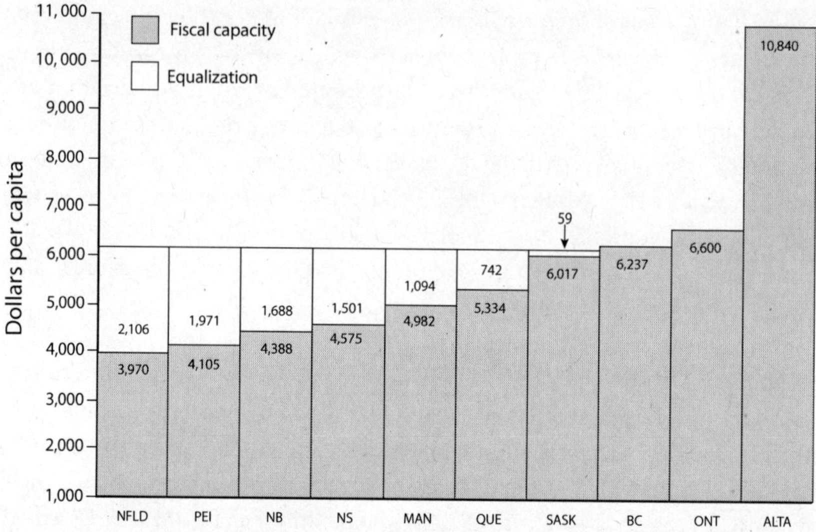

Figure 8.1 Per capita equalization by province, 2000-1
Source: Thomas J. Courchene, "Confiscatory Equalization: The Intriguing Case of Saskatchewan's Vanishing Energy Revenues," *IRPP Choices* 10, 2 (2004): 1-44.

From an original three-tax (or revenue) category base, the equalization program has expanded to include thirty-three categories. Calculations in each category establish potential provincial per capita yields, which are equalized by federal government transfers up to a designated national average per capita level. (The calculation also assumes that provinces apply an average tax effort, defined as the average rate of tax applied by the provinces occupying a tax category.) The provinces that are deficient in any given revenue source are thereby lifted to the standard level, though the provinces whose receipts are above the standard are not affected. The per capita equalization results for the fiscal year 2000-1, just prior to disputes between Canada and Nova Scotia, are captured in Figure 8.1. Seven provinces (including Nova Scotia) received equalization payments in varying degrees to raise their fiscal capacities, while three provinces (British Columbia, Ontario, and Alberta) did not qualify for equalization.

Evidently, much depends upon the elements of the averaging calculation. When equalization began, the standard was based on an average of the two richest provinces, which was later replaced by a ten-province national average standard. In 1982, this standard was supplanted by a five-province standard that included Ontario, Quebec, Manitoba, Saskatchewan, and British

Columbia. Oil-rich Alberta and the four poorer Atlantic provinces were omitted. In 2007, a ten-province standard was reinstated, together with some added provisions that exacerbated the Atlantic offshore conflict. Table 8.1 illustrates the way in which equalization served to lift Nova Scotia (and, by extension, other provinces) to a national average in the fiscal year 2000-1. As might be expected, the largest entitlements were based on personal income tax, business income tax, provincial local property tax revenues, and general sales taxes, which together accounted for more than 70 percent of Nova Scotia's equalization payment in that year. The shared offshore revenues in Nova Scotia are represented by a negative figure, signifying that the province fell above the national average in this entitlement (to be expected given that it is a single-province levy.) As will be seen, this line has become by far the most contentious fiscal element in offshore politics.

In the constitutional amendment known as the Constitution Act, 1982, the principle of Parliament making equalization payments to the provinces was enshrined in section 36. Titled "Equalization and Regional Disparities," the section affirmed the goals of promoting equal opportunities for Canadians and furthering economic development to reduce disparities in opportunities. In particular, section 36(2) affirmed "the principle of making equalization payments to ensure that provincial governments have sufficient revenues to provide reasonable comparable levels of public services at reasonably comparable levels of taxation."[2] This did not, however, freeze any particular version of the equalization program in place. The scheme has continued to evolve.

Some changes resulted from alterations to the formula at the political or technical level, for instance, at the general quinquennial review of the equalization scheme in 2006-7. This process might suggest that major decisions are bargained by federal and provincial delegates and result in an intergovernmental consensus. However, the equalization program is a federally legislated and funded program, confirmed in the Constitution and delivered by the Department of Finance. As Newfoundland Premier Roger Grimes put it, "Over the years, there has been a series of changes when the Government of Canada has decided that those changes are in the best interest of the Government of Canada and, in their view, in the best interest of the people of Canada."[3]

Other changes came from developments in provincial fiscal capacity – that is, in the real economy – that affected the equalization payments flowing through the formula. Clearly, one of the most dramatic examples is resource revenues, particularly from oil and gas. Beginning in 1962, Alberta

TABLE 8.1

Nova Scotia equalization entitlements, 2000-1

Revenue source	Entitlements ($000s)
Personal income tax revenues	429,830
Business income revenues	230,651
Capital tax revenues	34,332
General and miscellaneous sales taxes	100,325
Tobacco taxes	–6,966
Gasoline taxes	–17,153
Diesel fuel taxes	7,609
Non-commercial vehicle licences	–882
Commercial vehicle licences	6,653
Revenues from sale of alcoholic beverages	–1,094
Hospital and medical insurance premiums	2,234
Race track revenues	993
Forestry revenues	44,499
New oil revenues	15,593
Old oil revenues	1,605
Heavy oil revenues	4,712
Mined oil revenues	0
Third-tier oil revenues	4,373
Heavy third-tier oil revenues	2,520
Natural gas revenues	57,457
Sales of Crown leases	13,145
Other oil and gas revenues	1,908
Mineral resources	18,223
Water power rentals	38,495
Insurance premium revenues	10,157
Payroll taxes	55,761
Provincial local property tax revenues	274,193
Lottery ticket revenues	–1,169
Other games of chance revenues	879
Misc. provincial local taxes and revenues	79,780
Shared revenues: offshore activities (NFLD)	0
Shared revenues: offshore activities (NS)	–6,565
Shared revenues: preferred share dividends	186
Total equalization entitlements	1,402,284

Source: Thomas J. Courchene, "Confiscatory Equalization: The Intriguing Case of Saskatchewan's Vanishing Energy Revenues," *IRPP Choices* 10, 2 (2004): 30.

royalties were proposed for inclusion in the formula, though their status varied considerably: they were sometimes included and sometimes not, sometimes counted at a 50 percent level and other times at a 100 percent level. Then, as a result of the OPEC oil spike of 1973 (which roughly quadrupled the price of oil per barrel) and 1979 (which roughly doubled the price again), the fiscal capacities of producing provinces exploded in the categories of oil and gas revenues. Within the formula of the day, these developments promised to significantly boost the entitlements of non-petroleum-producing provinces and dramatically raise Ottawa's overall equalization bill in the process. To avoid this outcome, the federal government implemented a series of adjustments.[4] In 1974, for example, new (or post-OPEC priced) oil was included only to one-third of its revenue levels. In 1977, this share was increased to one-half. Later, following the second OPEC crisis, much of the impetus for the new five-province standard for revenue category bases was the desire to exclude Alberta's burgeoning petroleum returns from the resource revenue categories.

Offshore Revenues and Equalization

Once commercially promising discoveries began in the 1970s, the frontier lands of the Atlantic continental shelf posed another challenge to equalization. As seen in earlier chapters, the Canada–Nova Scotia dispute over offshore resource ownership was set aside in 1982 in favour of a negotiated deal on resource management and finance. By the Canada–Nova Scotia Agreement on Offshore Oil and Gas Resource Management and Revenue Sharing, Nova Scotia would receive 100 percent of offshore oil and gas revenues from a stipulated set of sources. The arrangement would continue until the province's overall fiscal capacity (as calculated by the equalization formula) reached 110 percent of the national average (plus a 2 percentage point capacity escalator for every percentage point that the province's unemployment rate exceeded the national average rate).

It is important to understand why Nova Scotia sought to bring these fiscal matters into the offshore agreement. Any increase in the offshore revenue base meant reduced equalization payments for the recipient province. Thus, the positive impact of rising oil or natural gas royalties and other payments was significantly dampened by a cut in federal equalization payments. This effect, known as a clawback because revenue gains in one stream were being cancelled out by reductions in another, was resented bitterly in traditional have-not provinces as they began to benefit from new "own source" revenues. The outlook of Nova Scotia (as well as Newfoundland and, sometimes, Saskatchewan) was that the have-not provinces remained far behind have provinces in all other fiscal capacities. Thus, it was punitive and offended the underlying ethic of equalization to neuter the only tax source in which the have-not provinces were poised to achieve an advantage. To meet provincial concerns, countermeasures were inserted into the offshore agreements to slow the erosion of revenues.

In effect, the 1982 agreement recognized that Nova Scotia's petroleum revenues should figure in the equalization scheme, but not until the province had enjoyed some gains from the new petroleum revenues. Only when the effect of oil and gas revenue became pronounced (defined by a Nova Scotia fiscal capacity of 110 percent of the national fiscal capacity plus the escalator) would offshore petroleum revenues start to replace equalization revenues. To provide a concrete example, Figure 8.1 shows that the national per capita average fiscal capacity was $6,026 in 2000-1, whereas that of Nova Scotia stood at $4,575. Oil and gas revenues would have to lift Nova Scotia to 110 percent, or $6,684 (i.e., above the level of Ontario), before oil and gas revenues would begin to be affected.

The question of how abruptly and how deeply the declining equalization effect could be still remained. Once Nova Scotia reached a fiscal capacity of 110 percent, the offshore agreement advised that "the intent is that resource revenues in the offshore region are reduced [by equalization] only gradually to ensure that Nova Scotia's fiscal and economic gains are lasting."[5] A complicated set of provisions governed Nova Scotia's receipt of resource revenues once its fiscal capacity ranged between 110 and 130 percent. A ceiling was stipulated by the rule that total offshore revenues should never have the effect of raising Nova Scotia's fiscal capacity beyond 140 percent of the national average.

These provisions were never activated during the life of the 1982 agreement because no offshore production commenced during this time (the first candidate, the Venture gas project, was suspended at the design stage in 1986 in the face of plummeting petroleum prices). Nonetheless, section 15 of the agreement provides an important insight not only into the intergovernmental thinking of the time but also into the expectations that were embedded in the initial round of the offshore fiscal settlement. The 1982 deal set several significant precedents. First, it acknowledged that offshore revenues and equalization were intertwined. Indeed, the 1982 agreement and a renewed national equalization formula were finalized at close to the same time. Second, the 1982 agreement failed to explicitly address the clawback possibility that the equalization scheme would set in motion once oil and gas revenues began to flow. Third, the need to remedy this oversight resulted in a side arrangement to the agreement being struck between the federal and provincial ministers of finance. Surprisingly, this side arrangement was not disclosed in 1982, and its content remained secret for several years. Premier John Buchanan alluded to the existence of this side deal several times but invoked confidentiality to justify his government's imprecise accounts of the forecast for offshore fiscal returns. Indeed, the terms of this putative deal were revealed only in 1984, when federal enabling legislation was introduced to implement the agreement.[6] It is not clear whether the detailed terms of the side deal were finalized at the time of the 1982 agreement or worked out in the period between March 1982 and May 1984.

In any event, Part 5 of the enabling bill dictated the interaction between offshore revenue flows and fiscal equalization. The intent was to limit the negative impact of oil and gas revenues on Nova Scotia's equalization entitlement through provisions for equalization offset payments. When offshore commercial oil or gas production commenced, Nova Scotia would receive an offset grant from Ottawa amounting to the difference between provincial equalization calculated with the full 100 percent of offshore revenues included and provincial equalization calculated with only 10 percent of those revenues included. In effect, 90 percent of offshore revenues were protected from clawback in that year. For each of the following eight years, an additional 10 percent was added to the second calculation until the offset payment was eliminated entirely in year ten. These arrangements were carried over to the 1986 accord and remain relevant today.[7]

The offset was first triggered in the 1993-94 fiscal year by the Cohasset-Panuke light oil project. By the time this rather small-scale project ceased production in 1999, the level of offset protection had declined to 30 percent of offshore revenues. This decline posed a serious problem for the province, since the much larger Sable project was poised to commence shipping in the final days of 1999. However, Nova Scotia had already used up the bulk of its offset protection. To those in Halifax, this seemed like a perverse false start that was depriving Nova Scotia of its just entitlements at the very moment when the Scotian Shelf was truly taking off. Frustration with the arrangement was a powerful spur for the province's campaign for new offshore revenue equalization terms.

Between the negotiation of the 1982 and 1986 Canada–Nova Scotia agreements, the equalization question also emerged in Newfoundland. The Government of Newfoundland had pursued a distinct offshore strategy since 1975, asserting a proprietorial claim to the continental shelf based on pre-Confederation law.[8] At the time that Nova Scotia was sitting down with Ottawa to negotiate joint management institutions in 1981-82, its neighbour was preparing court challenges to Ottawa's offshore jurisdiction. Despite the failure of this litigation, it was with considerable satisfaction that Premier Brian Peckford achieved his own offshore goals by negotiating the Canada-Newfoundland Atlantic Accord of 1985. Section 2 captured the spirit of the deal by designating the province as the "principal beneficiary of oil and gas resources off its shore, consistent with the requirement for a strong and united Canada."[9] The first phrase has since assumed totemic importance for Nova Scotia and Newfoundland. The latter phrase is seldom remembered or invoked by federal officials outside of the Department of Finance. For greater clarity, the accord affirmed that Newfoundland "can establish and collect resource revenues as if these were on land within the province."[10] For greater certainty, the list of eligible revenues included royalties, corporate income tax, sales tax, bonus payments, rental and licence fees, and other revenues. As in the Nova Scotia case, the Atlantic Accord was a bilateral deal with Newfoundland whose provisions were formalized by parallel federal and provincial enabling statutes.

In an explicit move to prevent dollar-for-dollar loss of equalization, section 39 of the Atlantic Accord set out provisions for equalization offset that would cushion, without entirely eliminating, the clawback effect. Triggered by the production of 15 million barrels of offshore oil or oil equivalent annually, the offset consists of two provisions. Part 1 guarantees Newfoundland a percentage of its overall equalization entitlement from the previous year; put another way, it inserts a floor level of equalization loss. The percentage varies according to the province's fiscal capacity relative to other provinces (a 95 percent floor at 70 percent capacity or less, a 90 percent floor at 70 to 75 percent capacity, and an 85 percent floor at 80 percent capacity or more). The provision extends for twelve years. Part 2 is a phase-out protection on the unprotected balance of the year-to-year equalization decline (the 5, 10, to 15 percent portion). Protection begins at 90 percent of the balance and declines to 0 percent after fourteen years. The offset protection will effectively end in the fourteenth year after production start-up. For Newfoundland, the offset provisions became operative with Hibernia oil production in 1999.[11]

Because Nova Scotia was guaranteed more favourable terms subsequently achieved by other offshore provinces, the Canada–Nova Scotia accord of

1986 transformed the 1982 agreement in light of the Atlantic Accord. As far as the equalization offset was concerned, however, the terms of the earlier offset scheme were carried forward.

One other significant provision that has affected the treatment of offshore revenue is known as the generic solution and was incorporated into the national equalization scheme in 1994, when it was backdated for one year. The solution grew out of Ottawa's concern for the distortions that could occur in cases in which a revenue tax base is highly concentrated in a single province.[12] This situation opened the possibility that a change in that province's tax rate could significantly alter the equalization distributions from that revenue category throughout the country. The precipitating case involved potash revenues in Saskatchewan, but the issue applied equally to Quebec's asbestos-mining revenues and to the case of offshore petroleum revenues in Nova Scotia and Newfoundland. The equalization revenue categories are listed in Table 8.1. Since neither province forms part of the five-province standard, the equalization standard for these bases is set at zero. Consequently, left on its own (and absent any protection from the East Coast offshore accords), the equalization formula would fully confiscate all offshore revenues in these categories, resulting in a negative entitlement or clawback.

To deal with this problem, Ottawa formulated the generic solution. In cases where an equalization-receiving province has 70 percent or more of a tax base, 30 percent of that actual tax revenue would be sheltered from the effects of the calculation. Put another way, the maximum negative offset or tax back through equalization in such a case (i.e., the maximum clawback) would be 70 percent. The generic solution is embedded within the equalization scheme and is open to any province that qualifies. For the eastern provinces, the generic solution offered an additional level of protection (to the 30 percent level) that would be available on a continuing basis, even after the accord offsets expired.

Notwithstanding these terms, Nova Scotia and Newfoundland nurtured an ongoing grudge against any clawback on the grounds that it violated the principal-beneficiary clause. The case was a familiar one, stretching back some fifteen years or more. For Nova Scotia and Newfoundland, the accord framework was primary – a set of bilateral agreements that had not been altered. The principal-beneficiary concept carried a clear expression of intent for coastal provinces with offshore jurisdiction to benefit from offshore development in a manner similar to provinces in the western sedimentary basin. It is difficult to argue that the confiscation of offshore fiscal gains, by means of the equalization clawback, is consistent with fulfillment of the principal-beneficiary clause.

Thus, the agreements that established the management and fiscal status of continental shelf petroleum acknowledged the realities of prevailing equalization clawbacks and inserted countermeasures. The principle was one of transitional protection, not to absolutely exclude offshore revenues from equalization but to ease the shift to major resource-revenue positives and lowered aggregate equalization. Once the offshore provinces became have provinces in terms of equalization (i.e., no longer eligible for net equalization transfers), a different calculus would apply. In retrospect, however, the assumption that this could be expected within a decade's time (at rates of growth so high that new revenue flows would not be skimmed away by equalization) was shaky. When reality failed to meet expectation, the offshore provinces saw that their one and best opportunity for sustainable growth was being pre-empted by the perverse consequences of a national program.

In addition, it was evident that the treatment of offshore revenues was neither scripted in gold nor carved in stone. Just as Ottawa pursued a panoply of national fiscal goals, adjusting the scheme to meet national needs, Nova Scotia and Newfoundland expected adjustments to meet their own interests.[13] Whether this took place within the equalization scheme or outside of it (through the offshore agreements) was part of the problem. For example, the equalization route could include the deletion of offshore revenues from the list of thirty-three revenue categories, the partial elimination of offshore revenues (to a third or a half level) from the base calculation, or the shift from a five- to a ten-province national standard. Alternatively, the offshore agreements' provisions could be amended to provide broader time frames and full compensation for offshore clawbacks, and termination could be based on aggregate per capita equalization levels well above the qualifying standard for equalization. It was precisely these proposals that framed the debate after 2001.

Over the last decade, a powerful contradiction has caused a widening chasm between the two Atlantic provinces and Ottawa over offshore revenues and equalization. This conflict is rooted in the fact that petroleum takeoff did not take place as expected in the years after the 1986 agreement. Instead, the global market decline brought a hiatus of a decade or more before significant production projects came on stream in the form of Sable offshore gas in Nova Scotia and Hibernia crude oil in Newfoundland. By that time, Nova Scotia was well on its way to exhausting its offset guarantees thanks to Cohasset-Panuke, even though the province's best offshore prospects still lay ahead. Newfoundland, contemplating multiple megaprojects with fifteen- to twenty-five-year lifespans, likewise viewed a ten- or twelve-year offset transition as manifestly insufficient. Both provinces recognized that the generic solution gave away far more than it preserved and was designed to meet Ottawa's needs alone. The stage was thus set for a renewed battle over the disposition of offshore revenues.

The "Offshore" Provincial Challenge

Soon after his accession to power in 1999, Nova Scotia premier John Hamm called on Ottawa to revise the fiscal treatment of provincial offshore revenues and, in so doing, fulfill the spirit of the 1980s agreements. In the fall of 2000, Hamm appealed to Nova Scotian voters to pressure federal Liberal ministers and MPs during the general election to end the looming 70 percent equalization clawback on offshore royalties and taxes.[14] Early in 2001, Hamm launched his "Campaign for Fairness," which was carried throughout the nation in the years that followed. The nub of the case was clear: "All that we are asking for is to be treated as others were before us. We are asking only for what Nova Scotians were promised. And that is – as the revenues from our offshore oil and gas grow, the additional financial benefits should flow to Nova Scotians."[15] The promise of the principal-beneficiary clause could only be realized by ending the equalization clawback and Ottawa's appropriation of four-fifths of the offshore take. A month later, the premier took his case to Ottawa, where he met with the national press and conferred with Liberal ministers Paul Martin, Stephane Dion, and Robert Thibault.[16]

The beginning of natural gas flow from the Sable project was a powerful spur to this initiative. With twenty-some years of projected royalties ahead, Nova Scotia was intensely frustrated by the prevailing 81-19 percent revenue split. Moreover, with record levels of interest in offshore exploration, including new plays such as the deepwater slope, there was a powerful sense in Halifax that Nova Scotia's energy sector was taking off. By June 2001, Hamm had attracted positive editorial support from the *National Post,* which saw fiscal balance as a path out of "a province-wide welfare trap."[17] In August, Newfoundland Premier Roger Grimes formally joined the cause. Former federal Conservative minister John Crosbie entered the lists in September, offering a detailed review of the political commitments embedded in the 1980s agreements and a spirited endorsement of the provincial case.[18]

However, the Chrétien Liberals, newly elected to their third term of office, proved to be completely uninterested. Despite ostensible support from Nova Scotia's Liberal ministers in Ottawa, the fairness file drew little more than a polite hearing. The federal department for implementing the East Coast energy accords, Natural Resources Canada, was a relatively junior agency in the Ottawa hierarchy. Far more important, given Nova Scotia's demands, was the federal Finance Department, which had jurisdiction over federal-provincial finance and a role as the guarantor of the venerable pan-Canadian equalization scheme.

Revisions to the equalization program were not unheard of. Indeed, many significant adjustments had been made, under federal leadership, in the decades since its inception in the 1950s. However, the program's complicated formulae and conditions represented a particular federal-provincial compromise, one not easily or casually reopened. When this did happen, the secret to consensus often lay in a carefully crafted bargain among the eleven parties that often emerged from months of bilateral or multilateral negotiations led by Ottawa. For example, one proposed solution to the offshore clawback problem, widely discussed in the 2001-3 period, was to shift the equalization formula from a five-province to a ten-province standard and, at the same time, eliminate non-renewable resources as a revenue category. Although this suggestion was supported by some provinces (including Nova Scotia and Newfoundland), it was opposed by others (including Quebec, Manitoba, and New Brunswick, for whom it would bring cuts in overall equalization returns). Ottawa often cited the lack of provincial consensus as a reason for rejecting new proposals. Although the need-for-unanimity argument does not square fully with the history of equalization changes, for the federal government both held and exercised ultimate authority, it does illustrate the difficulty of moving Ottawa in directions contrary to its own inclinations. Thus, the prospect of a single province (or even the East Coast pair, once Newfoundland made common cause in 2002) achieving bilateral success was not auspicious.

Stéphane Dion, minister of intergovernmental affairs in the Liberal government, emphasized this very fact in a September 2001 response to Crosbie. Dion's basic line was that Newfoundland and Nova Scotia were receiving 100 percent of petroleum revenues, as provided for in the agreements of the 1980s. Ottawa was thus meeting the terms of the deals. The equalization program, from which the two provinces had benefitted both before and after the agreements, was in this view an entirely separate matter. Indeed, Dion argued that the offshore revenues were partially shielded for precisely this purpose.[19] In effect, a stalemate had been reached. Nova Scotia lacked the means to break the deadlock, and Ottawa had little interest in doing so.

In 2002, a review of equalization by the Senate Standing Committee on National Finance kept the issue alive, though not exactly pressing. Three of the committee's eight recommendations dealt with offshore revenues. While advising against the elimination of non-renewable resource revenues from the formula, the senators called for changes in the generic solution to protect an increasing share of provincial revenues from clawback and for Ottawa to evaluate whether the intent, as distinct from the technical letter of the terms, had been achieved.[20]

In Newfoundland, the report of the Royal Commission on Renewing and Strengthening Our Place in Canada both highlighted and reframed the issue. Released in June 2003 to positive reviews in the province of Newfoundland and Labrador, the report outlined seven terms for a new partnership, including "new approaches to sharing offshore oil revenues in a way consistent with past promises."[21] Indeed, the urgency of redefining the terms of offshore petroleum development, along with those of fisheries and hydropower, runs throughout the two hundred pages of the report.

A graph that projected net Newfoundland revenues from offshore oil in the 2004-23 period dramatically illustrated the imbalance. It showed gross oil revenues from the three existing projects (Hibernia, Terra Nova, and White Rose) rising by a factor of six to peak production around 2010 then sliding precipitately back to initial levels by 2015 and tapering thereafter. By contrast, net provincial oil revenues barely rose because of equalization losses that ranged from $200 to $500 million annually during the boom phase and from $100 to $200 million for the decade-long tail-off to 2023. The conclusion was clear: "The existing revenue sharing arrangements of the Atlantic Accord are no longer a valid means of achieving the objectives of the Accord, and they must be amended to enable Newfoundland to become the principal beneficiary."[22] Moreover, the graph underlined the urgency of the report's call for immediate negotiations with Ottawa to revise the Atlantic Accord.

Fairness Revived

By 2003, Premier Hamm's discourse on fairness had become tired and perhaps faintly defeatist in the face of Ottawa's lack of interest. The only new twist was the election of the Newfoundland Conservative Party under the leadership of millionaire businessman Danny Williams. William's campaign

Blue Book, in terms reminiscent of Brian Peckford's Norwegian model of the 1980s, suggested the revival of a more activist offshore state.[23] With oil royalties from Hibernia, Terra Nova, and White Rose all at stake, the clawback was, for Williams, an early target.

Williams injected new life into the East Coast (Nova Scotia–Newfoundland) alliance, which was mobilized when Prime Minister Paul Martin called the June 2004 federal election. Although he had swept into the Liberal leadership with strong public approval, Martin's credibility had plummeted because of Chrétien's legacy and Martin's generally uninspiring style.[24] Martin's overwhelming advantage in the opinion polls for January 2004 had dissipated by April, and the hemorrhage of Liberal support continued into the campaign itself. By June, all prospects of a majority were abandoned, and Martin fought desperately to hold onto a Liberal minority.

In the campaign lead up, the federal Conservative Party pledged to end the offshore clawback by developing a ten-province equalization standard that would exclude resource revenues from the mix. The New Democrats made a similar commitment. Premier Williams seized the moment by demanding that Prime Minister Martin also promise to end the offshore clawback. Together with the mayor of St. John's, Williams urged Newfoundland voters to reject any party that refused to offer such a guarantee. The measure of the prime minister's desperation, and his need for at least five of the province's seven seats, was his abrupt reversal of form on the issue. On 4 June, Newfoundland minister John Efford declared that an election was no place to negotiate equalization policy. A day later, Paul Martin offered the requisite guarantee, declaring that "the proposal that [Mr. Williams] has put forth is a proposal that we can accept." However, with no details on just what the terms might be, even federal fisheries minister (and Halifax MP) Geoff Regan was left in the dark; but he did pledge that, whatever was involved, Nova Scotia would be given a similar deal.[25] It was later reported that Newfoundland had proposed that Ottawa make an annual reimbursement of the clawback but leave the equalization regime intact.[26] The estimates for reimbursement in the fiscal year 2004-5 were $140 million for Newfoundland and $14 million for Nova Scotia.

Danny William's blunt and aggressive populism therefore achieved, in the context of the 2004 federal campaign, what John Hamm's polite and reasoned noblesse had failed to deliver over the previous four years. Not surprisingly, Premier Hamm called immediately for a parallel guarantee for Nova Scotia. Although he expressed a preference for the ten-province standard with resource revenue excluded, Hamm indicated a willingness to accept the Newfoundland deal.[27] Only on the final day of the campaign did the prime minister confirm that a similar 100 percent reimbursement of the clawback would be provided to Nova Scotia.[28] Evidently, the fairness campaign's centre of gravity had shifted from Halifax to St. John's.

The Perils of Implementation

The Martin Liberals emerged from the election with a weak minority of 135 members in a 308-seat Parliament that included 6 Liberals from Nova Scotia and 5 from Newfoundland. All that remained, it seemed, was to hold Ottawa's feet to the fire until the necessary formalities were achieved. It was not long, however, before signs of dissent were evident. By the end of the summer of 2004, the federal lead role was assigned to Natural Resources minister John Efford. This was not surprising, given that the promised rebates were framed as an offshore accords matter rather than an equalization matter. However, the Department of Finance soon emerged as a key player on a series of intergovernmental files. Ottawa met with the provinces in September 2004 for a health policy summit that resulted in an extraordinary $18-billion commitment to new transfers over six years. A second meeting was scheduled for late October to consider changes to the national equalization scheme. Finance minister Ralph Goodale was given the lead federal role in these matters and even supplanted Efford in the clawback discussions.

Matters came to a head at the First Ministers' Conference on equalization on 26 October 2004. Ottawa's efforts to limit the prime minister's June election commitment were evident in the first federal clawback offer. The offer included several new conditions, including an eight-year sunset clause and a renewed clawback in the event that either Nova Scotia or Newfoundland surpassed Ontario's per capita fiscal capacity before 2012 as a result of burgeoning oil and gas revenues. Beyond this, Goodale offered a choice between two mechanisms for compensation: a set of guaranteed payments over eight years (totalling $640 million for Nova Scotia and $1.6 billion for Newfoundland) or annual payments equal to the clawback value, which would fluctuate from year to year. Condemning Ottawa's equivocation on the principal-beneficiary pledge, both provinces rejected the offer.[29] Williams accused Martin of a "breach of trust" and stormed out of the meeting. Hamm remained at the table but insisted that better terms would be required. Indeed, Nova Scotia calculated that the eight-year limit would cost the province $800 million over the life of the Sable project, not to mention potential future projects. As the premier put it, "there [should be] no sunset to being a principal beneficiary."[30]

Although Efford warned that Ottawa's offer was final, negotiations resumed in November. At least four sessions were held as the month progressed; sometimes they involved Goodale and the premiers and other times, Goodale and the energy ministers. However, there was no progress on the sticking points as various make-or-break meetings came and went.[31] Throughout this period, the level of public resentment in Newfoundland rose even higher, as Williams rode his defence of the provincial interest to new levels of celebrity. The two premiers continued the pattern of good cop–bad cop pronouncements. Newfoundland dismissed federal half-measures, while Nova Scotia insisted that progress was being made.

On 22 December 2004, the federal government doubled the length of its offer to sixteen years, so long as a province remained a net equalization recipient (i.e., a have-not province). Williams termed this a slap in the face and ordered the national flag to be removed from all provincial buildings. Hamm welcomed "significant progress" but declared that it was still insufficient. The provinces diverged on their prospects for achieving "have" status on the strength of oil and gas revenues. With three major petroleum projects firm and a fourth likely, Newfoundland, unlike Nova Scotia, would likely become a have province over the projected time frame. Federal officials accused Williams of moving the goal posts and refusing to accept terms in December that he himself had advanced months earlier. In early January, Williams ended his flag boycott and requested a face-to-face meeting with Prime Minister Martin. The meeting evolved into a new set of negotiations, a Martin-Williams-Hamm meeting in Ottawa, and a breakthrough agreement by month's end.

The central point of the agreement was the principle that both provinces retain full offshore revenues without clawbacks on the equalization side, so long as they continued to qualify for equalization.[32] The deal also specified federal offset payments over eight years to 2012, estimated at $2.6 billion for Newfoundland and $830 million for Nova Scotia, most of it prepaid, with the balance subject to several price- and production-volume variables. An eight-year extension to 2020 was authorized if either province was an equalization recipient in 2011 or 2012. Both agreements were subject to review by 2019. Although the official text was titled an arrangement between governments, it was universally tagged the Atlantic Accord (2005) in eastern

Canada. In contrast to the first generation of East Coast agreements, the accord was signed on 14 February 2005 not by first ministers, or even by finance ministers, but by federal Liberal Geoff Regan (Fisheries and Oceans) and provincial Conservative Cecil Clarke (Energy). Enabling legislation followed later in the year in a federal omnibus bill C-43.

Premier Hamm had won his long-standing campaign for fairness. Almost immediately, speculation within the province turned to possible targets for the new funds. This speculation was effectively neutralized when the premier announced that all offshore revenues, now and in the future, would be channelled away from general revenues into a dedicated fund for debt reduction. At the time, Nova Scotia's consolidated debt stood at more than $12 billion. At the spring 2005 session, the House of Assembly enacted the Financial Measures (2005) Act to this effect, which was accompanied by loud support from business circles.[33] Significantly, from a political point of view, the measure could be justified as a collective benefit for all Nova Scotians, today and tomorrow. The coupling of offshore fiscal benefits with debt payment became one of Hamm's most prominent legacies as politicians in all three major parties invoked the "John Hamm debt-reduction plan."

A Third Rupture, 2007

The transfer of federal power from Paul Martin to Stephen Harper in the January 2006 election did not complicate the issue. As Opposition leader, Harper had endorsed the 2005 accord. However, a regular five-year review of the equalization scheme was under way, and the review would end during the early years of Harper's government. A corresponding change in the premiership of Nova Scotia – Conservatives chose Rodney MacDonald to succeed Premier John Hamm, who was retiring in March – meant that the two prime movers in Nova Scotia offshore fiscal matters were new to office in 2006.

Within a year, however, the consensus broke with the most dramatic rupture of all. This conflict began to crystalize with the federal budget for the fiscal year 2007-8, which included Ottawa's acceptance of a new equalization deal. The fuel was the federal government's *O'Brien Report,* a technical review that proposed to place equalization on a principled national basis. A political discourse on Canada's fiscal imbalance had emerged, one that centred on Ottawa's mounting surpluses at the provinces' expense. O'Brien proposed a ten-province standard to calculate equalization and the exclusion of half the resource revenues. However, he also proposed an equalization cap to ensure that no receiving province could rise above the fiscal capacity of the lowest non-receiving province, which was then Ontario.[34]

These modifications to the national program, particularly the proposed cap, put the February 2005 agreements in jeopardy. They signified unilateral changes to the agreed-upon terms, and Finance Minister Flaherty confirmed that an offshore revenue clawback would be part of the new scheme. The federal Conservatives were pursuing a broader national fiscal goal for which they were willing to sacrifice the Atlantic deals. In particular, the federal government offered the Atlantic provinces a choice of the old or new formulas. Dismissing the cap as well as the so-called choice, the Government of Nova Scotia insisted that the proper denominator was an uncapped guarantee under the new equalization scheme, underscoring a phrase from the 2005 agreements that called for use of "the equalization formula as it exists at the time [of offset calculations]."[35] At the same time (and perhaps in an effort to cushion the blow), the federal budget announced increases in the equalization receipts for Nova Scotia and Newfoundland. On the eastern flank, reaction was vitriolic. Premier Rodney MacDonald declared that the 2007 budget had "effectively ripped up our offshore Accord." The changes were a complete surprise to Nova Scotia, which professed "no consultation, no notice, no reason why."[36] Although the first two points may not be strictly true, in the sense that the O'Brien report was already on the table for discussion, O'Brien's addition to the omnibus budget package was certainly abrupt and unilateral. As James Bickerton observes, political trust between Ottawa and the two provinces was broken by this chain of events.[37]

Despite the difficulty of successfully opposing an announced budget measure, the MacDonald government mounted a furious campaign through ministerial and bureaucratic contacts from March until June. The premier travelled to Ottawa before the budget's third reading to make his case and called on the Opposition in the House of Commons to defeat the offending clauses. (Liberals and New Democrats voted against the bill in the knowledge that support from the Bloc Québécois would sustain the minority Conservatives.) MacDonald then moved his case to the Senate.

One unlikely champion of the Nova Scotia position did surface in the House of Commons: Bill Casey, a long-serving Conservative backbench MP from the Nova Scotia riding of Cumberland-Colchester. Casey acknowledged that the Harper government had reneged on the 2005 agreement and estimated that the change would cost Nova Scotia $1.3 billion. He declared, "I could not vote to endorse the 2007 Budget which broke the contract with my province."[38] Casey's vote against the budget meant that he opposed his party on a matter of confidence. By his account, tremendous pressure was brought to bear from the Prime Minister's Office, Finance Minister Flaherty, and Nova Scotia regional minister, Peter MacKay.[39] However, during the vote on second reading on 5 June, Casey rose with a copy of the 2005 accord in hand and voted against the Harper-Flaherty budget. Within minutes, he was expelled from the Conservative caucus. In this unlikely way, Casey emerged as the contemporary conscience of Nova Scotia politics – a man of principle who had served his party loyally in the House of Commons since 1988 but was unwilling to accept the perfidy being inflicted on his struggling home province.

In Nova Scotia, there was little doubt where popular sentiment lay. Conservative MP's endured a tense summer as Casey was celebrated as a model public servant. Polling data by CRA Research for February and May 2007 captured the effects of the imbroglio, showing that satisfaction with the Harper government had plunged from 47 to 17 percent in Newfoundland and from 50 to 37 percent in Nova Scotia.[40] For its part, the Harper government denied all charges and insisted that the equalization terms in the budget were both legal and fair. As if to taunt the provincial government, Harper invited MacDonald to test his claim in a court challenge. Although he sat as an Independent MP, Casey was renominated in October by the Conservative constituency membership in Cumberland-Colchester. Ultimately, the party's national headquarters had to suspend the local executive to void Casey's selection. Bill Casey won handily as an Independent and served until April 2009, when he was appointed Nova Scotia's provincial agent-general in Ottawa.

The financial costs of the new equalization proposals were being totted up within weeks of the budget vote. Two eminent students of fiscal federalism, unattached to the governments, underlined the scale of the stakes. Paul Hobson and Wade Locke estimated that while Nova Scotia could benefit from the new scheme in the opening two years, its loss over the full period to 2019-20 would be $1.1 billion. For Newfoundland, the new framework would cost the province money in all but year three, for an aggregate shortfall of $1.4 billion (in comparison to the old program).[41]

As these events played out, the budget implementation bill was still before Parliament. On 10 October, however, the two governments announced a revised deal for Nova Scotia. By its terms, Nova Scotia could select from two options on annual offset payments – the new equalization scheme as outlined in the budget or the terms of the (now reinterpreted) 2005 accord. By choosing the latter, MacDonald argued that the province would receive a larger (by $68 million) 2008 allotment, a much larger (by 1.5 billion) allotment over the period to 2020, and a larger (by $229 million) allotment than the "original interpretation" of the 2005 accord would have provided to 2020.[42]

Perhaps an even more attractive carrot for the Nova Scotia government was Ottawa's new commitment to honour a long-standing financial obligation that had arisen out of the 1986 accord. Known as the Crown share commitment, it had enabled an offshore province to buy into the 25 percent Crown share that Ottawa asserted as part of the National Energy Program. When the Mulroney government terminated these measures, it acknowledged that compensation was due to the Atlantic provinces for loss of future Crown share opportunities (a point confirmed by the 1986 accord). Two decades later, however, the issue either remained dormant or lacked a sense of political urgency. Then, as part of the 10 October 2007 package, Ottawa committed to resolve the issue. Equally significantly, it also agreed to a settlement process. The federal and provincial estimates of the value of this lost opportunity were widely divergent: Ottawa proposed $200 million, while Nova Scotia estimated $1.8 billion.

The task of calculating the Crown share adjustment payment was, consequently, delegated to a three-person panel. Early in January 2008, the members were announced. Ottawa nominated Brian Crowley, former head of the neoliberal Atlantic Institute for Market Studies and a former visiting fellow at the Department of Finance. Nova Scotia nominated Halifax lawyer Dara Gordon, and the mutually agreed upon chair was retired chief justice Lorne Clarke of the Supreme Court of Nova Scotia. The panel reached a deadlock over final calculations. Crowley was inclined toward Ottawa's position, while Gordon leaned toward Nova Scotia's.[43] In the absence of consensus, Clarke proposed a compromise, which the two governments accepted.[44] The final total, calculated on the basis of existing projects for which the Crown share was not available for take-up, was approximately $860 million. Future projects would add to the amount.

It is hard to avoid the conclusion that the Crown share compensation, after decades in suspended animation, was the cost of the Harper government's budget debacle of 2007. Certainly, the federal Nova Scotia minister and Conservative MP's pressed the case privately while being excoriated publicly. Once the Crown share deal was signed on 13 July 2008 (by federal minister Peter MacKay and the Nova Scotia premier), Rodney MacDonald announced that the lion's share of the funds (except for the $75 million that the province had pre-spent on universities and offshore research) would follow other offshore payments into the debt-reduction scheme.[45] A long-running political saga had reached its end.

In less than a year, Premier MacDonald was gone from government, and the legacy of the offshore fiscal settlement played a significant role in his defeat. Nova Scotia's Conservative minority government was swept up in a controversy of its own, centred on debt retirement in general and the offshore offset payments in particular. Recall that Hamm had legislated that the cumulative offshore offset payment of 2006 be applied directly to debt reduction rather than general revenues. Because of certain accounting protocols, this payment had to be dispensed over a series of years, and the law required the budget to record stipulated surpluses in these years to ensure that future budgets were not balanced by the application of the offset funds. Although the province did report budget surpluses in the years from 2006 to 2009, the surpluses fell short of designated levels.[46] Not surprisingly, this shortfall figured in the 2009 provincial election campaign, when the opposition parties charged the Conservatives with breaking the terms of their own budget law and damaging Nova Scotia's long-term debt position. MacDonald was unable to deal effectively with the issue, and it likely played a part in his defeat.

When the New Democratic Party gained a solid majority and the economy turned decisively into decline after the global financial crash of 2008, offshore royalties surfaced once again. It soon became clear that the Sable project had passed its peak royalty flow, and a stream of revenues that had bolstered the MacDonald Conservatives was no more. Sable Offshore Energy Inc. royalties began modestly in 2000-1 at $19 million and remained at comparable levels for the next four years. However, in 2005-6 the royalty returns jumped four-fold to $124 million. This increase reflected a number of factors, including volumes and prices and the structure of the Sable royalty contract. (Corporate owners recovered their capital costs in the initial years, after which the province took a greater share in royalties.) The four years from 2005-6 to 2008-9 (which spanned the MacDonald government's tenure) yielded peak royalty returns of $124 million, $269 million, $400 million, and $452 million, respectively. Then payments fell to $126 million in 2009-10, and the downward trend was projected to continue until the project's end.[47] The Dexter government made a point of setting out the full implications in a 2009 budget discussion paper. Barring a revival of offshore exploration and discovery, offshore revenues would never again be more than a minor revenue source.[48]

Conclusion

Beginning in 1982, bilateral intergovernmental agreements began to define the terms of future offshore revenue sharing. Initially, the logic of the principal-beneficiary clause guaranteed Nova Scotia 100 percent of petroleum revenues. The implications for Canada's broader national equalization scheme were also recognized. Several triggers for revenue sharing were defined by the terminology and calculations of equalization. Yet there was no clear and forthright settlement on how offshore revenues interfaced with equalization. The first adjustment took the form of the secret side deal. The mechanism (the offset grant) was not spelled out until years later. In any event, a precedent had been set – Ottawa showed itself willing, under certain circumstances, to remedy unanticipated conflicts in fiscal policy goals, just as it had historically dealt with other equalization issues.

Despite the terms of the 1982 and 1986 agreements, a delay in production meant that the fiscal arrangements remained hypothetical and were relegated to the background as other policy sectors involving offshore exploration, industrial benefits, and project promotion took the lead. Over time, the broader equalization program continued to evolve. Federal caps were introduced in the 1990s, and the generic solution of 1994 applied to any concentrated, single-province revenue source.

Predictably, the offshore revenue file heated up in the 1990s with renewed exploration and the advent of Hibernia oil and Sable gas production. Resolution was important to each province but especially to Newfoundland, which had a legacy of failed management of resource benefits in electric power and the ground fishery, among others. The institutional landscape in 2000 was different. For Ottawa, the solution involved not breaking new ground but dusting off established arrangements, including perpetuating the bureaucratic segmentation by which the accords were administered by Natural Resources Canada while equalization fell under the federal Department of Finance. For the provinces, the need for wholesale modernization was overdue. Equalization payments needed to be adjusted for the effects of the five-province standard, for example. Similarly, the formula needed to take into consideration the delay in the onset of actual offshore production. And there were newly emerging needs. The provinces could invoke the spirit of accords that called for five-year policy reviews. They viewed bilateral deals such as the accords as charter agreements, whereas equalization was, by its past history, malleable. Moreover, the provinces interpreted Ottawa's fiscal surplus of 1997 as ushering in a new period of policy flexibility.

Each of the bargaining chips of the 2004 round was rooted in in past practice – the Ontario clause, for example, or the offset terms (current and revised). The advent of the Paul Martin regime, after the lengthy stonewall of the Chrétien years, signalled another opportunity for an offshore fiscal settlement. To a certain extent, Nova Scotia and Newfoundland worked together in a good cop–bad cop pairing. Their co-operation was furthered by the fact that changes to the terms of the two accords had to move in concert. After a point, however, the two jurisdictions diverged in terms of developmental timing and scale.

A new phase opened after 2000, when the question of fiscal fairness entered the public domain. The new policy discourse was defined in the Atlantic producer provinces. The good cop (Nova Scotia) set out the intellectual case, while the bad cop (Newfoundland) brought to bear brute force tactics that elicited federal responses. The electoral politics of minority governments also offered tactical openings and resulted in the Martin government's concessions of 2004.

Throughout these years, the residual political opposition of the Department of Finance is a striking. At every opportunity, departmental officials and ministers worked to minimize concessions or to eliminate hard-won provincial gains. The department's bureaucratic hegemony in Ottawa meant that other players, including Natural Resources Canada and regional political ministers, were constantly on the back foot. The preliminary settlement of 2004 was overturned following the change in federal government. It took the crisis triggered by the March 2007 budget measures to force yet another federal compromise, which involved Ottawa reviving the long-dormant Crown share compensation file as a substantial makeweight in the final settlement. In the end, the political subordination of the Department of Finance was most telling.

In Nova Scotia, the provincial government ultimately realized the ambitions of John Hamm's Campaign for Fairness, though not in the manner originally envisaged. Nonetheless, the campaign stands, alongside the successful promotion of the Sable projects and the eventual installation of a local gas distribution system, as one of the primary provincial political triumphs in the offshore domain. Fairness came at a cost, however. To the extent that provincial gains were realized in the form of intergovernmental fiscal transfers, it shifted the offshore political discourse in the direction of traditional politics. The fairness debate did little to accelerate exploration in the Scotian Basin, to deepen corporate production efforts, or to develop new policy tools for the sector's advancement. It can be argued that since offshore petroleum was the chief arena available for provincial government gains, its exploitation was not only timely but also necessary. It must also be acknowledged that in a policy sector so heavily knotted with federal-provincial overlays, the offshore fiscal file was always destined to be central. But there is a lingering sense that the provincial political class preferred to fight on familiar government-to-government terrain and to rely on traditional policy instruments rather than crafting new and innovative responses to the challenges thrown up by the Scotian Basin.

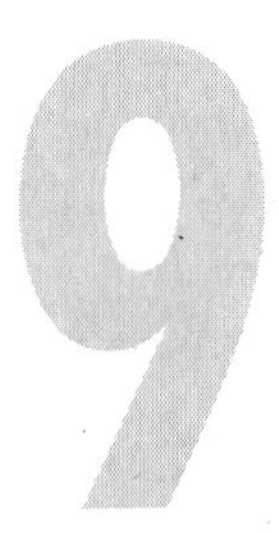

The Onshore Politics of Natural Gas Distribution

A separate political domain opens up once product begins to flow, one that centres on issues of onshore, in-province interests and outcomes. Some of these issues have been introduced in discussions of offshore revenue recovery and industrial linkages between the mainland and offshore sectors. This chapter explores another dimension of Nova Scotia benefits – the distribution of domestic natural gas for consumption by households and businesses.

From the earliest discovery of offshore petroleum, its exploitation has been justified by the advantages the new energy source would offer the province's consumers. The conference convened in Halifax in early 1980 to explore offshore opportunities flagged the importance of "decreased reliance on expensive imported oil to meet the province's energy needs."[1] Later in that year, the Nova Scotia legislature passed a new Gas Utilities Act to deal with "the establishment of fair prices and rates to be charged by a gas utility serving members of the public of Nova Scotia."[2] The appeal of offshore petroleum is not hard to appreciate in a province consigned by national energy policy to rely on imported oil. Although this reliance meant least-cost supplies in the 1960s, the OPEC-led oil spikes of the 1970s created unstable prices for heating fuel and electricity production. Similarly, the Canadian natural gas market was drawn, by regulatory policy, to supply markets from Quebec westward. Nova Scotia argued that western Canadian supplies should be made available by pipeline extensions to the Maritimes and also that a more balanced mix of primary energy fuels would enhance business efficiencies.[3] The benefits of natural gas feedstock for commercial, industrial, and residential consumers was a repeated theme in the provincial political discourse of the 1980s and 1990s.

However, the failure to extend the TransCanada trunk system eastward, together with the demise of the Venture gas project in 1987, meant that Nova Scotia continued to rely on imports. The province was still a greenfield natural gas jurisdiction when the Sable project was confirmed in 1997. The challenge for the provincial government was to orchestrate a new industrial sector from the ground up. That this challenge arose at a time when the underlying coordinates of the North American gas industry were in rapid flux, due partially to price deregulation, complicated the task. This chapter examines conflicts pertaining to gas distribution that arose after 1996. Gas distribution encompasses a striking variety of interests that operates in a separate political domain from upstream interests. Not surprisingly, the industrial precedents and policy paradigms of greatest interest were drawn from other provincial jurisdictions. However, the outcomes were determined in the final instance by the interplay of domestic interests under provincial state authority. Nova Scotia's experience suggests that a small province faces extraordinary challenges in delivering such a policy mandate. The state's capacity was deficient, both in the technical regulatory sense and in the wider curbs imposed by political and multinational business structures.

The lead players in the domestic arena are quite different from those on the production side of things. For in-province distribution, the important state authorities are agencies of the Government of Nova Scotia. The Petroleum Directorate (now the Department of Energy), already the custodian of provincial Crown interests in offshore assets and a prime interlocutor with the Canada–Nova Scotia Offshore Petroleum Board (CNSOPB), acquired the lead role for onshore systems. The Premier's Office, from John Buchanan to John Savage and beyond, also played an important role in petroleum issues, particularly during times when the premier chose to hold the petroleum portfolio personally. During Russell MacLellan's Liberal government, onshore gas distribution shot to the top of the political agenda. Other provincial bureaucracies with responsibilities that impinged on the distribution subsector included Environment, Transportation, and Municipal Affairs. Of paramount significance was the Nova Scotia Utilities and Review Board, or UARB, a quasi-independent agency that exercised regulatory powers over intraprovincial pipeline licensing.

The extent to which these discrete bureaus were drawn together in pursuit of a comprehensive strategy is a prime variable in policy outcomes. It can be seen by considering the government's overall goals for gas distribution, the legal and administrative mechanisms selected for advancing these goals, and the capacity to fit the onshore distribution subsector into Nova Scotia's (and Canada's) broader offshore petroleum framework.

The pool of business firms that sought the right to build and distribute inside Nova Scotia is likewise pertinent. These firms had a blank slate in 1996, when the Sable consortium gave the green light for offshore project development. The slate was again blank in 1998, when regulatory approvals were secured for both the offshore system and the onshore trunk transmission pipeline to the United States. At that time, no one was using natural gas in Nova Scotia for factory heating, electrical generation, or domestic use. There were, however, rival energy commodity suppliers of oil, propane, and electricity. But the possibility of a provincial gas industry opened up with some urgency when Sable Offshore Energy Inc. signed final contracts and began construction early in 1998. As the target date for first flow of offshore gas loomed at century's end, the Government of Nova Scotia discovered that much work was required to create a gas regulatory regime. In the end, Sable gas came ashore well before a provincial distribution system was in place to receive it.

The constellation of prospective corporate players was diverse. Nova Scotia Power Inc. (whose parent is Emera Inc.) was very interested in the prospect of installing natural gas turbines in various generating stations to move away from oil and coal. The company even considered applying for a gas distribution licence in 1998 but in the end declined. Out-of-province electricity generators such as TransAlta were also potential entrants to a liberalized power grid because of the competitive advantages of dual-cycle generating technologies, though this depended upon further regulatory terms and the Utilities and Review Board's consent to sell into the provincial grid. Even some Nova Scotia municipalities considered going into the power business. The large institutional energy users in both the private and public sectors were another group that could figure as anchors for local distribution. Finally, there was the need for an entirely new type of firm – a gas distribution company such as Consumers Gas in Ontario or Gaz Metropolitain in Quebec – to transport and sell gas between the Maritimes & Northeast Pipeline's (MNP) trunk line and final users.

Establishing the Policy Template

The years from 1995 to 1997 were formative ones for reviving offshore petroleum activity. The Savage government made several moves to kick-start production at the Sable field, including the negotiation of a royalty regime with the Sable rights holders (concluded in May 1996) and an agreement on a consolidated, single-panel regulatory process for environmental and social review (1996-97). Each of these matters drew significant political controversy. The Savage government, then in the second half of its mandate, was seen to be evasive in disclosing the royalty terms, which, it was alleged, were excessively concessionary.[4]

Even more dramatically, the appearance of a rival Quebec-based route for shipping Sable gas for export was publicly excoriated as undermining Nova Scotia's just entitlement.[5] Indeed, for the second half of 1996, the spectre of Quebec poaching the main transmission line (at the expense of the Sable-to-Maine proposal) dominated public discussion. Ambiguous comments from the Chrétien Liberals served to turn the problem into an intergovernmental issue and allowed Premier Savage to make some heavy running in federal-provincial circles as a champion of Nova Scotia's project.[6]

For much of this time, the question of provincial gas consumption as an offshore benefit was entirely ignored. This third major policy initiative, dealing with Nova Scotia gas distribution, slipped off the political radar. Perhaps it was not surprising, since the existence of a new provincial gas network was contingent upon offshore production in some form, and SOEP was not fully confirmed until late in 1997. At the same time, however, the very structure of the Nova Scotia gas business, not to mention its commercial prospects, depended closely upon the terms of state regulation. For this purpose, the provincial government had to fashion a regulatory regime *de novo*. An earlier gas statute from the Buchanan era was no longer relevant in light of industry restructuring. Given the leadtime required to fashion new policy structures, such delays were surprising, and public awareness was slow to manifest.

The provincial government began work on the gas distribution file in 1996. A consultant's report by Ziff Energy and the Stikeman, Elliott law firm outlined a framework in which natural gas sales (the commodity component) would be competitive, while the physical pipeline delivery system (the transportation component) would be regulated as a natural utility.[7] The Utilities and Review Board would assume the new regulatory functions, granting franchise rights to pipeline operators to build and operate systems, approving carrying tariffs, and licensing gas sellers. The two businesses would be separate from each other. A draft of this report was circulated publicly, with an invitation for comment, during the summer of 1996.[8]

In effect, the report captured dominant North American trends that had emerged in the midstream and downstream natural gas sectors since 1985. In both the United States and Canada, gas had been partially deregulated in a series of policy steps. Part of the impulse was to accelerate the growth of the gas industry and tackle the mounting problem of shut-in gas in western Canada (reserves that could not be exploited for lack of markets). The immediate challenge was to expand long-distance trunk pipeline infrastructure, thereby opening new geographic regions to gas delivery. One of the most dramatic industry transformations of recent decades, the story of natural gas restructuring is complex, nuanced, and difficult to encapsulate. In Canada, it began with the Mulroney government's agreement with the producing provinces to deregulate gas pricing.[9] Price deregulation was followed by a new, flexible policy orientation at the National Energy Board toward licensing gas exports to the United States.[10] Then, beginning in the 1990s, a flurry of major new trunk pipeline projects were proposed and approved by regulators.[11]

By 1995, a new model for the natural gas industry was evident. Upstream, prices were market sensitive, and producers could sell directly to distributors and end users. For their part, interprovincial and international trunk pipelines had become common carriers, offering open transport services at regulated rates. Further downstream, at the receiving end, gas distributors were also regulated carriers connecting directly to end-use customers. Distributors carried both their own gas and gas sold competitively by private marketers, a trade that the distributors could join through arms-length affiliates.[12] The prototypes were the larger gas-consuming provinces such as Alberta and Ontario. Yet, despite the appearance of a new model, many variations and uncertainties remained. The new business relationships were works in progress; they were modifications of earlier systems that continued to be shaped by those system's legacies. This point was not appreciated in Nova Scotia when attention turned to designing a greenfield gas distribution framework.

When the Nova Scotia government unveiled its draft Gas Distribution Act in the spring of 1997, it closely followed the consultants' advice. The Utilities and Review Board was designated the regulator, and any constructor or operator of a local distribution network required a franchise. Tolls for gas distribution (though not for commodity gas supply) were also regulated. The businesses of local gas transport and sale were separated to allow for the possibility of competitive marketing. More policy provisions would follow in the regulations issued under the act.

For the most part, the Opposition parties' critiques of Bill 6 were superficial. Complaints were raised about the premature timing of the bill, and calls for postponement were heard.[13] Only seven people appeared at the law amendments stage.[14] The Halifax Chamber of Commerce questioned the Utilities and Review Board's control over prices.[15] In addition, there were complaints about the partisan character of the board's membership, for two of the three members had Liberal affiliations, and the chair had served previously as Premier Savage's chief of staff.[16] Notwithstanding these concerns, the act was in place by the autumn of 1997.

In the meantime, however, the provincial leadership had changed after John Savage's retirement, when federal MP Russell McLellan was selected as Liberal Party leader and premier. McLellan chose to make Scotian Shelf development one of the pillars of his leadership campaign.[17] His call for improved provincial benefit terms was an implicit repudiation of the Savage government's offshore settlement. Once in office, McLellan staged a successful eleventh-hour intervention on the pricing terms of Sable gas in Nova Scotia. As described earlier, the premier secured a ten-year price premium as a compromise for the broader regulatory endorsement of postage-stamp tariffs along the Maritime trunk pipeline corridor to Maine.

The time-limited character of McLellan's gas price concession added urgency to achieving the prompt licensing of gas transporters and sellers. Although the Gas Distribution Act provided an overall framework, with the Utilities and Review Board serving as the chief regulatory agent, the more detailed parameters of licensing remained to be set. Legal regulations had to be developed by cabinet and issued by provincial Order-in-Council.

The Government of Nova Scotia spent more than a year developing the Gas Distribution Regulations of November 1998. In many respects, the period was a time when gas-supply politics erupted in all their complexity, for several reasons. First, although the act had spelled out a clear and logical structure for gas distribution, crucial questions remained that the regulations would have to address. Second, each successive policy statement – the Sable project's joint panel approval of November 1997, the memorandum of understanding between the province and MNP and Sable consortium of December 1997, the National Energy Board's export permit to MNP, and the Gas Distribution Act of September 1997 – constrained the question of in-province gas, though in ways not always evident at the time. These issues had to be reconciled as the regulatory process unfolded. Third, lobbyists exerted heavy pressure on the gas-distribution regulations from the beginning of the working-group deliberations. Conflicts arose between business and public interests at all stages of the gas-industry chain. Finally, that these events occurred very late in the Liberal government's electoral cycle (whose end point came in June 1998) served to intensify the pressure from lobbyists.

The opening of any new service region will draw interest from established system operators elsewhere, and Nova Scotia was no exception. By mid-1998, a number of aspiring consortia had been announced, including Nova Scotia Power and Consumer Gas, Irving Oil and Westcoast Transmission, and SaskEnergy. The fourth and final prospect to appear was Sempra Energy, a California conglomerate that was already constructing a distribution system in Bangor, Maine. Prospective new gas distributors also appeared at the subregional or municipal level. One of the earliest was an alliance of interests in Antigonish County that advanced a co-operative venture model to build a lateral pipe from the MNP's mainline to county customers. This group drew inspiration from the community co-operatives that dominated rural gas delivery in the province of Alberta. Other municipal initiatives were reported in Pictou and Halifax counties. For prospective applicants, the terms stipulated in the regulatory framework would be all important.

At the same time, potential industrial consumers of gas were positioning themselves for secure and inexpensive long-term supplies. These included firms in the pulp and paper, electrical power, and other manufacturing sectors. The possibility of direct sales to industrial customers (outside of the general commercial franchises) loomed large. Finally, commercial and residential markets were targets for gas sales. There was a widespread assumption that the arrival of a safe, clean, and inexpensive energy substitute in a market that had long suffered high-cost electricity and volatile oil pricing would sweep all rivals before it. This assumption neglected some significant barriers to entry, including the costs of system conversion to users, the competitive responses of rival industries (such as home-heating oil) during the installation period and after, and the impacts of competitive supply on gas prices.

Public debate escalated during and after the March 1998 provincial election. Gas industry interests played a part by broadly declaring the competitive advantages of their product to all energy users. Commonly quoted unit price differentials put natural gas at a level 40 percent cheaper than electricity or oil. As the political debate picked up, however, business spokesmen were at greater pains to qualify such sweeping statements by matching data to the geographic location, franchise type, and size of market to be served.

During the campaign itself, the New Democratic Party (NDP) expressed support for municipal interests who feared they were being marginalized by constituting a "rural gas working group" to ensure that their voices were heard.[18] Following the return of the Liberal minority government in 1998, NDP member John Holm introduced a private member's bill to ensure that approved franchisees were committed to broad, cross-province distribution and ease of application for local applicants. (Many municipalities argued that a proposed $50,000 application fee was an unfair barrier to local firms and co-operative groups.) Although Holm's bill was not enacted, it highlighted a growing concern that franchisees would seek to skim the cream by concentrating on large markets and high-volume customers.

The question of orderly development of the new gas system became increasingly politicized. As time passed, critics warned that the vision of a quick and comprehensive gas supply was a misconception. In part, this was a reaction to MacLellan's message of natural gas populism, centred on the promise of near-universal service. Calgary oilman James Gray challenged this rosy scenario, advising that "gas service will be phased in over an extended period with the areas of high-load concentration being serviced in the first several years ... Realistically, some of your citizens in less populated areas of your province will be beyond the reach of natural gas service ... Others will need to wait many years."[19]

Fear that the province would distort the shape of the gas market to win the support of municipalities and consumers was voiced frequently throughout 1998. One commentator warned that "wall-to-wall (or door-to-door) gas distribution in Nova Scotia is a sure loser ... [MacLellan] should try educating the mayors instead of placating them."[20] The corollary was that – to ensure a stable, reputable, and efficient system – the chances of greatest success lay with one comprehensive franchisee. By implication, local companies, municipal consortia, and co-operatives would be excluded, a possibility that was strongly though unsuccessfully resisted by a network of some forty local aspirants.

Another aspect of small-business and residential gas uptake was the cost of adapting from old to new energy sources. MacLellan plunged squarely into the debate in autumn 1998 when he called upon Ottawa to provide at least transitional gas price subsidies by way of support for future lateral pipelines (a proposal quickly rejected in Ottawa).[21] When talk of the need for retrofit grants and even price subsidies arose, the heating-oil supply industry was quick to condemn it. With more than 60 percent of the home-heating market (about 227,000 households), the oil supply business in Nova Scotia had much at stake. The message was that "the heating oil industry doesn't mind fighting natural gas suppliers in the marketplace, providing government doesn't give start-up money to the competition."[22]

Yet another theme was the adequacy of the Nova Scotia supply allotment of Sable gas. In October 1998, Conservative leader John Hamm warned that once large industrial consumers such as Nova Scotia Power and Stora Enso paper were contracted, the province's portion would be oversubscribed and the residual (commercial and residential) public would face short supply.[23] For some time, reports had circulated that prospective Maritime demand for gas far exceeded suppliers' expectations. Robert Chisholm, leader of the NDP, made a similar point, but the MNP declared that there was plenty of capacity available for residential and commercial customers.[24]

This debate tied in to another one on the adequacy of the lateral pipelines that would connect the mainline to local distributors. The question arose in the summer of 1998, when MNP filed applications for construction of the Halifax and Point Tupper laterals the following spring. According to the joint-tolling agreement, these two laterals were to be built by MNP, and their tariffs would be folded into the mainline tariff. Almost immediately, the capacity of these lines was challenged as being too small. The Halifax line, at 30 centimetres in diameter, was declared insufficient to meet both Halifax and other (southwestern Nova Scotia and Annapolis Valley) markets.[25] It was noted that the Saint John (New Brunswick) lateral was designed for a line 40 centimetres in diameter. The MNP replied that the Halifax lateral was designed to serve Nova Scotia Power's Tufts Cove power plant, along with metro consumers, and that additional laterals would be more appropriate for the regional markets. Premier MacLellan declared his support for the 40-centimetre design.

These points highlight the style of political debate that surrounded gas distribution during the critical year of 1998. Prospective franchise holders weighed alternative markets and user class demands and worked (largely behind the scenes) to influence the government's all-important class rules, which would guide the Utilities and Review Board's licensing deliberations. Tensions between user classes, subregional markets, and pipeline operators were well evident.

Through it all, the Utilities and Review Board prepared to assume a major new jurisdiction over gas pipelines. New staff were hired, training was arranged, and consultations with the Nova Scotia Petroleum Directorate about the upcoming gas distribution regulations were ongoing. Ultimately, however, the regulations were written by the government and approved by cabinet. Despite some early signals that the regulations would be released in the spring to allow for applications and public hearings in the autumn of 1998, the government seemed to be paralyzed when it came to the contradictory political demands. In October, a draft copy of the regulations found its way onto the webpage of the *Chronicle-Herald*.

On 9 November, the province released the long-anticipated Gas Distribution Regulations. The overriding design parameter, which would guide the Utilities and Review Board's deliberations, required the successful franchisee to offer service in all eighteen counties within the first seven years of operation, effectively making access available to at least 62 percent of all provincial households. This stipulation became known as the "18/62/7 target." A single, province-wide franchise was the preference. Mention was also made of the possible addition of supplemental franchises at a later date to incorporate areas without service.[26]

The Politics of Licensing Gas Distributors

Up to this point, the lead provincial agency for gas distribution policy had been the Petroleum Directorate. Since it reported directly to Premier MacLellan, it was tied into the central power axis in the cabinet. As the prospective regulator, the Utilities and Review Board was also integral to this policy network. However, during the lengthy germination of its statutory mandate, the board's point of reference was gas utility regulators in provinces such as Alberta and Ontario.

Members of the Utilities and Review Board were frustrated by delays in finalizing the regulations. Like all other informed interests in the province, the board was aware that time was precious: the Sable project and MNP expected to start shipping gas at the close of 1999. The board's main gas consultant, Paul DeWolfe, conceded on several occasions that the province's regulatory timetable was slipping as the year wore on.[27]

Through the assumption of gas distribution responsibilities, the Utilities and Review Board was forced into a fundamental transformation. Its success in managing this process would be one of the crucial factors determining the province's policy capacity. As in most Canadian provinces, utility regulation in Nova Scotia had a history dating back to the early twentieth century. The Nova Scotia Public Utilities Board was established in 1909 and had authority over intraprovince electricity and telephone services and the power to regulate both rates and the quality of services. In both sectors, the board tended to react to initiatives by the major regulated firms to trigger applications for rate change.[28] Board members tended to serve for long periods that spanned multiple governments, and their attention alternated between the several regulated sectors.

The Public Utilities Board was renamed the Utilities and Review Board during the major restructuring of 1992. Legislation merged the board with separate authorities that handled municipal affairs, compensation for expropriations, and tax review. However, the merger was just the beginning of a design to create an omnibus provincial super-regulator. When jurisdiction over gas distribution was added in 1997, so too was jurisdiction over intraprovincial pipelines. In 2000, the Utilities and Review Board's mandate was enlarged with the addition of licensing responsibilities for alcohol and gaming and short-haul railways. The panel of members was expanded to nine, and additional clerical staff was taken on board.[29] None of the traditionally regulated sectors were simple to handle, and a cross-sector authority faced serious challenges. In addition, the Utilities and Review Board experienced significant changes to its operational context in the closing decades of the twentieth century, when government utilities were privatized and industry conditions liberalized.

When the Utilities and Review Board's jurisdiction was extended to natural gas distribution in 1997, the board became responsible for an industry in the throes of restructuring. Not only were the board's skills and learning patterns less transferable than in earlier decades, outside knowledge about the new gas sector was itself in flux. Once the act was in place, the board embarked on its own preparatory process. During the year that it awaited the issuance of the all-important regulations, it hired consultants to train staff and board members in the natural gas dossier and augment its technical competence. Running against this positive capacity-building effort was the increasing frequency of turnover at the board level. Although the Savage government filled two vacancies on the seven-person board in 1997, the MacLellan government faced three vacancies only a year later. These vacancies, of course, took place in the newly politicized context of onshore gas politics. In addition, Savage's appointment of his former chief of staff as the board's chair raised the spectre of partisan reward in appointments. In less than a year, that chair departed for a (federally appointed) position on the Nova Scotia Supreme Court. With only a minority government following the March 1998 election, MacLellan was obliged to consult closely with the Opposition on the three appointments required to bring the board up to strength.[30] This too played a part in extending the date of issue for the Gas Distribution Regulations.

The closing months of 1998 saw extensive manoeuvring among the aspiring gas franchisees. Four contenders emerged for the single general franchise stipulated by the government. By this point, the contenders were household names in Nova Scotia, having spent the autumn season in province-wide publicity promotions. In order of announcement, they were Scotia Advantage (July), Maritime NRG (August), SaskEnergy (August), and Sempra Atlantic (September).

Scotia Advantage was an alliance between Nova Scotia Power (a prospective gas consumer at power-generating plants and a partner in Sable Offshore Energy Inc.) and Consumers Gas (a huge central Canadian distribution firm). Maritime NRG brought together the Irving industrial interests in New Brunswick (a prospective gas consumer at its pulp-and-paper and petroleum-refining operations) and Westcoast Transmission (a leading trunk gas transmission firm in the North American market). SaskEnergy was the state-owned gas utility in the province of Saskatchewan. Finally, Sempra Atlantic was a newly formed subsidiary of Sempra Energy, the giant California-based gas and electric utility. Sempra was already building a gas distribution network in Bangor, Maine, that would be supplied by the MNP's mainline.

Surprisingly, this field of four prospects was reduced by year end to two. On 11 December 1998, Scotia Advantage announced its decision not to apply, citing concerns about the viability of the 18/62/7 rule. Less than a week later, SaskEnergy also declined to proceed. In this case, the reasons were the government's approval of direct gas sales to large industrial plants outside of the distribution network and doubts about the capacity of the lateral pipelines that would feed local distributors.[31]

When the filing deadline arrived, there were only two full-service franchise aspirants. The first to declare was Sempra Atlantic, which unveiled a billion dollar plan to meet the 18/62/7 criteria, irrespective of the direct-sale option.[32] Indeed, it is possible that by staking out a maximal position early, Sempra might have convinced some potential rivals to throw in the towel. There were really two business models available for province-wide franchises. One depended on a maximum number of laterals being built under the joint-tolling provision and on local distribution clusters running from the end of laterals. The diameter of MNP's laterals was a critical consideration.

Although MNP might have engineered its laterals on the basis of direct-sales customers, the distributors required major gas-carrying capacity above direct sales. The denial of direct sales would work best of all, and this model had been accepted by all but Sempra. It is fair to assume that in the absence of an alternative distribution model, the regulatory hearings would have revolved around who best could make the model work and with what mix of revised conditions. Yet, with Sempra's stand-alone proposal (the company was apparently troubled by neither direct sales nor lateral size), rival applicants were in trouble. Regardless of whether the economics of Sempra's design held up, its politics were unassailable. Scotia Advantage and SaskEnergy withdrew in the face of this political *force majeure*. As the head of the Antigonsh co-operative put it, "Everyone else was thinking $500 to $600 million. If you were sitting on the fence, you'd get the hell off."[33]

Maritimes NRG likewise had doubts about the 18/62/7 criteria but devised a different tactic to deal with them. The Irving-Westcoast consortium announced that it would "comply with the intent of the legislation" but only within the confines of commercial sense.[34] In practice, this meant that Maritimes NRG outlined a system that fell well short of the mandatory access terms but asked the board for an exemption from that requirement. Indeed, Maritimes NRG aggressively challenged Sempra's proposal, contending that it constituted a gross and unrealistic overcommitment. Of the seven municipal or co-operative groups that also declared their intent to apply, only four submitted full proposals and carried through during the public hearing phase.

The Full Regulation Class Franchise Decision

It is difficult to do justice to the seven thousand pages of evidence and testimony that the board heard between April and August 1999. The discussion that follows focuses on the outcome as revealed by the Utilities and Review Board's November decision. By placing the power of franchise approval for gas delivery systems in the board's hands, the Government of Nova Scotia appeared to be following conventional practice in utility regulation throughout Canada. However, the province was not willing to delegate unconditionally, nor was the board the sole influence in shaping the new industry. The Gas Distribution Act spelled out the factors to be considered when determining the public interest in granting franchises. The Gas Distribution Regulations went further. They stipulated that the board's deliberations must conform to provincial policies. Reinforcing this point, the regulations incorporated the MacLellan government's November 1998 policy statement (on maximizing benefits from gas delivery) as an appendix.

The Nova Scotia regulatory style was clearly to design a policy structure and then hand off its implementation to the quasi-independent Utilities and Review Board. By contrast, in New Brunswick another approach was under way. Facing the development of a similar greenfield natural gas environment, the cabinet reserved the right to choose franchises but delegated rate and performance monitoring to the Public Utilities Board. Enjoying a majority, the New Brunswick Liberals asked the Select Legislative Committee on Energy to consult and recommend parameters for gas industry development. After two weeks of public hearings, the committee prepared a comprehensive review of the issues.[35] This review shaped the revision of pipeline policy the following year.

In 1999, the New Brunswick Department of Energy's invitation for proposals drew two general-class applications and, after a prompt and confidential review, the cabinet favoured Enbridge Gas New Brunswick (a partnership of Consumers Gas and provincial business partners) over Maritimes NRG. Not surprisingly, many of the issues paralleled the situation in Nova Scotia. However, the process in New Brunswick was far more direct and expeditious. The quality of the public policy discourse was notably more sophisticated and encouraged far more realistic public expectations as to the speed and scope of system coverage. It is true that MacLellan's minority status, from March 1998 to July 1999, accentuated partisanship and might even have precluded ratification of a discretionary cabinet choice. However, the New Brunswick process also avoided the highly damaging award-and-withdrawal syndrome that afflicted Nova Scotia.

As the Utilities and Review Board's hearings unfolded, there seemed little doubt that Sempra Atlantic would be the default choice. Only Sempra pledged to meet (and actually exceed) the 18/62/7 targets. In addition, Sempra Atlantic planned to finance the project internally, drawing on the capital of its Fortune 500 parent in California. Furthermore, Sempra had a track record of building and operating large distribution systems, so its bona fides were difficult to challenge. Maritimes NRG, on the other hand, adopted a more qualified approach. It stated flatly that the 18/62/7 targets were commercially prohibitive, and it countered with a proposal for a scaled-down system in the province's major urban areas. It asked the board to grant it an exemption from the mandatory access terms. On the financial front, Maritimes NRG was reluctant to divulge information about its principal sponsor, the privately held Irving group based in New Brunswick.

The Utilities and Review Board threaded its way through these issues in its dense and detailed decision. The decision was organized according to the terms of the public-interest criteria set out in section 8 of the Gas Distribution Act and additional factors stipulated by cabinet in the Gas Distribution Regulations. The two points on which the decision turned were financial capability and compliance with the mandatory access terms, both points on which Sempra's application bested that of Maritimes NRG. At the same time, the board conceded that there were some startling uncertainties and gaps in its foundational knowledge. Its members admitted that they did not understand lateral line finance, an element that would clearly be crucial to distribution prospects. The board's discussion of performance-based rate regulation was also fuzzy. Finally, the absence of MNP, the trunk pipeline carrier to New England, deprived the board of crucial expertise and evidence. As a federally regulated business, with ongoing hearings on lateral pipelines before the National Energy Board, MNP had opted not to appear. Table 9.1 summarizes the board's findings.

The outcome prompts a number of questions. Did Sempra Atlantic overcommit in its application to capture the franchise? If so, was this an error of unfamiliarity with local conditions or a deliberate strategy? Once rival proponents were chased off and business activities were under way, the act allowed a franchise holder to return to the board (and cabinet) to seek amendments to the terms of the franchise. At least one participant to the regulatory process warned publicly of this possibility. Byron MacDonald of the Central Annapolis Gas Cooperative stated, "I can see them coming back in a few years and saying it's not viable."[36] Similar sentiments were expressed by Brian Crowley of the Atlantic Institute of Market Studies. By this point, the regulatory bargain seemed to have shifted in favour of the licence holder, since the costs of project collapse and reset might be more than the provincial state could accept.

If the initial franchise decision is viewed through the lens of the board's capacities and responsibilities, several attributes stand out. First, the board's first foray into gas-distribution licensing dealt with the most fundamental possible decision – the choice of system carrier. In addition, the board tackled this decision at a time when it was still acquiring baseline technical competence by hiring new staff and consulting services. The situation was complicated further by the shifting membership of the board's panel and a minority government. To use Marver Bernstein's terms, the board seems to have been neither a newly empowered crusader for the public interest nor a simple captive of the regulated industry.[37] Aware of the fundamental character of

TABLE 9.1

Factors addressed by the Utilities and Review Board in its 1999 decision

Relevant section of Gas Distribution Act (GDA)	Decision	Finding
Section 8(a): existence of actual or potential markets.	Pt. 3	The projected penetration rates by both applicants are justifiable and reasonable (despite differences). Consumption estimates are supported by sufficient evidence (Maritimes NRG is lower, while Sempra Atlantic is more aggressive).
Section 8(b): availability of adequate gas supplies.	Pt. 2	Both applicants meet the criteria for demonstrating adequate supply (both submitted letters of intent with suppliers).
Section 8(c): economic feasibility of proposed gas-delivery system.	Pt. 4	1 Relative reliability of market-penetration rate (share of potential market achieved over first ten years) and consumption estimates (Maritimes NRG average residential estimate, 85 GJ/year; Sempra Atlantic estimate, 130 GJ/year). 2 Relative reliability of forecast price of fuel oil (the reference for gas price setting): since both forecasts are reasonable, the board asks which proposal carries less risk for consumers? Maritime NRG's loss-recovery mechanism imposes a higher burden. 3 Extent and cost of construction plans: see 8(f) below.
Section 8(d): financial capability of applicant.	Pt. 9	Sempra Atlantic satisfies its criterion, but Maritimes NRG does not. Irving Oil is the sole financial investor for Maritimes NRG, and insufficient financial data is provided on Irving Oil (a private company). Sempra Energy (the parent company) commits to finance system. Letters of endorsement from both sponsors.
Section 8(e): related experience of applicant.	Pt. 9	Both applicants have requisite experience.

Section 8(f): plans of applicant to provide service on terms stipulated by s. 5 of the Gas Distribution Regulations.	Pt. 5	Sempra Atlantic meets the terms of the 18/62 rule, but Maritimes NRG does not. Maritimes NRG considers that compliance with the mandatory access terms renders the project uneconomical. It proposes to invest $560 million over seven years to supply 14/18 counties and will use the MNP's laterals (see below), but without a financial commitment to build full base system. Maritimes NRG's request for an exemption from the Gas Distribution Regulations mandatory access terms (s. 10) is denied.
... on terms stipulated by s. 22 (approval of rates).	Pt. 6	The board applies a performance-based, as distinct from a cost-of-service, approach to rate scrutiny. Maritimes NRG does not, over ten years, achieve the benefits associated with a performance-based rate, while Sempra Atlantic has more of the elements of a performance-based rate, thereby best serving the public interest.
... on reliance of the MNP's laterals.	Pt. 7	The board asserts it does not know enough about the status of lateral financing. Maritimes MNP withdrew from the hearings. Laterals will be regulated by the National Energy Board on a case-by-case basis. The board is not convinced that Maritime NRG's proposed laterals will achieve maximum penetration in a timely manner and with lower tolls.
Section 8(g): other such factors as provided by governor-in-council (socio-economic impact and benefits).	Pt. 8	Packages are provided by both applicants, and the issue is decided on the comparative likelihood of actual implementation. Sempra Atlantic meets the standard, with modifications.
Section 8(g): other such factors as provided by governor-in-council (separation of delivery and sales).	Pt. 10	Both applicants propose to sell gas. Sempra Atlantic's request for sales subsidiary recognition is deferred until the Utilities and Review Board's Phase 2 hearings on selling agent licensing.

Source: Nova Scotia, Utilities and Review Board, "Re Gas Distribution Act, 1999," NSUARB-NG-98, November 1999.

the choice it faced but also cognizant of the emerging ethic of light-touch regulation and market incentives, the board opted to treat the applications at face value. Given a choice between ambitious overreach or skeptical under-commitment, the Utilities and Review Board opted for the former. However, its decision was taken up not by the MacLellan Liberals but by the new Conservative government of John Hamm.

The Sempra Franchise: Crisis and Collapse

When cabinet approved the Utilities and Review Board's franchise recommendation on 16 December 1999, the way was cleared for Sempra Atlantic. The approval marked twenty-seven months since passage of the Gas Distribution Act and more than a year since the regulations had been affirmed. Moreover, Sable gas was scheduled to begin flowing by the end of the month.

For Sempra Atlantic, however, the new phase entailed a shift in its commercial and political focus – from applicant to operator, from proposal to construction, and from the board's hearing room to the provincial bureaucracy. As it turned out, a series of critical regulatory issues remained outstanding, and the Government of Nova Scotia proved surprisingly unresponsive to their resolution, once again revealing the state's weak capacity for developmental planning on a major infrastructure priority.

The first signs of trouble arose on the question of municipal taxes. The board set a deadline of one month for the company to reach an agreement with local authorities, represented by the Union of Nova Scotia Municipalities. An agreement proved to be unattainable, and the ensuing months were filled with public rancour. Sempra proposed a tax rate of 1.5 percent on gross transportation revenues and 0.75 on its assets, levels comparable to those paid by other utilities such as Maritime Telegraph & Telephone Ltd. and Nova Scotia Power.[38] In dollar terms, these payments would yield an estimated $56 million over the first decade, with almost half going to the Halifax Regional Municipality.

In the internal politics of the Union of Nova Scotia Municipalities, Greater Halifax had a central though not exclusive voice. Since the earliest and most extensive gas build out would take place in that city, the Halifax Regional Municipality had high expectations. For several years, its Sable gas committee had monitored matters and recognized that its moment of maximum leverage had arrived.[39] Indeed, expectations were high throughout the local government sector, fed by MacLellan's 18/62/7 standard and the extended lobbying of prospective franchisees. As a result, the union proposed a tax rate averaging 3.5 percent over the decade but escalating to

7 percent by the tenth year. Sempra Atlantic's president, Andrew Rea, dismissed the proposal as commercially unviable and disproportionate with other utilities. In a blunt warning, he declared that prohibitive taxation "could cause us to give the franchise back and say we can't do business under these particular circumstances."[40]

The Utilities and Review Board eventually intervened to set a 10 April 2000 deadline for a negotiated settlement, after which the board would arbitrate. The intervention was welcomed by the company, though the municipalities feared a pro-project bias on the part of the board. Prior to this deadline, however, an agreement was struck between Sempra Atlantic and the Halifax Regional Municipality that would become a model for the rest of the province. In effect, the terms split the political difference. For the first decade, the company would pay 1 percent of gross revenues and 0.55 percent on assessed assets. During the second decade, it would pay 4 percent of gross revenues.[41]

The lengthy and rancorous course of this tax dispute is notable in several respects. First, the provincial government was absent as a positive broker of compromise. Although the government could claim that the dispute was a matter for the company and municipalities to resolve, the urgency that had been attached to gas distribution as a public benefit, and the almost triumphal nature of MacLellan's periodic assurances, implied a more profound developmental commitment. This commitment was not matched in efforts to reach an agreement on the central terms of project advancement. Time was lost, and goodwill dissipated. The end of the tax dispute also marked Andrew Rea's departure as Sempra Atlantic's chief executive. That moment may also mark the company's deepening awareness of the still incomplete nature of its political franchise.

The Utilities and Review Board's second licensing phase for gas marketers opened in June 2000. Part of the liberalized downstream natural gas system that emerged in the 1990s, gas marketers were firms that bought gas at the wellhead, contracted its transport to pipeline carriers, and sold it directly to end-use customers. Marketers were regarded as a valued source of competition to the traditional distribution utilities and useful agents of downstream price sensitivity. The major players at these hearings included Energy Source Canada Inc. (a Sempra affiliate), Enbridge Business Services (a subsidiary of Enbridge Consumers Gas), Enercom (a subsidiary of Nova Scotia Power), Irving Oil Inc., Wilson Fuel Co., and the Canadian Oil Heat Association (which had concerns about the impact of gas marketing on oil fuel sales).[42] Not surprisingly, concerns were raised about Sempra's possible dominance of gas sales. The board proposed to meet this concern with a code of conduct for all gas marketers. Rivals, however, sought to impose limits on Sempra's use of its name and logo in marketing gas on the grounds that it would confer an unfair advantage.[43]

A far greater operational and design problem was brewing in the field of pipe system design and installation. In its franchise application, Sempra Atlantic set out plans to lay high-pressure pipelines along the shoulders of provincial secondary highways. Roadside installation was a critical parameter for the rapid construction of the system and the rollout of service, beginning in Halifax. The matter did not provoke significant comment before the Utilities and Review Board. Indeed, Sempra Atlantic claimed that it was following a common practice in the North American industry. However, provincial highway officials found problems with this provision.

The issue came to public light in the autumn of 2000, when Sempra Atlantic's new president, Hal Snyder, told the Amherst Rotary Club, "I need you to help me convince ... the Department of Transportation and Public Works to be quicker in their decision-making."[44] Municipal leaders in Cumberland County lent their support to test Sempra Atlantic's proposed construction method in their area.[45] Others agreed, including the backers of the (failed) Antigonish co-operative franchise bid, declaring that the pipe-laying question "shouldn't be a make-or-break issue in bringing natural gas to rural Nova Scotia."[46]

Provincial officials were not to be swayed, however. After commissioning a national study from the Transportation Association of Canada and reviewing a risk analysis study by the Bercha Engineering Group of Calgary, the Department of Transportation and Public Works denied Sempra's request on 10 April 2001. Officials cited several concerns: the integrity of the roadbeds, increased maintenance costs to government, and safety risks to travellers. What linked them was a perceived need to modify "highway maintenance and construction activities to manage the risks from the pipeline presence ... Without incurring these impacts, and making the necessary safety provisions, risk from the pipeline generally would be unacceptable, producing a high probability of property damage and loss of life ... Some of the activities appear to be sufficiently large to make the activity unfeasible, or require (alternative) pipeline routings."[47]

The transportation minister, Ron Russell, contended that Sempra Atlantic had been aware of the concerns before launching its franchise application.[48] The company contested this claim, however, asking why the studies had been commissioned if the government already had a firm policy.[49] Sempra pointed out that it had been willing to discuss cost sharing.

The immediate terms of the dispute mask a more profound change that had overtaken Sempra's franchise. In the summer of 1999, MacLellan's minority government had been defeated by the Progressive Conservatives. By furnishing a new government, this time with a majority standing, the July election swept away the cabinet most closely identified with the Sempra project. In its place, Premier John Hamm's ministers brought to office years of criticism about the Liberal's perceived mishandling of the natural gas file. Faced with the prospect of additional hidden costs to government in facilitating a perceptibly flawed deal, the Conservatives simply said no. The stiffening of the government's backbone must be understood in this context. In many respects, the roadside pipe issue provided a substantial pretext to draw the line.

Just when Sempra became aware of the government's attitude is difficult to say. However, the company replied to Russell's rejection with the news that it planned to re-examine the entire gas distribution plan. There was no mistaking the pessimism of this announcement. As President Hal Snyder put it:

> Moving construction from the road shoulder adds tens of millions of dollars to overall project costs ... Those increased costs, in areas such as design, construction, land acquisition and new regulatory approvals, must be considered in evaluating the overall distribution plan ... To support extensive building of the distribution system, revenues are needed from customers ... Our construction has been delayed by two years and, as a result, we have lost a significant opportunity to engage customers through that period ... Acquiring customers in those two years would have helped support construction of the distribution system ... Shifts in the North American energy market also have placed pressure on the company's business plan.[50]

Coincident with this news, Sempra Atlantic gave notice of another delay in its construction schedule. Building plans were cancelled for Truro, Amherst, and New Glasgow, while engineering planning for all other areas outside of Halifax were suspended. Without roadside installation, gas appeared to be finished in rural Nova Scotia. As a follow-up to the review, more than half of Sempra's fifty-nine head office staff was laid off in June.[51] From a distance, former head of Sempra Atlantic Andrew Rea predicted that the deadlock was so fundamental that it would finish the project.[52]

By June 2001, the sense of urgency was palpable. In neighbouring New Brunswick, the first small business user of distributed gas had been hooked up. Sempra Atlantic decided to force the issue with a formal letter to the Nova Scotia Petroleum Directorate, which was responsible for policy. The company outlined two future scenarios: "One: if government supports [our] new business model, Sempra will go immediately to the UARB. Two: without that support, Sempra will drop the franchise 'and start the legal process to recover our investment in Nova Scotia.'"[53] In effect, Sempra was inviting the government to either be friends or be sued.

Petroleum minister Gordon Balser's response indicated conclusively that the Hamm government was willing to start with a clean slate. Declining any positive response to Sempra's invitation, Balser offered the following comment:

> Our primary responsibility is to look out for the interests of Nova Scotia, not Sempra ... Sempra won the right to distribute gas in Nova Scotia by agreeing to exceed government requirements at the time. They are now seeking to change those terms fundamentally. It wouldn't be fair to all the others who bid for the contract for us to endorse what is, in essence, a totally new deal ... Sempra has an exclusive franchise to distribute gas under an existing set of conditions. It's now Sempra's choice as to what they do with that franchise ... If Sempra is convinced of the merits of their new proposal, they should subject that plan to a public review before the UARB, recognizing that other parties may wish to pursue the franchise in its revised form.[54]

Weeks later, Sempra forced the issue with an application to the Utilities and Review Board for either the surrender or amendment of the franchise. Such a move was authorized under section 10 of the Gas Distribution Act, and it required decisions first by the board and then cabinet. In justifying its request, Sempra cited the fact that the roadside impasse had undermined its approved proposal, along with "the unprecedented, unforeseeable and unpredictable level of volatility" in the energy market and the proposed operation of the Point Tupper lateral at a pressure less than that allowed in Sempra's plan.[55] To cope with these challenges, Sempra requested four key modifications: (1) the replacement of the 18/62/7 requirements with a core commitment to build and operate a system in "certain communities" (presumably greater Halifax), (2) the adjustment of the rate plan while maintaining a minimum 5 percent savings over fuel oil, (3) the establishment of a mechanism to foster and fund widespread conversion to natural gas in spite of the current energy price volatility (i.e., establishment of a government incentive program), and (4) regulatory and policy streamlining in "recognition that Government support, and a shared interest in, the success of gas distribution is important."[56] Although the requests were addressed to the board, it was notable that at least half were directed at the provincial government. Similar points were restated the following month in Sempra's submission to the Hamm government's energy policy review. Two sentences summed up the company's position: "Nova Scotia needs a natural gas 'champion' [that] could spearhead the coordination of provincial resources and facilitate interactions in the natural gas sector ... It is a question of focus, attitude and supportive action."[57]

Simultaneous with the scheduling of public hearings on Sempra's application, the board invited alternative franchise applications from interested parties. (They were due on 30 August, but the deadline was extended to 1 October 2001.)[58] By 21 September, with no further show of support from the province, Sempra threw in the towel and filed for a full and formal surrender.[59]

Once Sempra Atlantic acknowledged its intention, the focus turned to a final settlement. Avoiding an ugly number of lawsuits, the company and government worked out terms on the value, maintenance, and sale or abandonment of Sempra's facilities and assets, which were mainly located in the Halifax Regional Municipality. A final agreement was announced on 25 October 2001. Upon surrender, an upper limit of $2.25 million would be put on the sale of Sempra's assets. The company would maintain the assets at its own expense until the end of June 2003, when it would be free to dispose of them as it saw fit. The "left over" inventory would not be bound by the upper price limit. If any assets remained unsold at the end of 2003, Sempra could either continue to maintain them at its own expense or abandon the installed pipe without any further liability.[60] At the end of February 2002, the Utilities and Review Board gave final approval to the deal, and Sempra's full regulation class franchise license passed into history.

New Beginnings: The Second Franchise Process

The Hamm Conservative government had treated the Sempra debacle as an unwanted inheritance from its predecessor. However, while the problem was being resolved, a broader effort was being made to launch a new Conservative plan for Sable gas development. This plan included many threads, including a boundary challenge with Newfoundland on the Laurentian Basin and John Hamm's "Fairness Campaign" on royalties and equalization payments. The Conservatives seemed more comfortable negotiating with governments than with business actors. In its effort to strike a new beginning and co-ordinate the necessary threads, the government launched a full-scale energy policy review in 2001. The review began with a discussion paper, included a number of written submissions, and culminated in the release of a new, two-volume policy statement, *Seizing the Opportunity*, in December 2001. The statement reaffirmed the government's goal: "to set the stage for expanded industrial, commercial, and residential use of gas and gas liquids in Nova Scotia."[61]

The new policy abandoned the 18/62/7 targets that had so pervasively deformed the politics of gas distribution during the MacLellan period. The energy review also coincided with the final throes of the Sempra story. Indeed, when the Utilities and Review Board invited new franchise applicants as part of its examination of Sempra's summer 2001 application, no less than thirteen potential rivals, corporate and municipal, emerged. Some of them were familiar faces from the first round, including municipalities and co-operatives in the Annapolis Valley, Antigonish, Yarmouth, Halifax, and Cape Breton and companies such as Enbridge Inc. and SaskEnergy and oil providers such as Wilson and Scotia Fuels. Among the new players were AltaGas and an investment group linked to Nova Scotia's Jodrey family (both were in association with SaskEnergy).

When the Sempra settlement was complete, the government turned its attention to revising the Gas Distribution Regulations that would guide future franchise awards. The new energy strategy set out the ongoing challenges facing gas distribution in terms that Sempra Atlantic might well have agreed with:

1 consumer reluctance to convert, as a result of lack of familiarity with the characteristics of the fuel, its delivery, and pricing
2 relatively high capital costs for consumers to convert from heating oil or electricity to natural gas
3 initial high capital costs for the distribution system, which in the early years will not have sufficient customer revenue to offset start-up costs
4 difficult construction conditions in several regions of the province where there is extensive bedrock close to the surface
5 existing regulatory systems that either were not designed for gas distribution or have yet to be thoroughly tested through ongoing operations
6 inability to rely on significant federal subsidies that were applied to the construction of gas distribution assets in other provinces.[62]

The answer was a more market-oriented framework with streamlined regulatory practices. The province committed to brokering key contracts between new franchise holders and the municipalities. Distributors would now be permitted to offer bundled services that combined gas sales, delivery, equipment sales, and service. In place of the 18/62/7 access targets, applicants would be assessed on their ability to service proposed franchise areas within ten years. Future Utilities and Review Board hearings would be divided into two phases. A primary distributor would be selected in the first round (minimum four counties serviced), and smaller secondary franchises could be awarded to areas that remained open. Finally, the province announced that it would participate directly (through the Department of Energy) in future franchise hearings to ensure that "the regulator clearly understands the position of the province with respect to its regulatory decisions."[63]

In effect, the new regulatory regime conceded that the gas infrastructure would develop more slowly and in the larger urban markets.[64] In addition, the political climate had changed, and the government was eager to dampen public expectations rather than feed them as in earlier times. Certainly, the failure of the Sempra project, together with the limits of past public policy, had had a chastening effect.

Yet several basic policy issues, carried over from the earlier era, remained, and prospective general franchise applicants pressed for clarification in 2002.[65] One continuing impediment was the question of direct access or "bypass" for major industrial users outside of a distribution franchise. Bypass would deprive a general franchisee of its largest potential contracts.[66] Facing political pressure from both sides, the Government of Nova Scotia struck a compromise. Bypass would be prohibited during the initial ten years of a franchise, but the four existing direct-sales beneficiaries would be exempted and direct sales would be permitted in non-franchise areas.[67]

Another old problem was the question of high-pressure gas line installation at roadside. During discussions with provincial officials prior to the second franchise round, both Enbridge and SaskEnergy indicated that they would like some access to highway shoulders.[68] Indeed, SaskEnergy (as a partner in the Heritage Gas consortium) asserted in its franchise application that it did not rule out roadside installation.[69] The Petroleum Directorate (later the Department of Energy) signaled its open-mindedness on the matter. This sudden volte-face sparked harsh criticism from the New Democrats, and energy critic John Holm asked the central question: "Why would it be appropriate for one and not for the other? What's different?"[70] The premier responded that roadside construction would only be considered as a final alternative.[71] It was clear, however, that the government was willing to negotiate for a new project, by a new operator, not encumbered with Sempra Atlantic's business and political history.

The municipal sector was also noticeably different in the post-Sempra era. Some municipalities looked forward to working with a new distributor under revised regulations. The favourite ally in early 2002 seemed to be SaskEnergy, which was in the process of signing memoranda of agreement with the Halifax Regional Municipality, the towns of Truro and Amherst, and Queen's County Regional Municipality. These agreements contained little substance but were a sign of support from those municipalities eager to receive gas. Evidently, the hope was that such accords might speed up (or at least reduce delays before) construction and service delivery.[72] Certainly, SaskEnergy's line was that co-operation was the way forward for business and local authorities. It was more than a rhetorical point, for local governments controlled a variety of building and operating powers that affected the gas business, and their support, in principle, set a positive climate for future dealings.

The same principle was applied to municipal taxation. SaskEnergy indicated at the 2002 franchise hearings before the Utilities and Review Board that it would, if successful, lobby the province for a standard revenue-based taxation system. The government had already made a commitment, in its new energy strategy, to address this issue. In the fall of 2004 the issue was finally settled with passage of the Gas Distribution System Municipal Taxation Act.

On 7 October 2002, the Utilities and Review Board opened formal hearings to select new gas distribution franchisees. By this time, however, many of the potential applicants from the previous year were not present. Enbridge Inc. had dropped out, citing economic factors. Others had opted for partnerships, as SaskEnergy did with AltaGas Inc. and Scotia Investments (the Jodrey group) to form Heritage Gas Inc., the first franchise applicant. The other primary franchise applicant was Strait Area Gas Inc. in eastern Nova Scotia. In this regulatory round, there were even more intervenors than before.[73]

The two applicants carved out separate franchise areas. Heritage Gas Inc. proposed to service Colchester, Cumberland, Halifax, Pictou, and Guysborough and parts of Hants, Inverness, and Richmond counties in the first ten years. It estimated that system expenditures in the period would be approximately $120 million, while the fully realized system would cost between $300 million and $400 million. By the close of the first decade, Heritage hoped to serve about ten thousand customers, one quarter of whom would be gained in the first seven years.[74] The point of commercial feasibility was estimated to be 35 percent of households in the franchise area. The company planned to have gas flowing into parts of Dartmouth and Amherst by 2003. A key part of Heritage's plan was to gain large industrial customers. Dalhousie University and several hospitals would anchor gas delivery to Halifax, and Heritage struck a deal with Nova Scotia Power to deliver gas to its Burnside plant.[75] Overall, Heritage hoped for a 14 percent return on its investment, based on the greenfield risks associated with the project, but the Utilities and Review Board later reduced this estimate by one point on the urging of the province.[76]

The Utilities and Review Board's response to this proposal can best be described as modest. It described the ten-year targets as "not terribly ambitious." Premier Hamm was more blunt in declaring himself very disappointed.[77] Nonetheless, the Utilities and Review Board chose to accept Heritage's application (the only one to cover metropolitan Halifax), with provisions for review of the company's progress and feasibility estimates (of viable service areas) in the future.[78]

By comparison, Strait Area Gas Inc. offered a more modest plan for a $4.4-million system over twenty-five years that would serve Guysborough, Antigonish, Inverness, and Richmond counties.[79] The first customer would be the Nautical Institute of Port Hawkesbury, which would receive service in late 2004.[80] Extensions to Port Hastings and Mulgrave would follow. Strait Area Gas projected it would have 350 customers in the first five years and 1,500 customers when by the end of the project. The gas supply would come from the surplus supply of a single end user – Stora Enso.

Strait Area Gas's application introduced a novel corporate structure that had not been seen before in the province. The distribution system would be built by Rocky Creek Canada Inc., a partnership between Nova Scotia firm GasWorks Installations and ARB Inc., a California construction company with ties to Sempra. It would be a BOOT project, in which Rocky Creek Canada Inc. would build, own, operate, and then transfer a lease-to-own system to Strait Area Gas. In a sequence of stages, Rocky Creek would build the system to specifications and operate it under contract. The capital infrastructure would then be leased to Strait Area Gas, which would pay down the capital lease over time and assume full ownership and operational rights at the time of transfer. The business model raised some concerns with both the board and the province. The arrangement was rare in North America and was more commonly used for utility projects in the developing world.[81]

Following nine days of public hearings, the board approved both applications on 7 February 2003. The Hamm cabinet confirmed the approvals by the end of the month. Heritage Gas was awarded five of the eight areas, including Cumberland, Colchester, Pictou, and Halifax counties and the Goldboro area of Guysborough County. Strait Area Gas earned approval for the four counties, but not the Goldboro area.[82] However, the company's approval was conditional on the board's approval of its six-month financial and operational report, which would pertain chiefly to its BOOT system agreement and operation. The Hamm government had insisted on this stipulation in return for its support of the application.[83] The stipulation, in turn, likely played a significant role in the board's decision to approve Strait Area Gas's plan.

Months passed before either applicant formally accepted its franchise. Heritage Gas did so in June 2003 and went on to forge an agreement with Sempra Atlantic to purchase intellectual property and install a pipeline in the Burnside area of Dartmouth. In September, the board made its final ruling on Strait Area Gas's application. Certain conditions were attached: (1) the attainment of adequate financing, including a minimum $150,000 of working capital, sixty days prior to obtaining its permit to construct; (2) the oversight of a general manager; and (3) construction within three years of cabinet approval of the board's decision.[84]

Heritage Gas as Provincial Champion

The year 2004 marked the second time that a franchised gas distributor had commenced to lay pipe and sell service. However, Heritage Gas offered only a fragment of the system promised in Sempra's timetable. In Dartmouth, service to the Burnside Industrial Park began in late 2003, and residential service began in Crichton Park in the spring of 2004, though the customer base remained below 150 by year's end. The following year, Heritage Gas installed another 20 kilometres of plastic lines in Dartmouth, and the customer base doubled to 302. Another 138 customers signed up and were waiting for service.[85]

Amherst was the second town to be serviced. Eighteen kilometres of steel lines and 14 kilometres of plastic lines were installed during the summer of 2005, and first gas flowed in September. By early 2006, the customer base was 66, and another 157 waited for service. These numbers fell far short of the estimates outlined in the company's application. Whereas the plan called for 10,000 customers in ten years, the actual system serviced fewer than 400 in the first two years (and 660 were under contract). The cautious build out continued with service to the Halifax International Airport and an extension to peninsular Halifax in 2007. Tentative plans were developed for the next stage, which would include service to smaller regional cities such as Truro and New Glasgow, located close to the MNP's mainline. These plans are presently on hold.

Heritage Gas's business strategy was the antithesis of Sempra Atlantic's. The two franchise areas are illustrated in Map 9.1. Heritage Gas began with the largest metropolitan region in the province, where one-third of the population resides. Its business plan depends on large institutional customers in either the public or private sector to anchor each new segment and only commences construction once commitments are in place.[86] Financial imperatives have dictated a conservative expansion plan. The market penetration of Halifax has been slower than expected: the total customer base was only 3,300 in 2009. As with any greenfield utility, capital expenses have run far ahead of revenues. Heritage Gas relies on a revenue deficiency account to handle losses to date, and the account is not expected to be eliminated until 2019, at the earliest. Another trend of the retail gas industry has been the decline in volume consumed per customer. In 2004, the volume was forecast at 131 gigajoules per year, but by 2008 the forecast had fallen to only 95 gigajoules per year. This decline is attributable to customer conservation practices and the adoption of more energy-efficient appliances.

Without question, natural gas price hikes in the winters of 2000-1 (when commodity prices doubled to US$4 per thousand cubic feet), 2002-3 (US$5 per thousand cubic feet), and 2005-6 (US$7 per thousand cubic feet) played havoc in the incipient gas distribution industry.[87] During each episode, the price of natural gas shot above oil (in equivalent measures). Most critically, this muddied the waters in the consumer gas market to the point where the fabled gas price savings of the 1990s were no longer relevant for residential users. Indeed, it was increasingly argued that the competitive cushion enjoyed by gas was a thing of the past. Fluctuations followed Hurricanes Katrina and Rita, the price spike of the autumn of 2007, price declines (to the US$6-7 per thousand cubic feet range) in 2006 and 2007, and the price spike of 2009, when prices peaked at $12 before sliding to a six-year low of $3.

For retail customers, the price of delivered gas includes gas acquisition or commodity costs and Heritage Gas's system-building and operating costs. The former are passed on from gas suppliers and recalculated monthly. The

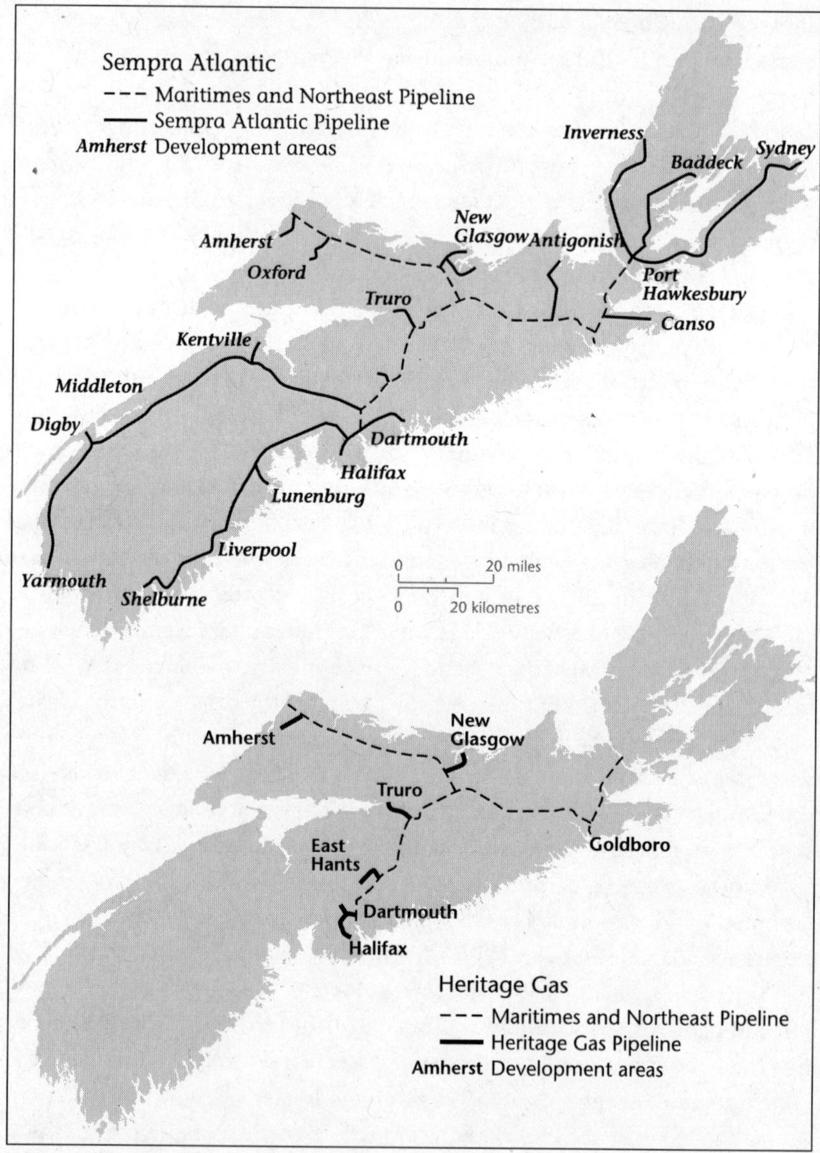

Map 9.1 Comparison of Sempra Atlantic and Heritage Gas proposals
Source: Sempra Atlantic Gas Service Territory, 2003; Heritage Gas, Nova Scotia Franchise Map.

latter appear in billings as a fixed monthly charge and a base energy charge, both of which are regulated by the Utilities and Review Board.

Conclusion

Even prior to the Venture discovery, the Nova Scotia government had declared its ambition that offshore gas would provide a significant consumer benefit to residents. A long-term supply of affordable gas would solve security problems and afford a competitive advantage to provincial businesses. In 1979, when security of supply loomed large, gas was conceived of as a resource that would supply regional needs. In the increasingly deregulated 1980s, this conception changed. However, even after the export-business paradigm was accepted, the need to reserve a share for Nova Scotia remained an article of faith. A lion's share of the product could be sold profitably in New England, but a residual share needed to be reserved and protected for consumption at home. What was missing was an appreciation of the complicated commercial and political logistics associated with creating an effective infrastructure. Indeed, when the history of domestic gas distribution is weighed by this standard, it is found seriously wanting.

Until the advent of an actual producing field, the issue of gas distribution remained largely dormant. It shot up the provincial petroleum agenda in 1996, however, when the Sable proposal became more firm. The organizational and intellectual context is important to the outcome. The province had no experience – commercial, regulatory, or political – in the wholesale or retail natural gas business. Arrangements would be drawn, in many respects, on a blank slate. Regulation occurred at the close of a period of radical restructuring in the continental natural gas industry, when old practices had been abandoned and new practices had not yet been fully settled. To the extent that knowledge can be imported from more experienced jurisdictions, the lessons for Nova Scotia were far from consensual. Legacy issues also played a role, most notably the joint-tolling bargain struck in 1997.

Yet the Government of Nova Scotia was in a strong position to direct and shape the character of gas distribution in strategic ways. Unlike natural gas exports, intraprovincial distribution fell unambiguously under the province's regulatory control. The same was true of ancillary policy fields such as municipal taxation, environmental protection, and highway management, fields that could be co-ordinated in Halifax through familiar executive mechanisms. Thus, gas distribution tested the capabilities of the provincial state, and the province's failure to deliver on commitments in a timely way calls for an explanation.

Party politics also played a role, from considerations of electoral strategy (the MacLellan Liberals' desire to target a rural voter base) to the fragility of minority governments and a rapid turnover among ministerial elites. The tension between the Savage and MacLellan Liberals was evident, as was the tension in the succession from Liberal to Conservative governments. The experience of neighbouring New Brunswick was likewise highly pertinent. As far as transmission and distribution are concerned, conditions in both provinces were strikingly similar. Indeed, New Brunswick offers an effective comparative policy case, one in which all of the variables are controlled except for public policy disposition. Where Nova Scotia vacillated, New Brunswick made strategic choices at the executive level and followed through on them. Political factors clearly made a difference in the two outcomes.

It is difficult to imagine a more fragmented and uncoordinated state response than that of the MacLellan government. The government was slow to formulate a legislative framework for gas distribution, and the eventual articles vested substantial new powers in a regulatory agent that lacked experience in the field. The cabinet then compounded the problem by declaring an ambitious province-wide installation agenda that it refused to support at administrative levels. Instead, it allowed a series of portfolio-driven complications to impede and eventually dislodge the natural gas distribution agenda. The absence of an effective lead agency or administrative champion was particularly evident. Perhaps the most obvious candidate was the Petroleum Directorate or Energy Department, but its expertise was chiefly on the upstream side of the industry chain. Its reluctance to instruct the Utilities and Review Board is striking.

This does not mean that the installation of gas infrastructure was simple or purely technical. The competitive economics of gas as a fuel fluctuated markedly throughout the period. These fluctuations complicated the calculations of aspiring distributors, as did the comprehensive scale of the government's system coordinates. Indeed it is hard to avoid the conclusion that prospective franchisees were seen as outsiders who were necessary if not entirely welcome. This posture was probably reinforced by the reactions of local interests – the municipal authorities and aspiring local franchisees and co-operatives that anticipated a role in the emerging system and feared being saddled with costly externalities.

Ultimately, the two-step sequence for franchise allotment entailed a mid-course policy correction, including scaled-back estimates and the need to fit gas distribution into the wider policy template of the Hamm government's 2001 energy paper. This correction came, however, at the cost of sacrificing some long-standing public welfare targets associated with offshore development. The mid-stream shift had another effect. Burnt by gas distribution, the Hamm government redoubled its determination to maximize Nova Scotia's rent returns in the upstream sector. The "Campaign for Fairness" gained added steam.

10 The Liquefied Natural Gas Factor in Nova Scotia

Coastal society is not always tightly connected to offshore petroleum enterprises. This was the point of the principal-beneficiary designation in the Canada–Nova Scotia agreements, which was intended to maximize both the number of points of onshore/offshore contact and their breadth. In the new millennium, however, the number of potential coastal nodes has multiplied. This expansion is linked to the emergence of a new segment in the global petroleum trade: liquefied natural gas (LNG). This chapter explores the potential influence of this new sector on the Scotian Basin. The offshore upstream industry has a contradictory relationship – both allied and at odds – with the LNG trade. At the same time, the Government of Nova Scotia appreciates the potential significance of the LNG industry and was broadly supportive of early movement in this sector.

The Maritimes became an LNG hotspot in the early 2000s. The sector is still new (the first LNG has only recently been delivered), but commercial and political events over the past decade have established the parameters of the sector's future development in critical ways. In this chapter, the structure of the global LNG industry is delineated as a complex product chain laced with corporate and political tensions. The three prospective Maritime Canada consortia seeking to import and process gas have had to develop strategies within this context. But their projects have also emerged within the regulatory arena of gas terminal and pipeline licensing. The interplay between the product chain and the regulatory nexus has resulted in only one of the three projects (the Repsol-Irving project in New Brunswick) coming to fruition to date.

The LNG trade is a distinct sector of the global hydrocarbon market that has expanded dramatically over the past twenty years. Its expansion has been driven by several factors: technological advances, relative price shifts, and a step-change reduction in production costs. As James Jensen puts it, "the global LNG market shows very little family resemblance to its two ostensible parents – the world oil market and the variously liberalized onshore natural gas markets."[1] Indeed, imported LNG should be viewed as an "offshore" product that happens to have a longer supply link than does, say, Scotian Basin gas. Since LNG can be globally sourced, it bypasses the North American continental shelf as an intermediate structure. Yet there are parallels: both have a politically sensitive relationship with the provincial coastal margin and economy and a complex interface with state regulatory structures at both the federal and provincial levels. For the host society, the interface begins at the point when the liquefied product is landed, when the particular requirements of the downstream LNG business come into play, including offloading facilities, storage capacity, and regasification plants. Transport networks to major markets are also important. In the Maritimes, LNG import would not be possible without the existence of certain infrastructure elements built to facilitate petroleum production in the Scotian Shelf. In particular, the Maritimes & Northeast Pipeline (MNP) offers a strategic link for potential LNG businesses on Canada's Atlantic coast that are premised on having access to the major industrial market in the northeastern United States.

The business relationship between indigenous and imported gas is both competitive and complementary, depending on the position in the product chain. Infrastructure that supports the offshore industry can also benefit LNG importers. On the other hand, a viable LNG segment can smooth out the supply bumps that sometimes attend an emerging offshore production sector and, by sustaining fixed-cost infrastructure, avoid the danger of losing critical facilities. In addition, new technological configurations in LNG may in the future alter the economic calculus for small and medium offshore field development, particularly at the unprecedented oil and gas price levels of the new millennium. For example, the floating liquefied natural gas production and storage ship, which was in the prototype stage in the mid-2000s, offers a mobile alternative that could alter the scale constraint posed by expensive seabed pipeline infrastructure.[2] When coupled with floating liquefaction technology, it is possible to imagine direct field-to-terminal shipments from within the Scotian Basin or elsewhere that dispense with offshore pipelines altogether and leave a far lighter offshore footprint at the project's end.

Finally, the LNG production and supply option has been assimilated into state energy and petroleum planning in Maritime Canada. Although LNG does not figure as an indigenous energy asset, it can play an important role in the energy supply equation, particularly to even out fluctuations in natural gas supply. The long distance LNG trade surged in the late 1990s. When signs emerged that the site selection process for new import and regasification terminals in the United States would be challenged, delayed, or even blocked by local communities, on both security and safety grounds, Maritime Canada's prospects warmed further. Indeed, state authorities recognized the strategic significance of LNG import at a relatively early date.

For all of these reasons, it is clear that the post-2000 LNG experience raises many pressing questions about power, institutions, and management. In addition, it offers a telling test of power relationships and policy capacity in Nova Scotia's state circles.

Liquefied Natural Gas as Commodity

Liquefied Natural Gas is one of dozens of hydrocarbon energy products in the contemporary global mix and a relatively recent one at that. It is a manufactured commodity based on the condensable properties of petroleum gas when treated by industrial processes. The scientific foundation of LNG emerged in the nineteenth century when Michael Farraday successfully liquefied various gases. In the case of natural gas (a predominantly methane compound), liquefaction occurred when the gas was cooled to –161°C (–259°F). Although Karl van Linde made the first compressor refrigerator in 1873, the industrial production of LNG only began in the twentieth century. The decisive physical transformation, which carries dramatic implications for energy commodity transport, is the concentration of volume. In liquid form, natural gas condenses to approximately one six-hundredth of its gaseous volume.

Natural gas presented formidable challenges for capture and transport from the beginnings of the petroleum industry, and liquefaction offered a powerful means to overcome them. In some respects, liquefaction renders gas into a more manageable and flexible commodity. The first North American LNG plant opened in 1912, and the first commercial plant followed in 1941. The first commercial application for LNG was as a medium of local gas stockpiling. Gas distributors (and some high-volume gas consumers in electricity and manufacturing) opted for on-site liquefaction and storage to guarantee adequate supplies at moments of peak energy demand. This practice continues today – there are more than a hundred LNG storage complexes in place throughout industrial North America.[3] The practice allows commercial gas users to engage in peak shaving, drawing on stockpiled LNG as additional fuel during periods of maximum demand, over and above regular contracted supplies.

In the late 1950s, a new LNG market emerged that had the possibility of long-distance transport and sales. The offshore commercial LNG trade began in 1959, when the tanker *Methane Pioneer* delivered a load of 7,000 barrels of oil equivalent or approximately 840 tonnes in weight from Louisiana to Britain. Algeria became the world's first major LNG exporter in 1964, when it shipped 260 million cubic feet (7 million cubic metres) per day to Britain. By 1975, the Japanese and Korean markets had caught up with Europe in shipped volume and soon established a dominant global position in LNG imports. Taiwan followed, and for the next two decades Asian demand grew by about 2.4 million tonnes (roughly the capacity of one new liquefaction train) per year.[4] Algeria and Libya were joined by new suppliers from Indonesia, Malaysia, Australia, and Brunei.

Beginning in the mid-1990s, the global LNG profile shifted, and the Atlantic Basin began to match the Pacific in import traffic and to challenge it on the export side. Major new supplies emerged from Nigeria, Trinidad and Tobago, Qatar, and Oman. These greenfield plants were greater in scale and used second-generation technology and larger tankers to cut costs and carve out new North American markets for LNG, particularly in supplying combined cycle electricity producers.

Obviously, the primary criterion of commerciality is LNG's price competitiveness in import markets. Here the key element is the relative cost of LNG per heating-unit value compared to alternative energy sources. Indeed, the price relationship between crude oil and natural gas (and LNG) is one of the most important drivers of upstream and midstream gas development. Within the gas sector specifically, transport distance is another significant element of commerciality. It has been suggested that an LNG supply has an advantage over pipeline gas beyond a distance of 1,200 kilometres (offshore) or 3,700 kilometres (onshore).[5]

The LNG Product Chain

To understand the prospects for the LNG sector, both commercially and politically, one must understand the structure of the international natural gas product chain. As in most contemporary energy markets, this chain consists of a series of discrete business stages that range from gas field discovery to final gas commodity sale. These stages are gas exploration and production, liquefaction, shipping, landing, storage and regasification, and transport to delivery. As businesses, these stages are sufficiently distinct to represent separate industry segments. Together, they constitute the LNG sector as one thread within global petroleum. The commercial prospects of LNG are a function of both economic and political relationships and market transactions and policy coalitions. The interests and strategies of both corporate and state actors are framed, in large degree, according to their locations on the chain.

When major fields are developed in close proximity to major markets, field and market are generally connected directly, and long-distance liquefaction does not figure into the equation. When large gas discoveries are stranded far from available markets, the prospects for LNG emerge. Even in these cases, however, the scale of proven gas reserves required to support a multi-billion-dollar complex, financed over twenty to thirty years, is vast. Not surprisingly, barely a dozen basins worldwide – in North Africa, the Persian Gulf states, the Caribbean, West Africa, Australia, and the Asia-Pacific – meet this standard. Typically, the producing interests maintain ownership of the raw gas product up to a point of sale, that is, during field delineation, gas extraction and gathering, and initial transport by pipeline to a (generally coastal) processing location.

The next and most capital-intensive stage is the manufacture of liquefied gas. The scale and costs of such operations pose risks beyond the scope of even large upstream producers. Consequently, as the LNG sector has evolved, the processing stage tends to be undertaken by separate corporate entities that combine owners, gas buyers, and occasionally other investors. The construction period usually lasts for three or more years after project sanction (the firm's decision to proceed). Financing and engineering precede construction and may add another two to three years to the project. The raw gas is cleaned, liquefied, and stored for shipping at an export facility. A liquefaction plant is known as a "train," and trains are scalable: the number of trains and total capacities are open to adjustment and staging. In the early years of the industry, train capacity averaged about 2 million tonnes per annum, and at least three trains were required for a commercially viable complex. With more sophisticated compressors, large trains today are double that size.[6] In the long-distance LNG trade, liquefaction plants and export-loading facilities are sited at tidewater to facilitate shipping. Historically, liquid gas supplies were committed by long-term (twenty years plus) contracts with end buyers.

Stage three is the marine transport of the liquid gas. Loading takes place at special-purpose wharves with high-speed flexible hoses. Specialized double-hulled, insulated vessels are the receiving medium. Two designs have predominated to date. The most readily recognizable is the MOSS-type tanker, which carries multiple spherical LNG-holding tanks, whose upper halves are visible above deck. The alternative is the membrane-type design, which involves a metal liner impervious to liquid being installed against insulation attached to the hull. Today, a typical tanker has a capacity of 125,000 to 140,000 cubic metres of LNG, though vessel capacity is constantly increasing. Because of rapid growth in this market segment, a high proportion of the global fleet of about 175 vessels in 2008 was less than ten years old. It is common for world-scale LNG producers to control their own fleets, thereby guaranteeing constant product flow to contracted customers. However, the commissioning of new ships has created a residual fleet of smaller and older vessels that can support independent shippers, particularly in the merchant segment of the trade. The tankers use auto-refrigeration techniques to keep gas near the boiling point (at atmospheric pressure), while gas vapour is captured to power the engines.[7] In contrast to crude oil shipping, liquid gas transport enjoys an exemplary safety record: there have been no major explosions or releases in more than thirty thousand voyages in over forty years. In the first generation of overseas LNG shipping, fleets are normally controlled by processor-sellers. The Australian North West Shelf consortium, for example, has a fleet of twelve ships ferrying product between Western Australia and Japan.

The next stage is reception, storage, and regasification. The LNG is off-loaded into pipelines, either at a shore-based wharf or at a floating bell buoy connected to land by subsea lines. The product moves directly to storage in giant refrigerated tanks that have a capacity ranging from 160,000 to 180,000 cubic metres (that is, somewhat larger than standard vessel capacity). The LNG is then returned to gaseous form in a regasification plant. It is warmed gradually, either by active heat or by ambient (air/water) heat transfer, in controlled facilities. At this stage, the volume advantage is recovered, and the product is simultaneously repressurized for release from the import plant. Although the scale of regasification operations can vary, many of the contemporary proposals and completions have a capacity of

1.0 to 1.5 billion cubic feet (28 to 42 million cubic metres) per day. In North America, investment in regasification terminals is most significant in coastal Atlantic, Gulf, and Pacific regions that have tie-ins to the major pipeline networks. In terms of safety, the most critical phase is the gas-to-liquid or liquid-to-gas conversion, since natural gas is flammable at concentrations of 5 to 15 percent, and a few rare plant explosions have occurred. The most damaging fire occurred in Cleveland in 1944, killing 138 people when liquid gas leaked into a sewer. For obvious reasons, state regulations on the siting, materials, and procedures of regasification plants are highly rigorous today. However, the politics of import terminal siting, particularly opposition from local communities, are among the most contentious in the entire LNG chain.

The final phase is onward shipment for sale to gas consumers. Receiving terminals are normally connected to long-distance gas supply grids by means of trunk pipelines. Indeed, proximity to trunk networks is a prime determinant in siting a regasification plant. For example, when LNG imports began in the United States in 1968, the first plant was built on the Gulf Coast at Lake Charles, Louisiana, where it tied into an existing network of continental pipelines. Similar considerations shaped three other first-generation US receiving plants in Massachusetts, Georgia, and Maryland. After an initial growth spurt associated with the energy price spike, which peaked in 1979, the LNG import business declined as the conventional gas supply bubble burst and prices slumped in the 1980s. By the time the business revived a decade later, the North American gas industry had been deregulated and de-integrated. These developments, in turn, shaped the 1990s pipeline boom, which was driven by new gas supplies, price recovery, and competitive pressures among the now-separate supplier, transport, and consumer segments. Furthermore, gas had emerged as a fuel of choice for the growing electric power sector and for many secondary manufacturers. Consequently, every LNG operator capable of delivering 1.0 to 1.5 billion cubic feet (28 to 42 million cubic metres) per day at competitive prices enjoyed the same status as two to three offshore projects on the scale of the Sable offshore energy consortium.

Obviously, the business and political strategies of LNG interests are shaped closely by their positions in the product chain. In terms of business organization, these segments can be both specialized and integrated. Even when corporate supermajors are active in all phases of the chain, the need for partnerships to secure investment means that business alliances (equity, long-term contracted, and technological) are the norm. Although the business

TABLE 10.1

Notional cost structure for a typical 5-million-tonne LNG project

Stage	Cost (US$ billion)	Percent cost	Typical return (%)
Upstream	1.000	30	15-20
Liquefaction	1.250	37	8-12 (tolling) 10-20 (non-tolling)
Shipping	0.800	24	8-10
Regasification	0.325	9	14
Total	3.375	100	

Sources: Angela Tu Weissenberger, "Casting a Cold Eye on LNG: The Real Possibilities and Pitfalls for Atlantic Canada," *AIMS Oil and Gas Papers* 4, Atlantic Institute for Market Studies (Halifax, January 2006), 13; see also James Jensen, *The Development of a Global LNG Market: Is It Likely? If So, When?* (Oxford: Oxford Institute for Energy Studies, 2004), 6.

economics of each LNG enterprise chain is distinct, the general characteristics are instructive. Table 10.1 presents notional cost structures for a typical LNG project with a capacity of 5 million tonnes per annum.

Markets

As already mentioned, the long-distance LNG trade became commercial in the 1960s, beginning with Algerian exports and expanding to Asia-Pacific and Persian Gulf suppliers. For the first generation, Japan was the principal destination, but both South Korea and western Europe took a share. Capital commitments were vast, and the risks to upstream producers and processors were profound. Not surprisingly, it was in this era that the predominant industry model was forged: LNG was sold under long-term contracts that cemented strong supplier-consumer alliances. When Alaskan natural gas began to flow in 1968, it was as LNG to Japan on a twenty-five-year contract.

The initial North American experience with LNG imports was mixed at best. Several terminals opened in the late 1970s but closed several years later when gas prices flattened during the OPEC recession. Shut-in Alberta gas then began to reach continental markets on terms that rendered LNG uneconomic. After 1983, total LNG imports in the United States dropped below 100,000 million cubic feet per year, a level that was sustained for the next fifteen years.[8] North American LNG imports appeared to be a failed experiment. There were no imports at all in 1987.

However, the worldwide upswing that began in the 1990s offered the industry a second life. From 1993 to 2004, world demand for LNG grew by 110 percent as the number of LNG-producing nations increased to more than a dozen. On the consumption side, the largest destinations by 2004 were Japan (44 percent of global demand) and South Korea (17 percent), followed by Spain (10 percent) and the United States (10 percent).[9] The industry is highly dynamic, however, and western Europe and China are now poised to become major LNG import rivals.

For the United States, the start of Trinidadian LNG shipments in 1999 led to a rapid five-fold jump in US total imports by 2004.[10] In recent years, Trinidad has supplied two-thirds of US imports, while Egypt, Nigeria, and Algeria provide the remainder.[11] The run-up in US LNG imports peaked in 2004 at 652 billion cubic feet, before slipping back to 452 billion cubic feet at the close of the decade.

Reflecting the rush to establish a foothold in this dynamic emerging sector, more than fifty-five regasification terminals were proposed for North America by 2004, of which ten were in the northeastern United States and a half dozen were in Canada. Most of these proposals were speculative and centred on securing site options physically and legally. Only a fraction of announced projects survive the rigours of financing, supply contracting, and regulatory review to reach the construction and operating stages. Indeed, if all terminals proposed for North America at the height of the boom were built, they would account for three-quarters of current North American gas consumption.[12] By mid-decade the principal constraint for new projects was clearly the availability of a long-term LNG supply. Even projects that had secured regulatory approval were being deferred or abandoned for lack of supply. Other proponents were in discussions about consolidating separate projects. Not only were LNG suppliers in a position to determine project viability, they were also pushing hard for equity participation as part of the deals.[13]

Developments in the United States were part of a broader global trend. In 2007, liquefaction capacity worldwide stood at 170 million tonnes per annum, with an additional 91 million tonnes per annum under construction and 285 million tonnes per annum planned. This capacity is split equally between the Pacific and Atlantic basin markets and reflects the international scramble to gain a position in an increasingly profitable energy trade. Over the next phase, major expansions in LNG global output are expected from new facilities in Equatorial Guinea, Norway, Nigeria, Qatar, and Yemen.

Traditionally, most new capacity has been committed to buyers on long-term contracts (twenty plus years) known as sale and purchase agreements. This pattern began with Japan and Korea in the Pacific market and continues today. As Jensen observes, "no new LNG train has been launched without at least some long-term contract coverage."[14] For obvious reasons, long contracts continue to be central to project finance on the production side. However, a number of recent LNG market trends – including a growing diversity of suppliers, declining delivery costs, and more competition between buyers in tight markets – have facilitated the emergence of a parallel, short-term market. An estimated 9 percent of global LNG now trades in this way. Cargoes can sail without a firm buyer and can be diverted en route between markets according to short-term price conditions.

Each type of contract embodies a different balance of risks. In long-term sales, the locked-in price means that the seller cannot benefit from capturing favourable price fluctuations, and the locked-in volume means that the buyer cannot benefit from adjusting supply needs. For the buyer, such contracts are take-or-pay deals that normally cover 90 percent of the contract volume. Elements of flexibility have been incorporated, however, through ramp-up and plateau provisions, together with options for short-term sales within the greater contract to cover contingencies.[15] As North American and European gas markets liberalized, however, and as commodity prices became subject to competitive pressures, the traditional sale and purchase agreement has given way to shorter terms and market-referenced pricing. These changes fit the newer LNG chain model, in which competition has penetrated the various links to differing degrees.

The short-term market affords producers greater flexibility to capture higher net-backs or margins between delivered LNG costs and sales revenues. In the early 2000s, these returns were substantial. One estimate of LNG production and delivery costs in 2007 put returns between US$2.60 and $4.80 per million British thermal units, depending on producer fiscals and delivery distance, a 30 percent increase from the comparable estimate of 2002. (Weissenburger suggests an average of $3.50 per million British thermal units.)[16] This cost structure can be compared to North American LNG sales prices for December, per thousand cubic feet, of US$4.78 (2003), $7.18 (2004), $10.47 (2005), and $7.81 (2006), $7.86 (2007), $8.86 (2008), and $4.63 (2009).[17] (The conversion rate of a thousand cubic feet to a million British thermal units is 1.03, thus allowing for a fairly rough comparison of volume and energy unit pricing.)

As new LNG supplies come on line, market terms are expected to become more flexible. For an LNG import enterprise, greater flexibility will likely mean qualified long-term contracts and incremental, short-term merchant purchases. Moreover a wider variety of marketers are likely to be involved, including LNG producers, LNG buyer-shippers, and merchant or arbitrage traders.[18]

Regulatory Regimes

As with other offshore petroleum projects, LNG terminals and regasification plants are subject to extensive legal regulatory requirements. Given the relatively recent resurgence of the North American LNG sector, new proposals in Canada and the United States have faced a variety of pre-existing regimes framed for marine petroleum shipping, import licensing, port facilities construction, processing and storage activities, and pipeline interconnection. For Canada-based terminals linked to US markets, export licensing needs to be added as well. In short, the range of state regulatory controls is extensive. Although the LNG sector parallels the offshore exploration and production regime in certain respects, it is *sui generis* in as much as it poses unique problems. A telling example is the extent to which the discrete components of LNG regulation have been integrated or consolidated into joint project licensing, as distinct from incremental review.

On the face of it, the regulatory agencies, statutes, and instruments in Canada's LNG regulatory regime remain highly dispersed. In 2005, a National Energy Board review considered a series of seven discrete business activities ranging from ship transport to pipeline flow and identified seventeen federal regulatory elements. Leading roles fell to six agencies: Transport Canada, Environment Canada, the Canadian Environmental Assessment Agency (CEAA), the National Energy Board, the Department of Fisheries and Oceans, and Natural Resources Canada. In addition, the province of Nova Scotia is responsible for nine regulatory elements, of which the departments of energy, environment, and the municipalities play the most prominent roles.[19]

Transport Canada regulates works in or over navigable waters as well as marine transport security planning, terminal proposal guidance, and tanker safety certification. Environment Canada exercises powers over LNG storage facilities, greenhouse gas emission reporting, and the disposal of (construction) sediments at sea. It has general oversight over reviews under the Canadian Environmental Assessment Act. The Department of Fisheries and Oceans is responsible for assessing potentially harmful alterations, destruction, or disruption (HADD) of fish habitats from new facilities such as jetties or pipeline watercourse crossings. The National Energy Board controls import licensing and certificates of public convenience and necessity for terminal facilities, and it is responsible for connecting pipelines and possible tariff and toll review. Natural Resources Canada advises the federal cabinet on final legal approvals of the National Energy Board decisions. Far from holistic licensing and review, the regulatory regime for LNG terminal facilities is fragmented and incremental.

Perhaps the most co-ordinated dimension of regulation occurs under the CEAA and centres on the environmental impacts of the project proposal. As seen earlier, an explicit CEAA goal is the coordination of federal agency involvement in major project assessment. Although federal environmental review obviously does not exhaust the full range of federal regulatory concerns, it has assumed an anchor role in the sense that the failure to win approval carries an effective veto on further steps. Proponents need environmental approvals in hand before a project can be deemed ready for the financial, engineering, and commercial negotiations that lead to final project sanction by corporate sponsors.

An energy project on the scale of an LNG terminal normally requires either a comprehensive study or a panel review under the act. This process is generally triggered by the proponent's formal submission of a project proposal outlining the scope of the new works. As responsible authorities under the CEAA, Transport Canada, the National Energy Board, Environment Canada, and the Department of Fisheries and Oceans are required to ensure that an environmental assessment is conducted in conjunction with any other necessary permits or approvals. A federal responsible authority prepares an environmental-scoping document to establish the range of concerns. The preliminary ruling is made by one or more responsible authorities and is confirmed or varied, after public consultation, in the final determination by the minister of the environment.

The proponent then prepares a comprehensive study report that is reviewed by federal agencies and during public consultations supported by participant funding. At the close of this process, permit decisions are made (possibly subject to conditions). In any event, construction cannot commence until all required permits and licenses have been approved.

A parallel environmental review takes place within the Nova Scotia government under the Environment Act. This process begins when the proponent submits a registration document to the Department of Environment. Following administrative scrutiny and the review of public submissions (normally over a three-month period), the minister of the environment comes to a decision, possibly with stipulating conditions. As seen earlier in connection with the Sable Offshore Energy Project panel review of the late 1990s, degrees of federal-provincial harmonization are possible, particularly when both parties agree to accept the proponent's documentary submissions. In terms of timing, processes, and ministerial decisions, however, they remain separate.

As environmental permits are acquired and as intercorporate business alliances on finance, ownership, and sales are formalized, an LNG project evolves toward final decision on construction. Before this stage, however, regulatory standards affecting the flow of products in trade must be satisfied. For receiving facilities in Maritime Canada, this involves regasification transmission and export approvals from the National Energy Board. The corporate applicant will vary according to facility or product ownership. For example, the importer of the liquid gas owns the product until it reaches the bulk liquid storage phase at terminal, though ownership can change as the gas moves through the regasification process. The owner of the gaseous plant outflow is subject to export controls, while the pipeline conveyor contracted to move the gas holds the certificate of public convenience and necessity on transmission lines. Ultimately, each LNG import project has a distinct profile, attributes, and needs.

LNG Project Politics in Maritime Canada

The story of LNG in Maritime Canada is one of converging vectors of continental supply and demand mediated by state regulatory networks. Hovering in the background were factors such as declining US domestic gas production and declining western Canadian imports, together with an explosive growth in natural gas demand in the power-generating sector. These trends led US industry and government authorities to forecast growth in LNG imports to help close the demand-supply gap. This opportunity was enhanced by investment markets after 2000. Natural gas wellhead prices in the United States rose dramatically above their decade-long trend of US$1.50 to 2.50 per thousand cubic feet. Not surprisingly, the early 2000s brought a cascade of new LNG import terminal proposals for coastal locations.

Maritime Canada was home to three proposals, two in Nova Scotia and one in New Brunswick. Liquefied natural gas represented an entirely new energy commodity in the region, one that found favour in different ways with provincial political authorities. New Brunswick looked positively on

LNG imports after 2001. Its policy statement, *Energy Strategy,* underlined the goal of securing supply and the contribution that LNG imports could make toward it.[20] No doubt the absence of significant indigenous gas supplies encouraged New Brunswick to highlight the value of imports. Tellingly, Nova Scotia's energy policy statement, which was also released in 2001, made no explicit mention of LNG prospects, even though it devoted whole chapters to offshore oil and gas.[21] It was only after the Scotian Basin cooled in 2003-4 – with the scale-down of the Sable project's lifespan, the suspension of the Deep Panuke proposal, and the tail-off of deepwater exploration on the Scotian slope – that Halifax began to pay more attention to liquefied gas. Be this as it may, the announcement of multiple import and regasification terminals in the early 2000s opened a significant new arena for political and commercial competition.

The Bear Head LNG Project

As seen earlier, the world of petroleum commerce is based on securing advantageous positions within complex product chains and business networks. In the rapidly expanding global trade in liquefied gas, advantage took a particular shape. Each prospective entrant in the North American LNG business faced a relatively short window of opportunity to find a niche that could last for a generation. For much of this time, the Bear Head project was considered one of the strongest regional contenders, but it foundered in 2006. The case illustrates the uncertainties of developing and implementing a back-end LNG import business based on corporate sponsorship.

In August 2003, a private Canadian start-up firm named Access Northeast Energy Inc. announced its proposal for an LNG import and regasification facility at Bear Head, Cape Breton Island. The proposed site is adjacent to an industrial zone at Port Hawkesbury, where the Strait of Canso provides a natural deepwater harbour. Access Northeast Energy had been founded a year earlier by Calgary-based ARC Financial. Its plan was to build a wharf and storage and regasification plant that would be connected by a 56-kilometre lateral pipeline to the MNP's trunk line to New England.[22] In May 2004, Access Northeast Energy submitted its environmental assessment registration document, thereby initiating the federal and provincial regulatory reviews. Three months later, on 9 August, Nova Scotia's minister of the environment announced approval of the application, subject to conditions.

Only days later, the shape of the project took a radical turn, when it was announced that Bear Head had been purchased by Anadarko Petroleum

Corporation, one of the leading independent US upstream companies. Anadarko Petroleum combined extensive assets on land in the United States, in the deepwater Gulf of Mexico, and in Algeria. Anadarko entered Canada in 2000 through the purchase of Union Pacific Resources Group (which had been formed by the takeover of Canadian independent Norcen in 1998). Although Anadarko Canada was a significant player in the western Canada sedimentary basin, its purchase of Bear Head LNG marked a new departure.

If anything, the new ownership enhanced the commercial credibility of the Bear Head project. In contrast to Access Northeast Energy, Anadarko was an established presence in the industry. Active globally, it was potentially in a position to orchestrate (on its own and through partnerships) long-term gas supplies at the upstream end. Consequently, the ownership change did not trouble political authorities. Premier Hamm welcomed Anadarko as a global leader with a reputation for making smart investments.[23] The shift of ownership was seamless, and work continued on the design, supply, and regulatory fronts.

The Bear Head project's specifications remained relatively unchanged. Phase 1 called for the construction of wharf and harbour unloading facilities capable of handling 70 to 135 ship visits a year. Two LNG storage tanks, each with a capacity of 180,000 cubic metres net, would receive the product, and a third tank would be added in Phase 2. The regasification plant was designed for an initial capacity of 1 billion cubic feet (28 million cubic metres) per day, which would increase to 1.5 billion cubic feet (42 million cubic metres) per day, and the total capital cost was estimated at $450 million.

During 2005, preliminary work progressed. The land and coastal frontage for the project site was assembled by the provincial Crown corporation Nova Scotia Business Inc. Consisting of 179 acres of land and a 67-acre water lot with access road, the parcel was sold in May 2005 to Anadarko's subsidiary Bear Head LNG Corporation for $4.62 million.[24] A three-year construction phase was expected to begin in the summer. In June, Anadarko reached an agreement with MNP for shipping space on an expanded mainline. Later in the year, an engineering, procurement, and construction contract was scheduled for issue. Already, however, there were reports of difficulties in securing liquefied gas for the Bear Head plant. Gas prices were reaching record levels, in part due to the carnage visited on Gulf of Mexico offshore facilities by summer hurricanes. In addition, the giant western European utilities were locking up huge blocks of new global LNG output in long-term exclusive contracts. After months of uncertainty, Anadarko officially froze its construction plans in March 2006.[25]

Then Bear Head was swept up into the broader corporate politics of its parent. Beginning in 1999, a series of corporate mergers established an elite of global supermajor firms, including BP-Amoco, ExxonMobil, Chevron-Texaco, and ConocoPhillips. The surviving large independent firms faced a dilemma. As some of the last free-standing exploration and production companies in the market sector, operating globally and holding significant reserves on their books, they were tempting targets for future consolidation. Yet the corporate cultures at these firms were often fiercely independent and far more entrepreneurial than at the bureaucratized petroleum giants. As a result, the dangers of acquisition were ever-present. One defensive alternative was the merger of multiple independents, the path that Anadarko chose to initiate in June 2006. It successfully completed takeovers of rivals Kerr-McGee and Western Gas Resources, for a combined US$21.1 billion, while assuming an additional $2.2 billion of their combined debts.[26] The new firm, Anadarko Petroleum Corporation, ranked as a leader among the remaining independents, reporting just over 3 billion barrels of oil equivalent of proved reserves at the close of 2006.

A standard follow-on of any huge corporate consolidation is a close review of all accumulated assets and the sale of redundant or non-core operations. Done effectively, such divestitures can generate significant revenues to retire shares of the debt incurred to close the deal. Anadarko announced in late June that the entire asset base of its Canadian subsidiary was up for sale. In September 2006, Anadarko made a deal with Canadian Natural Resources that generated $4.3 billion.[27]

Although it was structured separately from Anadarko Canada, Bear Head LNG Corporation was also subject to auction. On 10 July, it was announced that the subsidiary had been sold for US$125 million to US Venture Energy, a European private equity firm. The sale included an eighteen-month MNP shipping option on 350 million cubic feet (10 million cubic metres) per day of natural gas throughput at competitive rates.[28] However, this takeover deal collapsed within weeks, leaving Anadarko holding its supply-deprived project in Cape Breton.[29]

Bear Head LNG had faced a further setback that same summer when it lost its service contracts with MNP. A year earlier, the two firms had signed precedent and service agreements for gas transport that included termination provisions should Anadarko fail to secure an adequate gas supply. When Anadarko confirmed its lack of supply on 8 September 2006, MNP exercised its right of termination.[30] The Bear Head LNG prospect was effectively finished, though another five months passed before Anadarko Petroleum wrote off $111 million in costs against its fourth-quarter earnings.[31]

This episode underlines several defining features of the LNG import sector. First, the North American rush toward investment in inward-flowing LNG occurred in a highly compressed time frame. The elapsed time between Access Northeast's first filings and the Bear Head write-off was less than three years. Second, the field of players was diverse, ranging from speculative start-up firms to multinationals with global reach. The start-ups could stake out a position by securing a site and launching the regulatory reviews that preceded construction, with the option (or even the intention) to later sell the "approved" site to better capitalized firms. This enabled multinationals to join in later by means of acquisition. Both, however, faced a common constraint: the scarcity of supply. Ultimately, this scarcity would be a prime determinant of a project's progression to the building phase. Third, the absence of effective state leverage in Nova Scotia is striking. The owners of capital took the initiative. Apart from offering support for land assembly and environmental permitting, the provincial Crown had far less purchase in the LNG sector than on the offshore seabed.

The Keltic Petrochemicals Project

A second Nova Scotia LNG import project was proposed for Goldboro, Guysborough County, on the Nova Scotia mainland. The site was close to the Country Harbour landing point for Sable offshore gas and the receiving point for the MNP. From the outset, Keltic Petrochemicals' business strategy differed from the standard LNG import operation. The plan fashioned by founder W. Kevin Dunn, a Calgary oilman with Maritime roots, called for an LNG import facility that would provide feedstock for a petrochemical plant producing ethylene, polyethylene, propylene, and polypropylene, along with fuel for a co-generation energy plant. The estimated cost of the complex was US$4.5 billion and covered both the LNG import and regasification terminal and the petrochemical works.

Incorporated in March 2000, Keltic Petrochemicals Inc. predated other LNG proposals in the region. Its distinguishing feature and centrepiece was the petrochemical-manufacturing facility designed to sit between the import terminal and the onward shipment of revapourized gas. The facility represented a quantum jump from the standard LNG import facility; it lifted its capital cost, manufacturing value, and employment profile by a factor of ten. For some time, a vision of a secondary manufacturing industry based on offshore gas landings had been part of the regional policy debate, and Keltic Petrochemicals offered a means to fulfill it.

Keltic Petrochemicals' import, storage, and regasification facility included three storage tanks of 160,000 cubic metres each and had a send-out capacity of 1 billion cubic feet per day. This capacity could be doubled by the addition of three more tanks in the second phase. In effect, Keltic Petrochemicals' LNG throughput capacity mirrored that planned for Bear Head. What differed, of course, was the destination, for Keltic's vapourized gas would be directed principally to the adjacent petrochemical plant, where the wet elements would be separated. The residual gas would then flow to the MNP trunk line. Allowance was also made for the purchase of back-up supplies from Sable Offshore Energy Inc.'s landing point at Goldboro.

The chemical treatments are more complicated than this bare description conveys. Three compounds – ethane, propane, and butane (along with processed gas) – would be removed from the incoming LNG gas, leaving a purer methane-based gas to enter the shipping pipeline. Other required feedstocks, such as refinery propylene and methanol, would be shipped to Goldboro wharf and channelled directly to the chemical plant.

As in rival Maritime projects, Keltic Petrochemicals triggered environmental reviews in 2004. The CEAA notified the relevant federal agencies, and Transport Canada combined with the Department of Fisheries and Oceans to produce a scoping document that was released in May of the following year for public comment.[32] In January 2005, the federal environment minister, Stéphane Dion, ruled that a comprehensive study would be required. Two responsible departments would conduct internal reviews. The Department of Fisheries and Oceans would focus on the wharf component, and Transport Canada would focus on the full impact of the project.[33]

A parallel provincial review by the Nova Scotia Environmental Assessment Board began in January 2005, when Keltic Petrochemicals registered with the Department of Environment. However, at this point the process stalled. Various delays resulted in the provincial review not commencing until mid-2006, and public hearings were convened in the late autumn. From the outset, Keltic Petrochemicals enjoyed strong regional support in eastern Nova Scotia, which welcomed the prospect of a major industrial operation that built on the Sable precedent.[34] Reporting in February 2007, the Environmental Assessment Board held that "on balance, and in consideration of the positive and negative aspects of this proposal, the Panel recommends that the project should proceed," subject to additional commitments on air, noise, and water-quality monitoring; local employment incentives; and the protection of Aboriginal sites.[35] The following month, the minister granted provincial environmental approval, subject to conditions. By this stage, Keltic Petrochemicals faced a different problem in the form of gas feedstock supply.

In terms of corporate sponsorship, Keltic Petrochemicals' proposal bore certain parallels to the Bear Head proposal in its initial phase. The concept, site quality, and timeliness of the projects were undeniable, but major questions could be raised about the capacity of the founding interests to deliver what was promised. Although the technology of LNG import was well established, the challenge was for the start-up sponsors to break into an LNG supply chain that was tightening at the upstream stages with each passing year. Clearly, the answer involved business alliances, cemented either by supply contracts, equity investments, or both.

Keltic Petrochemicals' particular adaptation began to appear in late 2005, when it announced a memorandum of understanding with the Dutch firm Petroplus International "to advance the Nova Scotia project."[36] Petroplus International was established in 1993 and had evolved into a Europe-based independent oil company involved in the refining and storage of niche products such as marine fuels and lubricants. Its refineries were located in Belgium, Switzerland, and Britain. In 2001, it started the Tango brand of unmanned filling stations (subsequently sold to Kuwait Petroleum). In 2005, the private equity firm Carlyle Group combined with the founding partners of Petroplus International to buy all public shares and take Petroplus private.

By this time, Petroplus had identified the LNG trade as an added focus. In 2000, it established Dragon LNG to import and process LNG at Milford Haven, Wales. A deal in 2004 with BG Group (formerly British Gas) and Petronas of Malaysia booked the terminal's entire capacity of 6 billion cubic metres per year.[37] In 2002, Petroplus announced the LionGas LNG project in Rotterdam, which had a similar initial capacity and a planned expansion to more than double that level. Consequently, Petroplus International's interest in Keltic Petrochemicals (held by its LNG operating company, 4Gas) was its third foray into LNG development.

In March 2006, the structural form of the partnership became clearer. It was announced that the LNG import and regasification facility had been separated from Keltic Petrochemicals. It was sold to Maple LNG, which was owned jointly by 4Gas North America and Sunterra Canada. In effect, the integrated Keltic Petrochemicals business concept was abandoned. The newly segmented proposal gave Maple LNG control of the import phase and, by extension, the feedstock supply for Keltic Petrochemicals.

Despite these organizational adaptations, Keltic LNG dropped out of the group of contenders in 2005. Although Bear Head and Canaport LNG pressed ahead with environmental approvals, Keltic LNG slowed down. Where Canaport LNG and Bear Head seemed able to forge reputable upstream linkages, Keltic could not. Keltic completed preliminary site work for the storage tanks, but 4Gas still lacked a firm LNG supply. Company officials indicated in April 2007 that supplies remained disturbingly tight. To little surprise, the Keltic and Maple LNG projects were both abandoned in 2010.[38]

The Canaport LNG Project

The third prospective LNG project was located at Saint John, New Brunswick. The initiating sponsor was Irving Oil. The company had operated a deepwater crude oil import facility known as Canaport since 1973. It was located on the Bay of Fundy, a few miles east of Saint John Harbour. In July 2001, Irving Oil announced a plan to expand into LNG import, storage, and regasification at the site and began the permitting process. The process was suspended the following year during the chaos that followed the collapse of Enron Corporation (the world's leading commodity gas trader). In 2003, however, Irving Oil revived the project when Washington signalled its growing support for LNG imports. Throughout this period, Irving Oil acted on its own initiative. Although it completely lacked experience in liquefied gas, it had long been an international crude oil purchaser and enjoyed ready access to upstream suppliers. Consequently, the company sought an ally. Although Chevron-Texaco was most frequently mentioned as a possible partner, nothing came of the plan.[39]

Undeterred, Irving Oil proceeded with environmental approvals for its terminal site. In the spring of 2004, it submitted an impact assessment report to parallel federal and provincial authorities. The plan outlined plans for a 350-metre offloading pier with mooring facilities for vessels with capacity up to 200,000 cubic metres. Three storage tanks, holding 160,000 cubic metres apiece, would feed liquefied fuel to the regasification plant. At this stage, first gas was optimistically targeted for 2006. On 6 August 2004, Irving Oil received its environmental approvals with conditions attached.

A second crucial issue was hammered out at the same time. Irving Oil approached the City of Saint John for a property tax freeze on the Canaport site – \$500,000 per annum for a term of twenty-five years. The deal was controversial and met significant resistance from taxpayers. In May 2004, the critics petitioned the provincial legislature to overturn the favourable tax deal, but to no effect.[40]

Irving Oil's leverage stemmed from its ownership of a deepwater coastal site, its success in securing fiscal and environmental clearances that made it construction ready, and its alignment with provincial ambitions for enhanced gas markets. However, in the summer of 2004, it still lacked a long-term gas supply. As in the Bear Head project, the award of environmental approvals led directly to the arrival of international partners. In this case, the Spanish gas multinational Repsol YPF confirmed its participation with Irving Canaport in September 2004. Repsol YPF is the largest integrated Spanish petroleum firm and figures in the global top ten of privately owned oil and gas corporations. Its 1999 takeover of the Argentinian company YPF marked a major expansion into Latin America, an expansion that has since been extended to include LNG-producing projects in Venezuela and Peru.[41] With major stakes in several international LNG projects in Algeria, Spain, Trinidad, and the United States, as well as extensive processing and distribution networks in western Europe, Repsol YPF's interest marked a crucial step toward commerciality and catapulted Canaport to the front of the pack. In June 2005, the Canaport LNG processing partnership was formalized to build, own, and operate the terminal. The project, valued at US$750 million, is divided between Repsol YPF and Irving Oil on a 75 percent–25 percent basis. Repsol YPF undertook to supply all offshore LNG. It also retained ownership of the revapourized gas for sale anywhere outside of Canada. Irving Oil provided the site and holds the sales rights for the Maritime provinces.[42] Construction began in the autumn of 2005, and the engineering, procurement, and construction contract was awarded in May 2006 for a facility designed to ship 1 billion cubic feet (28 million cubic metres) per day.

The next critical hurdle for Canaport was the transportation link from terminal to markets. To service its anchor market in New England, Repsol YPF required pipeline connections. In March 2005, it approached MNP to build a stand-alone pipeline to the US border, where it would connect with the MNP's US mainline to Boston. However, negotiations broke down over tolling arrangements. Emera Brunswick Pipeline, a subsidiary of the Nova Scotia energy firm Emera, stepped in and was contracted to build a new line to carry Repsol gas on a twenty-year term.[43] Emera Brunswick applied to the National Energy Board in May 2006 for permits to construct and operate the pipeline and for approval of the pipeline tolls negotiated with Repsol. This was the final critical piece in Canaport's multiphase regulatory process.

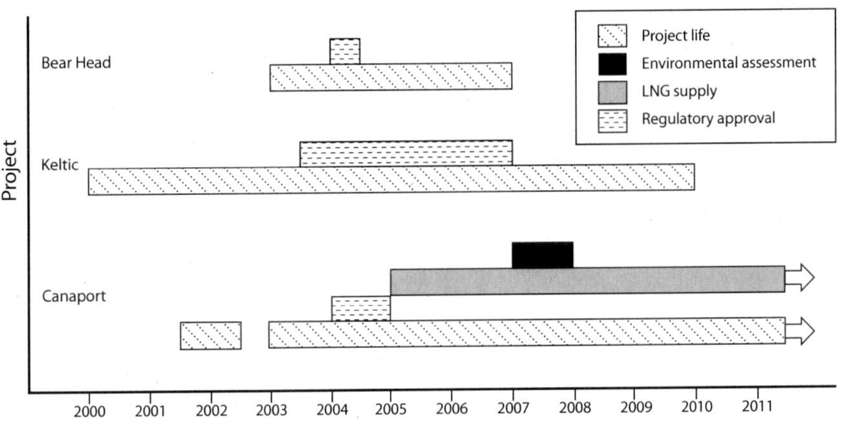

Figure 10.1 Critical-stage comparison of Maritime liquefied natural gas projects

After a sharply contested hearing before the National Energy Board, in which the stand-alone export pipeline concept was challenged, the board granted the required certificates in May 2007.[44] First gas flowed through Canaport in 2009.

In sum, three projects were advanced in Maritime Canada during this germinal phase of the LNG import industry. Figure 10.1 highlights their progression through the developmental phases. Ultimately, only Repsol-Irving (or Canaport) emerged from the complex gestation period as a fully vested candidate.

LNG Prospects and the Transport Question

The MNP's trunk pipeline was integral to the business strategies of all three projects, though not necessarily in identical ways. Since the New England market was the ultimate destination of the greater share of gas, the terms of connection to the MNP were crucial to the projects' viability. Consequently, the terms of pipeline access emerged as a critical regulatory focal point with the National Energy Board at its centre. In some respects, pipeline regulation was nothing new. Recall that back in 1996-97 MNP had been subject to political forces in both the province of origin and the province of transit. Russell MacLellan's Liberal minority government in Nova Scotia had been eager to ensure gas service to its major metropolitan areas by folding the costs of constructing lateral or spur pipelines into the rate base for the trunk line. In addition, the province contested the tolling structure for Sable gas, leading to a postage-stamp toll as opposed to a charge-by-distance toll. This toll effectively set a common tariff per unit volume to the US border, regardless of the point where gas was connected or taken off. It was on this basis that MNP acquired its regulatory approvals in Nova Scotia and has functioned since.

The supply conditions differed significantly from those of the Sable fields, however, insofar as a province seeking to host terminal facilities lacked the political leverage that could be derived from the Crown's title to gas in the ground. With LNG, the policy analogy lay closer to harbour or port management, for the province was simply a host to the importation, offloading, and shipping of gas from abroad. Although there was no guarantee that the pricing regime would carry over, the existence of the trunk line offered the opportunity to replicate the tariff economics of Sable supplies. Much depended, in the final analysis, on the orientation of the federal National Energy Board as the gatekeeper for transport and export permissions. For example, a decision to expand the capacity of the MNP line, either by adding new compressors or by looping the pipe by adding a parallel line, fell under the purview of the board.

Clearly, MNP was a strategic asset in the emergence of a new regional LNG industry. Indeed, without its prior existence, the business concept of landing liquid gas in Maritime Canada would never have arisen, and none of the three consortia would have located there. In legal, commercial, and regulatory terms, the MNP was a more strategic institution than it sometimes appeared. Although the pipeline system was a seamless physical entity from Goldboro to Dracut, in corporate terms it amounted to two sets of assets owned in common but operated by separate Canadian and US companies. Although their functional interdependence was acknowledged, each firm was a regulated enterprise within its political sphere of operations. The ownership relationships are mirrored in both companies. Duke Energy held 77.5 percent through the acquisition of founding partners Texas Panhandle and Westcoast Transmission. Minority holdings went to ExxonMobil and Emera/Scotia Power (12.92 percent). In December 2006, Duke Energy opted to separate its electricity and natural gas operations and spun off its pipeline holdings into the newly capitalized Spectra Energy, which presently holds the controlling bloc in MNP.

Maritimes & Northeast Pipeline contemplated expansion several times throughout its operating history as it adapted to changing supply and traffic conditions. For example, in 2001, MNP signed a conditional service agreement to transport newly discovered gas from the Deep Panuke formation.

This service would require the doubling of the MNP's capacity and would entail adding a series of new compressor stations on the US side of the trunk line. Despite regulatory approval from the National Energy Board, this plan was frozen when EnCana withdrew its offshore development plan from regulatory review (it was later revived). A few years later, the prospect of LNG import and regasification arose. During MNP's commercial open season in early 2005, it signed two precedent agreements: one with Repsol for 730,000 million British thermal units per day and another with Anadarko/Bear Head. The following year, when the parties began applications for regulatory approvals, proved to be pivotal.

The Critical Nexus: Pipeline and Export Politics

Regulatory authorities have long been recognized as powerful arbiters in the energy industries. Since 1960, the National Energy Board has exercised licensing authority for interprovincial and international petroleum pipelines and for the export of Canadian petroleum materials. In the early decades, the pipelines functioned as midstream enterprises, purchasing natural gas and transporting it to markets for sale. In the mid-1980s, however, a paradigm shift took place that altered the board's regulatory function in fundamental ways. The deregulation of natural gas prices unleashed a dramatic expansion of exploration, discovery, market demand, and pipeline construction to carry Canadian gas to the mainland United States.[45] In the new markets, producers could sell directly to consumers, and long-distance and local distribution pipelines assumed the role of transmission service providers to all eligible gas suppliers. The National Energy Board aptly captured the scale of the paradigm shift when it redefined its procedures: "In July 1987, the Board adopted a new procedure known as the Market-Based Procedure (MBP) ... The basic premise of the MBP is that the market will work to satisfy Canadian requirements for natural gas at fair market prices. For this to be fulfilled, markets must be competitive, there should be no abuse of market powers and all buyers should have access to gas on similar terms and conditions ... A necessary requirement for establishing a competitive gas market was that open, non-discriminatory access be provided to all shippers on interprovincial gas pipelines."[46]

As a national regulator, the National Energy Board is cognizant of a variety of markets defined by commodity, region of operations, and pricing environment. The board's views are conveyed to prospective applicants and to the public in published reports, among which the topics of Maritime natural gas and LNG have been addressed. However, it is not until formal applications have been lodged that formal deliberations and decision processes begin.

It is in the adjudication of licence applications that the political dimensions of the gas or LNG industry are decided. In effect, the regulatory proceeding should be seen as a forum for the political ordering of industry relations. The state agency seeks to reconcile certain public policy imperatives (the statutory grounds for judgment are "the public convenience and necessity") with commercial interests and the forward strategies of corporate operators. Regulatory deliberations can be a more or less contested environment, depending on the alignments of corporate and societal interests.

The regulatory process therefore needs to be understood as a distinct decision-making forum. It is a bounded contest in which the outcome is shaped by policy coordinates, stipulated procedures, and the interplay of stakeholder inputs. The limiting factors in the present case include the following: (1) the formal (National Energy Board) rules of procedure, (2) the backdrop of pertinent prior board policies and rulings, (3) the terms of the specific application, (4) the range of intervenors and the emergent structure of discourse, and (5) any overarching policy externalities that impinge in de facto, if not nominal terms, on the agency decision (see Table 10.2).

In the spring of 2006, Emera applied to the National Energy Board for a licence to build and operate a new pipeline to deliver three-quarters of Canaport's gas capacity to the United States. Hearings were held later in the year, and the decision was released in May 2007. The sequence of events ensured that, as the first entrant to the new sector, the Canaport-Emera project had the opportunity to define the preliminary terms for gas transport.[47] Rival projects, unable to file at that time, were placed in a reactive position of intervening to challenge Canaport-Emera on the basis of an as-yet unspecified future interest. The distinguishing feature of this application, of course, was the stand-alone Emera pipeline to move Canaport gas to the border.

Emera Brunswick sought three rulings from the National Energy Board. The first was on a certificate of public convenience and necessity to construct and operate a 145-kilometre line of 76-centimetre diameter with a capacity of 900,000 gigajoules per day. The line would extend from the Canaport terminal in Saint John to the Maine border, where it would connect to the MNP's US mainline. The second was an order to approve the

TABLE 10.2

Dimensions of the National Energy Board as a regulatory forum

Limiting factors	Content
Formal NEB rules of procedure	• Part 3 of the act requires decisions to be made in terms of "present and future public convenience and necessity." • Functioning as a quasi-judicial tribunal, the board may hold public hearings. • The board must comply with principles of natural justice (e.g., adequate opportunity for parties to be heard; decisions to be made by independent and unbiased decision makers). • NEB's filing manual governs the application process.
Pertinent prior NEB policies or rulings	• NEB adopts a market-based procedure to assess applications to export gas from Canada. • NEB decision on the MNP certificate for construction and operation (GH-4-1998). • NEB decision on province of New Brunswick application regarding short-term export order procedures (MH-2-2002). • *Maritimes Natural Gas Market: Overview and Assessment,* June 2003. • CEAA provisions for environmental impact approvals cover NEB jurisdiction projects.
Terms of the specific application	• Emera Brunswick seeks to construct and operate gas pipeline from Canaport (Saint John) to US border. • Emera Brunswick seeks approval of tolling agreement with Repsol for 792,292 GJ/d gas.
Range of intervenors and emergent discourse	• At GH-1-2006 hearing, Emera Brunswick was joined by Bear Head LNG, Enbridge Gas NB, Imperial Oil, Irving Oil, Repsol Energy Can., Shell Can., six groups, thirty individuals, and three government departments.
Overarching political externalities	• Beginning in 2000, the LNG import sector begins to emerge as an important new part of North American energy trade, attracting investment on the Atlantic, Gulf, and Pacific coasts. • The provinces of New Brunswick and Nova Scotia identify the LNG import business as strategic energy sector.

tolls that Emera would charge for carrying Repsol gas. The tolls were based on a deal negotiated between the two parties. Its terms obliged Repsol to pay all fixed charges applicable to the line for the twenty-five-year contract period, including a return on investment ranging from 11 to 14 percent. The third was an order to designate Emera Brunswick a Group 2 company under Part 4 of the National Energy Board Act, which would qualify the company, as a single customer enterprise, for a lighter form of regulatory oversight and monitoring. (As a federally regulated project, the pipeline also required an environmental review under the Canadian Environmental Assessment Act. The statute allowed, and the respective ministers agreed, that the National Energy Board hearings could substitute for a special Canadian Environmental Assessment Agency panel review on environmental impacts.)[48]

When the application moved to the public hearing stage, a number of intervenors challenged its terms. For example, local neighbourhood groups in Saint John expressed concern about the impact of constructing a new corridor through their city. In this, they were backed by many individuals. Another challenge came from Nova Scotia interests concerned about the impact of the dedicated export pipeline to the US border (which some intervenors dubbed the "bullet line") on the commercial economics and future viability of the MNP's system overall. Proponents of both the Bear Head terminal and the Keltic project depended on the MNP as their link to New England. To this end, Bear Head argued that Canaport should be required to utilize all available portions of the MNP trunk line, not just the US portion from Maine to Boston: "The level of excess capacity would suggest that with a mainline expansion and possible reversal of the Saint John lateral, the Canadian segment of the MNP system could readily transport the Repsol requirements and reduce the tolls for all shippers."[49] Bear Head estimated in this case that the prevailing toll on the Canadian segment would drop from Can$0.69 to Can$0.47 per million British thermal units, compared to a drop to Can$0.65 with the bypass.

A similar case was presented by the Nova Scotia Department of Energy. Officials argued that allowing Canaport to bypass the MNP's Canadian line would violate the original (1996) regulatory bargain on which the MNP's line had been approved – as an infrastructural work to seed the development of an expanding Maritime gas market for both domestic and export sales: "The infancy of the developing Maritimes Canadian market would, in and of itself, be sufficient to warrant special interest public considerations.

However this application compounds the problem of dealing with such issues by being associated with the building of Canada's first LNG facility. The connection of such a facility to the United States by a bullet line with no connections to other facilities in Canada also raises questions about what the Canadian public interest demands, in terms of necessary benefits, for allowing foreign companies to site facilities here to serve markets elsewhere."[50]

In response, Emera Brunswick and Irving-Repsol argued that the economics of the LNG project required a stand-alone pipeline to the border to connect with the MNP's US mainline. Thus, it should be seen by the National Energy Board as "a market-based contractual response of a pipeline service provider, Emera Brunswick, to the transmission service needs of a particular shipper, Repsol."[51] As far as the public interest was concerned, Repsol argued that the project's decisive contribution to Canada's Maritime market lay in its potential for 250,000 million British thermal units per day (to be marketed by Irving).

Broadly put, these were the parameters of debate before the board on the public interest criterion. Critics of the application argued that the bypass would disadvantage the future prospects of MNP Canada. Proponents rejected the notion that the prior MNP facility in Canada had any connection to the Canaport project and proffered a far narrower notion of public interest.

In its May 2007 decision, the board accepted the proponents' case. It ruled out arguments about MNP's system economics and future viability, partly on the grounds that MNP was not a party to the hearing and was therefore outside of the calculation of public interest and partly by invoking the notion that each project should be assessed by the terms of its application rather than by hypothetical alternatives. Implicitly at least, this decision relegated to the background earlier decisions such as the MNP's founding licence of 1997. It also required the board to ignore some central findings from its 2003 assessment of Maritime gas markets, particularly the finding that "there are a number of unique characteristics of the Maritimes gas markets that give rise to concern."[52] These characteristics included the single offshore supplier situation and the preponderance of export traffic on the line. This finding echoed a conclusion from another Maritime hearing a year earlier, in which the board judged that "the developing Maritime market faces many challenges that are not faced by buyers in the mature [i.e., western Canadian] export market."[53]

The National Energy Board panel that adjudicated the Emera Brunswick application heard evidence that required it to make choices about appropriate frameworks of interpretation and operational assumptions. The relative youth and uniqueness of the regional gas market, coupled with the clearly drawn principles from the initial MNP licence ten years earlier, could have allowed the board to give special attention to factors *sui generis*. This approach would, however, entail a shift from the sort of values applied more frequently over the previous decade to new export pipeline applications from the western sedimentary basin.

Ultimately, the fact that only one LNG project and one pipeline was under review proved crucial. Perhaps if rival applications had been advanced within the same time frame, the systemic considerations that Nova Scotia intervenors sought to inject into the debate might have gained greater traction with the board. In this sense, the earlier failures of Bear Head and Keltic to tie down the necessary supply links and the ensuing delays in filing export applications of their own proved fatal to them in the 2006-7 export pipeline proceeding.

Conclusion

When Nova Scotia chose to grasp the LNG energy mantle at the turn of the millennium, it entered a business sector and a policy field quite different from the more familiar world of offshore oil and gas extraction. This fact became evident as time progressed. Liquefied natural gas import and distribution is, in essence, a merchant operation. A commodity produced and procured elsewhere must be transported, processed, and resold to complete the value chain. Liquefied natural gas terminal operations in Maritime Canada sit at the final stages of this chain. Perhaps the sector's differences from upstream production in the Scotian Basin were initially obscured by the nominal commonality suggested by the term *natural gas*, regardless of its source. However, the policy instruments that governed offshore exploration and production, which derived ultimately from Crown title to the resource, were conspicuously absent when Nova Scotia became involved in downstream LNG imports. In fact, the political challenge that the authorities faced in shaping this new industry was closer to that of promoting secondary manufacturing investment onshore, but with a powerful federal regulatory agency added to the mix.

Structurally, there are two decisive thresholds that must be passed if an LNG import project is to move beyond the conceptual stage. Attaining these thresholds is what separated the forty plus proposed LNG terminal projects in North America in 2003 from the half dozen new enterprises that have been realized. The first requirement is securing sufficient long-term supplies of liquid feedstock. Doing so is the merchant's problem in a tight market. The problem can be solved by backward equity investment in the supply chain or by partnering with gas owners and processors in an integrated joint venture. In 2003, Anadarko appeared to be best placed to achieve the threshold. The company was an offshore exploration and production specialist of multinational scale. Certainly, the Government of Nova Scotia was confident that Anadarko's arrival rendered Bear Head a credible player. But it was Irving Oil, a refiner of imported crude, that landed the prize through its alliance with Repsol (a strategic alignment that echoed Irving Oil's pre-existing business model). In the meantime, the corporate restructuring that followed the Anadarko merger with Kerr-McGee rendered the Bear Head project marginal then irrelevant. As for the Keltic project at Goldboro, the prospect for success grew increasingly distant over time. The project lacked both an upstream ally and an independent foothold in gas liquids.

Securing long-term (twenty year plus) liquid gas supplies is critical to orderly project progression in several respects. This requirement must be satisfied before sponsors will access capital in sufficient quantities to move forward, for lenders treat guaranteed feedstock as a physical asset. Securing firm pipeline service contracts for transport also depends on meeting this requirement. Finally, a solution to the supply parameter is necessary before a project sponsor can apply for regulatory approvals.

Indeed, the second threshold for project viability involves winning regulatory consents for transit and export. At this stage, the project sponsor enters the world of a powerful federal agency with high levels of expertise that operates according to a hardened policy template. Each regulatory proceeding for new business licensing constitutes a discrete political episode. In effect, the applicant and application trigger an extended, multi-stakeholder review that takes place against the backdrop of a fixed regulatory mandate and procedure. In a newly emergent sector such as LNG, there may be advantages of first entry, particularly under the National Energy Board's prevailing philosophy of weighing specific business interests against the public interest. It is clear that new rules and precedents are being set at this regime-fashioning phase. As a result, the configuration of interests is critical. A multi-application hearing attracts more scrutiny than a single-application hearing. Interested parties can assert different pressures as applicants than they can as third-parties.

Significantly, Irving-Repsol grasped a singular advantage as first mover, capturing pipeline capacity and export permits before its rivals. The company was able to advance the bullet-line concept as a commercially superior choice, leaving the "MNP bypass" issue for others to articulate. Moreover, the rival sponsors' inabilities to launch applications within the formative time frame proved critical. When it came to an examination of pipeline system attributes, the board was left with a choice between Irving-Repsol's fait-accompli and Anadarko's unconfirmed aspiration. Faced with the choice of facilitating a new enterprise and a new sector start-up or postponing approval into an uncertain future, the National Energy Board chose the former, ending a critical episode in Maritime petroleum politics.

11

Offshore Politics and the Aboriginal Challenge

The Crown regime for offshore resource management has responded dynamically to economic and political pressures in recent decades. This flexibility is reflected in the shifting boundaries of sovereign jurisdiction, the disputes over the scope of federal and provincial powers, intrastate tensions at both levels of government, the administrative dynamics of the Canada–Nova Scotia Offshore Petroleum Board (CNSOPB), and the ebb and flow of offshore industry regulation.

Over time, however, the underlying foundation of the state's involvement – unburdened Crown title – has remained intact. That is, the Crown holds the power to dispose of offshore assets and regulate the terms of access as it wills, according to the political arrangements that it chooses to make. In this sense, the offshore polity, or more precisely that segment encompassed by the continental shelf, is a distinctive political formation.

This chapter explores the possibility that the Crown's strength is less absolute than is normally thought. The challenge comes from a rival title and a rival bundle of rights asserted by Aboriginal peoples. Prior to 1982, the possibility of such a claim would have been remote. However, the entrenchment of the Constitution Act in that year, section 35 in particular, transformed the status of Aboriginal citizens in fundamental ways. The provisions pertaining to Aboriginal and treaty rights, hard fought during the constitutional campaigns of the early 1980s, conferred significant new political status on Indian, Inuit, and Metis peoples.[1] Over the past thirty years, section 35 has opened important political avenues through litigation and judicial rulings on treaty rights, Aboriginal rights, and Aboriginal title. Matters dealing with resource use and ownership have been of particular importance. Perhaps it was only a matter of time before these questions were projected from terrestrial and aquatic contexts to those of seabed resources. Although a frontal challenge to offshore petroleum tenure has not yet been launched, the politico-legal context is at the very least suggestive.

To explore the roots, parameters, and prospects for the transformation of offshore political tenure, this chapter opens with a brief review of the history of the Mi'kmaq peoples in the territory known today as Nova Scotia. A discussion of the relevant terms of the 1982 constitutional provisions and the dominant paths of judicial challenge they engendered sets the stage for an exploration of the rolling frontier of Aboriginal-state relations and a number of litigation strategies for asserting Aboriginal people's offshore interest. Finally, the possibility for legal change is assessed. This chapter reveals how the shifting terms of legal politics are transforming the Nova Scotia offshore polity, why court findings on the Crown's duty to consult are now integral to offshore governance, and how, even without a successful title claim, Aboriginal peoples may well have a special place in the future of offshore petroleum exploration and production.

Mi'kmaq Peoples and Mi'kmaki

The history of Aboriginal society in Nova Scotia is complex and fascinating. For the past five hundred years, the Mi'kmaq encounter with Europeans has been central to the process of change. However, indigenous culture has been part of the wider Maritime region for a far longer duration. Some fourteen thousand years ago, a warming trend marked the end of the last ice age. Paleoindian peoples, organized in hunting societies, migrated eastward across the continent along the edge of the receding glaciers, finding their way to the east coast tundra. Some of these people settled in the territory of present-day New England and Maritime Canada, and artifacts at Debert in central Nova Scotia date from 10,600 BP.

The warming climate had at least two dramatic effects. Over the next eight millennia, it transformed the landscape from open tundra into woodlands. Initially, the forest was dominated by conifers such as spruce and pine. In the final stage of the archaic period, however, hardwood species such as beech, maple, ash, and elm established dominance and supported a substantial population of large mammals such as deer and moose.[2] Melting ice sheets also caused a steady rise in sea levels, averaging perhaps one metre every three centuries or 70 metres in total. As a result, the coastal plains were inundated, the Mi'kmaq land base was restricted, and much of the early hunting territory disappeared.

Harold Prins describes a durable culture of local hunting bands that tended to combine coastal and inland resources in a seasonal migratory round.[3] Larger bands of perhaps two hundred people congregated for much of the year at the coasts for fishing, clamming, birding, and sealing. During the winter, small groups of fewer than twenty people moved into the forests to hunt terrestrial game. These arrangements varied, of course, depending upon local resource endowments. However, the general pattern held true in the centuries prior to European contact in the 1700s, and it prevailed in an area stretching from the Gaspé Peninsula across New Brunswick, Prince Edward Island, and Nova Scotia.[4]

The Mi'kmaq shared not only a language and material culture but also a political structure. Kin group leaders known as *saqmaw* served as hunting group chiefs and gathered at the band or regional levels to deal with overlapping interests. Prins estimates that the late pre-contact Mi'kmaq population ranged from ten thousand to twenty thousand people, or ten to twenty persons per forty square miles. Seven distinct districts were recognized, and each held councils (see Map 11.1).[5] In addition, a grand council of district leaders was convened for all of Mi'kmaki.

The first Europeans encountered by Mi'kmaq may have been the Breton fishermen who found their way to Newfoundland and the Gulf of St. Lawrence beginning in 1504. They were joined by the Portuguese (1525-), the Normandy explorers (Cartier, 1534-), and the Basques. By the 1580s, the commercial interests of Europeans included fur products, fish, and seals. By 1600, the French Crown was issuing exclusive settlement land rights to seigneurs and trade rights to companies. The first Acadia settlement appeared in 1604, when Pierre Gua De Monts and Samuel de Champlain arrived at Port Royal in today's Annapolis region of Nova Scotia.

Even before the geopolitical rivalry between France and England began to intensify, the European presence had exerted a devastating impact.[6] The initial century of contact had exposed Aboriginal peoples to novel germs and viruses against which they had no defences. It is estimated that 75 to 90 percent of the population of Mi'kmaki at the time of contact had died out by 1600, leaving from two thousand to five thousand people. Such a harsh population swing must be factored into any legal appraisal of the Mi'kmaq contact experience, including court-directed references to contact-era activities.

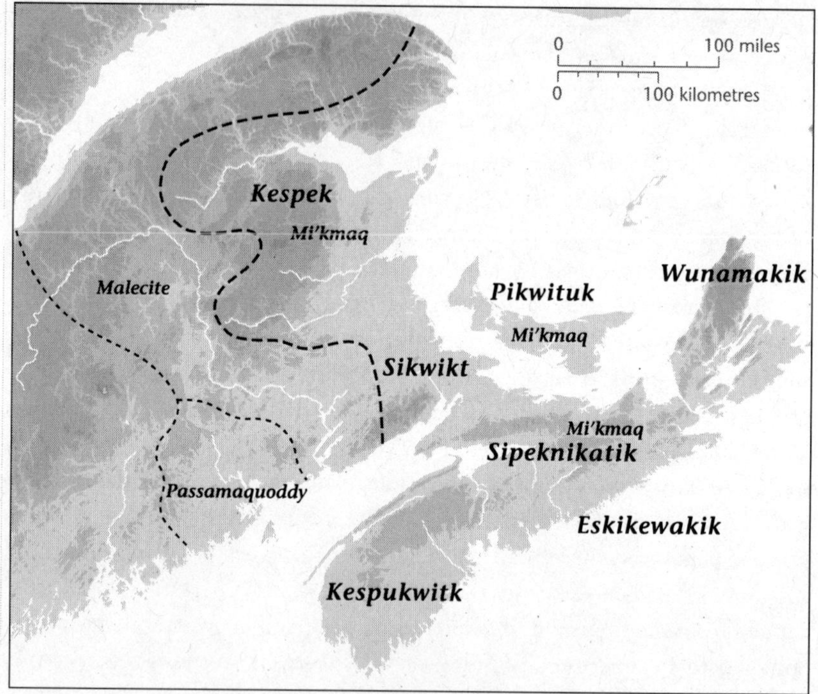

Map 11.1 Mi'kmaki lands and districts

As in any colonial encounter, the process of intercultural contact in Nova Scotia was spatially uneven and socially variable. Some Mi'kmaq people and band groups were involved early and served intermediary roles with their still isolated neighbours. In addition, the presence of multiple European agents brought diverse strategies and styles to Mi'kmaki.[7] France tended to treat Aboriginal peoples as autonomous societies and did not press for the assertion of sovereignty so much as military alliances and religious contact. England treated the Mi'kmaq as subjects and their resistance as rebellion. The Treaty of Utrecht in 1713 conferred both territory and sovereignty on England. This was not the only kind of treaty to affect Mi'kmaki. During the eighteenth century, a series of agreements was concluded between Mi'kmaq tribal leaders and English colonial officers, typically to halt hostilities, keep Mi'kmaq neutral, and set out a basis for future civil relations. These treaties of peace and friendship – signed in 1693, 1725, 1726, 1749, 1752, and 1761 – among others, typically stipulated an end to fighting, the return of captives, and guarantees of Aboriginal lands, hunting privileges, and trade. As tensions resurfaced with the advance of settlement, new treaties coincided with the close of various cycles.[8] It is these treaties of peace and friendship that provide the basis for a powerful thread of modern rights litigation, asserting continuing legal guarantees against infringements by statute law. Names such as Sylliboy, Simon, Isaac, Marshall, Peter Paul, and Bernard constitute landmarks for Mi'kmaq in the ongoing judicial process.

In 1763, England emerged triumphant from the Seven Years' War, ending French colonial occupancy in Canada. The Royal Proclamation of that year enunciated key principles for future Crown relations with Aboriginal people, declaring them under royal protection on all lands not yet ceded, prohibiting any land purchase without Crown licence, and regulating trade between immigrants and Aboriginal people. Within a decade, however, the force of immigrant settlement began mounting, and colonial authorities exercised Crown powers to grant and sell expanding portions of Indian land. By the time that land sales were discontinued after 1900, the Nova Scotia Crown holding was less than 25 percent of provincial territory. A series of small Indian Reserves, ranging from 500 to 2,000 acres, had been established by executive order, beginning in 1779. There were fourteen by 1825. In 1843, colonial politician Joseph Howe reported on land embezzlement and the political dominance of the settler faction. He estimated that there were only some 1,300 surviving Mi'kmaq. Concealed by his account of politico-legal exclusion, however, was the story of Mi'kmaq living on the land according to the ethical principles of *netukulimk*.[9]

Aboriginal Rights under Section 35

The Constitution Act, 1982, included several clauses that, for the first time, acknowledged Aboriginal rights at the constitutional level. In particular, section 35 provided that "the existing aboriginal and treaty rights of the aboriginal peoples of Canada are hereby recognized and affirmed."[10] Given that federal and provincial authorities (and national Aboriginal leaders) proved unable to elaborate on the substance of such existing rights in their post-1982 constitutional talks, the courts emerged as the principal forum for legal clarification. Furthermore, since there are striking variations of Aboriginal experience throughout the nation, both historical and legal, it is not surprising that the most promising paths of litigation would vary.[11] In British Columbia, for example, where most bands and tribes are not covered by treaties, cases centred on gaining judicial recognition of Aboriginal title over traditional lands or Aboriginal rights to resource-harvesting activities. On the Prairies – where the so-called numbered treaties ceded Indian land to the Crown in return for reserves, annuities, and other compensation –

litigation has concentrated on establishing the extent of treaty rights and securing their observance. In the Maritime provinces, where the peace and friendship treaties are silent on land title while confirming traditional rights of resource harvesting, there are grounds for pursuing treaty rights while also advancing possible Aboriginal and title rights outside of treaties.

To date, Canadian litigation on Aboriginal and treaty rights has tilted toward terrestrial matters – protected activities, land title, and Aboriginal governance. There are some landmark marine resource cases, especially in the fisheries. Indeed, one of the first Supreme Court rulings on the scope of section 35, *R. v. Sparrow,* dealt with the Pacific salmon fishery.[12] In many respects, it is the cultural practices of coastal Aboriginal groups that provide the legal link between the resources of land and sea. Aboriginal societies in coastal regions have varying histories of offshore activity prior to contact with Europeans. Moreover, to the extent that Crown authorities hold jurisdiction beyond the low-water mark, a path is open for Aboriginal rights to be explored as an underlying dimension of Crown holdings.

At the same time, there are significant differences between the onshore and offshore legal regimes. When explorers planted their sponsors' flags, when European peace treaties transferred New World colonies from one empire to another, or when colonial wars altered patterns of geopolitics in North America, the focus was overwhelmingly on terrestrial holdings. Whether the goal was strategic military positioning, overseas settlement, or a merchant trading hinterland, European interests viewed the New World as a set of natural assets centred on *terra.* Offshore waters were, in key respects, different. It is not that states were reluctant to assert sovereign claims to the sea in an era of expanding marine trade. However closed seas, sovereign sectors, and even zones of influence were impossible to enforce in an age when multiple marine powers contested such claims. In 1609, Hugo Grotius advanced the doctrine of *Mare Liberum* or open seas. Significantly, Grotius also favoured state control of a modest coastal strip. Over the next several centuries, a number of definitions were debated in European circles, including the lines-of-sight doctrine and the cannon shot rule.[13] Ultimately, it was the three-mile belt that was accepted as a diplomatic compromise, and Britain adopted it during its Age of Empire in the nineteenth century. The three-nautical-mile territorial sea came into use and remained a standard of offshore state sovereignty until it was revisited in the modern period.

This leaves open the question of how these arrangements affected Canada. Part of the uncertainty derives from the gradual evolution of Canadian sovereignty between Confederation in 1867 and the Statute of Westminster in 1931. Another part flows from the distinct attributes of sovereignty, legislative jurisdiction, and proprietary rights to territorial waters and their submerged lands.

The status of the territorial seabed and subsoil was addressed by the Supreme Court of Canada in 1967 in the Government of Canada's reference case on *Offshore Mineral Rights of British Columbia*. The court found that the submerged lands were the property of Canada and that jurisdiction to both these lands and the extended continental shelf to a depth of 200 metres also fell to the federal Crown. This ruling flowed from an examination of the powers of the Colony of British Columbia before it joined Confederation in 1871. The court found no colonial ownership of a territorial sea. The distinguishing British case was *Regina v. Keyn* (1876), which held that, unless stipulated by Parliament, the realm of England ended at the low-water mark. Although the three-nautical-mile sea might be British territory, it fell beyond the reach of common law. In response to this ruling, the Imperial Parliament passed the Territorial Waters Jurisdiction Act of 1878 to give the Admiralty Court a criminal jurisdiction in these waters. As the Supreme Court put it in the BC reference case, "the rights asserted by the British Crown in respect of the colony of British Columbia were after 1871 asserted by the British Crown in respect of the Dominion of Canada."[14]

Prior to 1919, Canada held limited rights to legislate for the territorial sea. Then, over a twelve-year period extending from Canada's separate signature on the Versailles Treaty to the enactment of the Statute of Westminster, sovereignty was consolidated in Ottawa.[15] From this point forward, the Government of Canada was in a position to join fully in international law developments, including the 1958 UN Convention on the Continental Shelf and the Parliament of Canada's Territorial Sea and Fishing Zones Act of 1964. The latter served to consolidate Canadian sovereignty over the three-mile sea (extended to twelve miles in 1970) as well as the rights to explore and exploit the broader continental shelf. In 1978, Canada asserted a fisheries economic exclusion zone extending to the 200-mile limit.[16]

Where does this leave Aboriginal groups interested in asserting rights or title to offshore activities or resources? The entrenchment of Aboriginal and treaty rights in 1982 was pivotal in the modern history of marine resource management, though it only became evident over time. Many of the legal benchmarks and guidelines mentioned in the Canadian terrestrial context carry over to the offshore context. In light of Crown jurisdiction and proprietary rights, Aboriginal peoples can advance an Aboriginal right or a title right in the same fashion as on land. Part of the process involves establishing that an activity was pursued at the time of contact and that the activity in question was central to the practices, customs, and traditions of the culture group. In a situation where a treaty encompassed activities such as hunting and fishing that were pursued offshore, Aboriginal people would have a parallel path for asserting an activity-based right. On the question of Aboriginal title per se, the standards of claim are different. The temporal marker shifts from point of contact to the point at which sovereignty was claimed, inviting exploration of the extent and duration of sovereignty over offshore areas and activities.

In Canada, the most notable offshore rights initiative to date is the March 2002 claim by the Haida Nation of British Columbia to ancestral lands and waters covering 5,800 square kilometres of the Hecate Strait. The first ever claim to title in offshore resources, the case was announced after years of inconclusive treaty negotiations with the Government of British Columbia. At that time, the Government of British Columbia was publicly considering ending a decades-long moratorium on offshore petroleum exploration, a move that the Haida and Tsimshian nations strenuously opposed.[17] The Queen Charlotte sedimentary basin covers 80,000 square kilometres, including the Haida claim, and the Geological Survey of Canada estimates that it is the most important West Coast offshore prospect with up to 10 billion barrels of oil and 40 trillion cubic feet (1.1 trillion cubic metres) of natural gas.

Should the Haida title claim proceed to court, it would follow a path similar to other title actions in the province, for instance, the Gitxsan and Wet'suwet'en action in the *Delgamuukw* case. At trial, the plaintiff has the burden of proving occupation prior to sovereignty, continuity between pre-sovereign and modern occupancy, and the exclusive character of traditional occupancy. None of these criteria is expected to present particular barriers to the Haida people, who inhabit an offshore archipelago with a rich evidentiary base in archaeological, historical, and cultural materials. The central connection of the people to both land and water is the nub of such a case. However, the trial stage of such a claim promises to be lengthy, as earlier cases have demonstrated. Regardless of outcome, the appeal process could extend the period of litigation by five to eight years.

A closely related question is what the Haida Nation seeks to affirm in its title claim? Prior to the actual petition of claim, the answer to this question must remain speculative. However, on the basis of Haida leadership commitments to protect the terrestrial and aquatic environments for the continued benefit of the First Nation and to achieve a management stake at all levels of resource planning, a variety of new governance structures can be expected, along with possible financial returns from past and future use. Although the Haida are not restricted by the pattern of past claim settlements negotiated between First Nations and Ottawa, the terms of Nunavut, Yukon, Northwest Territories, and Labrador agreements reveal a plethora of co-management arrangements for resources and environmental impacts, on both land and water.

Of particular interest is the impact on the offshore petroleum resource. In *Delgamuukw,* Chief Justice Antonio Lamer describes the content of Aboriginal title as encompassing "the right to exclusive use and occupation of the land held pursuant to that title for a variety of purposes, which need not be aspects of those aboriginal practices, customs and traditions which are integral to distinctive aboriginal cultures; and second that those protected uses must not be irreconcilable with the nature of the group's attachment to that land."[18] Lamer observes that the *Guerin* case established that Aboriginal title encompasses mineral rights. Yet, because Aboriginal title is *sui generis* and differs from fee simple, Lamer finds that there are limits to the prospective uses of Aboriginal lands to ensure compatibility of use with the nature of the group's attachment. A hunting ground cannot be destroyed by developing a strip mine, nor can a ceremonial site be turned into a parking lot.

Clearly, the terms of compatibility will be pivotal. Many exponents of the doctrine of zero-risk management would contend that any petroleum exploration and production activities are incompatible with marine-resource harvesting. At the same time, many corporate explorers and state regulators would argue that rigorous impact assessment and best-practice operational and mitigatory measures have significantly reduced the risk and facilitated the coexistence of multiple uses and users. Since Aboriginal and Crown title are bound together in contemporary Canadian judicial thinking, these tensions between users can be expected to persist under whatever title settlement terms and institutional arrangements are determined.

At the same time, it is clear that an offshore claim faces certain restrictions not applicable on land. The first of these is the potential limiting impact of the territorial sea, since this is the spatial area over which jurisdiction or sovereignty has been most continuously operative for legal purposes. On the one hand, it is possible and even probable that sea-based Aboriginal resource use has been concentrated in this coastal belt. Consequently, the possibility of building a legal case of strength is most likely in this area.

There are historical records that firmly indicate the Mi'kmaq's practice of using coastal waters, including sea fishing and hunting for seal, whale, and walrus.[19] Records also establish travel by boat over significant distances, such as from Cape Breton Island to the Iles de la Madeleine in the Gulf of St. Lawrence or from the mainland to Prince Edward Island.[20] There is also extensive evidence of coastal and estuary harvesting of both shellfish and fin fish during the spring and summer phases of the year.

If the Canadian case law on offshore Aboriginal rights remains undeveloped, the same cannot be said for Australia. Both countries share a common-law tradition, a history as settler Dominions, and the existence of indigenous cultures; therefore, it is not surprising that their respective paths of Aboriginal jurisprudence are mutually informed. In the 1990s, Australia too experienced watershed High Court decisions that advanced Aboriginal rights. *Mabo and Others v. Queensland (No. 2)* (1992) represented one such turning point in indigenous rights litigation. It conferred common law recognition of Aborigines' rights to possess and enjoy traditional lands, wherever a traditional connection to land and water is found and not extinguished.[21] Four years later, *Wik* (1996) extended Aboriginal title to Crown lands held by pastoral leaseholders. Title extended to a large proportion of Australia's rural grazing land, since pastoral leases had replaced land sales and grants as means of land conveyance at an early date.

As far as offshore rights are concerned, the next High Court ruling was the most dramatic. *Commonwealth v. Yarmirr* (2001) arose in the Croker Islands, located in the Timor Sea north of the Northern Territory. It involved a claim to 200 square kilometres of offshore sea. The court found an Aboriginal right to the offshore area, though not an exclusive right.[22] In light of common law rights to activities such as public navigation and fishing, the Aboriginal right was found to be shared with others. At the time, *Yarmirr* was seen as a historic breakthrough and was known as the "Mabo of the Sea." Although it made no explicit reference to petroleum, it did confirm Aboriginal people's rights to travel within and through the offshore claim area; to fish, trap, and hunt for noncommercial food needs; to visit places of cultural and spiritual significance; and to safeguard cultural and spiritual knowledge.

The momentum of this series of judgments was arrested, however, by *Western Australia v. Ward* (2002). The High Court found that, regardless of whether there had been traditional use of offshore petroleum rights, Aboriginal sea rights had been extinguished by the Petroleum Act of 1936 and the Mining Act of 1904. Therefore, there were no continuing seabed rights for Aborigines.[23]

Richard Bartlett points out that the High Court of Australia performed a striking turnabout between its rulings on *Mabo* and *Wik* and its ruling on *Ward,* that is, between 1996 and 2002. Several forces contributed to this change.[24] The Commonwealth Labor Government, which had fashioned the Native Title Act (1993) in a positive response to *Mabo,* was replaced three years later by the right-of-centre Liberal-National coalition government. The latter's platform called for the amendment of the Native Title Act to make it more workable, a commitment widely understood as a pledge to strengthen the status of resource titles, narrow the scope of Aboriginal land negotiations, and raise the bar for registration of title claims. The amendments came into effect late in 1998. At the same time, Bartlett notes that the shifting composition of the High Court and the appointment of a new chief justice in particular, coincided with this shift.

It is unlikely that Australian case law will provide guidance to break new ground in Canadian law in the near future. The era of greatest judicial dialogue between the Australia's High Court and the Supreme Court of Canada was between 1975 and 1995. During that time, the Supreme Court of Canada's *Calder* case influenced the High Court's recognition of Aboriginal rights in common law as found in *Mabo.* In a similar way, the Supreme Court of Canada's findings in fish-harvesting rights cases such as *R. v. Sparrow* and *R. v. Van der Peet* had a mark in Australia.

However, the two countries' underlying institutional differences cannot be discounted. In Canada, the Constitution Act, 1982, elevated existing treaty and Aboriginal rights possessed by "Indian, Inuit and Metis peoples" to constitutional status. It was this higher-level standing and subsequent litigation that led the Supreme Court of Canada to launch its ongoing exploration of the substantive meaning of such rights. No comparable constitutional standing applies to Australian Aboriginal rights. The Native Title Act of 1993 took the form of statute law alone. As such it has been transformed by subsequent Commonwealth Parliaments, an option not readily available in Canada.

Mi'kmaq Prospects for Offshore Oil and Gas

For Mi'kmaq, as for other Aboriginal peoples, the offshore rights and title issues do not exist in a vacuum. Rather, they are one part of a much larger project to secure a settlement on matters pertaining to Aboriginal lands, resources, and governance. As a consequence, the issue of offshore title and rights is likely to be approached strategically, insofar as it can advance and reinforce the more comprehensive political campaign. Moreover, since Aboriginal peoples have not been viewed in the past as central stakeholders in the oceans sector, their involvement is relatively recent. A brief review of the patterns of Mi'kmaq land and resource politics reveals the complex interplay of political organization, rights litigation, and formal negotiation driving the rights and title agenda.

The Union of Nova Scotia Indians was established in 1969, when the leadership of the eleven existing provincial bands opted for a united voice to respond to the perceived assimilative threats of Ottawa's White Paper on Indian Policy. This was the era of mass Aboriginal mobilization across the country, and the near-unanimous opposition of provincial, territorial, and national organizations to the white paper led to the withdrawal of the proposal one year later. The union's focus then turned toward securing positive Aboriginal rights in law and policy. In its *Calder* judgment of 1973, the Supreme Court of Canada indicated significant support for the recognition of ongoing Aboriginal title where it had not been explicitly extinguished. The case opened significant prospects not only in non-treaty areas but also for Aboriginal people in the Maritimes whose treaties did not involve land cession.

Buoyed by success in the Isaac hunting-rights case, the Mi'kmaq decided to prepare a land claim under the federal comprehensive claims policy. In 1976, the Union of Nova Scotia Indians formally presented two major documents to the federal and provincial governments: "The Nova Scotia Aboriginal Rights Position Paper" and "The Crown Land Rights and Hunting and Fishing Rights of the Micmac Indians."[25] In the paper on Crown land rights, the Mi'kmaq assert "an Aboriginal right to hunt and fish and trap animals, fish or fowl" on reserves or unoccupied Crown land and state "that this claim shall be acknowledged as partial claim of Aboriginal title."[26] The federal government took the position that treaty and Aboriginal rights had been superseded by law, while the province tended to view "Indian" affairs as a federal jurisdiction.[27] Following these dismissive positions by government, the land issue was deadlocked for several decades.

Although governments proved to be unresponsive, the courts provided a series of significant confirmations that advanced both treaty and Aboriginal rights. Some of these accrued across the country on a case-by-case incremental basis, but they had implications that often stretched well beyond the initiating jurisdiction. Others originated in Nova Scotia. In the 1975 *Isaac* ruling, the Nova Scotia Court of Appeal found a right to hunt on reserves irrespective of provincial regulation. A decade later, in *Simon,* the Supreme Court of Canada drew upon section 35(1) to find a right to off-reserve hunting based on the 1752 Treaty, reversing a half century of jurisprudence to the contrary. In *R. v. Denny, Paul, and Sylliboy* (1990) the Nova Scotia Court of Appeal recognized Mi'kmaq food-fishing rights. The following year, this precedent influenced the Nova Scotia Crown's decision to end a case on illegal moose hunting involving a group of Cape Breton Mi'kmaq.

In 1995, a new field of litigation opened in New Brunswick, when Thomas Peter Paul was charged with illegal logging on Crown land. By the time the appeal process concluded three years later, Peter Paul's treaty right to log had between affirmed twice. It was overturned, however, by the New Brunswick Court of Appeal. During this same time frame, Donald Marshall's claim of Mi'kmaq people's treaty right to fish and sell eels was under way.[28] The Supreme Court of Canada's favourable decision in 1999 marked a high point of Mi'kmaq treaty rights litigation. Other cases followed, including the Stephen Marshall and Joshua Bernard logging-rights cases of 2005, by which a treaty and Aboriginal right to cut and sell logs was affirmed by both the Nova Scotia and New Brunswick Courts of Appeal. The Supreme Court of Canada reversed the decisions the following year, however.

The scorecard of judicial victories and defeats cannot be easily summarized. It can be said, however, that over the twenty years stretching from the *Simon* judgment to *Bernard,* a series of constitutionally entrenched rights were recognized, including hunting on Crown land and fishing in rivers and coastal waters, but not logging on Crown lands. Along the way, the Supreme Court of Canada has vastly strengthened the application of certain seventeenth-century Mi'kmaq and Maliseet treaties. The court has also delineated new rules of interpretation and evidentiary standards in both treaty and Aboriginal right cases. Perhaps most importantly, there are now new principles and standards for determinations in a number of areas: the Crown's fiduciary responsibility, the intended purpose of section 35(1), the alignment of Aboriginal and Crown title, the compatibility of Aboriginal and treaty rights and Crown regulation, and the Crown's duty to consult Aboriginal people in the face of prospective title claims.[29]

One final sequence of litigation has a bearing on the question of offshore rights and title. Although these challenges involve terrestrial lands, they are connected to offshore petroleum production, and they signal another emerging thread in the recognition of Aboriginal resource rights. Recall that a Joint Public Review Panel was struck in 1996 to assess the various elements of the proposed Sable and Maritime & Northeast Pipeline (MNP) projects. In its report, the panel recommended that the proponents be required to submit a written protocol or agreement spelling out Aboriginal groups' roles and responsibilities in project monitoring. The National Energy Board made this a condition of granting MNP a certificate, and talks were held in 1998. Draft protocols were discussed with the Union of Nova Scotia Indians, but talks broke down. The union's legal action cited defects in the subsequent negotiations between the board and MNP (which ultimately led to the acceptance of the failed MNP protocol as sufficient consultation), which did not involve the Union of Nova Scotia Indians. In 1999, the Federal Court of Appeal ruled that the board had not acted fairly toward the Union of Nova Scotia Indians and had breached its duty of procedural fairness. The issue went back to the board for new consultations.[30]

Two years later, the Union of Nova Scotia Indians joined the Confederacy of Mainland Mi'kmaq to challenge the adequacy of the provincial government's consultations, particularly its use of the Crown Lands Act to grant options and easements to MNP for its onshore trunk pipeline. The plaintiffs sought a court order to block MNP's access to those lands, together with findings that the provincial Crown had a duty to protect Aboriginal and treaty rights and interests on those Crown lands and was in breach of this duty. At no time had there been notification, consultation, or compensation, nor had the bands offered their consent. At trial, the judge found that the legal action should be changed from an order of relief to a trial, in which the duty to consult could be broadly examined.[31] The Nova Scotia Court of Appeal upheld the decision. Politically, however, these cases underlined the Mi'kmaq's determination that the Crown discharge its duty. The Supreme Court of Canada's rulings the following year in *Haida Nation v. British Columbia (Minister of Forests)* and *Taku River Tlingit First Nation v. British Columbia (Project Assessment Director)* gave greater impetus to this need.

Litigation Strategies for the Offshore Region: A Hypothetical Reconnaissance

The statutory basis of offshore petroleum management has already been established. Authority for exploration and production in waters adjacent to the province of Nova Scotia is delegated to the Canada–Nova Scotia Offshore Petroleum Board. This jointly sponsored agency was established by the terms of an intergovernmental agreement known as the Canada–Nova Scotia Offshore Petroleum Resources Accord, signed on 26 August 1986. The territorial limit of the board's operations is defined by Schedule 1 of the Canada–Nova Scotia Offshore Petroleum Resources Accord Implementation Act of 1988 and covers provincial sectors in the Bay of Fundy, Gulf of St. Lawrence, and Cabot Strait, as well as the Atlantic continental shelf to the 200-mile limit. Under the provisions of this statute, the board is authorized to issue interests in the form of the exploration, production, and significant discovery licence.

The launch of an Aboriginal treaty or rights claim generally springs from a particular encounter between Aboriginal and non-Aboriginal interests that results in a legal challenge. The characteristics of the trigger event, as it were, are instrumental in transforming the political dispute into litigation. In any area of law, potential plaintiffs are well advised to select a strong case, one whose attributes embody the principles of law at issue. For example, James Matthew Simon's conviction for illegally possessing a hunting rifle in closed season was overturned on appeal on the grounds of a treaty right to hunt from 1752. Thomas Peter Paul's acquittal on charges of illegal logging on Crown land was first upheld and then overturned on the basis of a 1726 treaty right for traditional activities. Donald Marshall's conviction for fishing for eels without a licence and out of season was overturned on appeal on the grounds of a 1761 treaty right to trade in natural products, including fish.

There has yet to be an Aboriginal challenge on the issue of offshore petroleum; as a result, the following discussion is hypothetical. However, four scenarios can be considered, based on prior legal cases, to explore a possible Mi'kmaq position in subsea resources.

Assertion of a Treaty Right

Perhaps the strongest basis for a treaty right claim is the Treaty of Peace and Friendship of 1760-61. This treaty has been advanced in previous cases related to fishing and logging. In *R. v. Marshall* (1999), the Supreme Court of Canada found that this treaty contained a positive right to hunt, fish, and gather for trade to meet the necessaries of life. This was interpreted by Justice Binnie to mean the right to a moderate livelihood (though not to unlimited accumulation of wealth) through hunting, fishing, and trading. The case extended this right to eel fishing.

To date, the courts have been asked to address treaty rights to hunt, fish, and log. In general, it appears that, subject to the qualifying criteria, treaty guarantees such as those of 1760-61 extend readily to hunting and fishing. In each case, however, an argument for particular activities and uses must be made to the satisfaction of the court. The situation for the timber resource is somewhat different. In *R. v. Marshall; R. v. Bernard* (2005), Chief Justice Beverley McLachlin concluded in reference to the treaty of 1760-61:

> While the right to trade in traditional products carries with it an implicit right to harvest those resources, this right to harvest is the adjunct of the basic right to trade in traditional products. Nothing in the wording of the truckhouse clause comports a general right to harvest or gather all natural resources then used. The right conferred is the right to trade. The emphasis therefore is not on what products were used, but on what trading activities were in the contemplation of the parties at the time when the treaties were made. Only those trading activities are protected. Ancestral trading activities, however, are not frozen in time and the question in each case is whether the modern trading activity in issue represents a logical evolution from the traditional trading activities at the time the treaties were made.[32]

In the case of offshore petroleum, the activity in question extends beyond living resources. To address the question of subsurface petroleum, it may be helpful to recall the words of the Supreme Court of Canada in the *Marshall* clarification of November 1999:

> The September 17, 1999 majority judgment did not rule that the appellant had established a treaty right "to gather" anything and everything physically capable of being gathered. The issues were much narrower and the ruling was much narrower. No evidence was drawn to our attention, nor was any argument made in the course of this appeal, that trade in logging or minerals, or the exploitation of offshore natural gas deposits, was in the contemplation of either or both parties to the 1760 treaty; nor was the argument made that exploitation of such resources could be considered a logical evolution of treaty rights to fish and wildlife or to the type of things traditionally "gathered" by the Mi'kmaq in a 1760 Aboriginal lifestyle.[33]

This finding does not exclude arguments in favour of such exploitation and trade, but it does require that an evidentiary case be made for any such inclusions under treaty terms.

In this case, expert evidence might be adduced from a variety of fields and disciplines. For example, petroleum seeps, both crude oil and natural gas, have been part of Nova Scotia's terrestrial geology for thousands of years. Seeps occur in places where fractures in rock formations allow oil or natural gas to rise under pressure to the surface, where the oil pools and the gas disperses. Furthermore, it could be established that Mi'kmaq peoples have known of such sites both through discovery and through the transmittal of knowledge over generations. Indeed, the resource was likely of value to many Aboriginal people who followed a diversified seasonal round of hunting, trapping, and gathering activities sometimes situated at coastal locations and sometimes situated inland.

A case could turn on whether the modern activity of gathering and trading petroleum is a logical evolution from traditional trading activities. Citing McLachlin in *R. v Marshall; R. v. Bernard*, "Logical evolution means the same sort of activity, carried on in the modern economy by modern means. This prevents Aboriginal rights from being unfairly confined simply by changes in the economy and technology. But the activity must be essentially the same. 'While treaty rights are capable of evolution within limits, ... their subject matter ... cannot be wholly transformed' *(Marshall 2)*."[34] Absent such evidence, there likely will not be sufficient grounds for the logical evolution of a treaty right to subsurface petroleum.

Another possibility would be to base a claim on a treaty right to hunting and fishing that includes marine settings and stands to be infringed upon by the licensing of offshore exploration and production. For obvious reasons, this claim has not arisen in the distant offshore waters of the Scotian Shelf. However, the claim could well arise in the inshore waters affected by the controversial Cape Breton exploration licences. Assuming a successful grounding of the offshore fishing and hunting activity, the argument would turn on the extent of infringement imposed by the CNSOPB's regulation.

Assertion of Aboriginal Right

Members of the Mi'kmaq First Nations of Nova Scotia could also claim that they possess an Aboriginal right to subsurface resources by virtue of traditional and continuing use. This claim is distinct from treaty rights deriving from eighteenth-century treaties between the Crown and Mi'kmaq. Since the treaties stop short of acknowledging or enumerating all harvesting activities that formed part of the traditional life on the land, it follows that those not stipulated by treaty but practised in pre-contact times could continue as rights unless they were otherwise expressly extinguished. This was the finding of the Nova Scotia Court of Appeal in *Denny, Paul and Sylliboy* (1990). The accuseds' conviction for violating federal fisheries regulations for the catch of salmon and cod was reversed on the basis of an Aboriginal right to fish (the possibility of a treaty right to fish was not considered by the court).[35] It could be argued, for example, that Aboriginal peoples made use of subsurface petroleum as it rose to the surface by natural means. The petroleum provided waterproofing for boats and served as an inflammatory fuel, among other uses, and as such was integral to Aboriginal society.

The operative tests for recognition of an Aboriginal right under section 35(1) begin with the "practices, customs and traditions" criteria delineated by Chief Justice Lamer in *R. v. Van der Peet.* The burden of demonstrating that the activities in question formed part of Mi'kmaq customs, practices, and traditions at the time of European contact lies with the plaintiffs. It could be that the evidence relating to subsurface petroleum, accessible through seeps to the surface, faces two problems. First, the vagaries of geological structure mean that seeps are occasional and scattered phenomena. Across the territories inhabited by Mi'kmaq, they might not have been generally or sufficiently available to form part of regular use. These problems of extent and continuity could impede the successful assertion of petroleum gathering and use. Second, the purpose of the resource use is not certain. Even if the existence of a traditional gathering practice was accepted, it can be asked whether the practice applied to more than domestic consumption. The case law on fisheries and logging is clear on this point: it distinguishes between the activities of harvesting for subsistence and harvesting for commerce or exchange. In sum, it would be challenging, though perhaps not impossible, to meet the *Van der Peet* test in this case.

An alternative would be to focus not on the petroleum resource but on traditional marine resources, a strategy that would entail the assertion of a sea-based right to hunt and fish. Evidence could be brought that Mi'kmaq people were maritime harvesters. They fished as crews in traditional boats and hunted seals in the water and on ice. Indeed, Cape Breton Mi'kmaq travelled as far as Îsles de la Madeleine to harvest marine species. Such a claim could entail a continuous and exclusive occupancy of the sea surface and the harvest of animals supported by the saltwater column. A stable seabed is integral to the realization of such entitlements. Consequently, to the extent that petroleum exploration and development disrupt marine animal movements and their habitat, it infringes on Aboriginal people's marine hunting and fishing rights.

Assertion of Aboriginal Title

An alternative argument could be advanced in the form of a right to subsurface petroleum by virtue of Aboriginal ownership or title. The opinion of Chief Justice Lamer in *Delgamuukw v. British Columbia* is relevant to this argument. That action arose out of a claim by the Gitxsan and Wet'suwet'en peoples, whose forbears had never signed treaties with the Crown. In the present case, the plaintiffs could assert a similar claim. Since the eighteenth-century colonial treaties of peace and friendship had no bearing on land ownership or the transfer of title, this would appear to leave alive the question of ongoing Aboriginal title.

As defined by Chief Justice Lamer, Aboriginal title is sui generis: it falls somewhere between European fee simple (private property) title and Aboriginal rights of activity upon Crown lands. Lamer also points out that such title entails the right to use lands for certain purposes related to the traditional attachments to the land, though title is subject to the limitation that these uses not be incompatible with traditional attachments. To establish proof of title, an Aboriginal group must demonstrate a traditional occupancy at the time of sovereignty that was both continuing and exclusive. It is important to remember that these criteria must be applied in a manner that respects the culture of the Aboriginal peoples at the time, in order to uphold the honour of the Crown.

A successful argument would have to establish that ancestors of the plaintiffs, living on the lands now known as mainland Nova Scotia or Cape Breton Island, occupied the land in a manner both continuous and exclusive. The plaintiffs would not need to establish a permanent and fixed occupancy of a particular tract of land in the fashion of a pioneer settler or colonist with a grant of fifty acres. In a migratory culture, the standard of continuity could be met by the regularity of the seasonal rounds pursued by families and bands. The traditional use of rivers for spring fishing, wooded valleys for fall hunting, or coastal plains and inlets for sealing, whaling, and ceremonial gatherings is well established in tribal narratives and archaeological artifacts. That such practices were pursued over centuries and in some cases millennia could lend a force to the concept of continuity that the more recently established European culture could scarcely rival. The quality of exclusive occupancy would also have to be met. In the period prior to the assertion of British sovereignty (for Cape Breton Island, before 1763) the Mi'kmaq peoples were primary occupants of the territory. Certain enclaves were assumed by the French – at Louisbourg and several coastal settlements – but never to the detriment of ongoing Aboriginal occupation.

The next step would be to determine which traditional attachments to the land formed part of Mi'kmaq occupancy related to title. In particular, what is the role of the gathering, use, and trade of the offshore petroleum resource? It is important to keep in mind that offshore petroleum as distinct from terrestrial petroleum is at issue here. There may be two possible avenues to establish this attachment.

The weighing of the evidence would likely be guided by McLachlin's observation in *R. v. Marshall; R. v. Bernard* that "to insist that the pre-sovereignty practices correspond in some broad sense to the modern right claimed, is not to ignore the aboriginal perspective. The aboriginal perspective grounds the analysis and imbues its every step. It must be considered in evaluating the practice at issue, and a generous approach must be taken in matching it to the appropriate modern right. Absolute congruity is not required, so long as the practices engage the core idea of the modern right."[36] It might yet be a challenge to establish "the core idea of the modern right" to petroleum use. The question of a sea-based fishery is a different matter, and the plausibility of a sea-based right to petroleum ownership or use would have to be made.

An alternative avenue of connection to offshore petroleum may be proposed by way of geological contiguity. In this argument, some sedimentary formations that underlie coastal waters may be shown to be connected integrally to land-based formations. An Aboriginal title that extends to terrestrial petroleum could thereby carry over to its offshore counterpart. While the question need not turn simply on the state of geological science, it could be argued that the petroleum potential of the Atlantic continental shelf derives precisely from its offshore character. Its geology is distinct from that found onshore, and the offshore region is a geological "province" distinct from those of terrestrial Canada. Even more importantly, considerations of the core idea concept apply here as well.

In sum, while it is not impossible to assert a Mi'kmaq Aboriginal title to the subsea resources of the region in question, it may not be the strongest avenue of advance.

The Crown Duty to Consult and Accommodate

As seen above, the right to Aboriginal title is one possibility that can be portrayed along a spectrum of Aboriginal rights. Title conveys a form of ownership, albeit a type different from fee simple. The courts describe Aboriginal title as sui generis – of its own kind – to stress its distinguishing features. In contemporary times, the pivotal Supreme Court decision on title has been *Delgamuukw*, in which Chief Justice Lamer reviews past case law before enunciating a defining position that "what Aboriginal title confers is a right to the land itself."[37] Accordingly, the tests for proof of Aboriginal title must be adapted from the *Sparrow* and *Van der Peet* criteria for Aboriginal rights. Title claimants must prove occupancy prior to the time when sovereignty was asserted and that occupation was exclusive to that Aboriginal group.

At the same time, Lamer reiterates that "the Aboriginal rights recognized and affirmed by section 35(1), including Aboriginal title, are not absolute."[38] Since the rights may be justifiably infringed by either the federal or provincial Crowns, the criteria of justification are of first order of importance. As developed in *Sparrow* and in *Van der Peet,* the first test is that the legislative objective in question be "compelling and substantial." Second, the infringement must be "consistent with the special fiduciary responsibility between the Crown and aboriginal peoples."[39] Fiduciary duty, Lamer observes, may be articulated in many ways, depending on the nature of the Aboriginal right in question. If we take Aboriginal title, for instance, the relevant aspects are that it is an exclusive right to use and occupy land, that it encompasses a right to choose the uses to which the land can be put, and that such lands have an inescapable economic component.[40]

For Lamer, it follows that "the fiduciary duty between the Crown and aboriginal peoples may be satisfied by the involvement of aboriginal peoples in decisions taken in respect to their lands. There is always a duty of consultation."[41] In certain cases, where the infringement is relatively minor, this may be sufficient, provided that the consultation is conducted in good faith. However, "in most cases, [the fiduciary duty] will be significantly deeper than mere consultation. Some cases may even require the full consent of an aboriginal nation."[42] Finally, given the economic dimension of title, "fair compensation will ordinarily be required when aboriginal title is infringed."[43] The *Delgamuukw* ruling therefore altered the basis of Aboriginal title law and the role of Crown authorities in meeting it. As the province directly affected, British Columbia spent several years overhauling its resource administrative and managerial regimes to align sufficiently with the Supreme Court's criteria.[44] Although other Crown authorities paid varying degrees of attention to this judicial finding, Aboriginal litigants reconsidered their prospects in light of the decision.

One of the first cases to follow *Delgamuukw* was the Haida's claim for Aboriginal title to their homelands, Haida Gwaii (the Queen Charlotte Islands), and associated waters. The point at issue in *Haida Nation v. British Columbia (Minister of Forests)* was the transfer of a tree farm licence to Weyerhaeuser Company in the face of an Aboriginal title claim and without the consent (indeed, over the objections) of the Haida. The legal challenge to the licence transfer was launched in 1999 and sought to have the transfer set aside on the grounds of non-consultation.

Just as *Delgamuukw* required the Crown to expand its duty to consult (beyond that contemplated in *Sparrow* and *Van der Peet*), so too did *Haida Nation*. Writing for the majority, Chief Justice McLachlin held that "depending on the circumstances ... the honour of the Crown may require it to consult and reasonably accommodate Aboriginal interests pending resolution of the [title] claim."[45] This conclusion is rooted in Lamer's purposeful interpretation of section 35(1) as the reconciliation of the pre-existence of Aboriginal society with the sovereignty of the Crown. Influenced by the commentary of legal scholars Sonia Lawrence and Patrick Macklem, Chief Justice McLaghlin offered a new view of reconciliation as less of an outcome and more of a process of conflict resolution. In particular, "the duty to consult and accommodate is part of a process of fair dealing and reconciliation that begins with the assertion of sovereignty and continues beyond formal claims resolution. Reconciliation is not a final legal remedy in the usual sense. Rather, it is a process flowing from rights guaranteed by sec. 35(1)."[46]

This finding sprang in part from the danger that unilateral Crown decisions, taken during the time when title claims are under preparation and negotiation but not yet settled, may reduce the benefits to future title holders. It also raised the corollary issue of when the duty to consult is triggered? In *Haida Nation*, the answer is that "the duty arises when the Crown has knowledge, real or constructive, of the potential existence of the Aboriginal right or title and contemplates conduct that might adversely affect it."[47] Recognizing the problem faced by the Crown in not knowing the actual extent in law of the asserted right, the court offered advice on possible Crown responses to a knowledge of potential existence. For the Crown, the scope of the duty is proportionate to (1) the preliminary assessment of the strength of the Aboriginal case for the existence of the right and (2) the seriousness of the potential adverse effect. Accordingly, a spectrum of duties can be envisaged, ranging from weak claims and limited rights that carry low infringement to strong claims and significant rights that carry high infringement. While the Crown is under no obligation to reach agreement (i.e., consultation does not equal achieving agreement), it is obliged to engage in a meaningful process of consultation in good faith. For McLachlin, accommodation arises when consultation "suggests amendment of Crown policy." Furthermore, situations at the "strong consequence" end of the spectrum may "reveal a duty to accommodate." At the same time, McLachlin noted, Aboriginal groups do not possess a veto: "The accommodation that may result from pre-proof consultation is just this – seeking compromise in an attempt to harmonize conflicting interests and move further down the path of reconciliation."[48] In the case of the tree farm licence, since the Haida had advanced a good prima facie case, and since the provincial Crown had recognized the implications of its decision for Aboriginal rights, there was a duty to both consult and accommodate.

Of equal note is *Taku River Tlingit First Nation v. British Columbia (Project Assessment Director)*, released simultaneously with *Haida Nation*. In this case, the First Nation challenged a provincial Crown decision to permit construction of a road to a mine site across lands subject to an Aboriginal title claim.[49] The court found the impacts of the road to be high, thereby justifying more than minimal consultation. The Supreme Court found that the Crown's duties to consult and accommodate had been fulfilled: a formal environmental review had been convened under the terms of legislation, the Taku River Tlingit had been full participants in the process, and mitigative measures had been stipulated in issuing the road permit. Together, the *Haida Nation* and *Taku* decisions demarcated a range of rights-claiming situations and acceptable responses.

Prior to the Supreme Court's decisions in *Haida Nation* and *Taku River Tlinglit*, certain lower court decisions held that such duties were not triggered until a section 35 right had been confirmed either politically or juridically. It could be argued that *Haida Nation* and *Taku River Tlinglit* have rendered this position untenable. The Crown must now only be aware of the Aboriginal claim, and the claim must be supported by a good prima facie case.

The next step would be to consider the scope of the duty and the possible accommodation. This process would begin with a preliminary assessment of the strength of the asserted right or title and would continue with a parallel assessment of the seriousness of its potential impact. In *Haida Nation*, McLachlin suggests the existence of a spectrum of consultation. If the case is weak, then formal notice to Aboriginal peoples, together with an opportunity to discuss (i.e., learn more) about the proposed decision, may suffice. However, faced with a stronger case for a right or title, there is a case for deeper consultation, including possible consent.

The "consultation trilogy" was completed by a 2005 case that amplified the Supreme Court's view on the necessary processes of consultation. *Mikisew Cree First Nation v. Canada (Minister of Canadian Heritage)* addressed the issue of how consultation affected a treaty right. In the case in question, the federal Crown had exercised its taking-up right to land under

Treaty 8 to build a winter road in northern Alberta that reduced the hunting and fishing territory on which the Cree held a treaty right to harvest. The Crown had approved and then modified the road proposal without targeted band consultation. It justified its actions on the grounds that its taking-up right was itself treaty-based and, therefore, could not infringe on an Aboriginal treaty right. The court held that the Crown's duty had not been met and continued:

> While [the Crown] has a right to "take up" surrendered lands, [it] is nevertheless under the obligation to inform itself on the impact its project will have on the exercise by the Mikisew of their treaty hunting, fishing and trapping rights and to communicate its findings to the Mikisew. The crown must then attempt to deal with the Mikisew in good faith and with the intention of substantially addressing their concerns. The duty to consult is triggered at a low threshold, but adverse impact is a matter of degree, as is the extent of the content of the crown's duty.[50]

Although the court found that not every take up of land would necessarily infringe on treaty rights and thus trigger a duty to consult, the duty does apply wherever the take up adversely affects the exercise of those rights. Furthermore, the sliding scale of consultation obligations applies to treaty issues. Although the road taking fell at the lower end of the consultation continuum, the Crown was deficient in notice, engagement, and effort to minimize adverse impacts on the Mikisew Cree.

The Supreme Court also offered a clarification that had implications for Maritime Canada about the potential scope of Crown consultation with First Nations signatories in large treaty territories. Treaty rights to hunt, fish, and trap are not held for the entire treaty area but are held on the basis of lands traditionally or presently used by a band. In effect, "the Crown is not required to consult with a First Nation about activities located outside those lands."[51]

The Nova Scotia Offshore Setting

As far as Nova Scotia is concerned, an opportunity for a challenge to the Crown duty (though not taken up at the time) was the Cape Breton Public Review Commission of 2000-1. At the close of an exploration licensing round on 1 July 1998, the CNSOPB granted two licences to Hunt Oil Company of Canada. Licences 2364 and 2365 conferred the right to explore

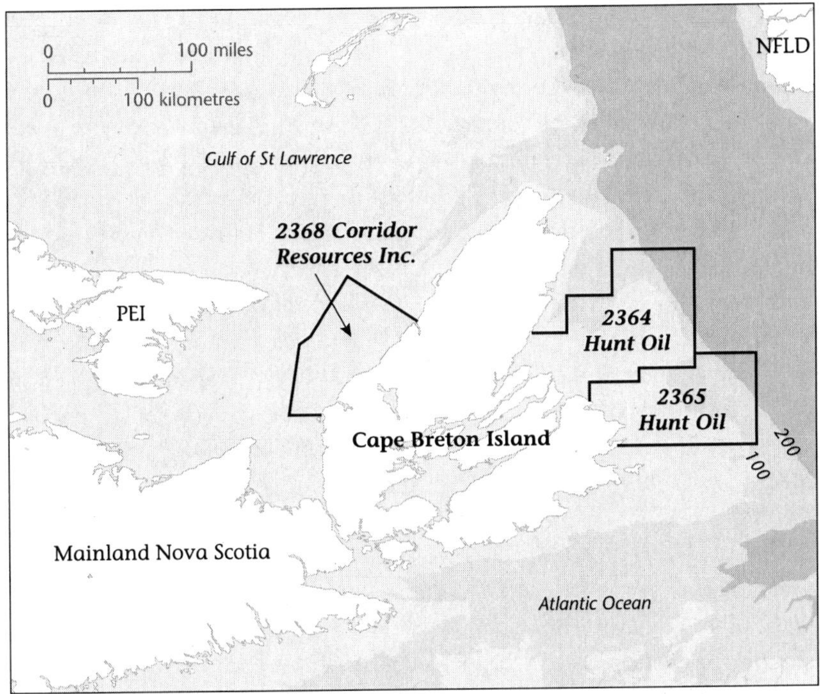

Map 11.2 Cape Breton offshore exploration licences, 1998-99
Source: Teresa MacNeil, Commissioner's Report (Halifax: CNSOPB, 2002), 7.

on 5,800 square kilometres in the area known as the Sydney Bight, situated in the Atlantic Ocean off the northeast coast of Cape Breton Island. In a subsequent round one year later, the board awarded Licence 2368 to Corridor Resources Inc. for exploration on 2,470 square kilometres in the Gulf of St. Lawrence off the west coast of Cape Breton Island. As is illustrated in Map 11.2, all three blocks began at the coastal margin. Although the board has issued hundreds of licences to offshore tracts within its jurisdiction, these were the first licences issued in coastal margin waters since the establishment of the board.

The licence holders then filed plans with the board, outlining programs of seismic activities within their licence areas. In such operations, specially equipped ships cruise in designated grid-like patterns, dragging arrays of sensing devices through the water behind them. Sound blasts are emitted at regular intervals, and the echoes that bounce back from subsea geological formations are collected and analyzed for evidence on petroleum prospects.

Throughout 2000, public concerns about seismic operations – and, more broadly, drilling in the licence areas – were voiced by fishing interests, environmental activists, Aboriginal organizations, and other citizen groups who warned of potential damage to the health of aquatic animals in the coastal margin and alterations to their behaviour. In response, the board ordered the license holders to cease seismic activities in the fall of 2000. In addition, the responsible federal and provincial ministers instructed the board to convene a public inquiry on the effects of potential exploration and production activities in the areas in question. Dr. Theresa MacNeil was appointed as a commissioner in 2001. Public hearings were held one year later, and a report was submitted in March 2002.[52] Following receipt of the public review report, and in response to its suggestion, the board encouraged a multi-stakeholder forum to pursue an understanding on abatement measures. The Ad Hoc Working Group brought together fifteen representatives from interested groups. Although many areas of consensus were reached, the representatives differed on "whether the level of potential risk was acceptable."[53] As a result, there was no unanimous recommendation on whether the board should allow seismic testing. Ultimately, the CNSOPB authorized the licence holders to proceed in 2004. Since then, limited seismic activity has been conducted.

The Union of Nova Scotia Indians chose to participate in the public review by submitting a written brief and following up with an oral submission. In December 2001, the Union stressed that the two Crown authorities "each owe a duty to the Mi'kmaq to consult with them about projects, developments and activities for which they may have any regulatory or decision-making authority that might impact on their constitutional rights."[54] Furthermore, the Union contended that "the duty to consult requires that consultations, discussions and negotiations take place in good faith, with the substantive objective of reaching an accommodation that recognizes and takes account of Mi'kmaq rights and interests." The brief noted the extent of traditional marine fishing activities and the fact that Aboriginal title has been asserted to all of Nova Scotia. In her report, MacNeil drew attention to the offshore title claims of Mi'kmaq and advised the two Crowns to engage in "early and full consultation" to explore the implications of these assertions. The Union of Nova Scotia Indians also joined in the deliberations of the Ad Hoc Working Group in 2002-3.

Then and now, Aboriginal plaintiffs could possibly seek a declaration from the courts that the initiatives of the CNSOPB, such as issuing coastal exploration licences, are violating a treaty or Aboriginal right or Aboriginal title enjoyed by the Mi'kmaq. Plaintiffs could seek a declaration from the court that their treaty and Aboriginal rights to the petroleum resource remain intact. Furthermore, they could seek an order to enjoin the Crown and the board from authorizing any further operations on the licences in question and any further issuance of offshore petroleum interests until these treaty and Aboriginal rights are satisfactorily acknowledged.[55]

Returning to the terms of the duty to consult laid out in *Haida Nation* and *Taku River Tlinglit,* a decision on the sufficiency of the public review commission, as a consultative mechanism on Aboriginal rights, would begin with the strength of the rights claim. The Union of Nova Scotia Indians might contend that, in light of an extensive traditional fishery right, a deep form of consultation – undertaken by the two Crowns rather than by a delegated inquiry – was required. On the other hand, the Crown would likely contend that, in light of the limited history of offshore rights recognition in Canada, the channels offered by the public review commission and the ad hoc consultation are commensurate with the state of the claims at the time.

The seriousness of the potential impact of the regulatory decisions under consideration must then be assessed. If exploration activity is allowed to proceed on the designated licences, what will be the consequences? The first stage of exploration entails two-dimensional seismic testing. Although it is distinct from and preliminary to exploratory drilling, much less production, there is a logical connection between seismic testing and drilling inasmuch as positive results in one will lead inexorably to the other. For this reason, concentrating on the seismic stage in isolation may be too narrow. The two leading impacts would appear to be (1) the risk of damage to coastal ecosystems and habitats supporting valued resources other than petroleum and (2) the risk of the pre-emptive capture of a petroleum asset whose ultimate title is shared with Aboriginal claimants. The financial impact of the latter could be mitigated through revenue-sharing arrangements calculated and assigned at any time in the exploitative cycle. The former, however, may be deemed to carry a more absolute risk. If seismic testing has lethal effects on commercial species or the food chain species related to them or sub-lethal effects on larval and juvenile animals that undercut resource availability in subsequent generations, such damage is not remediable.

The licensing of offshore exploration blocks may lead to a moderately strong case and a highly serious potential impact. If so, the spirit of the Crown's fiduciary obligation might well elevate the substance of the case to the highest level. In seeking a standard of duty in this case, a form of deep consultation may be deemed necessary, geared toward finding a satisfactory interim solution.

Attention would then turn to an examination of the consultation undertaken by the board and other Crown representatives in their licensing functions. Because the CNSOPB's activities are regulatory in nature, the weight of factors in *Taku River Tlingit* is both analogous and instructive. In that case, it was determined that the Crown was not required to establish a separate regulatory consultation strictly with Aboriginal people. The British Columbia Environmental Assessment process was already available to channel these concerns. However, the British Columbia Act explicitly directs Crown agents to include Aboriginal consultation in any environmental review.

It is significant that no similar procedure or statutory directive informs the board's procedure for opening new subregions within its purview to exploration. To clarify, the board and its predecessors have superintended petroleum activities in the Sable Island subregion since the 1970s. In the late 1980s, proposals were advanced by corporate explorers seeking to commence work in the Georges Bank subregion (well-apart from Sable). More recently, Corridor and Hunt Canada opened, by their licence nominations, yet another subregion not previously placed under permit. This Cape Breton initiative occurred at a time when section 35 rights are broadly being asserted in the Atlantic provinces. Parenthetically, these circumstances could point toward the need for an explicit direction, either in a statute or subordinate legislation, to acknowledge Aboriginal interests in the process.

The absence of formal directives or a formal scheme for consultation may be viewed as a significant omission. Certainly, the option was open, to both federal and provincial Crowns, to direct their joint agent (the board) to modify its regulatory procedures in this way. In effect, the obligation for Aboriginal consultation could have been integrated into the pre-existing duties of the board. The National Energy Board, in other petroleum-related deliberations, adopted a memorandum of guidance on consultation with Aboriginal peoples in 2002.

The Crown respondents to this sort of action would presumably document the pertinent consultative processes. This would cover actions from the year 2000. The public inquiry headed by Dr. MacNeil, together with the subsequent Ad Hoc Working Group consultation, offered avenues for Aboriginal input, along with that of other regional stakeholders. These were not insignificant measures. However, the central question would be whether they squared with the level of consultation and accommodation required in the present case – a combination of a moderately strong case and a highly serious potential impact.

By this measure, the Crown may face difficulty in meeting the necessary standards of the duty to consult, opening the way to granting an Aboriginal application. This need not, however, quash the board's licensing orders in their entirety. The court could grant a declaration that the government has a duty to consult, at the requisite levels, and perhaps suspend the operation of this decision for a transitional period to enable the Crown and Aboriginal interests to continue consultations. The present, a time when exploration activity on the Scotian Shelf is at an all-time low, might be a politically expeditious moment for this to occur.

An Alternative Political Pathway

The cases described above were all complex, lengthy, and expensive legal struggles that were only initiated or defended after careful strategic consideration. Given the unpredictable character of such litigation, it would also be wrong to infer that the process was simply linear. A sort of dialectical interplay characterizes legal and political streams of action. For example, the *Calder* decision drove the Government of Canada to acknowledge the continuing existence of Aboriginal title, and the *Simon* and *Denny* decisions forced the Government of Nova Scotia to abandon its denial of contemporary treaty rights in resource harvesting. Landmark judicial rulings also sparked political and administrative remedies within governments. *Sparrow* led the Department of Fisheries and Oceans to develop an Aboriginal fisheries strategy, while *Marshall* prompted a new implementation program for Atlantic Mi'kmaq.

In a cumulative sense, the litigation of the 1990s also catalyzed new institutional initiatives in an effort to shift the resolution of questions about land, resource, and governance rights from the courts into negotiated political channels. In Nova Scotia this was formalized in January 2001, when federal and provincial ministers and Mi'kmaq leaders agreed to convene talks to develop an umbrella agreement to resolve constitutional issues of rights, title, and governance. An agreement was signed eighteen months later in June 2002. The agreement sketched out three distinct work plans: one that continued a tripartite forum established in 1997 to deliberate on non-constitutional issues (such as education, health, justice, and economic development); a new initiative on section 35 treaty and Aboriginal rights (to be elaborated by a subsequent framework agreement); and a new initiative to agree on a consultation process that would enable government authorities and Mi'kmaq to hold working discussions connected to proceedings at the larger table.[56]

The following year, the process gathered momentum. In June 2003, the three parties named their negotiators for the talks. In the autumn, work on the framework agreement began. Four years later the Framework Agreement was signed by the three parties.[57]

Progress was also made on the consultation process, which would govern contacts between the governments and Mi'kmaq authorities on a range of matters pursuant to land and resource administration. The purpose of the consultation process aligns closely with the federal and provincial Crown's duty to consult on any issue pertinent to Aboriginal title. The need for a defined process grew more urgent following the *Haida Nation* and *Taku River Tlinglit* decisions of 2004. Under the process outlined in the umbrella agreement, the goal was to agree on terms of reference for consultative activities. The governments reviewed the draft terms during the winter of 2005-6.

As further evidence of the accommodative arrangements that could be agreed upon below the framework negotiating table, a bilateral preconsultation protocol was struck between the Mi'kmaq negotiating office (Kwilmu'ke Maw-klusuaqn) and Nova Scotia. The underlying premise was to enable the parties to have contact prior to the formal consultation period and off-the-record or "without prejudice" talks prior to formal negotiations. The Kwilmu'ke Maw-klusuaqn established a standing committee to serve as a conduit. As a result of the committee's work, the Government of Nova Scotia has expressed regret for not consulting Mi'kmaq prior to the transfer of Crown forestry rights from Kimberly-Clark to Neenah Paper. The government has also invited Mi'kmaq consultations on energy issues (including offshore petroleum). The CNSOPB has invited the Assembly of Nova Scotia Mi'kmaq Chiefs to name a representative to the board's Fisheries Advisory Committee. The Department of Natural Resources has invited Mi'kmaq involvement in several strategic deliberations affecting wildlife, forestry, and lands.[58]

Most recently, the Kwilmu'ke Maw-klusuaqn has launched an intensive consultation with members of the thirteen First Nations on their goals and priorities for the substantive talks that will follow the framework agreement. Each party will submit an interests statement to guide the definition of negotiating mandates along with approval of the framework agreement.

Conclusion

It is evident that the judicial interpretations of section 35 rights in the Constitution Act, 1982, have the potential to transform the offshore polity, just as they have the management of terrestrial natural resources in Canada. This potential underlines the importance of the courts as a discrete venue of state power, particularly the Supreme Court of Canada, where the tensions between constitutional rights and statute law are most prominently arbitrated. This is not an entirely new development. British Columbia's reference case on offshore mineral rights in 1967 strengthened Ottawa's legal position vis-à-vis the coastal provinces. Two decades later, questions of offshore jurisdiction were again adjudicated in British Columbia and in Newfoundland.

However, the cutting edge of Aboriginal rights rulings since 1985 is of a different order. They have enabled a new set of non-governmental interests to contest some of the basic coordinates of Crown title to lands and resources. This process began with a set of claims to activity-based rights in which various Aboriginal pursuits – hunting, fishing, gathering, and logging – were weighed in terms of constitutional protection. Landmark rulings over the past thirty years have begun to carve out the substantive protections that are contained within section 35(1), although the process is ongoing. Within this spectrum of activities, there may be room for offshore title rights, to the petroleum resource itself or to marine hunting and fishing, which could be jeopardized by offshore exploration and production. A second path to protection has also emerged, starting in 1997 with the Supreme Court's ruling in *Delgamuukw*. This option is based on the Crown's duty to consult with Aboriginal peoples whose constitutional rights may be undermined by administrative action under statute. It entails an obligation of specific and meaningful consultation with those Aboriginal groups that stand to be affected and, in some cases, a possible requirement to secure the consent or compensate the affected groups, according to the scale of the infringement. The duty was initially outlined in relation to Aboriginal title (and title claims) but has since been broadened to include treaty rights. The limitations on Crown power by virtue of the duty are potentially profound and remain in the early stages of judicial scrutiny. At a minimum, they constitute a form of procedural restraint in the obligations to notify and consult seriously. There may also be a substantive dimension to the duty insofar as the obligation extends to integrating Aboriginal considerations into plans and policies (in effect, a substantive right to a particular outcome).

Richard Devlin describes such combined substantive and procedure protections as a body of prostantive rights.[59]

As far as offshore petroleum is concerned, the nature and extent of Mi'kmaq rights remains legally untested. The pattern of litigation of section 35 rights has grown to encompass multiple resources, by virtue of Aboriginal challenges that were often given little initial chance of success. The federal Department of Fisheries and Oceans was caught by surprise by the *Sparrow* ruling on domestic Aboriginal fisheries in 1990 and was obliged to rework its licensing priorities and fashion an Aboriginal fisheries strategy. A similar bureaucratic catharsis followed the *Marshall* case on eel fishing in Atlantic Canada in 1997. In the aftermath of the *Delgamuukw* ruling on Aboriginal title to Gitxsan and Wet'suwet'en tribal territories, the province of British Columbia was obliged to rework its administrative protocols to meet the standard of meaningful consultation on any resource project. The New Brunswick timber management regime was shaken momentarily by Thomas Peter Paul's victory in asserting in the lower courts a treaty right to log on Crown land. It is not beyond possibility that offshore petroleum could in the future be added to this list.

A challenge could be mounted on several grounds. A treaty case could be made on the basis of traditional use of oil seeps in domestic, and perhaps traded, cultural goods. An alternative path may see a claim advanced on the basis of an unextinguished Aboriginal right or title, particularly in light of the limited surrenders involved in the treaties of peace and friendship. Apart from a direct claim for subseabed petroleum, a potentially promising line would assert marine hunting and fishing rights in jeopardy of infringement by petroleum exploration and production. Perhaps the most promising line of challenge, in light of recent Supreme Court of Canada rulings, may involve the Crown's failure to consult meaningfully before licensing offshore exploration and production in settings subject to title claims. In any event, it would seem that Crown title to offshore submerged lands may prove to be more complicated than is conventionally thought.

12 Conclusion

The dialectic that drives offshore petroleum development is an intricate distillation of regulations and risks. Some rules are framed as part of the offshore regulatory regime, inscribed in statute, intergovernmental accord, or agency order. Others are the products of wider state policy measures whose application impinges on petroleum exploration and production. The laws on environmental assessment, federal-provincial equalization, liquefied natural gas pipeline licensing, and Aboriginal rights come to mind. The same can be said of risks, which can take many forms. There is the geological uncertainty involved in exploration and the price and earnings uncertainty that arises from fluctuating market values. There is also risk in the political realm associated with the choice of governing instruments and the timing of policy interventions. The Scotian Basin's prospects for oil and gas production have played out on this complex political and economic canvas.

At the centre of Nova Scotia's offshore sector is an elaborate system of governance. To some, this governance system is a ponderous and clumsy structure that is, at best, neutral and, at worst, dysfunctional in its developmental impacts. To others, the system is a tenuous and uneven compromise between the competing interests of petroleum capital, host governments, and regional publics – the best system that could be created under the circumstances. This book suggests that there is no single resolution to such debates. The breadth of state policy and long history of the offshore industry requires a nuanced and qualified approach.

Any jurisdiction that enters into the world of offshore petroleum encounters diverse economic, social, and political interests. More accurately, that jurisdiction will both confront and create an interest-group universe of mounting diversity. The politics of offshore petroleum development in the Scotian Basin came to light in a series of issue areas or policy subsectors that changed over time. Among these subsectors, the lead role has shifted as new challenges have surfaced, new problems have been discovered, and new crises have erupted.

Many of the driving forces of political challenge and policy response are endogenous to the offshore upstream petroleum domain. These forces arise as exploration and production activity unfolds, and the notion of the basin development cycle is a valuable analytic tool to capture them. The notion not only captures the range of activities that simultaneously take place within an offshore region, it also underlines the engineering, commercial, and political correlates of distinct phases of development and their inevitable interpenetration. It also helps to explain how the upstream sector fits into the wider hydrocarbon economy. Scotian Basin products can only be realized in markets that are political as well as commercial constructs.

At the same time, there are exogenous pressures that originate outside of the offshore oil and gas system but impinge on its operations in profound ways. Some of these pressures arise from the prior presence of social and political interests in adjacent subsystems. This book establishes the significance of claimants in various circles: fisheries, the environmental movement, onshore business and labour, and Aboriginal groups. Other pressures arise from the extension of pre-established state instruments – statutes and policies of general application – to the emerging offshore domain. For example, petroleum royalty and tax collection needed to be fit into an existing intergovernmental fiscal paradigm that included equalization. The arrival of a new class of offshore vessels in the form of drill platforms and ships had to be assimilated into the marine environmental framework. Perhaps the most dramatic instances of policy spillover were triggered in the international oil market and in successive generations of federal environmental regulation. The foundations of the federal government's petroleum policy were redrawn three times in the period between 1973 and 1985. In addition, the unfolding of the federal government's environmental assessment regime in the late 1990s transformed the environmental protocols for offshore activities. Somewhat less dramatically, the Oceans Act of 1997 inaugurated a period of marine planning and protection that led to Sable Gully's designation as a protected site and an integrated ocean management policy. Finally, when currents of regulatory "reform" swirled periodically in Ottawa and Halifax in the early 2000s, the Nova Scotia petroleum regime was not exempt.

Parameters of the Offshore State

Two of the most powerful political force fields affecting Scotian Basin petroleum are those of federalism and the market. Under federalism, national and provincial state authorities interact as they assert jurisdictional claims. Under the market, the forces of capital interact with those of the states as they make investments in exploration and production.

The tension between the federal government and the provincial government can be captured as it shifts over time. The balance point between the two levels is dynamic and capable of moving from a highly centralized state (to 1980) to a more balanced or intermediate position (the 1980s) to a more decentralized position (1995-2010).

The capital-state relationship enjoys primacy because of the privileged position of market interests, which enter politics with a variety of structural advantages. Leverage may spring from a cultural bias toward property interests (the investor's prerogative), the disciplining impact of markets (the pricing factor), or the superior organizational resources of corporations and their capacity for collective action, to name only a few. At the same time, capital is not always hegemonic, as this book shows. Electoral and interest-group politics enable non-business interests to influence and, occasionally, control policy agendas. Conflicts inevitably arise among particular fractions of offshore and onshore capital that can undermine its collective strength. Also, state agencies can assert institutional interests of their own that can take precedence over societal and capital claims. Finally, within a policy subsector, political relationships can change over time, as with the obsolescing bargain.

By adding a temporal dimension, this book underscore's the cumulative character of policy making and power relations. The notion of path dependency captures the way in which prior decisions shape present and future options. The accumulation of vested interests shape the limits of the possible – put another way, the weight of past decisions limits the range of future possibilities. A closer attention to temporal sequences also highlights the interplay of factors at critical moments. Figure 12.1 summarizes the cumulative developments, intersections, and contradictions of the past five decades. In particular, it highlights trends in exploration and production

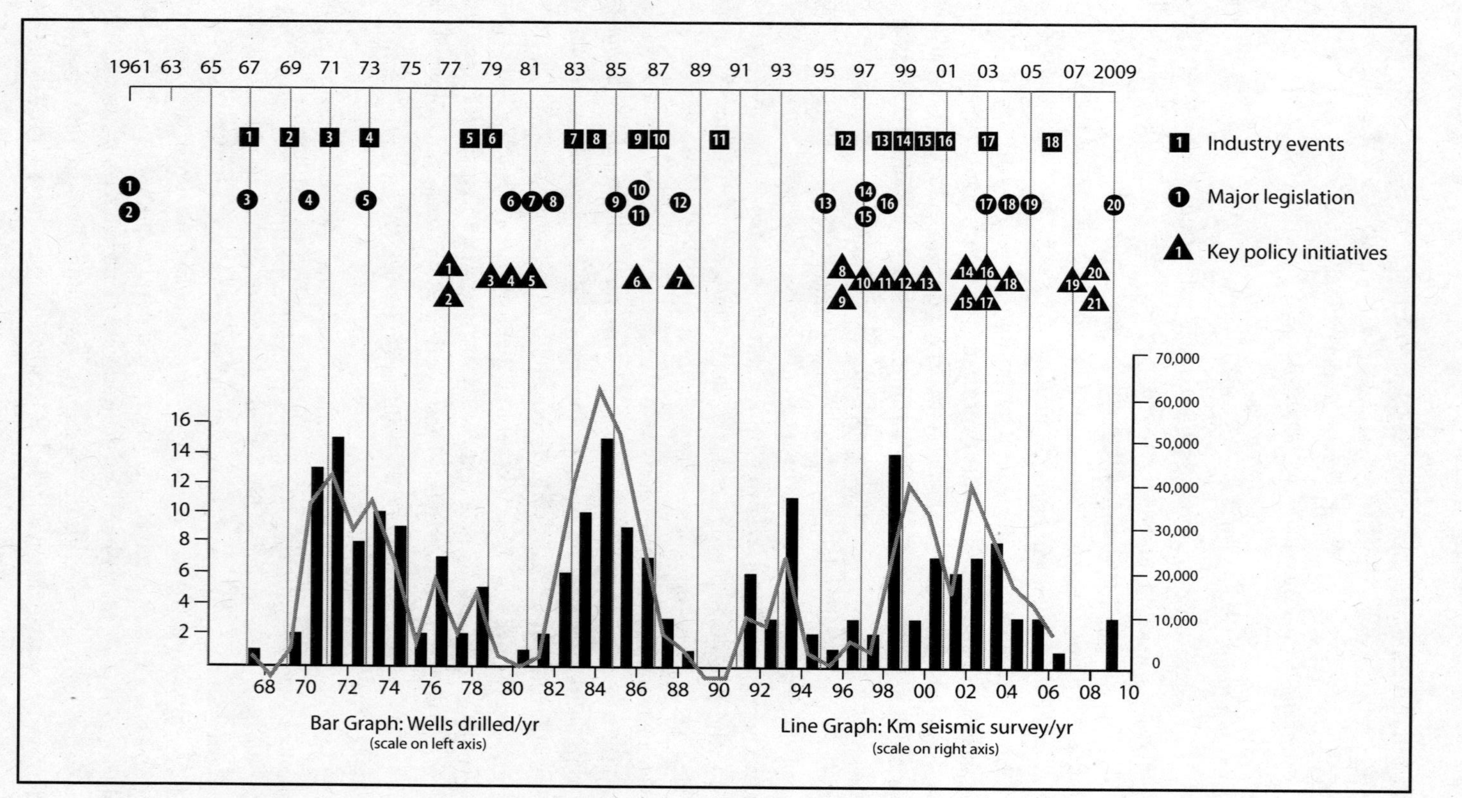
Industry events
Major legislation
Key policy initiatives
Bar Graph: Wells drilled/yr
(scale on left axis)
Line Graph: Km seismic survey/yr
(scale on right axis)

■ Industry events		● Major legislation		▲ Key policy initiatives	
1	1st Sable Well 67	1	Can O&G Land Regs 61	1	Frontier Super-D incentives 77
2	1st gas disc 69	2	Can O&G Drilling & Prod Regs 61	2	MOU Min Resources Offshore 77
3	Sable E-48 71	3	*Re: Offshore Min Rights of BC 67*	3	NSRL established 79
4	Cohasset oil disc 73	4	O&G Prod & Con Act 70	4	National Energy Program 80
5	1st deepwater well 78	5	Petro-Canada Act 73	5	COGLA established 81
6	Venture D-23 gas disc well 79	6	NS Pet Res Act 80	6	PIP terminated 86
7	Venture gas project applic 83	7	Can O&G Act 81	7	Georges Bank moratorium 88
8	Uniacke & W Venture gas blowouts 84	8	Can-NS OOGR Accord 82	8	NS Generic Royalty Scheme 96
9	Panuke B-90 oil disc 86	9	Atlantic Accord 85	9	SOEP Joint Public Review Panel 96
10	Venture gas project withdrawal 87	10	Can-NS Off Accord 86	10	GNS-SOEP MOU 97
11	COPAN oil flows 92	11	Can Petrol Resources Act 86	11	Jt Review Report and SOEP/MNP go-ahead 98
12	Sable Offshore Energy Project applic 96	12	Can-NS Off Accord Acts 88/9	12	Gas Distrib Franchise to Sempra Atlantic 99
13	Deep Panuke J-99 gas disc 98	13	CEAA 95	13	NS Fairness Campaign 00
14	COPAN last oil 99	14	NS Gas Distrib Act 97	14	Cape Breton Public Review 02
15	SOEI first gas 00	15	SCC: *Delgamuukw v BC* 97	15	Atlantic Energy Roundtable established 02
16	1st LNG (Keltic) proposal 01	16	NS Gas Distrib Regs 98	16	Gas distrib franchise to Heritage Gas 03
17	1st deepwater gas disc 03	17	CEAA amendments 03	17	NSRL assets sold 03
18	Well #204 (Dominion J-14) 06	18	Can-NS Fiscal Accord 04	18	Sable Gully Marine Protected Area 04
		19	SCC: *Mikisew Cree v Canada* 05	19	Deep Panuke Pt1 Approved 07
		20	Revised drill/production regs 09	20	NS Crown Share settlement 08
				21	GNS Offshore Renewal Plan 08

Figure 12.1 Political and economic trends and events in the Scotian Basin, 1961-2009

activity, significant industry milestones, legislative interventions, and policy initiatives.

The offshore petroleum state is a cumulative construct. In the Scotian Basin, there is no single blueprint for an offshore governance regime. Instead, it is an uneasy amalgamation of separate institutional layers. There was no moment when authorities convened to map out a unified and comprehensive system. Rather, a variety of departments and agencies acquired jurisdiction at differing times. Even before the 1958 UN Convention on the Continental Shelf, coastal states asserted jurisdiction over subsea oil and gas and enacted legislation to better secure their claims. Canada joined in this trend, first at the national and later at the provincial level. The process opened with a focus on Crown title and the issuance of exploration rights. As vessels appeared, wells were drilled, and discoveries were made, the pace of regulation accelerated. Agencies in charge of transportation, economic development, worker health and safety, fiscal relations, environmental protection, onshore infrastructure, and other areas asserted legislative and administrative mandates.

The closest approximation to a unified and consolidated offshore authority came in the 1980s with the creation of joint federal-provincial management structures. But the experiment was tentative and multi-staged. The Canada–Nova Scotia Offshore Oil and Gas Conservation Board, established by the 1982 Agreement on Offshore Oil and Gas Resource Management and Revenue Sharing, injected a new principle of shared decision-making but in a manner that tilted heavily toward federal paramountcy. In the 1985 Atlantic Accord, Newfoundland won a bolder design that was more genuinely intergovernmental: there was parity in the board's representation and a dedicated staff group that functioned independently of federal agencies. A year later, Nova Scotia gained a similar arrangement, by virtue of an updated accord and the Canada–Nova Scotia Offshore Petroleum Board (CNSOPB). The new policy provisions of the 1980s agreements went well beyond rights management to include a significant package of fiscal measures and industrial linkage targets. These measures were integral to achieving the central provincial goal of being the principal beneficiary of offshore petroleum development. In addition, terms were inserted for special consultative recognition of non-petroleum interests – in the fisheries sector and the onshore industrial workforce, as well as the public interest in environmental security.

Even though these new institutional arrangements went well beyond any previous bid for coordinated administration, there were definite limits to integration that were acknowledged as additional policy instruments were fashioned. When the advent of major projects triggered multiple statutory reviews, the logic of coordinated action was extended to the staging of joint regulatory proceedings. For the more mundane aspects of public administration, in which informal notification and information sharing would ease the pursuit of mandates, departments and agencies signed memorandums of understanding. When the perceived burden of cumulative regulation threatened to cloud the business climate, multi-stakeholder roundtable proceedings were launched.

The notion of the policy subsector helps to clarify the varied and specialized settings in which decision making takes place. As argued in the chapters above, the number of discrete subsectors has multiplied over the decades of offshore activity.

The analysis and comparison of policy subsectors offer an insightful means of establishing patterns of change. The subsectors identified in this study include Crown rights administration, offshore activity licensing, industrial benefits regulation, environmental security, fiscal relations, state entrepreneurship, onshore distribution, liquefied gas import and Aboriginal title. All impinge directly on the shape of offshore politics, of course. But at the same time there is value in distinguishing moments when the political priority or the issue-driving initiative shifts among them. For example, in the formative decades of the 1960s and 1970s, the imperative was the promotion of prospecting and discovery. Achieving a functional rights and title regime was central to this goal, and it proved far from an easy task given the undeveloped nature of offshore law and jurisdiction. Interstate rivalries also played a part as the ambition to control a new industry and capture a new revenue stream sometimes overpowered the need for stable and predictable corporate incentives. From 1965 onward, governments were also affected by a wider agenda of constitutional reform, and offshore jurisdiction figured as one of many bargaining points in the drive for consensus.

In October 1973, the political climate changed abruptly with the convulsions in the international petroleum market associated with the Arab-Israeli War and OPEC's response to it. National oil security emerged as a dominant political concern. This policy frame drove Canadian petroleum policy for the next ten years through successive iterations of federal policy and provincial response. It elevated the importance of offshore or frontier basins, particularly the fiscal matters of product pricing, royalty collection, and the capitalization of new ventures. Ultimately, this policy frame included the design of the joint management approach to the offshore resource.

During this time, other subsectors impinged on offshore exploitation with greater force. One subsector advanced the industrial-policy approach to upstream exploration and production and the determination to gain regional supply and employment benefits from the granting of offshore rights. Another subsector applied the environmental-assessment and protection techniques that were already gaining force in other settings. A third called for direct state equity investment as a technique to augment resource rents and shape the pace of commercial events. A fourth opened up new approaches to megaproject regulation and staging as the focus expanded from exploration to actual production.

The prolonged slump that hit the Atlantic offshore petroleum industry between 1987 and 1993 affected public authorities as well as private firms. The earlier sense of confidence and inevitability was punctured by the withdrawal of investment and the lapse of major projects. By the time that momentum began to recover in the 1990s, the range of market-driven forces had grown. Governments were grappling with budgetary crises that undercut many traditional expenditure tools, and continental petroleum markets were reconditioning business forces for an era of free trade. By this time, offshore authorities had a greater awareness of the complicated policy interconnections required for a well-rounded offshore production sector. The new offshore state relied more heavily on regulatory instruments rather than instruments of expenditure. Business-government bargaining over development plans, benefits plans, royalties, and infrastructure licensing were the new pacing levers of development in the Scotian Basin.

Beyond the familiar policy files and players, however, different sets of political relationships were building. A new site of political adjudication emerged in the Canadian courts of appeal, particularly the Supreme Court of Canada. This trend was driven by questions of Aboriginal rights and title and their degree of protection under the 1982 Constitutional Act. Aboriginal bands and citizens were the catalysts, and Crown authorities were largely reactive. The past three decades of litigation under section 35 have had a profound impact on resource management in fisheries, forestry, wildlife, and (as this book shows) oil and gas. By its nature, policy development through litigation is dispute driven, and the extent of change depends on the terms of judicial ruling. Prior cases, from *R. v. Simon* and *R. v. Sparrow* to *Haida Nation v. British Columbia* and *R. v. Bernard* have set the stage for a potentially profound recasting of offshore Crown title.

As gas production came onshore in 2000, the attention of provincial policy makers turned toward downstream issues such as provincial distribution and consumption. Long latent in the thinking of Nova Scotia's government officials, gas delivery assumed more urgent form as the Sable project progressed. This was a new subsector, and the answers lay in bureaus and agencies outside the orbit of the CNSOPB. That natural gas markets had recently been liberalized and that the policy-learning curve was steep, exacerbated the challenge. The initial general-licensing round ended in failure, and the process had to be reset on more modest terms.

The same can be said for the newly emerging industry of liquefied natural gas, in which a transformation in the global gas trade was injecting new competitive pressures. Nova Scotia figured as a potential landing site at a time when other North American coastal regions resisted the trend on political grounds. Of equal significance was the new industry's potential to sustain the onshore gas infrastructure at a time when the offshore primary supply remained uncertain. As with local gas distribution, the provincial government had a stronger potential role, though Ottawa remained pivotal through the powers of the National Energy Board. The regulatory nexus proved particularly complex, and the province also faced a challenge, ultimately successful, from a neighbouring, non-producing province.

The question arises, then, do any of these subsectors have critical status? This arises when a subsector holds a sufficiently central place in decision-making that its outputs constrain outputs in other subsectors and the trajectory of the policy sector as a whole. It is tempting to point to the rights-management and operational-regulations fields at the core of the CNSOPB as the critical subsector, given their gate-keeping role in offshore investment. However, the evidence points in a different direction. At key moments, the resource exploitation mandate has been overridden by other subsectors. Also, many of the critical regulatory levers are exercised by agencies outside of the joint management framework and operate independently of them. At the same time, no other subsector has consistently demonstrated a nodal character in the offshore field. Thus, when it comes to Scotian Basin petroleum, a striking feature is the absence of a critical subsector capable of constraining or ordering diffuse policy impulses.

The Nova Scotia Offshore State: Capacities and Outcomes

Throughout this book, the provincial state figures as a prominent animator of offshore politics. This raises the question, how successful has it been in realizing its goals? The sheer breadth of the offshore petroleum domain – spatially, temporally, and functionally – makes blanket judgments difficult, if not impossible. However, some conclusions are possible.

As far back as the mid-1960s, the Government of Nova Scotia announced its intentions for offshore petroleum at federal-provincial talks. The province sought to administer offshore petroleum just as it did in the onshore domain. Its goal was confounded by the Supreme Court of Canada's ruling in *Re: Offshore Mineral Rights, 1967*, which assigned to Ottawa jurisdiction for seabed resources. But it was the Mobil Canada strike of October 1971 that galvanized Premier Gerald Regan's excitement. Much of the early euphoria was dampened by Ottawa's energy policy responses to the OPEC oil boom. Indeed, Nova Scotia opted into the proposed Maritime Offshore Resources Board in 1977 to preserve a foothold in offshore developments. Conservative John Buchanan had other ideas, and Nova Scotia's subsequent withdrawal rendered the board stillborn. One conclusion was clear: in the newly politicized world of Canadian petroleum, there would be no watertight jurisdictions.

The upstream oil and gas industry mounted a significant commitment to the Scotian Basin in the 1970s that culminated with the Venture D-23 gas strike in 1979. Within a year, the Buchanan government had outlined a bold development vision. It convened conferences, issued strategy documents, enacted legislation, and established Nova Scotia Resources Limited. Prospects of industrial and employment prosperity, inspired by hasty visits to Galveston and Aberdeen, beguiled cabinet ministers.

Late in 1980, Nova Scotia and Ottawa clashed again following the release of the sweeping National Energy Program. For the province, the program was a double-edged sword. It brought powerful new tools to bear upon offshore exploration: Petroleum Incentive Payments, the Crown back-in option for Petro-Canada (or Nova Scotia Resources Limited), Canadian corporate content rules, and the Canadian Oil and Gas Lands Administration, a powerhouse agency for Canada Lands. At the same time, the National Energy Program largely pre-empted the province's role as Crown title holder and administrator.

Initially, it seemed that Nova Scotia would test its jurisdictional powers in court, as neighbouring Newfoundland was gearing up to do, but an exploration revival took hold on the Scotian Shelf. Buchanan changed tack, and Nova Scotia opted for a novel version of the joint management model. The 1982 agreement created the Canada–Nova Scotia Offshore Oil and Gas Board, sweeping away the legal and political uncertainties to tenure. The agreement also declared Nova Scotia's status as primary beneficiary for offshore development and ensured that the province would accrue royalties and enjoy leverage through board deliberations on licensing and benefits.

Nova Scotia Resources Limited was also unleashed as a provincial vehicle for an entrepreneurial stake. If the goal at this point was to kick-start basin exploration and steal a march on Newfoundland, it must be counted a success. The Scotian Shelf became a hot prospect in the early 1980s.

Almost immediately, Venture gas firmed up as a production prospect, and the sponsors made an application in 1983. These events seemed to vindicate concerted federal and provincial plans for early offshore petroleum supply. However, the volatile oil and gas markets shifted once again, this time in a downward direction that undermined the competitiveness of frontier supplies. The Scotian Basin began to cool by 1986, and the Venture project was suspended. Of parallel significance, the federal state's commitment to continental shelf petroleum and energy nationalism was reversed under the Mulroney Conservative government, elected in 1984. A business-oriented, market-leaning cabinet cancelled Petroleum Incentive Payments, abandoned Canadian content rules, rewrote the offshore tenure law, and began to deregulate the natural gas sector. Although the implications for the future of the joint management boards were not immediately evident, the shift in federal energy policy regimes was profound. As Ottawa stepped back from dirigiste frontier oil and gas management, the opportunities (and the imperative) for provincial management mounted.

In 1990, the CNSOPB became fully operative. Despite quiescent conditions in the basin, the Cohasset-Panuke (COPAN) oil project was tabled and ultimately approved. In this case, both the board and the Government of Nova Scotia learned valuable lessons about policy and management without the risk of being overwhelmed by industry pressures. As it turned out, the COPAN initiative was something of a swan song for Nova Scotia Resources Limited. Its decline was one more indicator that a Crown investment vehicle, so naturally a part of the nationalist past, was not suitable for a more market-driven petroleum strategy.

Nonetheless, the Government of Nova Scotia began to reassert itself and assume a more strategic role. John Savage's government took the initiative with the prospective partners to the Sable project. The new royalties deal enabled the partners to rapidly recover their capital costs before an enhanced profit-sharing royalty kicked in. From 1995, the provincial Petroleum Development Agency and later the Petroleum Directorate were designated lead actors for upstream policy matters. It is notable that, by this point, the application of the continental export business model went unquestioned for future offshore supply projects. For Nova Scotia, the range of new strategic issues expanded to include trunk pipelines, pipeline tariffs, and onshore gas distribution franchising. Later, the agenda was extended to include liquefied natural gas imports, offshore revenues and equalization, and a more integrated provincial energy strategy.

Throughout such encounters, the Government of Nova Scotia did not always prevail, nor did it always choose to fight. Halifax experienced repeated setbacks on the issue of the fairness of offshore royalties, waging an eight-year campaign in the face of prolonged federal resistance. The province failed absolutely to secure liquefied natural gas import terminal facilities to bolster the gas transportation infrastructure and ensure future domestic gas supplies. The lack of interest in an upstream Crown enterprise was bipartisan, and persistent misgivings about the value of Nova Scotia Resources Limited led to its somewhat disorderly unwinding. The Government of Nova Scotia also launched tripartite negotiations over the Mi'kmaq role in land and resource utilization, though without major results.

On the other hand, the Government of Nova Scotia has experienced some definite political gains. In its heyday, Nova Scotia Resources Limited was the prime mover for the first offshore oil production project at COPAN. Soon after, the government was the indispensable catalyst for the much more consequential Sable Offshore Energy Project. The province achieved some advantageous terms on the tariff regime for the Maritimes & Northeast Pipeline, setting the stage for gas distribution licensing. Nova Scotia defended the concept of the CNSOPB when the Chrétien Liberals were contemplating the board's abolition in the early 1990s. The province also strongly backed the benefits mandate that the board administered over almost three decades. On another front, Nova Scotia ultimately won (albeit with Newfoundland's weight added) a fair deal for offshore revenues. In the Department of Energy, the province forged a more reflective and innovative lead department in which offshore management retains a significant place.

Most of these accomplishments occurred while the federal government's interest in Scotian Basin resources was declining. In Ottawa, the national frame of reference for energy matters shifted elsewhere, overwhelmingly to the Alberta oil sands, a world-scale endowment whose second coming after 1995 has transformed the shape of Canadian petroleum production. Ottawa also turned its attention back to the Arctic, though a close study of northern pipeline regulation might suggest there is ambivalence here as well.

At present, Ottawa seems to see the Scotian Basin as a minor adjunct within the frontier lands envelope. The federal government frequently tolerates long delays in filling its seats on the CNSOPB when they come vacant.

A similar underestimation of the Scotian Basin is evident in Ottawa's persistent (and bipartisan) hardline on the offshore revenues issue. Indeed, a pattern can be discerned in federal involvement in basin politics since the Sable gas cycle began. Responsibility for Crown title was vested in the low-ranking Natural Resources Canada, while more senior departments and agencies (such as Finance, the National Energy Board, and even the Canadian Environmental Assessment Agency) were permitted to extend national policies without squarely addressing the legal and political priorities that were conferred on this region by the accords.

Looking forward, an intriguing question is whether the offshore policy and management template could be redirected, perhaps toward a regional focus under provincial direction? In other words, might the post-2005 slump give way, as it did in earlier slumps, to a new approach? This new approach would begin by reassessing the appropriateness of the term *slump* to point out that, despite a hiatus of exploration drilling, one major gas-producing enterprise is under way and a second (Deep Panuke) is in the advanced construction stage. Even on the exploration side, the re-evaluation of seismic data and the reconceptualization of Scotian Basin plays proceeds. Realistically, it seems appropriate to treat Scotian Basin petroleum as less than national-scale but nonetheless commercially meaningful in regional-marketing terms. Put this way, a sedimentary basin of small gas fields may, with modern technology for remote gathering and processing, nevertheless be a profitable endowment going forward. In political terms, an effective strategy would entail several new approaches, including the following: appropriate incentives for renewed exploration, policies for the maintenance and protection of critical infrastructure such as pipelines and processing facilities, mobilizing exploration and production capital on the optimal enterprise scales, and dealing with rights holders who opt to delay forward movement on commercial discoveries (the "fallow fields" issue). Clearly, such questions imply departures from an essentially market-driven approach in which the prerogatives of private capital are everywhere privileged.

Looking Forward

The Scotian Basin experience is an unfinished story. In a global commercial context, basins rise and fall and revive again. In 2011, natural gas prices are oscillating in the range of $4 to $5 per thousand cubic feet (or million British thermal units). This price decline is not auspicious for a gas-prone basin on the Atlantic coast. In addition, a North American gas supply bubble has developed since 2005 that is closely related to the rapid emergence of land-based shale gas, which offers a more favourable cost equation than does offshore gas.

The Scotian Basin also offers lessons for future offshore governance for other Canadian coastal settings. In macro-institutional form, there would appear to be several possibilities. One possibility is to accept the status quo and install the East Coast management model in new jurisdictions. The advantage would be to draw upon the accumulated experience of Nova Scotia and Newfoundland, enabling a relatively prompt and coherent start-up, should the way be cleared politically for an offshore launch. Both levels of government have found advantage in the joint board compromise, which has demonstrated its durability and resilience. The likelihood of this option seems remote, however, for several reasons. First, the political preconditions of the 1980s will be difficult to reproduce, and reaching an accord bargain may be the highest hurdle. Second, there is no compelling evidence that senior governments value the board's unique contribution. As this book reveals, each successive elected government has identified its own priorities for offshore petroleum development, and they seem to be increasingly pursued and resolved outside of the board structure. Third, there are defects in the existing model that may be sufficient to rule out its re-creation. For example, the joint board structure is more an administrative than a political success. Viewed as a political forum, there is a clear representational deficit when it comes to the access of interest groups. The periodic adoption of consultative committees for fishers and environmentalists serves only to underline this defect. Looking beyond these established clienteles, the general public has few points of access. As an inherently regulatory mechanism, the CNSOPB relies on higher ministerial direction for its political legitimacy.

Another option would recognize existing deficiencies and seek a remedy by expanding the delegated joint management formula to a broader range of responsibilities. New mandates have been grafted once before and could be added again. The evidence suggests, however, that the joint board works best in areas such as rights issuance and operational oversight, areas where its mandate is strongest and most exclusive. Moreover, the representational failings noted above will continue to apply. For every Sable Offshore Energy Project that is successfully adjudicated by a stacked panel review, there is a Georges Bank moratorium decision or a Cape Breton coastal protest, where ultimate decisions fall to ministers.

A third option would be to disestablish the existing boards or open new territorial basins without a joint authority. This scenario recalls the dilemmas of the early 1970s, and it is worth remembering that offshore capital has not faced this situation for more than a generation. On the British Columbia coast, the absence of a political accord is one of the key reasons (along with unsettled Aboriginal claims) that the corporate sector will not seriously consider a return. Also, the future development of prospects in the Gulf of St. Lawrence will turn on the resolution of a joint management deal. Offshore operators may not always be happy with the CNSOPB regime, but they may be far less comfortable in its absence.

Should heightened prospectivity return to the Scotian Basin or occur on other Canadian coasts in the aftermath of the one big find, these will be matters of high consequence. Alternatively, should the logic of more integrated ocean management take hold, the pressure for effective petroleum management structures will build once again.

The challenge for next-generation offshore management is neither to circle the wagons nor surrender past gains but to preserve the best of work to date while adapting to emerging imperatives. The traditional prescriptive regulatory philosophies have been overtaken, at least in part, by newer approaches in which policy goals are defined by performance-based targets that delegate compliance strategies to licensees. This new approach has taken hold particularly in areas where it can be plausibly argued that new technical and commercial practices have superseded those of old to offer significant operational cost savings without compromising public policy goals.

At the same time, there are definite limits to regulatory delegation, and corporate management systems will never fully replace a focused regulatory agency as the arbitrator and defender of the public interest. The 2010 Macondo blowout in the Gulf of Mexico has reignited this debate, and the political fallout will be felt for years to come. This book brings to light instances when the commercial imperatives of certain fractions of petroleum capital did not correspond with national or regional public interests. For instance, given a choice, the exploration and production sector prefers to operate free of state codes and audits for industrial and employment benefits. Yet this is obviously not compatible with any form of social license for offshore exploitation.

Finally, the unfolding of a basin development cycle means different things to offshore capital than it does to public authorities. In the sophisticated world of Norwegian state regulation, the maturing of first-generation fields was greeted not with passive resignation; rather, a carefully calibrated scheme was adopted to identify and protect critical field infrastructure while at the same time offering new licensing incentives to firms capable of profitably exploiting the residual resources even after the supermajors withdraw. Perhaps a new and invigorated approach to the direct regulation of the offshore industry is a new frontier of the public interest.

The future, then, may well lie in a blend of negotiated network governance coupled with North Sea-style regulatory leadership. Government involvement can be indirect or direct. Offshore authorities will need to cultivate new skills and disciplines that enable them to standardize what can be standardized and to achieve higher compliance by corporate adaptation where possible, but always according to rigorous performance standards. They will need to align procedures more systematically with the Crown duty to Aboriginal peoples and to build working relationships with a wider array of civil actors in the offshore polity. At the same time, they must maintain sovereign prerogatives to assert a public interest and pursue the appropriate strategies. As always, the challenge will involve an intricate and patient search for answers that balance the dictates of regulation and risk.

Notes

CHAPTER 1: INTRODUCTION

1 John Richards and Larry Pratt, *Prairie Capitalism: Power and Influence in the New West* (Toronto: McClelland and Stewart, 1979), Chap. 9.

2 Max Keddy, "Mobil Hit on Sable," *Chronicle-Herald* (Halifax, NS), 5 October 1971, 1.

3 John Gray, "The Making of Danny Chavez: Newfoundland's Rebellious Premier Takes on Big Oil and 'Steve" Harper,'" *Report on Business Magazine,* February 2008.

4 J.D. House, *The Last of the Free Enterprisers: The Oilmen of Calgary* (Toronto: Macmillan of Canada, 1980), chaps. 1 and 7.

5 Richard Schultz, "Interest Groups and Intergovernmental Relations: Caught in the Vice of Federalism," in *Canadian Federalism: Myth or Reality,* 3rd ed., ed. J. Peter Meekison, 375-96 (Toronto: Methuen, 1977).

6 This section draws extensively from an earlier discussion in Peter Clancy, "Offshore Petroleum Politics: A Changing Frontier in a Global System," in *Canada's Resource Economy in Transition: The Past, Present and Future of Canadian Staples Industries,* ed. Michael Howlett and Keith Brownsey, 255-77 (Toronto: Emond Montgomery, 2008).

7 Vern Baxter, "Political Economy of Oil and Exploitation of Offshore Oil," in *Impact of Offshore Oil Exploration,* ed. Shirley Laska (New Orleans: Mineral Management Service, 1993); Gary Lore, *Exploration and Discoveries, 1947-1989: An Historical Perspective,* MMS Gulf of Mexico Region Report 91-0078 (New Orleans: Minerals Management Service, 1992).

8 Douglas V. Fant, *An Analysis and Evaluation of Rules and Procedures Governing OCS Operations* (Washington, DC: American Bar Association, 1990); Richards and Pratt, *Prairie Capitalism.*

9 D.A. Fee and John O'Dea, *Technology for Developing Marginal Offshore Fields* (London: Elsevier Applied Science, 1986); Don E. Kash et al., *Energy under the Oceans: A Technology Assessment of the Outer Continental Shelf Oil and Gas Operations* (Norman: University of Oklahoma Press, 1973).

10 See also Aldo Chircop and Bruce A. Marchand, "Oceans Act: Uncharted Seas for Offshore Development in Atlantic Canada?" *Dalhousie Law Journal* 24 (2001): 23-50; Richard Hildreth, "Ocean Resources and Intergovernmental Relations in the 1980s: Outer Continental Shelf Hydrocarbons and Minerals," in *Ocean Resources and US Intergovernmental Relations in the 1980s,* ed. Maynard Silva, 155-96 (Boulder, CO: Westview Press, 1986); Neil Stalport, "Canadian Offshore Renewable Resources: Law and Policy Issues," in *Canadian Ocean Law and Policy,* ed. David VanderZwaag, 193-234 (Toronto: Butterworths, 1992).

11 Biliana Cicin-Sain and Robert Knecht, *The Future of US Ocean Policy: Choices for the New Century* (Washington, DC: Island Press, 2000); Joan Goldstein, *The Politics of Offshore Oil* (New York: Praeger, 1982).

12 National Research Council, *Striking a Balance: Improving Stewardship of Marine Areas* (Washington, DC: National Academy Press, 1997).

13 Robert Gramling, *Oil on the Edge: Offshore Development, Conflict, Gridlock* (Albany, NY: State University of New York Press, 1996).

14 Fred Dunning, *Britain's Offshore Oil and Gas* (London: UK Offshore Operators Association, 1989).

15 Oystein Noreng, *The Oil Industry and Government Strategy in the North Sea* (London: Croom Helm, 1980); Brent Nelsen, *The State Offshore: Petroleum Politics and State Intervention on the British and Norwegian Continental Shelves* (New York: Praeger, 1991).

16 Richard Cullen, *Federalism in Action: The Australian and Canadian Offshore Disputes* (Sydney: Federation Press, 1990); Constance D. Hunt, *The Offshore Petroleum Regimes of Canada and Australia* (Calgary: Centre for Resource Law, 1989).

17 Richard A. Bartlett, *Native Title in Australia*, 2nd ed. (Brisbane: LexisNexis Butterworths, 2004).

18 Graeme Atherton, *Fifty Years of Woodside's Energy* (Perth: WS Petroleum Ltd., 2004).

19 Nicholas Shaxson, *Poisoned Wells: The Dirty Politics of African Oil* (New York: Palgrave Macmillan, 2007); John Ghazvinian, *Untapped: The Scramble for Africa's Oil* (Orlando, FL: Harcourt, 2007).

20 Tony Rice and Paula Owen, *Decommissioning the* Brent Spar (New York: Routledge, 1999), and Grant Jordan, *Shell, Greenpeace and* Brent Spar (New York: Palgrave, 2001).

21 Les Dauterive, *Rigs to Reefs: Policy, Progress and Perspectives* (New Orleans: Mineral Management Service, 2000).

22 Judith Gurney, *The Gulf of Mexico: Revival and Opportunity in the Oil Industry* (London: Financial Times, 1997).

23 House, *The Last of the Free Enterprisers.*

24 John N. McDougall, *Fuels and the National Policy* (Toronto: Butterworths, 1982).

25 Deborah Yedlin, "Oil Patch Sale," *Globe and Mail,* 31 May 2004.

26 Gurney, *The Gulf of Mexico;* National Research Council, Marine Board, *Outer Continental Shelf Frontier Technology* (Washington, DC: National Academy Press, 1980).

27 John Samuel Szell, *Innovations in Energy: The Story of Kerr-McGee* (Norman: University of Oklahoma Press, 1979).

28 Offshore Technology Conference, annual meeting, Houston, 2002-2011, http://www.otcnet.org/.

29 United States, Department of Energy, Office of Natural Gas and Petroleum Technology, *Oil and Gas Programs* (Washington, DC: Department of Energy, 1977; United States, Department of Energy, Office of Fossil Energy, *Environmental Benefits of Advanced Oil and Gas Exploration and Production Technology* (Washington, DC: Department of Energy, 1999).

30 Kash et al., *Energy under the Oceans,* 3-4.

31 Michael Gibbons and Roger Voyer, *A Technology Assessment System: A Case Study of East Coast Offshore Petroleum Exploitation* (Ottawa: Science Council of Canada, 1974); Robert F. Keith et al, *Northern Development and Technology Assessment Systems: A Study of Petroleum Development Programs in the Mackenzie Delta–Beaufort Sea Region and the Arctic Islands* (Ottawa: Science Council of Canada, 1976).

32 William R. Freudenburg and Robert Gramling, *Blowout in the Gulf* (Cambridge MA: MIT Press, 2011).

33 National Commission on the BP Deepwater Horizon Oil Spill and Offshore Drilling, *Deepwater: The Gulf Disaster and the Future of Offshore Drilling* (Washington, DC: Government Printing Office, 2011).

34 Coalition to Restore Coastal Louisiana, *Coastal Louisiana: Here Today and Gone Tomorrow?* (Baton Rouge, LA: Coalition to Restore Coastal Louisiana, 1989); William R. Freudenberg and Robert Gramling, *Oil in Troubled Waters: Perceptions, Politics and the Battle over Offshore Drilling* (Albany, NY: SUNY Press, 1994); Hank C. Jenkins-Smith and Gilbert K. St. Clair, "The Politics of Offshore Energy: Empirically Testing the Advocacy Coalition Framework," in *Policy Change and Learning,* ed. Paul Sabatier and Jenkins-Smith, 149-75 (Boulder, CO: Westview Press, 1993).

35 Chris C. Oynes, "The Role of Deep Gas from the Shelf"(paper presented to the Offshore Technology Conference, Houston, Texas, 4 May 2003), http://www.gomr.boemre.gov/.

36 For more on industry self-regulation and third-party certification, see Joseph A. Pratt, William H. Becker, and William M. McClenahan, *Voice of the Marketplace: A History of the National Petroleum Council* (College Station, TX: Texas A&M University Press, 2002).

37 John Erik Fossum, *Oil, the State and Federalism: The Rise and Demise of Petro-Canada as a Statist Impulse* (Toronto: University of Toronto Press, 1997); David Milne, *Tug of War: Ottawa and the Provinces under Trudeau and Mulroney* (Toronto: James Lorimer, 1986); J.D. House, *The Challenge of Oil: Newfoundland's Quest for Controlled Development* (St. John's: Institute of Social and Economic Research, 1985); G. Bruce Doern and Glen Toner, *The Politics of Energy: The Development and Implementation of the NEP* (Toronto: Methuen, 1985); and Hunt, *The Offshore Petroleum Regimes.*

38 Cynthia Lamson, ed., *The Sea Has Many Voices: Oceans Policy for a Complex World* (Montreal/Kingston: McGill-Queen's University Press, 1994); Edward A. Fitzgerald, *The Seaweed Rebellion: Federal-State Conflicts over Offshore Energy Development* (Lantham, MD: Lexington Books, 2000).
39 Elizabeth Mann Borghese, *The Ocean Circle: Governing the Seas as a Global Resource* (New York: United Nations University, 1998).
40 Canada, Department of Fisheries and Oceans, *Canada's Oceans Strategy* (Ottawa: Fisheries and Oceans Canada, 2002); Cicin-Sain and Knecht, *The Future of US Ocean Policy.*
41 John G. Ikenberry, *Reasons of State: Oil Politics and the Capacities of American Government* (Ithaca, NY: Cornell University Press, 1988).
42 Jeanne N. Clarke and Daniel C. McCool, *Staking Out the Terrain: Power and Performance among Natural Resource Agencies* (Albany, NY: SUNY Press, 1996).
43 Svein S. Andersen, *The Struggle for North Sea Oil and Gas: Government Strategies in Denmark, Britain and Norway* (Stockholm: Scandinavian University Press, 1993).
44 Nelsen, *The State Offshore.*
45 Linda Weiss, *The Myth of the Powerless State: Governing the Economy in a Global Era* (Cambridge: Polity Press, 1998), 4.
46 Peter Clancy, "Political Devolution and Wildlife Management," in *Devolution and Constitutional Development in the Canadian North,* ed. Gurston Dacks, 71-120 (Ottawa: Carleton University Press, 1990), and "The Politics and Administration of Aboriginal Claims," in *Public Administration and Policy*, ed. Martin W. Westmacott and Hugh Mellon, 55-72 (Scarborough: Prentice Hall/Allyn and Bacon, 1999).
47 John C. Crosbie, "Overview Paper on the 1985 Canada-Newfoundland Accord Act," prepared for the Royal Commission on Renewing and Strengthening Our Place in Canada, 2003.
48 J.D. House, "Myths and Realities about Petroleum-Related Development: Lessons for British Columbia from Atlantic Canada and the North Sea," *Journal of Canadian Studies* 37, 4 (2002): 9-32.
49 Douglas M. Brown, "Sea Change in Newfoundland: From Peckford to Wells," in *Canada: The State of the Federation, 1990,* ed. R.L. Watts and D.M. Brown, 199-229 (Kingston: Institute of Intergovernmental Relations, 1991).
50 Derek Fee, *Petroleum Exploitation Strategy* (London: Belhaven Press, 1988), 32.
51 Jeremy Rayner et al., "Privileging the Sub-Sector: Critical Sub-Sectors and Sectoral Relationships in Forest Policy-Making," *Forest Policy and Economics* 2, 3-4 (2001): 319.

CHAPTER 2: THE POLITICS OF OFFSHORE BASIN DEVELOPMENT

1 R.A. Sandy MacMullin, "The Potential of the Nova Scotia Offshore for Northeast Markets" (presentation to New York Gas Group and New York Energy Association, New York, 21 May 2002).
2 United States, Minerals Management Service, Department of the Interior, *Deepwater Gulf of Mexico 2004: America's Expanding Frontier* (New Orleans, LA: Minerals Management Service, 2004).

3 Atlantic Geoscience Society, *The Last Billion Years: A Geological History of the Maritime Provinces of Canada* (Halifax: Nimbus Publishing, 2001), Chap. 7.
4 Ibid., Chap. 1.
5 Gerald Baier and Paul Groake, "Arbitrating a Fiction: Canadian Federalism and the Nova Scotia/Newfoundland and Labrador Boundary Dispute," *Canadian Public Administration* 46, 3 (2003): 315-38.
6 J.A. Wade and B.C. MacLean, "The Geology of the Southeastern Margin of Canada," in *Geology of the Continental Margin of Eastern Canada*, ed. M.J. Keen and G.L. Williams, 193-94 (Ottawa: Geological Survey of Canada, 1990).
7 Arthur G. Kidston et al., *Hydrocarbon Potential of the Deep-Water Scotian Slope* (Halifax: CNSOPB, 2002).
8 Wade and MacLean, "The Geology of the Southeastern Margin," 171.
9 Richard C. Selley, *Elements of Petroleum Geology*, 2nd ed. (San Diego, CA: Academic Press, 1968).
10 Ibid.
11 "Oil Exploration," *The Handbook of Texas Online*, http://www.tshaonline.org/handbook.
12 J.A. Wade et al., "Petroleum Resources of the Scotian Shelf," Paper 88-19 (Geological Survey of Canada, 1989), 20.
13 Canada–Nova Scotia Offshore Petroleum Board, *Cohasset-Panuke Project: Benefits Plan Decision Report and Development Plan Decision Report* (Halifax: CNSOPB, 1990), 5-8.
14 B.C. MacLean and J.A. Wade, "Petroleum Geology of the Continental Margin South of the Islands of St. Pierre and Miquelon, Offshore Eastern Canada," *Bulletin of Canadian Petroleum Geology* 40, 3 (1992): 252.
15 Kidston et al., *Hydrocarbon Potential*, 7, and Kidston et al., *Nova Scotia Deepwater Post-Drill Analysis, 1982-2004* (Halifax: CNSOPB, 2007).
16 L.F. Ivanhoe, "Future World Oil Supplies: There Is a Finite Limit," *World Oil* 216, 10 (1995): 77-88.
17 Paul D. Newendorp and John Schuyler, *Decision Analysis for Petroleum Exploration*, 2nd ed. (Aurora, CO: Planning Press, 2000), 137.
18 Mobil Oil Canada et al., *Venture Development Project: Development Plan Submission*, vol. 1 (Halifax: Mobil Oil Canada, 1983), 1.
19 Patricia Mohr, "Scotiabank Commodity Price Index," *Global Economic Research*, 27 November 2008, 2.
20 PanCanadian Energy, *Deep Panuke Offshore Gas Development: Project Summary*, vol. 1 (Halifax: PanCanadian Energy Corp, 2002), i-8.1.
21 R.M. Proctor, G.C. Taylor, and J.A. Wade, "Oil and Natural Gas Resources of Canada: 1983," Paper 83-31, Geological Survey of Canada.
22 Kidston et al., *Hydrocarbon Pontential*, 7.
23 Daniel Yergin, *The Prize: The Epic Quest for Oil, Money and Power* (New York: Free Press, 2008), 708.
24 One recent study is Jerome Davis, ed., *The Changing World of Oil: An Analysis of Corporate Change and Adaptation* (Aldershot: Ashgate Publishing, 2006).

25 Matthew R. Simmons, *Twilight in the Desert: The Coming Saudi Oil Shock and the World Economy* (New York: John Wiley and Sons, 2005), 131.
26 Neil Stalport, "Canadian Offshore Non-Renewable Resources: Law and Policy Issues," in *Canadian Ocean Law and Policy,* ed. David Vanderzwaag (Toronto: Butterworths Canada, 1992), 198.
27 See, for example, Terence Daintith, *Finders Keepers? How the Law of Capture Shaped the World Oil Industry* (Washington, DC: Earthscan, 2010).
28 *Canada–Nova Scotia Offshore Petroleum Resources Accord*, 26 August 1986, 2, http://www.cnsopb.ns.ca/pdfs/Accord.pdf.
29 Gaffney, Cline and Associates, "A Review of Regulatory Cycle Times in Certain Jurisdictions," report prepared for the Regulatory Issues Steering Committee of the Atlantic Energy Roundtable, August 2003.
30 "Board Chair Discusses Nova Scotia's Proactive Exploration Agenda," *World Oil* 228 (2007), supplement on "Nova Scotia Canada: The Next Play."
31 Michael Enachescu, "Searching for Offshore Nova Scotia Elusive Reservoirs and Large Traps," *Nova Scotia Energy R&D Forum*, 24 May 2006.
32 Malcolm Wicks, UK Minister of State for Energy, "Market and Project Opportunities in a Mature Basin" (presentation at "INSTOK International Oil and Gas Conference," Stavanger, Norway, 21 August 2006).
33 Jon Erik Fossum, *Oil, the State and Federalism: The Rise and Demise of Petro-Canada as a Statist Impulse* (Toronto: University of Toronto Press, 1997), Chaps. 2, 4, and 6.
34 J.D. House, *The Challenge of Oil: Newfoundland's Quest for Controlled Development* (St. John's: Institute for Social and Economic Research, 1985), Chap. 4.
35 John Gray, "The Making of 'Danny Chavez': Newfoundland's Rebellious Premier Takes on Big Oil and 'Steve' Harper," *Report on Business Magazine,* February 2008.
36 Eric Kierans, *Report on Natural Resources Policy in Manitoba* (Winnipeg: Planning and Priorities Committee of Cabinet, 1973).
37 Peter Foster, *Other People's Money: The Banks, the Government and Dome* (Don Mills, ON: Collins, 1983), 50.
38 Canada, Department of Energy Mines and Resources, *National Energy Program, 1980* (Ottawa: Supply and Services Canada, 1980), 38-40.
39 Nova Scotia, Department of Energy, "Nova Scotia Oil and Gas Corporate Taxation Summary," 2008, http://www.gov.ns.ca/energy/resources/RA/offshore/NS-Oil-and-Gas-Corporate-Taxation-Summary-Updated-feb-19-08.pdf.
40 See for example, Atlantic Energy Roundtable, *Report from the "Lessons Learned Workshop" Hosted by the Regulatory Issues Steering Committee,* June 2003, and Regulatory Issues Steering Committee and Industrial Opportunities Task Force, *Submission to Atlantic Energy Roundtable II,* October 2003.
41 Another informative account of Nova Scotia's offshore business development can be found in Jim Meek and Eleanor Beaton, *Offshore Dream: A History of Nova Scotia's Oil and Gas Industry* (Halifax: Nimbus Publishing, 2010).
42 This concept is closely associated with the work of biologist Stephen Jay Gould. For an account of its migration into public policy, see Peter John, "Is There Life after Policy Streams, Advocacy Coalitions and Punctuations: Using Evolutionary Theory to Explain Policy Change" *Policy Studies Journal* 31, 4 (2003): 481-98.

43 Hal Mills, "Eastern Canada's Offshore Resources and Boundaries: A Study in Political Geography," *Journal of Canadian Studies* 6, 3 (1971): 36-50.
44 Wade et al., "Petroleum Resources of the Scotian Shelf."
45 Max Keddy, "It's Oil: Mobil Hit on Sable," *Chronicle-Herald* (Halifax, NS), 5 October 1971, 1.
46 Tyler Priest, *The Offshore Imperative: Shell Oil's Search for Petroleum in Postwar America* (College Station: Texas A&M Press, 1967), 167.
47 Robert Gramling, *Oil on the Edge: Offshore Development, Conflict, Gridlock* (Albany, NY: State University of New York, 1996), 72.
48 Foster, *Other People's Money,* 50.
49 Jack MacDonald, "Setting the Stage: An Historical Perspective" (presentation at the Nova Scotia Offshore Basin Forum 2007, Halifax, 2007), http://www.offshorenergyresearch.ca/.
50 Wade et al., "Petroleum Resources of the Scotian Shelf."
51 Mobil Oil Canada et al., *Venture Development Project.*
52 Theresa MacNeil, *Commissioner's Report: Results of the Public Review on the Effects of Potential Oil and Gas Exploration Offshore Cape Breton* (Halifax: CNSOPB, 2002).
53 Richard DeWolf, *Scotian Shelf Gas Supply Region, 2002 Report* (Calgary: Ziff Energy Group, 2002).
54 Michael E. Enachescu and John R. Hogg, "Exploring for Atlantic Canada's Next Giant Petroleum Discovery," *CSEG Recorder* 30, 5 (2005): 19-30.
55 Nova Scotia, Department of Energy, *Nova Scotia Offshore Renewal Plan* (Halifax: Department of Energy, 2008).

CHAPTER 3: POLITICAL CONSTRUCTION OF ADMINISTRATIVE INSTITUTIONS

1 E.E. Schattschneider, *The Semi-Sovereign People* (New York: Holt, Rinehart and Winston, 1960), 30.
2 Keith Archer et al., *Parameters of Power: Canada's Political Institutions,* 2nd ed. (Scarborough: ITP Nelson, 1999), 11.
3 Don Axford, *Oil and Gas Oral History Project* (Calgary: Glenbow Institute, 1983).
4 William R. Freudenberg and Robert Gramling, *Oil in Troubled Waters: Perceptions, Politics and the Battle over Offshore Drilling* (Albany, NY: SUNY Press, 1994), 19-21.
5 Edward A. Fitzgerald, *The Seaweed Rebellion: Federal-State Conflicts over Offshore Energy Development* (Lanham, MD: Lexington Books, 2001); Geoffrey Laendner, *A Failed Strategy: The Offshore Oil Industry's Development of the Outer Continental Shelf* (New York: Garland Publications, 1993).
6 Richard Cullen, *Federalism in Action: The Australian and Canadian Offshore Disputes* (Sydney: Federation Press, 1990).
7 Ibid., 65.
8 *Reference re Offshore Mineral Rights of British Columbia,* [1967] S.C.R. 792.
9 Arbitration tribunal between Newfoundland and Labrador and Nova Scotia, Award of the Tribunal in the First Phase, 2001: 11, http://www.nr.gov.nl.ca/mines&en/publications/offshore/dispute/decision.pdf.
10 Ibid., 15.

11 The text of the memorandum appears in the *Chronicle Herald* (Halifax, NS), 2 February 1977, 1.

12 Rowland J. Harrison, "The Offshore Mineral Resources Agreement in the Maritime Provinces," *Dalhousie Law Journal* 4, 2 (1977-78): 245-76.

13 Nova Scotia, Department of Mines and Energy, *Offshore Oil and Gas: A Chance for Nova Scotians* (Halifax: Department of Mines and Energy, 1980), 27-28.

14 Canada, Department of Energy, Mines and Resources, *Offshore Exploration: Information and Procedures for Offshore Operators,* Report EI 79-4 (Ottawa: Energy, Mines and Resources, 1979).

15 Daniel Yergin, *The Prize: The Epic Quest for Oil, Money, and Power,* 2nd ed. (New York: Free Press, 2008).

16 Nova Scotia, Voluntary Economic Planning, *Oil and Natural Gas Offshore Development: The Opportunities and the Challenge* (Halifax: Voluntary Economic Planning, 1980).

17 Nova Scotia, Department of Mines and Energy, *Offshore Oil and Gas.*

18 For the Newfoundland approach, see J.D. House, *The Challenge of Oil: Newfoundland's Quest for Controlled Development,* Social and Economic Studies 30 (St. John's: Institute of Social and Economic Research, 1985).

19 G. Bruce Doern and Glen Toner, *The Politics of Energy: The Development and Implementation of the NEP* (Toronto: Methuen, 1985).

20 Canada, Department of Energy, Mines and Resources, *National Energy Program, 1980* (Ottawa: Supply and Services Canada, 1980), 42-44.

21 On the broad outlines of these federal constitutional initiatives, see David Milne, *Tug of War: Ottawa and the Provinces under Trudeau and Mulroney* (Toronto: James Lorimer, 1986), and Robert Shepard and Michael Valpy, *The National Deal: The Fight for a Canadian Constitution* (Toronto: Fleet Books, 1982).

22 For a review of the legal issues involved in this proposal, see Lawrence L. Herman, "The Need for a Canada Submerged Lands Act: Some Further Thoughts on Canada's Offshore Mineral Rights Problems," *Canadian Bar Review* 58, 3 (1980): 518-44.

23 Paul A. Sabatier and Hank C. Jenkins-Smith, *Policy Change and Learning: An Advocacy Coalition Approach* (Boulder, CO: Westview Press, 1993).

24 *Canada–Nova Scotia Agreement on Offshore Oil and Gas Resource Management and Revenue Sharing,* 2 March 1982, Schedule 2.

25 Nova Scotia, Department of Mines and Energy, *Offshore Oil and Gas,* 28.

26 *Canada–Nova Scotia Agreement,* 1982, Schedule 2, sec. 3.

27 Nova Scotia, Department of Mines and Energy, *Offshore Oil and Gas,* 19.

28 *The Atlantic Accord* (*Memorandum of Agreement between the Government of Canada and the Government of Newfoundland and Labrador on Offshore Oil and Gas Resource Management and Revenue Sharing),* 11 February 1985, sec. 2(c).

29 *Canada–Nova Scotia Agreement,* 1982, Schedule 2, p. 5.

30 A series of court cases was triggered by the Seafarers' International Union, which asked the Federal Court of Canada whether Ottawa had jurisdiction over offshore labour law. While this was underway, the Newfoundland government initiated a reference question on its jurisdiction over continental shelf resources. The Newfoundland

Court of Appeal found it had jurisdiction to the limits of the (twelve-mile) territorial sea. See *Re Mineral and Other Natural Resources on the Continental Shelf* (1983), 145 D.L.R. (3d) 9 (Nfld. C.A.). Ottawa's separate reference to the Supreme Court of Canada raised the question of federal jurisdiction over the Hibernia oil field. The question was answered in the affirmative in *Re Newfoundland Continental Shelf*, [1984] 1 S.C.R. 86.

31 House, *The Challenge of Oil*, 305.
32 *Atlantic Accord*, 1985, ss. 3-15.
33 Ibid., s. 12.
34 Ibid, ss. 16-22.
35 Ibid., s. 24.
36 Ibid., ss. 21-25.
37 Canada, Department of Energy, Mines and Resources, *National Energy Program*, 2.
38 *Atlantic Accord*, ss. 26-31.
39 "Preface," *Canada–Nova Scotia Offshore Petroleum Resources Accord*, 26 August 1986.
40 Gurston Dacks, ed., *Devolution and Constitutional Development in the Canadian North* (Ottawa: Carleton University Press, 1990).
41 Ibid., "The Quest for Northern Oil and Gas Accords," 225-56.
42 BC Ministry of Energy, Mines and Petroleum Resources, "Offshore Oil and Gas in BC: A Chronology," http://www.empr.gov.bc.ca/OG/offshoreoilandgas/OffshoreOilandGasinBC/Pages/AChronologyofActivity.aspx.
43 C.B. Pamenter, "Shell Takes 25 Million Dollar Gamble," *Canadian Petroleum*, June 1967.
44 Douglas M. Johnston and Erin N. Hildebrand, eds., *BC Offshore Hydrocarbon Development: Issues and Prospects* (Victoria: Maritime Awards Society of Canada, 2001), 1.
45 *Reference re: Ownership of the Bed of the Strait of Georgia and Related Areas* [1984] S.C.R. 338.
46 Al Hudec and Van Penick, "British Columbia Offshore Oil and Gas Law," *Alberta Law Review* 41 (2003): 112-15.
47 Canada and British Columbia, West Coast Offshore Exploration Environmental Assessment Panel, *Report and Recommendations*, April 1986.
48 Ibid., 2.
49 Dale Marshall, *Should BC Lift the Offshore Oil Moratorium?* (Ottawa: Canadian Centre for Policy Alternatives, n.d.).
50 British Columbia, Scientific Review Panel, "Report of the Scientific Review Panel," January 2002, http://www.empr.gov.bc.ca/OG/offshoreoilandgas/ReportsPresentationsandEducationalMaterial/Reports/Pages/BCHydrocarbonDevelopmentReport.aspx; Jacques Whitford, *BC Offshore Oil and Gas Technology Update* (Burnaby: Jacques Whitford, 2001).
51 See, for example, J.D. House, "Myths and Realities about Petroleum-Related Development: Lessons for British Columbia from Atlantic Canada and the North Sea," *Journal of Canadian Studies* 37, 4 (2003): 9-32.

52 British Columbia, *The Province of British Columbia's Perspective on the Federal Moratorium on Oil and Gas Activities, Offshore BC* (Victoria: Province of British Columbia, 2004).
53 See Canada and Nova Scotia, NRCanada and NS Petroleum Directorate, Georges Bank Review Panel, *Report*, June 1999; and Lucia Fanning, "Understanding the 1999 Georges Bank Moratorium Decision," *Marine Affairs Policy Forum* 1, 1 (2008): 1-4.
54 Douglas M. Brown, "Sea Change in Newfoundland: From Peckford to Wells," in *Canada: The State of the Federation, 1990*, ed. R.L. Watts and D.M. Brown (Kingston: Institute of Intergovernmental Relations, 1991), 212.
55 Confidential interview with former Nova Scotia official, 20 October 2004.
56 Neil Gunningham and Darren Sinclair, *Leaders and Laggards: Next-Generation Environmental Regulation* (Sheffield: Greenleaf Publishing, 2002), 111.
57 See Michael Harris, *Lament for an Ocean: The Collapse of the Atlantic Cod Fishery* (Toronto: McClelland and Stewart, 1998), and Peter Clancy "Chasing Whose Fish? Atlantic Fisheries Conflicts and Institutions," in *Canadian Water Politics: Conflicts and Institutions*, ed. Mark Sproule-Jones, Carolyn Johns, and B. Timothy Heinmiller, 261-85 (Montreal/Kingston: McGill-Queen's University Press, 2008).
58 Cynthia Lamson, ed., *The Sea Has Many Voices: Oceans Policy for a Complex World* (Montreal/Kingston: McGill-Queen's University Press, 1994).

CHAPTER 4: THE CNSOPB IN ACTION

1 Mark Sproule-Jones, *Governments at Work: Canadian Parliamentary Federalism and Its Public Policy Effects* (Toronto: University of Toronto Press, 1993), 24.
2 CNSOPB, annual reports, 1989-90, 2001-2, 2009-10.
3 *Canada–Nova Scotia Offshore Petroleum Resources Accord Implementation Act*, S.C. 1988, c. 28, s. 49.
4 Ibid., s. 49.
5 Ibid., s. 83.
6 For details on program management during the 1970s, see Canada, Department of Energy, Mines and Resources, *Offshore Exploration: Information and Procedures for Offshore Operators*, Report EI 79-4 (Ottawa: Energy, Mines and Resources, 1979).
7 Canada, Department of Energy, Mines and Resources, *Statement of Policy: Proposed Petroleum and Natural Gas Act and New Canada Oil and Gas Land Regulations* (Ottawa: Supply and Services Canada, 1976).
8 For a broader discussion, see G. Bruce Doern and Glen Toner, *The Politics of Energy: The Development and Implementation of the National Energy Program* (Toronto: Methuen, 1985), 88-95.
9 CNSOPB, annual report, 1984, p. 4.
10 Ibid., 1987, p. 3.
11 Ibid., 1987, p. 4.
12 Ibid., 1990-91, p. 3.
13 A.D. Hunt, "Land Management in the Canadian Arctic," *Proceedings of the Southwestern Legal Foundation*, National Institute for Petroleum Landmen, 1970, 177.
14 Pilot Task Force, http://www.pilottaskforce.co.uk/.

15 Atlantic Energy Roundtable, *Report from the "Lessons Learned Workshop" Hosted by the Regulatory Issues Steering Committee,* June 2003.
16 "Regulatory Impact Analysis Statement for Proposed Canada Oil and Gas Drilling and Production Regulations and Nova Scotia Offshore Petroleum Drilling and Production Regulations," Part 1, *Canada Gazette,* 18 April 2009, 1,096-1,105.
17 Canada, Frontier and Regulatory Renewal Initiative (FORRI), "Draft Drilling and Production Regulations – Stakeholder Consultation 2007," 27 August 2007, http://www.neb-one.gc.ca/clf-nsi/rpblctn/ctsndrgltn/rgltnsndgdlnsprsnttthrct/frntrff-shrrgltrrnwlnttv/drftcnslttn20070427-eng.pdf.
18 Canada, FORRI, "Draft Drilling."
19 Robert Gramling, *Oil on the Edge: Offshore Development, Conflict, Gridlock* (Albany, NY: SUNY Press, 1996), 89-90.
20 James Woodford, *The Violated Vision: The Rape of Canada's North* (Toronto: McClelland and Stewart, 1972), 11-13.
21 G. Bruce Doern and Thomas Conway, *The Greening of Canada: Federal Institutions and Decisions* (Toronto: University of Toronto Press, 1994), Chaps. 1 and 10.
22 Douglas Pimlott, Dougald Brown, and Kenneth Sam, *Oil under the Ice* (Ottawa: Canadian Arctic Resources Committee, 1976), Appendix 1.
23 Ibid., 124.
24 *Canada–Nova Scotia Agreement on Offshore Oil and Gas Resource Management and Revenue Sharing,* 1982, Schedule 2, p. 8.
25 National Energy Board, Canada-Newfoundland Offshore Petroleum Board, and Canada–Nova Scotia Offshore Petroleum Board, "Offshore Waste Treatment Guidelines," 2010 http://www.cnsopb.ns.ca/pdfs/owtg_redraft.pdf.
26 LGL Ltd. and S.L. Ross Ocean Research, *Environmental Assessment of Exploration Drilling Off Nova Scotia* (Halifax: Canada-Nova Scotia Offshore Petroleum Board, 2000).
27 Bram F. Noble, "Promise and Dismay: The State of Strategic Environmental Assessment Systems and Practices in Canada," *Environmental Impact Assessment Review* 29 (2009): 66-69.
28 CEF Consultants, *Strategic Environmental Assessment of the Misaine Bank Area* (Halifax: CEF Consultants 2006); Canada-Nova Scotia Offshore Petroleum Board, *Strategic Environmental Assessment of Potential Exploration Rights for the Eastern Sable Island Bank, Western Banquereau, the Gully Trough and the Eastern Scotian Slope* (Halifax: CNSOPB, 2003); Jacques Whitford, *Strategic Environmental Assessment: Laurentian Subbasin* (St. John's: CNOPB and CNSOPB, 2003).
29 Mark Butler, "Offshore Licensing Process Flawed," *Chronicle Herald* (Halifax, NS), 1 December 2000.
30 Teresa MacNeil, *Commissioner's Report: Results of the Public Review on the Effects of Potential Oil and Gas Exploration Offshore Cape Breton* (Halifax: CNSOPB, 2002).
31 "Regulatory Impact Analysis Statement," *Canada Gazette,* 24 July 2003, accompanying SOR/2003-280.
32 Canada, Department of Industry, Trade and Commerce and Regional Economic Expansion, "Major Projects Benefits Board to be Formed," news release, 20 May 1982.

33 *Canada–Nova Scotia Offshore Petroleum Resources Accord,* 26 August 1986, art. 31.01.a.
34 CNSOPB, annual report, 2000-1, p. 15.
35 Canadian Oil and Gas Lands Administration (COGLA), annual report, 1986, p. 8.
36 Ibid., 1987, p. 15.
37 CNSOPB, annual reports, 1989-90 to 1991-2.
38 Lasmo NS Ltd. and Nova Scotia Resources (Ventures) Ltd., Cohasset/Panuke Development Project, Preliminary Development Application, Halifax, 1990.
39 A Catenary Anchor Leg Mooring (CALM) buoy is held in place by long, curved anchor chains attached to the seabed.
40 Canada–Nova Scotia Offshore Petroleum Board, *Cohasset-Panuke Project: Benefits Plan Decision Report and Development Plan Decision Report,* Halifax, 1990.
41 CNSOPB, annual report, 1990-91.
42 J.R. Ellis, "Report of the Cohasset/Panuke Environmental and Socio-Economic Review Commission" (Halifax: Province of Nova Scotia, 1990).
43 CNSOPB, annual report, 1990-91, p. 17.
44 Ibid., 1991-92.
45 Leslie S. Eliuk, "History of the Practical Application of a Failed (?) Dolomite Model (Mixing Zone) to the 'Demascota Dolomite Beds' of the Abenaki Formation, Nova Scotia," *Dolomites,* 2004, http://*www.cspg.org/conventions/abstracts/2004Dolomites/C030.pdf*; Michael E. Enachescu and John R. Hogg, "Exploring for Atlantic Canada's Next Giant Petroleum Discovery," *CSEG Recorder* 30, 5 (2005): 19-30.
46 Canada-Nova Scotia Offshore Petroleum Board, *Cohasset-Panuke Project: Benefit Plan Decision Report; Development Plan Decision Report* (Halifax: CNSOPB), 59.
47 Canada–Nova Scotia Offshore Petroleum Board, *Environmental Screening Report: Cohasset Phase II Decommissioning* (Halifax: CNSOPB, 2004), 2.
48 EnCana and Jacques Whitford, "CEAA Screening Environmental Assessment, Cohasset Project Phase II Decommissioning," April 2004, viii, http://www.cnsopb.ns.ca/pdfs/CEAA_Screening_Cohasset_Decommissioning.pdf.
49 Canada–Nova Scotia Offshore Petroleum Board, *Application to Amend the Cohasset Development Plan: Decision Report* (Halifax: CNSOPB, 2004), 1.
50 See, for example, Barbara Jenkins, "Reexamining the 'Obsolescing Bargain': A Study of Canada's National Energy Program," *International Organization* 40, 1 (1986): 139-65.

CHAPTER 5: THE PROVINCIAL STATE AND THE ENTREPRENEURIAL IMPULSE

1 Canada, Auditor General of Canada, *Report of the Auditor General of Canada, 1988* (Ottawa: Supply and Services Canada, 1988), Chap. 10.
2 Mark C. Baetz, "Texaco and Georges Bank (A)," in *Readings and Canadian Cases in Business, Government, and Society,* ed. Mark C. Baetz, 475-97 (Scarborough, ON: Nelson Canada, 1993).
3 Nova Scotia, Department of Natural Resources, annual report, 1996.
4 Nova Scotia Petroleum Directorate, "Government Role," 2000, http://www.gov.ns.ca/.

5 Nova Scotia, Department of Energy, *Nova Scotia Offshore Renewal Plan* (Halifax: Department of Energy, 2008).
6 David Crane, *Controlling Interest: The Canadian Gas and Oil Stakes* (Toronto: McClelland and Stewart, 1982), 161-63.
7 For example, see Peter Kavanagh, *John Buchanan: The Art of Political Survival* (Halifax: Formac, 1988).
8 Theda Skocpol, "Bringing the State Back In: Strategies of Analysis in Current Research," in *Bringing the State Back In*, ed. Peter Evans, Dietrich Rueschemayer, and Theda Skocpol (New York: Cambridge University Press, 1985), 9.
9 John Ikenberry, *Reasons of State: Oil Politics and the Capacities of American Government* (Ithaca, NY: Cornell University Press, 1988).
10 The full text of this agreement appears in the *Chronicle-Herald* (Halifax, NS), 2 February 1977, 34.
11 Canada, Department of Energy, Mines and Resources, *Offshore Exploration: Information and Procedures for Offshore Operators*, Report EI 79-4 (Ottawa: Energy, Mines and Resources, 1979), Appendix B.
12 Nova Scotia, Voluntary Economic Planning, *Oil and Gas Offshore Development: The Opportunities and the Challenge* (Halifax: Voluntary Economic Planning, 1980).
13 *An Act Respecting Petroleum Resources*, S.N.S. 1980, c. 12.
14 Other bills included the Pipeline Act, which regulated construction of works between the wellhead and the consumer; the Gas Utilities Act, which delegated gas-rate regulation to the provincial Public Utilities Board; and the Energy and Mineral Resources Conservation Act, which established a new board to oversee efficient offshore production and prevent pollution.
15 Nova Scotia, Department of Mines and Energy, *Offshore Oil and Gas: A Chance for Nova Scotians* (Halifax: Department of Mines and Energy, 1980), 29-31.
16 For details, see G. Bruce Doern and Glen Toner, *The Politics of Energy: The Development and Implementation of the NEP* (Toronto: Methuen, 1985), Chap. 10.
17 Brian O'Neill, "Laughing Gas," *New Maritimes* 4, 6 (1986): 4.
18 *Reference re: Newfoundland Continental Shelf*, [1984], 1 S.C.R. 86.
19 Nova Scotia, Auditor General, annual report, 1991, p. 69.
20 Ibid., 1996, p. 69.
21 Nova Scotia, House of Assembly, *Debates*, 23 February 1981, p. 135.
22 Hattie Dyck, "Crown Corporations Will Not Be Used as a Political Tool, Claims President," *Chronicle-Herald* (Halifax, NS), 24 November 1981.
23 Michael Cope, "NSRL to Be 'Heavily Involved' in Offshore," *Chronicle-Herald* (Halifax, NS), 6 July 1982, 7.
24 Brian O'Neill, "The Nova Scotia Offshore: A Case Study in the Political Economy of Underdevelopment," in *Oil and Gas Development in "Have-Not Regions,"* ed. A. Winson (Halifax: Gorsebrook Research Institute, 1984), 3.
25 Nova Scotia Resources Limited, annual report, 1982-83, p. 1.
26 Ibid., 1983-84, p. 5.
27 Canada, Department of Energy, Mines and Resources, *Offshore Exploration*, 73-83.
28 Nova Scotia Resources Limited, annual report, 1982-83, p. 3.

29 Ibid., 1982, p. 2.
30 Nova Scotia, House of Assembly, *Debates,* 21 April 1982, pp. 1765-66.
31 Fred McMahon, "NSRL's First Sale Was to Nova Scotians," *Chronicle-Herald* (Halifax, NS), 10 May 1983, 7.
32 Sable Island Environmental Assessment Panel, *Venture Development Project: Report of the Sable Island Environmental Assessment Panel* (Ottawa: Sable Island Environmental Assessment Panel, 1983).
33 Nova Scotia Resources Limited, annual report, 1985-86, pp. 4-5.
34 Ibid., 1986-87, p. 8.
35 Ibid., p. 3.
36 John Erik Fossum, *Oil, the State and Federalism: The Rise and Demise of Petro-Canada as a Statist Impulse* (Toronto: University of Toronto Press, 1997), 217.
37 Nova Scotia Resources Limited, annual report, 1986-87, p. 5.
38 Ibid., 1985-86, p. 9.
39 Nova Scotia, Auditor General, annual report, 1996, p. 175.
40 Ibid., p. 180.
41 Ibid., 183-85.
42 Nova Scotia, House of Assembly, Standing Committee on Public Accounts, *Proceedings,* 18 November 1999.
43 Peter Clancy et al., *The Savage Years: The Perils of Reinventing Government in Nova Scotia* (Halifax: Formac Publishing, 2000).
44 Nova Scotia, House of Assembly, Standing Committee on Public Accounts, *Proceedings,* 18 November 1999.

CHAPTER 6: CORRIDOR POLITICS

1 Brian Galligan, *Utah and Queensland Coal: A Study in the Micro Political Economy of Modern Capitalism and the State* (Brisbane: University of Queensland Press, 1989), 2.
2 For an early appreciation of the diversity of the Sable project's interests, see Jennifer Henderson, "Power Play: A Sable Primer," *Atlantic Progress* (September-October 1998): 225-37.
3 Peter Clancy, *Micro-Politics and Canadian Business: Paper, Steel and the Airlines* (Peterborough, ON: Broadview Press, 2004), Chap. 1.
4 Mobil Oil Canada et al., *Venture Development Project: Development Plan Submission,* vol. 1 (Halifax: Mobil Oil Canada, 1983).
5 Norm Wiens, "Sable Comes of Age," *GeoCanada2000,* May-June 2000.
6 G. Bruce Doern and Glen Toner, *The Politics of Energy: The Development and Implementation of the NEP* (Toronto: Methuen, 1985), Chap. 6.
7 Wiens, "Sable Comes of Age."
8 John Erik Fossum, *Oil, the State and Federalism: The Rise and Demise of Petro-Canada as a Statist Impulse* (Toronto: University of Toronto Press, 1997), 89-94.
9 Canada, National Energy Board, *The Maritimes Natural Gas Market: An Overview and Assessment* (Calgary: National Energy Board, 2003).
10 Sable Offshore Energy Project, "Timeline," 5 January 1995, http://www.soep.com/.

11 After subsequent adjustments, the new equity shares were as follows: Mobil 50.8 percent, Shell 31.3 percent, Imperial 9 percent, Nova Scotia Resources Limited 8.4 percent, and Mosbacher Operating Ltd. 5 percent.

12 For an illustrated description of Sable Offshore Energy operations, see the project's website.

13 Maritimes & Northeast Pipeline, *NEB/Joint Review Panel Facilities and Tolls Application,* vol. 1 (Halifax: Maritimes and Northeast Pipeline, 1996).

14 See, for example, the discussion of utilities in John N. McDougall, *Fuels and the National Policy* (Toronto: Butterworths, 1982), Chap. 6.

15 G. Bruce Doern and Monica Gattinger, *Power Switch: Energy Regulatory Governance in the Twenty-First Century* (Toronto: University of Toronto Press, 2003).

16 Canada and Nova Scotia, Joint Public Review Panel, *Report: Sable Gas Projects* (Halifax: Environment Canada and Nova Scotia Environment and Labour, 1997), 64.

17 The formal terms of association between the SOEP and the Maritimes & Northeast Pipeline were formalized in a memorandum of understanding on 3 December 1997. See Appendix 6 in Canada, National Energy Board, "Reasons for Decision: Maritimes and Northeast Pipeline Management Ltd.," Hearing Order GH-4-98, pp. 52-58, Calgary: National Energy Board.

18 Sable Offshore Energy Project, "Additional Written Evidence to the Joint Panel," n.d., but submitted in 1996.

19 "Joint Position on Tolling and Laterals Among: Province of Nova Scotia, Province of New Brunswick, Sable Offshore Energy Project and Maritimes & Northeast Pipeline," 19 June 1997, printed as Appendix 6, in Canada and Nova Scotia, Joint Public Review Panel, *Report,* 127.

20 Canada and Nova Scotia, Joint Public Review Panel, *Report,* 127.

21 Ibid., 9.

22 Nova Scotia, Premier's Office, "Better Gas Deal Reached, Premier Says," press release, 10 December 1997.

23 Offshore petroleum royalty regulations made under sec. 23 of the *Offshore Petroleum Royalties Regulations,* O.I.C. 1999-337 (17 June 1999), N.S. Reg. 71/99, as amended by O.I.C. 2007-89 (19 February 2007), N.S. Reg. 55/2007.

24 For further details, see Nova Scotia, *Seizing the Opportunity: Nova Scotia's Energy Strategy,* vol. 2, Part 10, "Energy and Fiscal and Taxation Policy" (Halifax: Department of Energy, 2001), 5-8.

25 Government of Nova Scotia, press release, 23 May 1996.

26 Nova Scotia, Department of Energy, "Offshore Petroleum Royalty Regime," http://www.gov.ns.ca/energy/resources/RA/offshore/Offshore-Petroleum-Royalty-Regime.pdf.

27 "Agreement for a Joint Public Review of the Proposed Sable Gas Projects," in Canada and Nova Scotia, Joint Public Review Panel, *Report,* Appendix 1, 111-20.

28 Canada and Nova Scotia, Joint Public Review Panel, *Report.*

29 John T. Sears, *Report of the Commissioner on the Sable Offshore Energy Project* (Halifax: Province of Nove Scotia, 1997).

30 Kevin Cox, "Sable Project in Peril: Official," *Globe and Mail,* 6 February 1997.

31 Judy Myrden, "Rival Bid for Gas Line Gets Hearing," *Chronicle-Herald* (Halifax, NS), 18 March 1997, A1, A2.
32 Canada and Nova Scotia, Joint Public Review Panel, *Report*, Appendix 6, 132.
33 Sable Offshore Energy Project, press release, 8 July 1996, http://www.soep.com/.
34 Ibid., 25 November 1996, http://www.soep.com/.
35 Graham Thomson, "Project Alliances," in *AMPLA Yearbook 1997* (Melbourne: Australian Mineral and Petroleum Law Association, 1997), 127-46.
36 Geoff King, "Cooperative Project Delivery," in *AMPLA Yearbook 1997* (Melbourne: Australian Mineral and Petroleum Law Association, 1997), 147-58.
37 Sable Offshore Energy Project, press release, 11 February 1998, http://www.soep.com/.
38 Ibid., 4 January 2000, http://www.soep.com/.
39 The announcements began early in 2002, when Shell Canada announced a downward revision of Sable sales gas reserves from 1.1 trillion cubic feet to 800 billion cubic feet (Shell Canada, press release, 31 January 2002).
40 To illustrate the methodology involved: Shell Canada cut reserve estimates on "its" Sable fields by 90 billion cubic feet to a new total of 700 billion cubic feet. In addition, another 200 billion cubic feet of sales gas was reclassified from proven developed to proven undeveloped. One year later, Shell went further, cutting its ultimate recoverable (sale gas) total by some 300 billion cubic feet, for a new projected total of only 430 billion cubic feet.
41 CNSOPB, annual report, 2003-4, p. 6.
42 Judy Myrden, "Future of Sable Gas Dims," *Chronicle Herald* (Halifax, NS), 9 July 2010, 1-2.
43 Canada, National Energy Board, "Reasons for Decision," Hearing Order GH-3-2002, 24 March 2002 (Calgary: National Energy Board).

CHAPTER 7: THE POLITICS OF BACKWARD LINKAGE

1 The issue of industrial benefits has a closely related parallel in employment benefits, a topic beyond the scope of this study.
2 For a comprehensive description of offshore technologies, see Don E. Kash et al., *Energy under the Oceans: A Technology Assessment of the Outer Continental Shelf Oil and Gas Operations* (Norman: University of Oklahoma Press, 1973).
3 Michael Jenkin, *British Industry and the North Sea: State Intervention in a Developing Industrial Sector* (London: Macmillan Press, 1981), 14.
4 Ibid.
5 Brent F. Nelson, *The State Offshore: Petroleum, Politics and State Intervention on the British and Norwegian Continental Shelves* (New York: Praeger, 1991), Chap. 5 and passim.
6 Among other studies, see Eric Hanson, *Dynamic Decade* (Toronto: University of Toronto Press, 1961); John N. MacDougall, *Fuels and the National Policy* (Toronto: Butterworth, 1982); and William Kilbourn, *Pipeline* (Toronto: Clarke Irwin, 1970).
7 Roger Voyer, *Offshore Oil: Opportunities for Industrial Development and Job Creation* (Toronto: Canadian Institute for Economic Policy, 1983), 33.
8 Ibid.

9 J. Bruce Doern and Glen Toner, *The Politics of Energy: The Development and Implementation of the NEP* (Toronto: Methuen, 1985); and Jon Erik Fossum, *Oil, the State and Federalism: The Rise and Demise of Petro-Canada as a Statist Impulse* (Toronto: University of Toronto Press, 1997).
10 Bill C-48, Canada Oil and Gas Act, Statutes of Canada, 1980-83, c.81, s. 10(3) and s. 76 3.2.(2).
11 Stephen Clarkson, *Canada and the Reagan Challenge* (Toronto: Canadian Institute for Economic Policy, 1982), Chap. 4 and passim.
12 J.D. House, *The Last of the Free Enterprisers: The Oilmen of Calgary* (Toronto: Macmillan, 1980).
13 Vern Baxter, "Political Economy of Oil and Exploitation of Offshore Oil," in *Impact of Offshore Oil Exploration and Production on the Social Institutions of Coastal Louisiana,* ed. Shirley Laska (Baton Rouge: Department of the Interior, 1983), 26.
14 Offshore Operators Committee, "Who Is the Offshore Operators Committee?" n.d., http://www.offshoreoperators.com/who_is.shtml.
15 "Canadian Petroleum Association fonds," Glenbow Archives, Calgary, Alberta.
16 An interesting commentary on ongoing offshore activities can be found in the *Eastern Offshore News,* produced by the EPOA/OOC/Frontier Division thrice annually from 1979 to 1992.
17 Barry Beale, *Energy and Industry* (Toronto: Canadian Institute for Economic Policy, 1980).
18 For two perspectives on the industrial strategy, see Richard French, *How Ottawa Decides: Planning and Industrial Policy-Making, 1968-80* (Toronto: Canadian Institute for Economic Policy, 1980), and Mark C. Baetz, "Tier One/Tier Two" in *Canadian Cases in Business-Government Relations,* ed. Mark Baetz and Donald H. Thain (Toronto: Methuen, 1985).
19 Offshore/Onshore Technologies Association of Nova Scotia, "History," http://www.otans.com/.
20 Ibid.
21 Canada, Department of Industry, Trade and Commerce and Regional Economic Expansion, *Sector Profile: The Ocean Industry in Canada* (Ottawa: Industry, Trade and Commerce, 1977), 1.
22 Canada, Department of Industry, Trade and Commerce and Regional Economic Expansion, *Report by the Sector Task Force on the Canadian Ocean Industry* (Ottawa: Industry, Trade and Commerce, 1978).
23 Nova Scotia, Department of Development, *NS Ocean Industry Directory, 1984-85* (Halifax: Department of Development, 1985), viii.
24 Consultative Task Force on Industrial and Regional Benefits, *Major Canadian Projects, Major Canadian Opportunities: A Report* (Ottawa: s.n., 1981).
25 Canada, Department of Industry, Trade and Commerce, "Industrial and Regional Benefits Objectives," news release, 20 May 1982.
26 Senate of Canada, Special Senate Committee on the Northern Pipeline, *Proceedings,* No. 35 (14 September 1982), quoted in *Eastern Offshore News* 5, 2 (August 1983): 6.
27 "East Coast Petroleum Industry and Canada and Regional Benefits," *Eastcoast Offshore News* 7, 2 (1985): 15.

28 Nova Scotia, Voluntary Economic Planning, *Oil and Natural Gas Offshore Development: The Opportunities and the Challenge* (Halifax: Voluntary Economic Planning, 1980).

29 Nova Scotia, Department of Mines and Energy, *Offshore Oil and Gas: A Chance for Nova Scotians* (Halifax: Department of Mines and Energy, 1980).

30 Stevenson, Thorne and Kellogg and Gardner Pinfold, *Scotian Shelf Gas Development: The Economic Impact on Nova Scotia* (Halifax: Stevenson, Thorne and Kellogg, 1981).

31 *Canada–Nova Scotia Agreement on Offshore Oil and Gas Resource Management and Revenue Sharing,* 1982, s. 21(a).

32 The impact of this fund is addressed in Canada, Auditor General of Canada, *Report of the Auditor General of Canada, 1988* (Ottawa: Supply and Services Canada, 1988), Chap. 10.

33 Voyer, *Offshore Oil,* 58.

34 Peter Foster, *From Rigs to Riches: The Story of Bow Valley Industries* (Calgary: Bow Valley Industries, 1985), Chap. 18.

35 See, for example, Canadian Petroleum Association, "Discussion Paper on Supplier Development," 25 July 1983, CPA File 1,687. Canadian Petroleum Association Fonds, Glenbow Archives, Calgary (hereafter designated by title and CPA file number).

36 Canadian Petroleum Association, "Submission Regarding the Canada Oil and Gas Act," May 1985; and "Response to COGLA re 'An Operational Framework for Canada Benefits,'" 31 July 1985; CPA File 1,882.

37 Canadian Petroleum Association, "Designated Item Process" 5 March 1985, CPA File 1,882.

38 "Eastcoast Petroleum Industry and Canada and Regional Benefits," *Eastern Offshore News* 7, 2 (1985): 14-17.

39 Isautier to Carney and Crombie, 21 May 1985, "Submission Regarding the Canada Oil and Gas Act," p. 4, CPA File 1,882.

40 Mercier to Smyth, 6 December 1985, CPA File 1,882.

41 The CNSOPB was established by the terms of the Canada–Nova Scotia Accord of August 1986. However, because the mirror legislation required to authorize the board was not enacted until the close of 1989, the COGLA, together with the Government of Nova Scotia, continued to administer benefits until the board opened its doors in January 1990. The 1986 guidelines were revised in 1994 and continue to shape industrial benefits plans. For the current guidelines, see "Benefits Plans," CNSOPB, http://www.cnsopb.ns.ca/benefits_plans.php.

42 Canadian Association of Petroleum Producers, "Atlantic Energy Roundtable," presented to Atlantic Canada Energy Roundtable by Gerald Protti, 22 November 2002, http://www.capp.ca/default.asp?V_DOC_ID=642.

43 Regulatory Issues Steering Committee and Industrial Opportunities Task Force, "Submission to Atlantic Energy Roundtable II," 31 October 2003.

44 Canadian Association of Petroleum Producers, "Submission: Atlantic Energy Roundtable," November 2002, p. 22.

45 Paul Barnes, Canadian Association of Petroleum Producers, "Atlantic Canada Activity and Procurement Overview," 11 March 2004.

46 Nova Scotia, Department of Energy, *Seizing the Opportunity* (Halifax: Department of Energy, 2002), 2:12.

47 Wade Locke, "Offshore Oil and Gas: Is Newfoundland and Labrador Getting Its 'Fair Share'?" (paper presented at Leslie Harris Centre of Regional Policy and Development, St. John's, Newfoundland, 15 November 2006).

48 Nova Scotia, Department of Energy, *Seizing the Opportunity,* 2:21.

49 *Offshore Strategic Energy Agreement between Nova Scotia and EnCana,* 22 June 2006, p. 4.

50 Gerald Protti, EnCana Executive Vice-President, Corporate Relations and President, Offshore and International Affairs, "Speech to OTANS 25th Anniversary Dinner," Halifax, Nova Scotia, 20 February 2007.

CHAPTER 8: THE POLITICS OF FISCAL ENTITLEMENT

1 *Constitution Act, 1982,* s. 36(2), being Schedule B to the *Constitution Act 1982* (U.K.), 1982, c. 11.

2 Canada, Constitution Act, 1982.

3 Canada, Senate Standing Committee on National Finances, *Proceedings,* No. 22 (18 October 2001), 3.

4 For a historical survey of the equalization program in its early decades, see Robin W. Boadway, *Intergovernmental Transfers in Canada* (Toronto: Canadian Tax Foundation, 1980), 10-18. For a discussion of contemporary equalization developments, see Douglas M. Brown, "Fiscal Federalism: Searching for Balance," in *Canadian Federalism: Performance, Effectiveness and Legitimacy,* ed, Herman Bakvis and Grace Skogstad (Don Mills, ON: Oxford University Press, 2008), 63-88.

5 *Canada–Nova Scotia Agreement on Offshore Oil and Gas Resource Management and Revenue Sharing,* 1982, s. 15, p. 19.

6 Herman Bakvis, R.L Mazany, and A. Sinclair, "Energy Policy," *Governing Nova Scotia,* ed. Barbara Jamieson, 65-79 (Halifax: Dalhousie School of Public Administration, 1984).

7 *Canada–Nova Scotia Offshore Petroleum Resources Accord,* 26 August 1986, art. 27 (hereafter *Canada–Nova Scotia Accord*).

8 J.D. House, *The Challenge of Oil: Newfoundland's Quest for Controlled Development* (St. John's: Institute for Social and Economic Research, 1985).

9 *The Atlantic Accord* (*Memorandum of Agreement between the Government of Canada and the Government of Newfoundland and Labrador on Offshore Oil and Gas Resource Management and Revenue Sharing*), 11 February 1985, s. 2(c) (hereafter *Atlantic Accord*). Parallel language appears in the *Canada–Nova Scotia Accord,* s. 1.02(c).

10 *Atlantic Accord,* s. 2(e) and *Canada–Nova Scotia Accord,* s. 1.02(e).

11 For descriptions of the mechanism, see Canada, Department of Finance, "Federal Transfers to Provinces and Territories," http://www.fin.gc.ca/access/fedprov-eng.asp, and Wade Locke and Paul Hobson, "An Examination of the Interaction between Natural Resource Revenues and Equalization Payments: Lessons for Atlantic Canada," Working Paper 2004-10, Institute for Research on Public Policy, Montreal, 2004.

12 For details on the workings of the generic solution, see Thomas J. Courchene, "Confiscatory Equalization: The Intriguing Case of Saskatchewan's Vanishing Energy Revenues," *Choices* 10, 2 (2004): 1-44.

13 Premier Grimes of Newfoundland and Labrador captured the East Coast's position aptly, stating "we are led to believe by other provincial politicians in other jurisdictions and by federal politicians ... that changes to equalization can occur only if the provinces and territories agree. I would like to speak about that absolute fallacy and remind people that it is a program of the government of Canada, completely and totally within its control." Canada, Senate Standing Committee in National Finance, *Proceedings,* No. 22 (18 October 2001): 3.

14 Hon. John F. Hamm, Remarks to the Nova Scotia Chamber of Commerce, Halifax, 24 October 2000.

15 Hon. John F. Hamm, Remarks to the Metropolitan Halifax Chamber of Commerce, Halifax, 17 January 2001.

16 Hon. John F. Hamm, Newsmaker Breakfast Series, Ottawa, 7 February 2001.

17 Editorial, "Nova Scotia's Due," *National Post,* 13 June 2001.

18 John Crosbie, "Boom or Bust?" *Globe and Mail,* 12 September 2001.

19 Stéphane Dion, "Offshore Accords: Setting the Record Straight," *Chronicle-Herald* (Halifax, NS), 28 September 2001.

20 Canada, Senate Standing Committee on National Finances, "The Effectiveness of and Possible Improvements to the Present Equalization Policy," 14th Report, March 2002.

21 Newfoundland, *Royal Commission on Renewal and Strengthening Our Place in Confederation* (St. John's: Royal Commission, 2003), 9.

22 Ibid., 148-49.

23 Progressive Conservative Party of Newfoundland, *The PC Plan,* Chap. 2, http://www.pcparty.nf.net/plan2003d.htm.

24 See, for example, Paul Wells, *Right Side Up: The Fall of Paul Martin and the Rise of Stephen Harper's New Conservatism* (Toronto: McClelland and Stewart, 2006); John Gray, *Paul Martin: In the Balance* (Toronto: Key Porter Books, 2004); and Stephen Clarkson, *The Big Red Machine: How the Liberal Party Dominates Canadian Politics* (Vancouver: UBC Press, 2005).

25 Amy Fraser, "Regan Wants PM to Rethink Offshore," *Chronicle Herald* (Halifax, NS), 7 June 2004.

26 Stephen Maher, "Revenue Deal Won't Change NS Equalization Payments," *Chronicle Herald* (Halifax, NS), 8 June 2004.

27 Amy Smith and Stephen Maher, "NS Sure to Win on Offshore – Hamm," *Chronicle Herald* (Halifax, NS), 11 June 2004.

28 Stephen Maher, "NS Can Keep All Offshore Cash, Martin Says," *Chronicle Herald* (Halifax, NS), 28 June 2004.

29 Stephen Maher, "Hamm Doesn't Buy Offshore Pact," *Chronicle Herald* (Halifax, NS), 26 October 2004.

30 Canadian Press, "Premier Looks for New Deal on Offshore," *Chronicle Herald* (Halifax, NS), 28 October 2004.

31 Stephen Maher, "Offshore Talks Move to Nfld," *Chronicle Herald* (Halifax, NS), 20 November 2004.

32 Bank of Nova Scotia, Global Economic Research, "The Agreement on Offshore Revenues," *Fiscal Pulse,* 31 January 2005 (revised 29 June 2005).
33 Brian Crowley, "Nova Scotia Premier Invests Wisely upon Sales of Assets," *Chronicle Herald* (Halifax, NS), 2 September 2005.
34 James Bickerton, "Equalization, Regional Development, and Political Trust: The Section 36/Atlantic Accords Controversy," *Constitutional Forum constitutionnel* 17, 3 (2008): 99-111.
35 Canada and Nova Scotia, *Arrangement between the Government of Canada and the Government of Nova Scotia on Offshore Revenues,* 14 February 2005, 1.
36 Rodney MacDonald, "A Deal Is a Deal: Protecting Our Offshore Accord," *What's New in Nova Scotia,* pamphlet, Halifax, Summer 2007, p. 1, 3.
37 Bickerton, "Equalization."
38 Bill Casey, "Letter," June 2007, http://www.billcasey.ca/.
39 Casey claims that at a meeting immediately before the budget vote, he was locked in a room and hectored about loyalty and was promised a last-minute breakthrough. Ibid.
40 CTV Newswire, "Poll Shows Atlantic Accord Has Hurt Tories," 8 June 2007.
41 Paul A.R. Hobson and L. Wade Locke, "Assessing the Equalization options of Budget 2007 for the Atlantic Provinces," *APEC Commentary,* 13 June 2007.
42 Rodney MacDonald, "Our Offshore Accord," *What's New in Nova Scotia,* pamphlet, Halifax, Fall 2007, p. 1.
43 John Ivison, "Tories Set to Hand N.S. $850m Windfall," *National Post,* 7 July 2008.
44 Canada–Nova Scotia Panel on Crown Share Adjustment Payments, *Report of the Panel,* 4 July 2008, http://www.fin.gc.ca/n08/data/08-053_5-eng.asp.
45 Stephen Maher and David Jackson, "Millions Coming Our Way," *Chronicle Herald* (Halifax, NS), 9 July 2008, A1, A5.
46 For details, see Deloitte Touche LLP, *Province of Nova Scotia Financial Review: Interim Report* (Halifax: Deloitte Touche, 2009), 5-8.
47 David Jackson, "Not Much Gas Left in the Tank," *Chronicle Herald* (Halifax, NS), 9 August 2010, 1-2.
48 Nova Scotia, Department of Finance, *Getting Back to Balance* (Halifax: Department of Finance, 2009).

CHAPTER 9: THE ONSHORE POLITICS OF GAS DISTRIBUTION

1 Nova Scotia, Voluntary Economic Planning, *Oil and Gas Offshore Development: The Opportunities and the Challenge* (Halifax: Voluntary Economic Planning, 1980), 5.
2 Nova Scotia, Department of Mines and Energy, *Offshore Oil and Gas: A Chance for Nova Scotians* (Halifax: Department of Mines and Energy, 1980), 14.
3 Nova Scotia, Department of Mines and Energy, *The Natural Gas Pipeline: Toward Energy Security for Nova Scotia* (Halifax: Department of Mines and Energy, 1980).
4 Roger Taylor, "Suspense Unwelcome in Offshore NS Agreement, *Chronicle-Herald* (Halifax, NS), 17 September 1996, C1; Jim Meek, "Missing in Action," *Chronicle-Herald* (Halifax, NS), 22 October 1996, C1.
5 For example, see Dale Madill, "Savage Vows Pipeline Fight," *Chronicle-Herald* (Halifax, NS), 29 June 1996, A7; Brian Underhill, "Let Economics Dictate Sable Gas Route," *Chronicle-Herald* (Halifax, NS), 13 July 1996, A13.

6 Judy Myrden, "Keep Sable Gas Off Agenda Says Savage," *Chronicle-Herald* (Halifax, NS), 22 August 1996, A1; Brian Ward, "Savage Gears Up for Gas War," *Chronicle-Herald* (Halifax, NS), 6 September 1996, A5.
7 Elliott Stikeman and Ziff Energy Group, "Regulation of Gas Distribution Systems in Nova Scotia," 23 July 1996, Nova Scotia Department of Natural Resources.
8 Byline, "Ideas on Natural Gas Regulation Sought," *Chronicle-Herald* (Halifax, NS), 3 August 1996, A15.
9 Jon Erik Fossum, *Oil, the State and Federalism: The Rise and Demise of Petro-Canada as a Statist Impulse* (Toronto: University of Toronto Press, 1997), 212.
10 Canada, National Energy Board, *NEB: Ten Years After* (Ottawa: National Energy Board, 1996).
11 G. Bruce Doern, "Moved Out and Moving On: The National Energy Board as a Reinvented Regulatory Agency," in *Changing the Rules: Canadian Regulatory Regimes and Institutions*, ed. G. Bruce Doern et al., 82-97 (Toronto: University of Toronto Press, 1999).
12 For a description of these changes as they affected the electricity and natural gas sectors, see G. Bruce Doern and Monica Gattinger, *Power Switch: Energy Regulatory Governance in the Twenty-First Century* (Toronto: University of Toronto Press, 2003).
13 Cameron MacKeen, "Gas Bill Gets a Rough Ride," *Chronicle-Herald* (Halifax, NS), 18 April 1997, A6.
14 Dale Madill and Cameron MacKeen, "House Bids Premier Farewell: Premier Proud to Have Served," *Chronicle-Herald* (Halifax, NS), 10 May 1997, A1.
15 Cameron MacKeen, "NS Urged to Go Slower on Gas Distribution Act: Chamber Letter Lists Several Problems with Legislation," *Chronicle-Herald* (Halifax, NS), 3 May 1997, A9.
16 Cameron MacKeen, "Board Given Power to Select Gas Distributors," *Chronicle-Herald* (Halifax, NS), 16 April 1997, A3, 6.
17 Dale Madill, "Liberal Leadership Race Begins to Run on Sable Gas," *Chronicle-Herald* (Halifax, NS), 25 June 1997, A4.
18 Susan LeBlanc, "NDP Would Not Axe the Gas Deal," *Chronicle-Herald* (Halifax, NS), 18 March 1998, A10.
19 Brian Medel, "Premier Promises Region Won't Suffer Steep Gas Prices," *Chronicle-Herald* (Halifax, NS), 23 October 1998, A6.
20 Jim Meek, "Greed, Gullibility and Sable Island Natural Gas," *Chronicle-Herald* (Halifax, NS), 25 October 1998, A3.
21 Jim Meek, "Premier Wants Gas Subsidy: MacLellan to Lobby Ottawa," *Chronicle-Herald* (Halifax, NS), 1 November 1998, A1.
22 Eva Hoare, "Oil Heat Group Warns against Gas Subsidies," *Chronicle-Herald* (Halifax, NS), 18 November 1998, C2.
23 Brian Medel, "Too Little Gas for All, Hamm Tells Delegates," *Chronicle-Herald* (Halifax, NS), 24 October 1998, A4.
24 Bruce Erskine, "NDP Slams Gas Deal: Premier Says Agreements Will Lower Consumer Costs," *Chronicle-Herald* (Halifax, NS), 27 October 1998, A1; Bruce

Erskine, "Lateral Projections Come under Scrutiny," *Chronicle-Herald* (Halifax, NS), 27 November 1998, D1.

25 Steve Harder, "Panel Hears Differing Views on Conditions for Gas Lateral," *Chronicle-Herald* (Halifax, NS), 2 December 1998, C5.

26 Nova Scotia, Petroleum Directorate, news release, Halifax, 9 November 1998.

27 Judy Myrden, "Government Hearings Put on Hold – Consultant," *Chronicle-Herald* (Halifax, NS), 3 July 1998, B1.

28 Howard Windsor and Peter Aucoin, "The Regulation of Telephone Service in Nova Scotia," in *The Regulatory Process in Canada,* ed. G.B. Doern, 237-58 (Toronto: Macmillan of Canada, 1978).

29 Nova Scotia, Utilities and Review Board, "History and Jurisdiction," http://www.nsuarb.ca/.

30 Cameron MacKeen, "Parties See Eye to Eye on UARB Appointments," *Chronicle-Herald* (Halifax, NS), 28 November 1998, A3.

31 Bruce Erskine and Eva Hoare, "NSP, Enbridge Back Out of Gas Bid: Provincial Distribution 'Not Economically feasible,'" *Chronicle-Herald* (Halifax, NS), 12 December 1998, B5.

32 Bruce Erskine, "Gas Distribution Projected at $1b: Sempra Wants Figure to Exceed 62%," *Chronicle-Herald* (Halifax, NS), 3 December 1998, D10.

33 Bruce Erskine, "Gas Distribution Race Heats Up: Applicants Range from Large Companies to Local Co-ops," *Chronicle-Herald* (Halifax, NS), 15 December 1998, C1.

34 Bruce Erskine, "SaskEnergy Drops Out of Sable Bid: Irving Group Enters Fray," *Chronicle-Herald* (Halifax, NS), 16 December 1998, B1.

35 New Brunswick, Legislative Assembly, Select Committee on Energy, "Report on Public Policy and Legislative Issues Surrounding Natural Gas in New Brunswick," Fredericton, November 1998.

36 Bruce Erskine, "Gas Distribution Deadline Passes: Seven Local Groups Apply," *Chronicle-Herald* (Halifax, NS), 17 December 1998, A.9, 11.

37 Marver Bernstein, *Regulating Business by Independent Commission* (Princeton, NJ: Princeton University Press, 1955).

38 Steve Maich, "Parties Miles Apart on Gas Utility Deal," *Chronicle-Herald* (Halifax, NS), 6 Jan 2000, A6.

39 Steve Maich, "Halifax Gas Unlikely This Year: Sempra," *Chronicle-Herald* (Halifax, NS), 20 January 2000, A2.

40 Steve Maich, "Sempra: Taxes May Kill Gas Deal," *Chronicle-Herald* (Halifax, NS), 9 February 2000, A1.

41 Bruce Erskine and Steve Maich, "Sempra, Municipality Settle Tax Differences," *Chronicle-Herald* (Halifax, NS), 7 April 2000, C5.

42 Bruce Erskine, "Natural Gas Marketing Hearings Begin June 6," *Chronicle-Herald* (Halifax, NS), 25 May 2000, C7.

43 Judy Myrden, "Sempra Advantage Feared; Rivals Seek Limits on Use of Name," *Chronicle-Herald* (Halifax, NS), 7 July 2000, A1.

44 Tom McCoag, "Sempra Lobbies to Cut Red Tape," *Chronicle-Herald* (Halifax, NS), 17 Oct 2000, B3.

45 Tom McCoag, "Amherst, Cumberland Politicians Lobby for Gas Pipeline Tests," *Chronicle-Herald* (Halifax, NS), 17 Nov 2000, B3.

46 Bruce Erskine, "Highway Pipe Idea Supported by Consultant," *Chronicle-Herald* (Halifax, NS), 8 December 2000, D3.

47 Bruce Erskine, "Roadway Pipelines Not Forbidden, Sempra Says," *Chronicle-Herald* (Halifax, NS), 12 April 2001, C4.

48 Bruce Erskine, "Province Puts a Crimp in Sempra Pipes: Road Shoulders Off Limits," *Chronicle-Herald* (Halifax, NS), 11 April 2001, A1.

49 Bruce Erskine, "Roadway Pipes Not Forbidden, Sempra Says: Gas Distributor Was Willing to Help with Cost," *Chronicle-Herald* (Halifax, NS), 12 April 2001, C4.

50 Sempra, "Sempra Atlantic Gas Re-examines Distribution Plan," news release, 10 April 2001.

51 Bruce Erskine, "Sempra Lays Off 35 as Impasse Continues," *Chronicle-Herald* (Halifax, NS), 9 June 2001, A1.

52 Bruce Erskine, "Ex-Sempra Boss Can Forsee Firm Leaving Nova Scotia," *Chronicle-Herald* (Halifax, NS), 8 June 2001, B1.

53 Bruce Erskine, "Sempra Presses for New Deal: Company to Leave NS This Month," *Chronicle-Herald* (Halifax, NS), 2 June 2001, A1.

54 Nova Scotia, Petroleum Directorate, "Government Asks Gas Distributors to Go to UARB for Changes," news release, 1 June 2001.

55 Sempra Atlantic, "Notice of Application to the UARB for Franchise Surrender or Amendment by Sempra Atlantic," 29 June 2001, http://www.gov.ns.ca/petro/documents/SempraApplication.pdf.

56 Ibid.

57 Sempra Atlantic Submission to N.S. Provincial Energy Strategy Committee, Letter from James L. Connors to Scott Swinden and Paul Taylor, 10 July 2001, 5 pp.

58 Nova Scotia, Utilities and Review Board, "Natural Gas Distribution: Directions on Procedure for Sempra Atlantic's Surrender," 6 August 2001, http://www.gov.ns.ca/petro/documents/uarddirectionsonprocedure.pdf.

59 Bruce Erskine, "Sempra Pulls Plug on Gas Franchise," *Chronicle-Herald* (Halifax, NS), 22 September 2001, A1.

60 Nova Scotia, Utilities and Review Board, "Sempra Atlantic's Surrender," 25 February 2002.

61 Nova Scotia, Department of Energy, *Seizing the Opportunity: Nova Scotia's Energy Strategy* (Halifax: Department of Energy, 2001), 1:12.

62 Nova Scotia, Department of Energy, *Seizing the Opportunity,* 2:13.

63 Ibid., 2:16

64 Bruce Erskine, "Province Revamps Gas Rules; Service a Long Shot outside of Cities," *Chronicle-Herald* (Halifax, NS), 31 January 2002, A15.

65 Bruce Erskine, "Enbridge Needs Details before Bidding for NS Franchise," *Chronicle-Herald* (Halifax, NS), 14 December 2001, C2, and Judy Myrden, "SaskEnergy Eager to Deliver Gas; System Construction Could Begin in the Fall," *Chronicle-Herald* (Halifax, NS), 2 February 2002, C1.

66 Judy Myrden, "SaskEnergy Frowns on Gas 'Cherry-Pickers': Distribution System Not Compatible with Bypass Option," *Chronicle-Herald* (Halifax, NS), 22 February 2002, C1.

67 Amy Smith, "NS Eases Rules for Gas Distribution," *Chronicle-Herald* (Halifax, NS), 9 April 2002, A1.
68 Bruce Erskine, "Province Reconsiders Roadside Pipeline," *Chronicle-Herald* (Halifax, NS), 9 April 2002, A1.
69 Heritage Gas Inc., "Application for Full Regulation Class Franchise," Vol. 1, August 2002, s. 6.4.1.4, p. 46, Nova Scotia Utilities and Review Board records, Halifax.
70 Erskine, "Province Reconsiders."
71 Bruce Erskine, "Enbridge Needs Details before Bidding for NS Franchise," *Chronicle-Herald* (Halifax, NS), 14 December 2001, C2.
72 Jeffrey Simpson, "Some in HRM May Get Offshore Gas by Fall," *Chronicle-Herald* (Halifax, NS), 10 January 2002, A4.
73 In addition to the applicants, the list of intervenors included the Town of Amherst, the Canadian Association of Petroleum Producers, the Canadian Oil Heat Association (NS chapter), Emera Energy and its subsidiary Nova Scotia Power, GasWorks Installations, the Halifax Regional Municipality, Imperial Oil Resources, Industrial Cape Breton Board of Trade and Grow Cape Breton Partnership Inc., Irving Energy Services Ltd., Maritimes NRG Nova Scotia Ltd., the NDP Caucus, the Nova Scotia Department of Energy, the Union of Nova Scotia Municipalities, and an unknown intervenor.
74 Bruce Erskine, "Heritage Gas Plan Unwrapped," *Chronicle-Herald* (Halifax, NS), 16 August 2002, C1.
75 Judy Myrden, "No Gas in Halifax for a Few Years," *Chronicle-Herald* (Halifax, NS), 12 October 2002, A18; Judy Myrden, "NSP Changed Mind Over 'Unfair' Heritage Rates," *Chronicle-Herald* (Halifax, NS), 18 October 2002, C1.
76 Judy Myrden, "Heritage Has Profits in Sights," *Chronicle-Herald* (Halifax, NS), 8 October 2002, C1.
77 Judy Myrden, "Modest Heritage Gas Proposal Touted as 'Sustainable,'" *Chronicle-Herald* (Halifax, NS), 9 October 2002, C1; Judy Myrden, "Gas Plan Disappoints Premier," *Chronicle-Herald* (Halifax, NS), 10 October 2002, B3.
78 Nova Scotia, Utilities and Review Board, "Franchise Applications for the Distribution of Natural Gas in the Province of Nova Scotia," Decision NSUARB-2003-8, 7 February 2003, p. 19, http://www.canlii.org/ns/cas/nsuarb/2003/2003nsuarb8.html.
79 Strait Area Gas Inc., "Submission to the Nova Scotia Utilities and Review Board for the Natural Gas Distribution Franchise for the Strait Area," NG-02, received 16 August 2002, Halifax.
80 Judy Myrden, "Strait Are to Make Last Gas Pitch," *Chronicle-Herald* (Halifax, NS), 25 September 2002, B11.
81 Judy Myrden, "Strait Area Gas Plan Common in Third World," *Chronicle-Herald* (Halifax, NS), 17 October 2002, A14.
82 Judy Myrden and Eva Hoare, "Strait Towns, Heritage win gas franchise" *Chronicle-Herald* (Halifax, NS), 8 February 2003, A1.
83 Judy Myrden, "NS backs Strait Area gas plan" *Chronicle-Herald* (Halifax, NS), 8 November 2002, C1.
84 Judy Myrden, "Towns Move into Big Leagues," *Chronicle-Herald* (Halifax, NS), 30 September 2003, F1.

85 Heritage Gas Ltd., *Heritage Gas Pipeline News*, January 2006, http://www.saskenergy.com/.
86 Heritage Gas, "Who We Are," http://www.heritagegas.com/.
87 Rich Ferguson, "North American Natural Gas Crisis" (presentation to California State Committee on Energy, Utilities and Communications, Sacramento, CA, 27 October 2005).

CHAPTER 10: THE LIQUEFIED NATURAL GAS FACTOR

1 James Jensen, *The Development of a Global LNG Market: Is It Likely? If So, When?* (Oxford: Oxford Institute for Energy Studies, 2004), 1.
2 Adrian Cottrill, "Liquefaction Dips Toes in Water," *LNG Inside Upstream*, 5 April 2007, 8-9.
3 Michelle M. Foss, "Introduction to LNG: An Overview," Centre for Energy Economics, Houston, 2003, updated 2007, p. 12.
4 Jensen, *Development of a Global*, 8.
5 Foss, "Introduction to LNG: An Overview" p. 13.
6 Jensen, *Development of a Global*, 6.
7 Irving Oil Limited, "LNG Marine Terminal/Multi-purpose Pier Project: Environmental Impact Statement," Saint John, March 2004.
8 Sophia Ruester and Anne Neumann, *Next Year, Next Decade, Never? The Prospects of Liquefied Natural Gas Development in the US* (Berlin: German Institute for Economic Research, 2007), 37.
9 Angela Tu Weissenberger, "Casting a Cold Eye on LNG: The Real Possibilities and Pitfalls for Atlantic Canada," AIMS Oil and Gas Paper #4, Atlantic Institute for Market Studies, Halifax, January 2006, p. 5.
10 Ruester and Neumann, *Next Year*, 37.
11 Damien Gaul and Kobi Platt, *Short-Term Energy Outlook Supplement: U.S. LNG Imports – the Next Wave* (Washington, DC: Energy Information Administration, 2007).
12 Weissenberger, "Casting a Cold Eye," 1.
13 Anthony Guegel, "Culling Season on the Gulf Coast," *LNG Inside Upstream*, 1 September 2006, 9-10.
14 Jensen, *The Development of a Global*, 1.
15 Ibid., p.17. It should be noted that buyers were often restricted in reselling contracted gas.
16 Weissenburger, "Casting a Cold Eye," 1.
17 US Energy Information Agency, "Natural Gas Navigator," http://www.eia.doe.gov/dnav/ng/hist/n9103us3m.htm.
18 Weissenberger, "Casting a Cold Eye," 15-17.
19 Canada, National Energy Board, "LNG Regulatory Requirements," 9 August 2005, Calgary.
20 New Brunswick, *Energy Strategy* (Fredericton: Department of Natural Resources and Energy, 2001), 35.
21 Nova Scotia, Department of Energy, *Seizing the Opportunity: Nova Scotia's Energy Strategy*, 2 vols. (Halifax: Department of Energy, 2001).

22 Access Northeast, "Access Northeast Energy Plans Bear Head LNG Terminal," news release, 26 August 2003.

23 Premier's Office, "Nova Scotia Welcomes New Energy Investment," press release, 12 August 2004.

24 Nova Scotia Business Inc., "NSBI Land Sale to Bear Head Corporation Completed," press release, 2 May 2005.

25 "Anadarko Updates Bear Head LNG Terminal Status," *OilOnline*, 14 March 2006, http://www.oilonline.com/.

26 Deborah Yedlin, "Anadarko's Big Deal Will Be a Tough Sell," *Globe and Mail*, 3 August 2006, B2.

27 Anadarko Petroleum Corp., "Anadarko Announces Sale of Canadian Subsidiary," press release, 14 September 2006.

28 "Bear Head New Boys Brave Supply Squeeze," *LNG Inside Upstream*, 4 August 2006, p. 9.

29 "Anadarko Unable to Complete Sale of Bear Head LNG Site," *Alexander's Gas and Oil Connections*, 29 September 2006.

30 Maritimes & Northeast Pipeline, SEC Information Filing, Maritimes & Northeast Pipeline to Anadarko Petroleum Corp., 8 September 2006.

31 Michael Tutton, "Anadarko Out of Gas," *Chronicle Herald* (Halifax, NS), 8 February 2007, C3.

32 Transport Canada and Fisheries and Oceans Canada, "Environmental Assessment Track Report for the Petrochemical and Liquefied Natural Gas Facilities at Goldboro, N.S.," submitted to minister of the environment, 14 October 2005.

33 Canadian Environmental Assessment Agency, "Proposed Keltic LNG Project Environmental Assessment to Continue as a Comprehensive Study," Notice, Ottawa, 5 January 2005.

34 "The Keltic Hearings," *East Nova Business Report*, 1, 9 (2006): 1, 3, 5-12.

35 Nova Scotia, Environmental Assessment Board, *Report and Recommendations for the Review of Keltic Petrochemicals Inc.* (Halifax: Environmental Assessment Board, 2007).

36 Petroplus International B.V., "4Gas and Keltic Petrochemicals Inc. to Advance the Nova Scotia LNG Terminal," press release, 19 December 2005.

37 "Dragon LNG Limited," 29 October 2004.

38 Judy Myrden, "Falling Demand Puts LNG Terminal Plans Up in Air," *Chronicle Herald* (Halifax, NS), 19 June 2010, C4; Judy Myrden, "Goldboro LNG Plant a No Go," *Chronicle Herald* (Halifax, NS), 25 August 2010, A1, A2.

39 Reuters, "Irving Oil Revives Eastern Canada LNG Plan," 18 June 2003.

40 Adam Bruns, "Hitting for the Cycle: Atlantic Canada, South American Prospects Bring Repsol into North American LNG Picture," *Site Selection*, 20 June 2005, http://www.siteselection.com/ssinsider/pwatch/pw050620.htm.

41 Repsol YPF, "History of Repsol YPF," http://www.repsol.com/.

42 Canaport LNG, "Who We Are," http://www.canaportlng.com/.

43 Canada, National Energy Board, "Argument of Repsol Energy Canada Ltd," Hearing Order GH-1-2006, 15 December 2006, pp. 11-16.

44 Canada, National Energy Board, "Reasons for Decision: Emera Brunswick Pipeline Co. Ltd.," GH-1-2006, Calgary, May 2007.

45 G. Bruce Doern and Monica Gattinger, *Power Switch: Energy Regulatory Governance in the Twenty-First Century* (Toronto: University of Toronto Press, 2003).

46 Canada, National Energy Board, *Natural Gas Market Assessment: Ten Years after De-regulation* (Calgary: National Energy Board, 1996), v.

47 The Atlantic Institute for Market Studies drew attention to the advantages accruing to the "first mover" in the Maritime LNG market.

48 Canada, National Energy Board, "Reasons for Decision: Emera Brunswick Pipeline Co. Ltd.," NEB Hearing GH-1-2006, Calgary, May 2007, 1-3.

49 Peter J. Milne & Associtcs Inc., "Written Evidence of Peter J. Milne filed on behalf of Bear Head Corporation and Anadarko," NEB Hearing GH-1-2006, Calgary, 25 August 2006, p. 12.

50 Nova Scotia Department of Energy, "Closing Submissions," NEB Hearing GH-1-2006, 15 December 2006, p. 7.

51 Repsol Energy Canada Ltd., "Argument of Repsol Energy Canada Ltd.," NEB Hearing GH-1-2006, 15 December 2006, p. 34.

52 Canada, National Energy Board, *The Maritimes Natural Gas Market: An Overview and Assessment* (Calgary: National Energy Board, 2003), 7.

53 Canada, National Energy Board, "Reasons for Decision," Hearing Order MH-2-2002, Calgary p. 42.

CHAPTER 11: OFFSHORE POLITICS AND THE ABORIGINAL CHALLENGE

1 For the struggles over the definition of the Aboriginal clauses, see Douglas Sanders, "The Indian Lobby," in *And No One Cheered: Federalism, Democracy and the Constitution Act,* ed. Keith Banting and Richard Simeon (Toronto: Methuen, 1983). The literature on the legal implications of these sections is vast and includes Michael Asch, ed., *Aboriginal and Treaty Rights in Canada* (Vancouver: UBC Press, 1997); William Pentney, "The Rights of Aboriginal Peoples of Canada in the Constitution Act, 1982, Part II – Section 35: The Substantive Guarantee," *UBC Law Review* 22 (1988): 207-78; and Brian Slattery, "The Constitutional Guarantee of Aboriginal and Treaty Rights," *Queen's Law Journal* 8 (1982-83): 232-73.

2 Ralph Johnson, *Forests of Nova Scotia: A History* (Halifax: Department of Lands and Forests, 1986), Chaps. 1 and 2.

3 Harald E.L. Prins, *The Mi'kmaq: Resistance, Accommodation and Cultural Survival* (Fort Worth, TX: Harcourt Brace, 1996), 22-24. See also Robert M. Leavitt, *Maliseet and Micmac: First Nations of the Maritimes* (Fredericton, NB: New Ireland Press, 1995).

4 Philip K. Bock, "Micmac," in *Handbook of North American Indians,* vol. 15, *Northeast,* ed. Bruce G. Trigger, 109-22 (Washington, DC: Smithsonian Institution Scholarly Press, 1978).

5 "Seven Micmac Chieftaincy Districts According to Pacifique," n.d., http://www.aboriginalcanada.com/history/sevmic.htm.

6 Virginia P. Miller, "The MicMac: A Maritime Woodland Group," in *Native Peoples: The Canadian Experience,* 2nd ed., ed. R. Bruce Morrison and C. Roderick Wilson, 326-31 (Toronto: McClelland and Stewart, 1986).

7 Olive Patricia Dickason, "Amerindians between French and English in Nova Scotia, 1713-1763," in *Sweet Promises: A Reader on Indian-White Relations in Canada,* ed. J.R. Miller, 45-67 (Toronto: University of Toronto Press, 1991).

8 Bill Wicken offers an incisive portrait of the 1726 Treaty in *Mi'kmaq Treaties on Trial: History, Land, and Donald Marshall Junior* (Toronto: University of Toronto Press, 2002). On the decade before the Royal Proclamation, see L.F.S. Upton, *Micmacs and Colonists: Indian-White Relations in the Maritimes, 1713-1867* (Vancouver: UBC Press, 1979).

9 An important documentary account, based on the 1930-31 photographs of anthropologist Frederick Johnson, is Confederacy of Nova Scotia Mainland Mi'kmaq and Robert S. Peabody Museum of Anthropology, *Mikwite'lmanej Mikmaqi'k: Let Us Remember Old Mi'kmaq* (Halifax: Nimbus Publishing, 2001). On *netukulimk,* see Russel Lawrence Barsh, "*Netukulimk* Past and Present: Mikmac Ethics and the Atlantic Fishery," *Journal of Canadian Studies* 37, 1 (2002): 15-44.

10 Canada, Constitution Act, 1982.

11 A comprehensive survey of the legal and political variations is Bradford W. Morse, ed., *Aboriginal Peoples and the Law: Indian, Inuit and Metis Rights in Canada* (Ottawa: Carleton University Press, 1985). See also Peter A. Cumming and Neil H. Mickenberg, eds., *Native Rights in Canada,* 2nd ed. (Toronto: General Publishing, 1972).

12 M.E. Turpel, "Aboriginal Peoples and Marine Resources: Understanding Rights, Directions for Management," in *Canadian Ocean Law and Policy,* ed. David Vanderzwaag (Toronto: Butterworths, 1992), 398.

13 Robert Jay Wilder, *Listening to the Sea* (Pittsburgh: University of Pittsburgh Press, 1998), Chap. 1.

14 "Re Offshore Mineral Rights of British Columbia," *Reports of the Supreme Court of Canada,* 1967, 815.

15 For a documentary approach to this period, see "Part VIII: External Affairs and Defence" in C.P. Stacey, ed., *Historical Documents of Canada,* vol. 5, *The Arts of War and Peace, 1914-1945* (Toronto: Macmillan of Canada, 1972).

16 Dawn Russell, "International Ocean Boundary Issues and Management Arrangements," in *Canadian Ocean Law and Policy,* ed. David Vanderzwaag, 463-505 (Toronto: Buttersworth, 1992).

17 Gary Reece, "Speaking Notes: Oil and Gas Conference, 2 October 2001," in "First Nations Positions on the Offshore Oil and Gas Moratoriums" Appendix 2, *BC Offshore Oil and Gas Technology Update,* by Jacques Whitford Environment Ltd. (Burnaby: Jacques Whitford, 2001).

18 *Delgamuukw v. British Columbia,* [1997] 3 S.C.R. 1010, para. 117.

19 James A. Tuck, *Maritime Provinces Prehistory* (Ottawa: National Museums of Canada, 1984), 71-81.

20 Prins, *Mi'kmaq: Resistance,* Chap. 3.

21 *Mabo and Others v. Queensland (No. 2)* [1992] HCA 23.

22 *Commonwealth v. Yarmirr, Yarmirr v. Northern Territory* [2001] HCA 56.

23 *Western Australia v. Ward, Attorney-General (NT) v. Ward, Ningarama v. NT* [2002] HCA 28.

24 Richard Bartlett, *Native Title in Australia,* 2nd ed. (Brisbane: LexisNexis Butterworths, 2004).

25 Union of Nova Scotia Indians, "Nova Scotia MicMac Aboriginal Rights Position Paper," *MicMac News* 5, 12A (1976): 1-44; Union of Nova Scotia Indians, *Crown Land Rights and Hunting and Fishing Rights of Micmac Indians,* rev. ed. (Halifax: Union of Nova Scotia Indians, 1976).

26 Ibid., 19.

27 For details on the Union of Nova Scotia Indians land claim, see Adrian Tanner and Sákéj Henderson, "Aboriginal Land Claims in the Atlantic Provinces," in *Aboriginal Land Claims in Canada: A Regional Perspective,* ed. Kenneth Coates, 131-65 (Toronto: Copp Clark Pitman, 1992).

28 On the *Paul* and *Marshall* cases, see Ken Coates, *The Marshall Decision and Native Rights* (Montreal/Kingston: McGill-Queen's University Press, 2000).

29 For a fuller discussion, see Thomas Isaac, *Aboriginal and Treaty Rights in the Maritimes: The Marshall Decision and Beyond* (Saskatoon: Purich Publishing, 2001).

30 *Union of Nova Scotia Indians v. Maritime and Northeast Pipeline Management Ltd.*, [2000] 1 F.C. D-1.

31 *Union of Nova Scotia Indians et al v. Nova Scotia (Attorney General)*, 2001 NSCA 110.

32 *R. v. Marshall; R. v. Bernard,* 2005 SCC 43, [2005] 2 S.C.R. 220 at 6 [*Marshall; Bernard*].

33 *R. v. Marshall,* [1999] 3 S.C.R. 533 at para 20.

34 *Marshall; Bernard* at para. 25.

35 Turpel, "Aboriginal Peoples," 400-1.

36 *Marshall; Bernard* para. 50.

37 Ibid., para. 138.

38 Ibid., para. 160.

39 Ibid., para. 162.

40 Ibid., para. 166.

41 Ibid., para. 168.

42 Ibid.

43 Ibid., para. 169.

44 Peter Clancy, "*Delgamuukw v. British Columbia:* Redefinig Relations between Aboriginal Peoples and the Crown," in *Political Dispute and Judicial Review: Assessing the Work of the Supreme Court of Canada,* ed. Hugh Mellon and Martin W. Westmacott, 102-22 (Scarborough, ON: Thomson Nelson, 2000).

45 *Haida Nation v. British Columbia (Minister of Forests),* 2004 SCC 73, [2004] 3 S.C.R. 511 at para. 27 [*Haida Nation*].

46 Ibid., para. 32. See Sonia Lawrence and Patrick Macklem, "From Consultation to Reconciliation: Aboriginal Rights and the Crown's Duty to Consult," *Canadian Bar Review* 79 (2000): 252-79. See also Thomas Isaac and Anthony Knox, "The Crown's Duty to Consult Aboriginal People," *Alberta Law Review* 41, 1 (2003-4): 49-78, and Richard F. Devlin and Ronalda Murphy, "Reconfiguration through Consultation? A Modest (Judicial) Proposal," in *Reconfiguring Aboriginal-State Relations,* ed. Michael Murphy, 267-93 (Montreal/Kingston: McGill-Queen's University Press, 2003).

47 *Haida Nation* para. 35.
48 Ibid., para. 49.
49 *Taku River Tlingit First Nation v. British Columbia (Project Assessment Director),* 2004 SCC 74, [2004] 3 S.C.R. 550.
50 *Mikisew Cree First Nation v. Canada (Minister of Canadian Heritage)* 2005 SCC 69, [2005] 3 S.C.R. 388.
51 Lawson Lundell, "The Mikisew Cree Decision: Balancing Government's Power to Manage Lands and Resources with Consultation Obligations under Historic Treaties," 27 November 2005, http://www.hg.org/articles/article_882.html.
52 Theresa MacNeil, *Commissioner's Report: Results of the Public Review on the Effects of Potential Oil and Gas Exploration Offshore Cape Breton* (Halifax: Canada-Nova Scotia Offshore Petroleum Board, 2002).
53 Ad Hoc Working Group, "Report to the Canada–Nova Scotia Offshore Petroleum Board" (Halifax: CNSOPB, 2003), 4.
54 Bruce Wildsmith, "Submission to Public Review Commission," 27 December 2001, p. 2, unpublished document in Public Review Commission records.
55 For a discussion of how the duty to consult may affect the licensing of aquaculture operations, see Diana Ginn, "The Potential Impact of Aboriginal Title on Aquaculture Policy," in *Aquaculture Law and Policy: Towards Principled Access and Operations,* ed. David L. VanderZwaag and Gloria Chao, 271-92 (London: Routledge, 2006); and Ronalda Murphy, Richard Devlin, and Tamara Lorincz, "Aquaculture Law and Policy in Canada and the Duty to Consult with Aboriginal Peoples," in *Aquaculture Law and Policy,* ed. VanderZwaag and Chao, 293-330.
56 *Mi'kmaq – Nova Scotia – Canada Umbrella Agreement,* 2002.
57 Framework Agreement between the Mi'kmaq of Nova Scotia, Her Majesty the Queen in Right of Nova Scotia and Her Majesty the Queen in Right of Canada, http://www.ainc-inac.gc.ca/al/ldc/ccl/agr/nsf/nsfa-eng.asp.
58 "Achievements and Initiatives," *Micmac and Maliseet News* 16, 10 (2005).
59 Richard F. Devlin and Ronalda Murphy, "Reconfiguration through Consultation? A Modest (Judicial) Proposal," in *Canada: The State of the Federation, 2003: Reconfiguring Aboriginal-State Relations,* ed. Michael Murphy (Kingston: McGill-Queen's University Press, 2003).

Selected Bibliography

Ad Hoc Working Group. "Report to the Canada–Nova Scotia Offshore Petroleum Board". Halifax: Canada–Nova Scotia Offshore Petroleum Board, 2003.

Andersen, Svein S. *The Struggle for North Sea Oil and Gas: Government Strategies in Denmark, Britain and Norway*. Stockholm: Scandinavian University Press, 1993.

Arbitration Tribunal between Newfoundland and Labrador and Nova Scotia Concerning Portions of the Limits of Their Offshore Areas. *Award of the Tribunal in the First Phase.* Ottawa, May 2001.

Archer, Keith, Roger Gibbons, Rainer Knopf, and Leslie A. Pal. *Parameters of Power: Canada's Political Institutions.* 2nd ed. Scarborough: ITP Nelson, 1999.

Asch, Michael, ed. *Aboriginal and Treaty Rights in Canada.* Vancouver: UBC Press, 1997.

Atherton, Graeme. *Fifty Years of Woodside's Energy*. Perth: WS Petroleum Ltd., 2004.

Atlantic Canada Petroleum Institute. *Offshore Oil and Gas Land Approvals in Atlantic Canada.* Halifax: Atlantic Canada Petroleum Institute, 2001.

Atlantic Energy Roundtable. "Report from the 'Lessons Learned Workshop' Hosted by the Regulatory Issues Steering Committee". June 2003.

–. Regulatory Issues Steering Committee and Industrial Opportunities Task Force. "Submission to Atlantic Energy Roundtable II," 31 October 2003, http://mediaroom.acoa-apeca.gc.ca/e/library/reports/RoundTableSubmissionEn.pdf.

Atlantic Geoscience Society. *The Last Billion Years: A Geological History of the Maritime Provinces of Canada*. Halifax: Nimbus Publishing, 2001.

Axford, Don. *Oil and Gas Oral History Project.* Calgary: Glenbow Institute, 1983.

Baetz, Mark C. "Texaco and Georges Bank (A)." In *Readings and Canadian Cases in Business, Government and Society,* edited by Mark C. Baetz, 475-97. Scarborough: Nelson Canada, 1993.

–. "Tier One/Tier Two." In *Canadian Cases in Business-Government Relations,* edited by Mark Baetz and Donald H. Thain, 336-89. Toronto: Methuen, 1985.

Baier, Gerald and Paul Groarke. "Arbitrating a Fiction: Canadian Federalism and the Nova Scotia/Newfoundland and Labrador Boundary Dispute." *Canadian Public Administration,* 46, 3 (2003): 315-38.

Bakvis, Herman, R.L. Mazany, and A. Sinclair. "Energy Policy." In *Governing Nova Scotia,* edited by Barbara Jamieson, 65-79. Halifax: Dalhousie School of Public Administration, 1984.

Bakvis, Herman, and Grace Skogstad, eds. *Canadian Federalism: Performance, Effectiveness, and Legitimacy.* Don Mills, ON: Oxford University Press, 2008.

Barsh, Russel Lawrence. "*Netukulimk* Past and Present: Mikmaw Ethics and the Atlantic Fishery." *Journal of Canadian Studies* 37, 1 (2002): 15-44.

Bartlett, Richard A. *Native Title in Australia.* 2nd ed. Brisbane: LexisNexis Butterworths, 2004.

Baxter, Vern. "Political Economy of Oil and Exploitation of Offshore Oil." In *Impact of Offshore Oil Exploration and Production on the Social Institutions of Coastal Louisiana,* edited by Shirley Laska, 15-75. Baton Rouge: Department of the Interior, 1983.

Beale, Barry. *Energy and Industry.* Toronto: Canadian Institute for Economic Policy, 1980.

Bernstein, Marver. *Regulating Business by Independent Commission.* Princeton, NJ: Princeton University Press, 1955.

Bickerton, James. "Equalization, Regional Development and Political Trust: The Section 36/Atlantic Accords Controversy." *Constitutional Forum constitutionelle* 17, 3 (2008): 99-111.

Boadway, Robin. *Intergovernmental Transfers in Canada.* Toronto: Canadian Tax Foundation, 1980.

Bock, Philip K. "Micmac." In *Handbook of North American Indians.* Vol.15, *Northeast,* edited by Bruce G. Trigger, 109-22. Washington: Smithsonian Institution, 1978.

Borghese, Elizabeth Mann. *The Ocean Circle: Governing the Seas as a Global Resource.* New York: United Nations University, 1998.

British Columbia. *The Province of British Columbia's Perspective on the Federal Moratorium on Oil and Gas Activities, Offshore BC.* Victoria: Province of British Columbia, 2004.

British Columbia. Scientific Review Panel. "Report of the Scientific Review Panel." January 2002. http://www.empr.gov.bc.ca/OG/offshoreoilandgas/ReportsPresentationsandEducationalMaterial/Reports/Pages/BCHydrocarbonDevelopmentReport.aspx.

Brown, Douglas M. "Sea Change in Newfoundland: From Peckford to Wells." In *Canada: The State of the Federation, 1990,* edited by R.L. Watts and D.M. Brown, 199-229. Kingston: Institute of Intergovernmental Relations, 1991.

Canada. Auditor General of Canada. *Report of the Auditor General of Canada, 1988.* Ottawa: Supply and Services Canada, 1988.

Canada. Department of Energy, Mines and Resources. *National Energy Program, 1980.* Ottawa: Supply and Services Canada, 1980.

–. *Offshore Exploration: Information and Procedures for Offshore Operators.* Report EI 79-4. Ottawa: Energy, Mines and Resources, 1979.

–. *Statement of Policy: Proposed Petroleum and Natural Gas Act and New Canada Oil and Gas Land Regulations.* Ottawa: Supply and Services Canada, 1976.

Canada. Department of Fisheries and Oceans. *Canada's Oceans Strategy.* Ottawa: Fisheries and Oceans Canada, 2002.

Canada. Department of Industry, Trade and Commerce and Regional Economic Expansion. *Report by the Sector Task Force on the Canadian Ocean Industry.* Ottawa: Industry, Trade and Commerce, 1978.

–. *Sector Profile: The Ocean Industry in Canada.* Ottawa: Industry, Trade and Commerce, 1977.

Canada. National Energy Board. "LNG Regulatory Requirements," 9 August 2005. http://www.neb.gc.ca/clf-nsi/rthnb/lnk/lqfdntrlgs/lngrgltryrqrmnts-eng.pdf.

–. *The Maritimes Natural Gas Market: An Overview and Assessment.* Calgary: National Energy Board, 2003.

–. *Natural Gas Market Assessment: Ten Years after De-regulation.* Calgary: National Energy Board, 1996.

Canada. National Energy Board, Canada–Newfoundland Offshore Petroleum Board, and Canada–Nova Scotia Offshore Petroleum Board. "Offshore Waste Treatment Guidelines," 2010. http://www.cnsopb.ns.ca/pdfs/owtg_redraft.pdf.

Canada. Parliament. Senate Standing Committee on National Finances. "The Effectiveness of and Possible Improvements to the Present Equalization Policy." 14th Report. Ottawa: Senate of Canada, 2002.

Canada. Transport Canada and Fisheries and Oceans Canada. *Environmental Assessment Track Report for the Petrochemical and Liquefied Natural Gas Facilities at Goldboro, N.S.* Submitted to minister of the environment, 14 October 2005.

Canada and British Columbia. West Coast Offshore Exploration Environmental Assessment Panel. *Report and Recommendations.* April, 1986.

Canada and Nova Scotia. Joint Public Review Panel. *Report: Sable Gas Projects.* Halifax: Environment Canada and Nova Scotia Environment and Labour, 1997.

–. NRCanada and NS Petroleum Directorate. Georges Bank Review Panel, *Report.* June 1999.

Canada–Nova Scotia Offshore Petroleum Board (CNSOPB). *Application to Amend the Cohasset Development Plan: Decision Report.* Halifax: Canada–Nova Scotia Offshore Petroleum Board, 2004.

–. *Cohasset-Panuke Project: Benefits Plan Decision Report and Development Plan Decision Report.* Halifax: Canada–Nova Scotia Offshore Petroleum Board, 1990.

–. *Environmental Screening Report: Cohasset Phase II Decommissioning.* Halifax: Canada–NovaScotia Offshore Petroleum Board, 2004.

Canada–Nova Scotia Panel on Crown Share Adjustment Payments. *Report of the Panel,* 4 July 2008. http://www.fin.gc.ca/no8/data/08-053_4-eng.asp.

Canadian Association of Petroleum Producers. "Atlantic Energy Roundtable." Presented to the Atlantic Canada Energy Roundtable by Gerald Protti, 22 November 2002. http://www.capp.ca/default.asp?V_DOC_ID=642.

Chircop, Aldo, and Bruce A. Marchand. "Oceans Act: Uncharted Seas for Offshore Development in Atlantic Canada?" *Dalhousie Law Journal* 24 (2001): 23-50.

Cicin-Sain, Biliana, and Robert Knecht. *The Future of US Ocean Policy: Choices for the New Century.* Washington, DC: Island Press, 2000.

Clancy, Peter. "Chasing Whose Fish? Atlantic Fisheries Conflicts and Institutions." In *Canadian Water Politics: Conflicts and Institutions,* edited by Mark Sproule-Jones, Carolyn Johns, and Timothy B. Heinmiller, 261-85. Montreal/Kingston: McGill-Queen's University Press, 2008.

–. "*Delgamuukw v. British Columbia:* Redefining Relations between Aboriginal Peoples and the Crown." In *Political Dispute and Judicial Review: Assessing the Work of the Supreme Court of Canada,* edited by Hugh Mellon and Martin W. Westmacott, 102-22. Scarborough, ON: Thomson Nelson, 2000.

–. *Micro-Politics and Canadian Business: Paper, Steel and the Airlines.* Peterborough, ON: Broadview Press, 2004.

–. "Offshore Petroleum Politics: A Changing Frontier in a Global System." In *Canada's Resource Economy in Transition: The Past, Present and Future of Canadian Staple Industries,* edited by Michael Howlett and Keith Brownsey, 255-77. Toronto: Emond Montgomery, 2008.

–. "Political Devolution and Wildlife Management." In *Devolution and Constitutional Development in the Canadian North,* edited by Gurston Dacks, 77-120. Ottawa: Carleton University Press, 1990.

–. "The Politics and Administration of Aboriginal Claims." In *Public Administration and Policy,* edited by Martin W. Westmacott and Hugh Mellon, 55-72. Scarborough, ON: Prentice Hall/Allyn and Bacon, 1999.

Clancy, Peter, James Bickerton, Rodney Haddow, and Ian Stewart. *The Savage Years: The Perils of Reinventing Government in Nova Scotia.* Halifax: Formac Publishing, 2000.

Clarke, Jeanne N., and Daniel C. McCool. *Staking Out the Terrain: Power and Performance among Natural Resource Agencies.* Albany: SUNY Press, 1996.

Clarkson, Stephen. *The Big Red Machine: How the Liberal Party Dominates Canadian Politics.* Vancouver: UBC Press, 2005.

–. *Canada and the Reagan Challenge.* Toronto: Canadian Institute for Economic Policy, 1982.

Coalition to Restore Coastal Louisiana. *Coastal Louisiana: Here Today and Gone Tomorrow?* Baton Rouge, LA: Coalition to Restore Coastal Louisiana, 1989.

Coates, Ken. *The Marshall Decision and Native Rights.* Montreal/Kingston: McGill-Queen's University Press, 2000.

Confederacy of Nova Scotia Mainland Mi'kmaq and Robert S. Peabody Museum of Anthropology. *Mikwite'lmanej Mikmaqi'k: Let Us Remember Old Mi'kmaq.* Halifax: Nimbus Publishing, 2001.

Consultative Task Force on Industrial and Regional Benefits. *Major Canadian Projects, Major Canadian Opportunities: A Report.* Ottawa: s.n., 1981.

Courchene, Thomas J. "Confiscatory Equalization: The Intriguing Case of Saskatchewan's Vanishing Energy Revenues." *IRPP Choices* 10, 2 (2004): 1-44.

Crane, David. *Controlling Interest: The Canadian Gas and Oil Stakes.* Toronto: McClelland and Stewart, 1982.

Crosbie, John C. "Overview Paper on the 1985 Canada-Newfoundland Accord Act." Prepared for the Royal Commission on Renewing and Strengthening Our Place in Canada, 2003.

Cullen, Richard. *Federalism in Action: The Australian and Canadian Offshore Disputes.* Sydney: Federation Press, 1990.

Cumming, Peter A., and Neil H. Mickenberg, eds. *Native Rights in Canada.* 2nd ed. Toronto: General Publishing, 1972.

Dacks, Gurston. "The Quest for Northern Oil and Gas Accords." In *Devolution and Constitutional Development in the Canadian North,* edited by Gurston Dacks, 225-56. Ottawa: Carleton University Press, 1990.

Daintith, Terence. *Finders Keepers? How the Law of Capture Shaped the World Oil Industry.* Washington, DC: Earthscan, 2010.

Dauterive, Les. *Rigs to Reefs: Policy, Progress and Perspectives.* New Orleans: Mineral Management Service, 2000.

Davis, Jerome, ed. *The Changing World of Oil: An Analysis of Corporate Change and Adaptation.* Aldershot: Ashgate Publishing, 2006.

Deloitte Touche LLP. *Province of Nova Scotia Financial Review: Interim Report.* Halifax: Deloitte Touche, 2009.

Devlin, Richard F., and Ronalda Murphy. "Reconfiguration through Consultation: A Modest (Judicial) Proposal." In *Canada: The State of the Federation, 2003 – Reconfiguring Aboriginal-State Relations,* edited by Michael Murphy, 267-93. Montreal/Kingston: McGill-Queen's University Press, 2003.

DeWolf, Richard. *Scotian Shelf Gas Supply Region, 2002 Report.* Calgary: Ziff Energy Group, 2002.

Dickason, Olive Patricia. "Amerindians between French and English in Nova Scotia, 1713-1763." In *Sweet Promises: A Reader on Indian-White Relations in Canada,* edited by J.R. Miller, 45-67. Toronto: University of Toronto Press, 1991.

Doern, G. Bruce. "Moved Out and Moving On: The National Energy Board as a Reinvented Regulatory Agency." In *Changing the Rules: Canadian Regulatory Regimes and Institutions,* edited by G. Bruce Doern, Margaret M. Hill, Michael J. Prince, and Richard J. Schultz, 82-97. Toronto: University of Toronto Press, 1999.

Doern, G. Bruce, and Thomas Conway. *The Greening of Canada: Federal Institutions and Decisions.* Toronto: University of Toronto Press, 1994.

Doern, G. Bruce, and Monica Gattinger. *Power Switch: Energy Regulatory Governance in the Twenty-First Century.* Toronto: University of Toronto Press, 2003.

Doern, G. Bruce, and Glen Toner. *The Politics of Energy: The Development and Implementation of the NEP.* Toronto: Methuen, 1985.

Dunning, Fred. *Britain's Offshore Oil and Gas.* London: UK Offshore Operators Association, 1989.

Ellis, J.R. *Report of the Cohasset/Panuke Environmental and Socio-Economic Review Commission.* Halifax: Province of Nova Scotia, 1990.

Enachescu, Michael E. "Searching for Offshore Nova Scotia's Elusive Reservoirs and Large Traps." *Nova Scotia Energy R&D Forum*, 24 May 2006.

Enachescu, Michael E., and John R. Hogg. "Exploring for Atlantic Canada's Next Giant Petroleum Discovery." *CSEG Recorder* 30, 5 (2005): 19-30.

EnCana and Jacques Whitford. "CEAA Screening Environmental Assessment, Cohasset Project Phase II Decommissioning," April 2004. http://www.cnsopb.ns.ca/pdfs/CEAA_Screening_Cohasset_Decommissioning.pdf.

Evans, Peter B., Dietrich Rueschemayer, and Theda Skocpol, eds. *Bringing the State Back In.* New York: Cambridge University Press, 1985.

Fanning, Lucia. "Understanding the 1999 Georges Bank Moratorium Decision." *Marine Affairs Policy Forum* 1, 1 (2008): 1-4.

Fant, Douglas V. *An Analysis and Evaluation of Rules and Procedures Governing OCS Operations.* Washington, DC: American Bar Association, 1990.

Fee, D.A., and John O'Dea. *Technology for Developing Marginal Offshore Fields.* London: Elsevier Applied Science, 1986.

Fee, Derek. *Petroleum Exploitation Strategy.* London: Belhaven Press, 1988.

Fitzgerald, Edward A. *The Seaweed Rebellion: Federal-State Conflicts over Offshore Energy Development.* Lantham, MD: Lexington Books, 2000.

Fossum, John Erik. *Oil, the State and Federalism: The Rise and Demise of Petro-Canada as a Statist Impulse.* Toronto: University of Toronto Press, 1997.

Foster, Peter. *Other People's Money: The Banks, the Government and Dome.* Don Mills, ON: Collins, 1983.

French, Richard. *How Ottawa Decides: Planning and Industrial Policy-Making, 1968-80.* Toronto: Canadian Institute for Economic Policy, 1980.

Freudenberg, William R., and Robert Gramling. *Blowout in the Gulf: the BP Oil Disaster and the Future of Energy in America.* Cambridge, Mass: MIT Press, 2011.

–. *Oil in Troubled Waters: Perceptions, Politics and the Battle over Offshore Drilling.* Albany, NY: SUNY Press, 1994.

Gaffney, Cline and Associates. "A Review of Regulatory Cycle Times in Certain Jurisdictions." Report prepared for the Regulatory Issues Steering Committee of the Atlantic Energy Roundtable, August 2003.

Galligan, Brian. *Utah and Queensland Coal: A Study in the Micro Political Economy of Modern Capitalism and the State.* Brisbane: University of Queensland Press, 1989.

Gaul, Damien, and Kobi Platt. *Short-Term Energy Outlook Supplement: U.S. LNG Imports – the Next Wave.* Washington: Energy Information Administration, 2007.

Ghazvinian, John. *Untapped: The Scramble for Africa's Oil.* Orlando, FL: Harcourt, 2007.

Gibbons, Michael, and Roger Voyer. *A Technology Assessment System: A Case Study of East Coast Offshore Petroleum Exploitation.* Ottawa: Science Council of Canada, 1974.

Ginn, Diana. "The Potential Impact of Aboriginal Title on Aquaculture Policy." In *Aquaculture Law and Policy: Towards Principled Access and Operations,* edited by David L. VanderZwaag and Gloria Chao, 271-92. London: Routledge, 2006.

Goldstein, Joan. *The Politics of Offshore Oil.* New York: Praeger, 1982.

Gramling, Robert. *Oil on the Edge: Offshore Development, Conflict, Gridlock.* Albany: State University of New York Press, 1996.

Gray, John. "The Making of 'Danny Chavez': Newfoundland's Rebellious Premier Takes on Big Oil and 'Steve' Harper." *Report on Business Magazine,* February 2008.

–. *Paul Martin: In the Balance.* Toronto: Key Porter Books, 2004.

Gunningham, Neil, and Darren Sinclair. *Leaders and Laggards: Next-Generation Environmental Regulation.* Sheffield: Greenleaf Publishing, 2002.

Gurney, Judith. *The Gulf of Mexico: Revival and Opportunity in the Oil Industry.* London: Financial Times, 1997.

Hanson, Eric. *Dynamic Decade.* Toronto: University of Toronto Press, 1961.

Harris, Michael. *Lament for an Ocean: The Collapse of the Atlantic Cod Fishery.* Toronto: McClelland and Stewart, 1998.

Harrison, Rowland J. "The Offshore Mineral Resources Agreement in the Maritime Provinces." *Dalhousie Law Journal* 4, 2 (1977-78): 245-76.

Henderson, Jennifer. "Power Play: A Sable Primer." *Atlantic Progress* (September-October 1998): 225-37.

Herman, Lawrence L. "The Need for a Canada Submerged Lands Act: Some Further Thoughts on Canada's Offshore Mineral Rights Problems." *Canadian Bar Review* 58, 4 (1980): 518-44.

Hildreth, Richard. "Ocean Resources and Intergovernmental Relations in the 1980s: Outer Continental Shelf Hydrocarbons and Minerals." In *Ocean Resources and US Intergovernmental Relations in the 1980s,* edited by Maynard Silva, 155-96. Boulder, CO: Westview Press, 1986.

Hobson, Paul A.R., and L. Wade Locke. "Assessing the Equalization Options of Budget 2007 for the Atlantic Provinces." *APEC Commentary,* 13 June 2007.

House, J.D. *The Last of the Free Enterprisers: The Oil Men of Calgary.* Toronto: McClelland and Stewart, 1980.

–. "Myths and Realities about Petroleum-Related Development: Lessons for British Columbia from Atlantic Canada and the North Sea." *Journal of Canadian Studies* 37, 4 (2003): 9-32.

–. *The Challenge of Oil: Newfoundland's Quest for Controlled Development.* St. John's: Institute for Social and Economic Research, 1985.

Hudec, Al, and Van Penick. "British Columbia Offshore Oil and Gas Law." *Alberta Law Review* 41 (2003): 101-58.

Hunt, A.D. "Land Management in the Canadian Arctic." *Proceedings of the Southwestern Legal Foundation.* National Institute for Petroleum Landmen, 1970: 161-210

Hunt, Constance D. *The Offshore Petroleum Regimes of Canada and Australia.* Calgary: Centre for Resource Law, 1989.

Ikenberry, John G. *Reasons of State: Oil Politics and the Capacities of American Government.* Ithaca, NY: Cornell University Press, 1988.

Isaac, Thomas. *Aboriginal and Treaty Rights in the Maritimes: The Marshall Decision and Beyond.* Saskatoon: Purich Publishing, 2001.

Isaac, Thomas, and Anthony Knox, "The Crown's Duty to Consult Aboriginal People." *Alberta Law Review* 41, 1 (2003-4): 49-78.

Jenkin, Michael. *British Industry and the North Sea: State Intervention in a Developing Industrial Sector.* London: Macmillan Press, 1981.

Jenkins, Barbara. "Reexamining the 'Obsolescing Bargain': A Study of Canada's National Energy Program." *International Organization* 40, 1 (1986): 139-65.

Jenkins-Smith, Hank C., and Gilbert K. St. Clair. "The Politics of Offshore Energy: Empirically Testing the Advocacy Coalition Framework." In *Policy Change and Learning,* edited by Paul Sabatier and Hank C. Jenkins-Smith, 149-75. Boulder, CO: Westview Press, 1993.

Jensen, James. *The Development of a Global LNG Market: Is It Likely? If So, When?* Oxford: Oxford Institute for Energy Studies, 2004.

John, Peter. "Is There Life after Policy Streams, Advocacy Coalitions and Punctuations: Using Evolutionary Theory to Explain Policy Change," *Policy Studies Journal* 31, 4 (2003): 481-98.

Johnson, Ralph. *Forests of Nova Scotia: A History.* Halifax: Department of Lands and Forests, 1986.

Johnston, Douglas M., and Erin N. Hildebrand, eds. *BC Offshore Hydrocarbon Development: Issues and Prospects.* Victoria: Maritime Awards Society of Canada, 2001.

Jordan, Grant. *Shell, Greenpeace and Brent Spar.* New York: Palgrave, 2001.

Kash, Don E., et al. *Energy under the Oceans: A Technology Assessment of the Outer Continental Shelf Oil and Gas Operations.* Norman: University of Oklahoma Press, 1973.

Kavanagh, Peter. *John Buchanan: The Art of Political Survival.* Halifax: Formac, 1988.

Keith, Robert F., et al. *Northern Development and Technology Assessment Systems: A Study of Petroleum Development Programs in the Mackenzie Delta–Beaufort Sea Region and the Arctic Islands.* Ottawa: Science Council of Canada, 1976.

Kidston, Arthur G., David E. Brown, Brian Altheim, and Brenton M. Smith. *Hydrocarbon Potential of the Deep-Water Scotian Slope.* Halifax: Canada–Nova Scotia Offshore Petroleum Board, 2002.

Kidston, Arthur G., Brenton M. Smith, David E. Brown, Carl Makrides, and Brian Altheim. *Nova Scotia Deepwater Post-Drill Analysis, 1982-2004.* Halifax: Canada–Nova Scotia Offshore Petroleum Board, 2007.

Kierans, Eric. *Report on Natural Resources Policy in Manitoba.* Winnipeg: Planning and Priorities Committee of Cabinet, 1973.

Kilbourn, William. *Pipeline.* Toronto: Clarke Irwin, 1970.

King, Geoff. "Cooperative Project Delivery." In *AMPLA Yearbook 1997,* 147-58. Melbourne: Australian Mineral and Petroleum Law Association, 1997.

Laendner, Geoffrey. *A Failed Strategy: The Offshore Oil Industry's Development of the Outer Continental Shelf.* New York: Garland Publications, 1993.

Lamson, Cynthia, ed. *The Sea Has Many Voices: Oceans Policy for a Complex World.* Montreal/Kingston: McGill-Queen's University Press, 1994.

Lasmo NS Ltd. and Nova Scotia Resources (Ventures) Ltd. *Cohasset/Panuke Development Project. Preliminary Development Application.* Halifax: Lasmo/NSRL, 1990.

Lawrence, Sonia, and Patrick Macklem. "From Consultation to Reconciliation: Aboriginal Rights and the Crown's Duty to Consult." *Canadian Bar Review* 79 (2000): 252-79.

Leavitt, Robert M. *Maliseet and Micmac: First Nations of the Maritimes.* Fredericton: New Ireland Press, 1996.

LGL Limited and S.L. Ross Ocean Research. *Environmental Assessment of Exploration Drilling Off Nova Scotia.* Halifax: CNSOPB, 2000.

Locke, Wade, and Paul Hobson. "An Examination of the Interaction between Natural Resource Revenues and Equalization Payments: Lessons for Atlantic Canada." Working Paper 2004-10. Montreal: Institute for Research on Public Policy, 2004.

Lore, Gary. *Exploration and Discoveries, 1947-1989: An Historical Perspective.* MMS Gulf of Mexico Region Report 91-0078. New Orleans: Minerals Management Service, 1992.

MacDonald, Rodney. "A Deal Is a Deal: Protecting Our Offshore Accord." In *What's New in Nova Scotia.* Pamphlet. Halifax: Province of Nova Scotia, 2007.

MacDougall, John N. *Fuels and the National Policy.* Toronto: Butterworth, 1982.

MacLean, B.C., and J.A. Wade. "Petroleum Geology of the Continental Margin South of the Islands of St. Pierre and Miquelon, Offshore Eastern Canada." *Bulletin of Canadian Petroleum Geology* 40, 3 (1992): 222-53.

MacMullin, Sandy R.A. "The Potential of the Nova Scotia Offshore for Northeast Markets." Presentation to New York Gas Group and New York Energy Association. New York, 21 May 2002.

MacNeil, Theresa. *Commissioner's Report: Results of the Public Review on the Effects of Potential Oil and Gas Exploration Offshore Cape Breton.* Halifax: Canada–Nova Scotia Offshore Petroleum Board, 2002.

Maritimes & Northeast Pipeline. *NEB/Joint Review Panel Facilities and Tolls Application.* Vol.1. Halifax: Maritimes & Northeast Pipeline, 1996.

Marshall, Dale. *Should BC Lift the Offshore Oil Moratorium?* Ottawa: Canadian Centre for Policy Alternatives, n.d.

McDougall, John N. *Fuels and the National Policy.* Toronto: Butterworths, 1982.

Meek, Jim and Eleanor Beaton. *Offshore Dream: A History of Nova Scotia's Oil and Gas Industry.* Halifax: Nimbus Publishing, 2011.

Miller, Virginia P. "The MicMac: A Maritime Woodland Group." In *Native Peoples: The Canadian Experience,* 2nd ed., edited by R. Bruce Morrison and C. Roderick Wilson, 326-31. Toronto: McClelland and Stewart, 1986.

Mills, Hal. "Eastern Canada's Offshore Resources and Boundaries: A Study in Political Geography." *Journal of Canadian Studies* 6, 3 (1971): 36-50.

Milne, David. *Tug of War: Ottawa and the Provinces under Trudeau and Mulroney.* Toronto: James Lorimer, 1986.

Mobil Oil Canada, Petro-Canada, Texaco Canada Resources, Nova Scotia Resources (Ventures), and East Coast Energy. *Venture Development Project: Development Plan Submission.* Vol. 1. Halifax: Mobil Oil Canada, 1983.

Mohr, Patricia. "Scotiabank Commodity Price Index." *Global Economic Research,* 27 November 2008.

Morse, Bradford W., ed. *Aboriginal Peoples and the Law: Indian, Inuit and Metis Rights in Canada.* Ottawa: Carleton University Press, 1985.

Murphy, Ronalda, Richard Devlin, and Tamara Lorincz. "Aquaculture Law and Policy in Canada and the Duty to Consult with Aboriginal Peoples." In *Aquaculture Law and Policy: Towards Principled Access and Operations,* edited by David L. VanderZwaag and Gloria Chao, 293-330. London: Routledge, 2006.

National Commission on the BP Deepwater Horizon Oil Spill and Offshore Drilling. *Deepwater: The Gulf Disaster and the Future of Offshore Drilling.* Washington DC: Government Printing Office, 2011.

National Research Council. *Striking a Balance: Improving Stewardship of Marine Areas.* Washington, DC: National Academy Press, 1997.

–. Marine Board. *Outer Continental Shelf Frontier Technology.* Washington, DC: National Academy Press, 1980.

Nelsen, Brent F. *The State Offshore: Petroleum, Politics and State Intervention on the British and Norwegian Continental Shelves.* New York: Praeger, 1991.

New Brunswick. *Energy Strategy.* Fredericton: Province of New Brunswick, 2001.

Newendorp, Paul D., and John Schuyler. *Decision Analysis for Petroleum Exploration.* 2nd ed. Aurora, CO: Planning Press, 2000.

Newfoundland. *Royal Commission on Renewal and Strengthening Our Place in Confederation.* St. John's: Royal Commission, 2003.

Noble, Bram F. "Promise and Dismay: The State of Strategic Environmental Assessment Systems and Practices in Canada." *Environmental Impact Assessment Review* 29 (2009): 66-75.

Noreng, Oystein. *The Oil Industry and Government Strategy in the North Sea.* London: Croom Helm, 1980.

Nova Scotia. Department of Development. *NS Ocean Industry Directory, 1984-85.* Halifax: Department of Development, 1985.

Nova Scotia. Department of Energy. *Nova Scotia Offshore Renewal Plan.* Halifax: Department of Energy, 2008.

–. "Offshore Petroleum Royalty Regime," n.d. http://www.gov.ns.ca/energy/resources/RA/offshore/Offshore-Petroleum-Royalty-Regime.pdf.

–. *Seizing the Opportunity: Nova Scotia's Energy Strategy.* 2 Vols. Halifax: Department of Energy, 2001.

Nova Scotia. Department of Finance. *Getting Back to Balance.* Halifax: Department of Finance, 2009.

Nova Scotia. Department of Mines and Energy. *The Natural Gas Pipeline: Toward Energy Security for Nova Scotia.* Halifax: Department of Mines and Energy, 1980.

–. *Offshore Oil and Gas: A Chance for Nova Scotians*. Halifax: Department of Mines and Energy, 1980.

Nova Scotia. Department of Natural Resources. *Annual Report, 1996*. Halifax: Department of Natural Resources, 1996.

Nova Scotia. Environmental Assessment Board. *Report and Recommendations for the Review of Keltic Petrochemicals Inc*. Halifax: Environmental Assessment Board, 2007.

Nova Scotia. Utilities and Review Board. "Franchise Applications for the Distribution of Natural Gas in the Province of Nova Scotia." Decision NG-02 NSUARB 8 2003, 7 February 2003. http://www.canlii.org/en/ns/nsuarb/doc/2003/2003nsuarb8/2003nsuarb8.html.

–. "Natural Gas Distribution: Directions on Procedure for Sempra Atlantic's Surrender," 6 August 2001. http://www.gov.ns.ca/petro/documents/uarddirections onprocedure.pdf.

Nova Scotia. Voluntary Economic Planning. *Oil and Natural Gas Offshore Development: The Opportunities and the Challenge*. Halifax: Voluntary Economic Planning, 1980

Offshore/Onshore Technologies Association of Nova Scotia. "History." http://www.otans.com/pages/history.asp.

O'Neill, Brian. "Laughing Gas." *New Maritimes* 4, 6 (1986): 4-5.

–. "The Nova Scotia Offshore: A Case Study in the Political Economy of Underdevelopment." In *Oil and Gas Development in "Have-Not Regions,"* edited by A. Winson, 1-13. Halifax: Gorsebrook Research Institute, 1984.

Oynes, Chris C. "The Role of Deep Gas from the Shelf." Paper presented to the Offshore Technology Conference, Houston, TX, 4 May 2003. http://www.gomr.boemre.gov/homepg/whatsnew/speeches/speeches.htm.

PanCanadian Energy. *Deep Panuke Offshore Gas Development: Project Summary*. Vol. 1. Halifax: PanCanadian Energy Corp, 2002.

Pentney, William. "The Rights of Aboriginal Peoples of Canada in the Constitution Act, 1982, Part II – Section 35: The Substantive Guarantee." *UBC Law Review* 22 (1988): 207-78.

Pimlott, Douglas, Dougald Brown, and Kenneth Sam. *Oil under the Ice*. Ottawa: Canadian Arctic Resources Committee, 1976.

Pratt, Joseph A., William H. Becker, and William M. McClenahan. *Voice of the Marketplace: A History of the National Petroleum Council*. College Station, TX: A&M University Press, 2002.

Priest, Tyler. *The Offshore Imperative: Shell Oil's Search for Petroleum in Postwar America*. College Station: Texas A&M Press, 1967.

Prins, Harald E.L. *The Mi'kmaq: Resistance, Accommodation and Cultural Survival*. Fort Worth, TX: Harcourt Brace, 1996.

Proctor, R.M., G.C. Taylor, and J.A. Wade. "Oil and Natural Gas Resources of Canada: 1983." Paper 83-31, Geological Survey of Canada, 1984.

Rayner, Jeremy, Michael Howlett, Jeremy Wilson, Benjamin Cashore, and George Hoberg. "Privileging the Sub-Sector: Critical Sub-Sectors and Sectoral Relationships in Forest Policy-Making." *Forest Policy and Economics* 2, 3-4 (2001): 319-32.

Reece, Gary. "Speaking Notes: Oil and Gas Conference, 2 October 2001." In "First Nations Positions on the Offshore Oil and Gas Moratoriums," Appendix 2, *BC Offshore Oil and Gas Technology Update,* by Jacques Whitford Environment Ltd. Burnaby: Jacques Whitford, 2001.

Rice, Tony, and Paula Owen. *Decommissioning the* Brent Spar. New York: Routledge, 1999,

Richards, John, and Larry Pratt. *Prairie Capitalism: Power and Influence in the New West.* Toronto: McClelland and Stewart, 1979.

Ruester, Sophia, and Anne Neumann. *Next Year, Next Decade, Never? The Prospects of Liquefied Natural Gas Development in the US.* Berlin: German Institute for Economic Research, 2007.

Russell, Dawn. "International Ocean Boundary Issues and Management Arrangements." In *Canadian Ocean Law and Policy,* edited by David Vanderzwaag, 463-505. Toronto: Buttersworth, 1992.

Sabatier, Paul A., and Hank C. Jenkins-Smith. *Policy Change and Learning: An Advocacy Coalition Approach.* Boulder, CO: Westview Press, 1993.

Sanders, Douglas. "The Indian Lobby." In *And No One Cheered: Federalism, Democracy and the Constitution Act,* edited by Keith Banting and Richard Simeon, 301-32. Toronto: Methuen, 1983.

Schattschneider, E.E. *The Semi-Sovereign People.* New York: Holt, Rinehart and Winston, 1960.

Schultz, Richard. "Interest Groups and Intergovernmental Negotiations: Caught in the Vise of Federalism." In *Canadian Federalism: Myth or Reality?* 3rd, ed., edited by J. Peter Meekison, 375-96. Toronto: Methuen, 1977.

Sears, John. T. *Report of the Commissioner on the Sable Offshore Energy Project.* Halifax: Province of Nova Scotia, 1997.

Selley, Richard C. *Elements of Petroleum Geology.* 2nd ed. San Diego, CA: Academic Press, 1968.

Sempra Atlantic. "Notice of Application to the UARB for Franchise Surrender or Amendment by Sempra Atlantic," 29 June 2001. http://www.gov.ns.ca/petro/documents/SempraApplication.pdf.

Shaxson, Nicholas. *Poisoned Wells: The Dirty Politics of African Oil.* New York: Palgrave Macmillan, 2007.

Shepard, Robert, and Michael Valpy. *The National Deal: The Fight for a Canadian Constitution.* Toronto: Fleet Books, 1982.

Simmons, Matthew R. *Twilight in the Desert: The Coming Saudi Oil Shock and the World Economy.* New York: John Wiley and Sons, 2005.

Slattery, Brian. "The Constitutional Guarantee of Aboriginal and Treaty Rights." *Queen's Law Journal* 8 (1982-83): 232-73.

Sproule-Jones, Mark. *Governments at Work: Canadian Parliamentary Federalism and Its Public Policy Effects.* Toronto: University of Toronto Press, 1993.

Stacey, C.P., ed. *Historical Documents of Canada.* Vol. 5, *The Arts of War and Peace, 1914-1945.* Toronto: Macmillan of Canada, 1972.

Stalport, Neil. "Canadian Offshore Non-Renewable Resources: Law and Policy Issues." In *Canadian Ocean Law and Policy,* edited by David Vanderzwaag, 193-234. Toronto: Butterworths Canada, 1992.

Stevenson, Thorne, and Kellogg and Gardner Pinfold. *Scotian Shelf Gas Development: The Economic Impact on Nova Scotia*. Halifax: Stevenson, Thorne and Kellogg, 1981.

Stikeman, Elliott, and Ziff Energy Group. "Regulation of Gas Distribution Systems in Nova Scotia," 23 July 1996. Nova Scotia Department of Natural Resources.

Szell, John Samuel. *Innovations in Energy: The Story of Kerr-McGee*. Norman: University of Oklahoma Press, 1979.

Tanner, Adrian, and Sákéj Henderson. "Aboriginal Land Claims in the Atlantic Provinces." In *Aboriginal Land Claims in Canada: A Regional Perspective*, edited by Kenneth Coates, 131-65. Toronto: Copp Clark Pitman, 1992.

Thomson, Graham. "Project Alliances." In *AMPLA Yearbook 1997*, 127-46. Melbourne: Australian Mineral and Petroleum Law Association, 1997.

Tuck, James A. *Maritime Provinces Prehistory*. Ottawa: National Museums of Canada, 1984.

Turpel, M.E. "Aboriginal Peoples and Marine Resources: Understanding Rights, Directions for Management." In *Canadian Ocean Law and Policy*, edited by David Vanderzwaag, 439-49. Toronto: Butterworths, 1992.

Union of Nova Scotia Indians. *Crown Land Rights and Hunting and Fishing Rights of Micmac Indians in the Province of Nova Scotia*. Rev. ed. Halifax: Union of Nova Scotia Indians, 1976.

–. "Nova Scotia MicMac Aboriginal Rights Position Paper." *MicMac News*, 5, 12A (1976): 1-44.

United States. Department of Energy, Office of Fossil Energy. *Environmental Benefits of Advanced Oil and Gas Exploration and Production Technology*. Washington, DC: Department of Energy, 1999.

United States. Department of Energy, Office of Natural Gas and Petroleum Technology. *Oil and Gas Programs*. Washington, DC: Department of Energy, 1977.

United States. Minerals Management Service, Department of the Interior. *Deepwater Gulf of Mexico 2004: America's Expanding Frontier*. New Orleans: Minerals Management Service, 2004.

Upton, L.F.S. *Micmacs and Colonists: Indian-White Relations in the Maritimes, 1713-1867*. Vancouver: UBC Press, 1979.

Voyer, Roger. *Offshore Oil: Opportunities for Industrial Development and Job Creation*. Toronto: Canadian Institute for Economic Policy, 1983.

Wade, J.A., G.R. Campbell, R.M. Proctor, and G.C. Taylor. "Petroleum Resources of the Scotian Shelf." Paper 88-19, Geological Survey of Canada, 1989.

Wade, J.A., and B.C. MacLean. "The Geology of the Southeastern Margin of Canada." In *Geology of the Continental Margin of Eastern Canada*, edited by M.J. Keen and G.L. Williams, 167-238. Ottawa: Geological Survey of Canada, 1990.

Weiss, Linda. *The Myth of the Powerless State: Governing the Economy in a Global Era*. Cambridge: Polity Press, 1998.

Weissenberger, Angela Tu. "Casting a Cold Eye on LNG: The Real Possibilities and Pitfalls for Atlantic Canada." *AIMS Oil and Gas Papers* 4, Atlantic Institute for Market Studies, Halifax, January 2006.

Wells, Paul. *Right Side Up: The Fall of Paul Martin and the Rise of Stephen Harper's New Conservatism.* Toronto: McClelland and Stewart, 2006.

Whitford, Jacques. *BC Offshore Oil and Gas Technology Update.* Burnaby: Jacques Whitford, 2001.

Wicken, Bill. *Mi'kmaq Treaties on Trial: History, Land, and Donald Marshall Junior.* Toronto: University of Toronto Press, 2002.

Wilder, Robert Jay. *Listening to the Sea.* Pittsburgh, PA: University of Pittsburgh Press, 1998.

Wildsmith, Bruce. "Submission to Public Review Commission." 27 December 2001. Public Review Commission.

Windsor, Howard, and Peter Aucoin. "The Regulation of Telephone Service in Nova Scotia." In *The Regulatory Process in Canada,* edited by G.B. Doern, 237-58. Toronto: Macmillan of Canada, 1978.

Woodford, James. *The Violated Vision: The Rape of Canada's North.* Toronto: McClelland and Stewart, 1972.

Yergin, Daniel. *The Prize: The Epic Quest for Oil, Money, and Power.* New York: Free Press, 2008.

Index

Printed and bound in Canada by Friesens
Set in Futura Condensed and Warnock by Artegraphica Design Co. Ltd.
Copy editor: Lesley Erickson
Proofreader: Michael O'Hearn
Cartographer: Eric Leinberger